£23-95
(2)

ONE WEEK
LOAN

GIVE TO
PROCESSING
ON RET
TB

7th Apr 1997

10 JAN 1997
12 FEB 1999
10 FEB 1997
11 APR 1997
1 3 DEC 1999

2 7 SEP 1996
26 SEP 1997
31 JUL 97
- 5 MAY 2000

1 7 OCT 1996
- 9 DEC 1997
1 1 SEP 2000
- 9 JAN 1998
2 2 SEP 2000

2 5 NOV 1996

0 2 DEC 1996
- 6 MAR 1998
- 8 FEB 2001

0 9 DEC 1996
2 3 MAR 1998
11 MAY 1999

Numerical Analysis
and
Graphic Visualization
with
MATLAB®

Shoichiro Nakamura

The Ohio State University

For book and bookstore information

http://www.prenhall.com

Prentice Hall PTR, Upper Saddle River, NJ 07458

Library of Congress Cataloging-in-Publication Data

Nakamura, Shoichiro, 1935–

    Numerical analysis and graphic visualization with MATLAB /
        Shoichiro Nakamura.
           p.   cm.
    Includes bibliographical references and index.
    ISBN 0-13-051518-3
      1. Computer graphics.   2. MATLAB   I. Title.
    T385.N34   1996
    519.4'0285'53--dc20   95-32597
                                     CIP

Acquisitions editor: M. Franz
Editorial assistant: Noreen Regina
Cover design: Shoichiro Nakamura and Mark Weiss
Cover design director: Jerry Votta
Copyeditor: Roger Stern
Art production manager: Gail Cocker-Bogusz
Manufacturing manager: Alexis R. Heydt

©1996 Prentice Hall PTR
Prentice-Hall, Inc.
A Simon and Schuster Company
Upper Saddle River, New Jersey 07458

The publisher offers discounts on this book when ordered in bulk
quantities. For more information, contact Corporate Sales Department,
Prentice Hall PTR, 1 Lake Street, Upper Saddle River, NJ 07458.
Phone: 800-382-3419; FAX: 201-236-7141.
E-mail (Internet): corpsales@prenhall.com.

10 9   8   7   6   5   4   3   2   1

ISBN 0-13-051518-3

Prentice-Hall International (UK) Limited, *London*
Prentice-Hall of Australia Pty. Limited, *Sydney*
Prentice-Hall Canada Inc., *Toronto*
Prentice-Hall Hispanoamericana, S.A., *Mexico*
Prentice-Hall of India Private Limited, *New Delhi*
Prentice-Hall of Japan, Inc., *Tokyo*
Simon & Schuster Asia Pte. Ltd., *Singapore*
Editora Prentice-Hall do Brasil, Ltda., *Rio de Janeiro*

Contents

Preface

WHAT THIS BOOK DESCRIBES

This book is intended to introduce numerical analysis and graphic visualization using MATLAB to college students in engineering and science. It can also be a handbook of MATLAB applications to professional engineers and scientists.

With its unique and fascinating capabilities, MATLAB has changed the concept of programming for numerical and mathematical analyses. It has been found difficulty, however, to teach its application in numerical analysis with a text written previously. For this reason, developing a text that fully implements the mathematical and graphic tools of MATLAB in application of numerical analysis became desirable.

The following four fundamental elements are integrated in this book: (1) programming in MATLAB, (2) mathematical basics of numerical analysis, (3) application of numerical methods to engineering, scientific, and mathematical problems, and (4) scientific graphics with MATLAB.

The first two chapters are comprehensive tutorials of MATLAB commands and graphic tools. Chapters 3 through 11 cover numerical methods with their implementations with MATLAB. All the numerical methods described are illustrated with applications on MATLAB. Using the lists of the scripts and functions or copying from the diskette (available to readers free from MathWorks), readers can run most examples and figures on their own computers. Appendices describe special topics, including advanced three-dimensional graphics with colors, motion pictures, image processing, and graphical user interface.

This book is based on MATLAB Student Edition 4, or MATLAB Professional Edition 4.1 or higher.

WHAT IS UNIQUE ABOUT MATLAB?

MATLAB may be regarded as a programming language like Fortran or C, although describing it in a few words is difficult. Some of its outstanding features for numerical analyses, however, are:

Significantly simpler programming
Continuity among integer, real, and complex values
Extended range of numbers and their accuracy
Comprehensive mathematical library
Extensive graphic tools including graphic user interface functions
Capability of linking with traditional programming languages
Transportability of MATLAB programs

An extraordinary feature of numbers in MATLAB is that there is no distinction among real, complex, integer, single, and double. In MATLAB, all these numbers are continuously connected, as they should be. It means that in MATLAB, any variable can take any types of numbers without special declaration in programming. This makes programming faster and more productive. In Fortran, a different subroutine is necessary for each of single, double, real or complex, or integer variable, while in MATLAB there is no need to separate them.

The mathematical library in MATLAB makes mathematical analyses easy. Yet the user can develop additional mathematical routines significantly more easily than in other programming languages because of the continuity between real and complex variables. Among numerous mathematical functions, linear algebra solvers play central roles. Indeed, the whole MATLAB system is founded upon linear algebra solvers.

IMPORTANCE OF GRAPHICS

Visual analysis of mathematical analyses helps understand mathematics and makes it enjoyable. Although this advantage has been well known, presenting computed results with computer graphics was not without substantial extra effort. With MATLAB, however, graphic presentations of mathematical material is possible with a few commands. Scientific and even artistic graphic objects can be created on the screen using mathematical expressions. It has been found that MATLAB graphics motivate and even excite students to learn mathematical and numerical methods that could otherwise often be dull.

MATLAB graphics is easy and will be great fun for readers. This book also illustrates image processing and production of motion pictures for scientific computing as well as for artistic or hobby material.

COMMAND AND FUNCTION NAMES IN THIS BOOK

The command and function names peculiar to this book all include _ for example `rotx_.m`. The functions and commands that do not include the underscore are original from MATLAB.

WILL MATLAB ELIMINATE THE NEED FOR FORTRAN OR C?

The answer is no. Fortran and C are still important for high-performance computing that requires large memory or long computing time. The speed of MATLAB
computation is significantly slower than that with Fortran or C because MATLAB
is paying the high price for the nice features. Learning Fortran or C, however, is
not a prerequisite for understanding MATLAB.

REFERENCE BOOKS THAT ARE IMPORTANT TO LEARN MATLAB

This book explains many MATLAB commands but is not intended to be a complete
guide to MATLAB. Readers interested in further information on MATLAB are
advised to read the following literature on MATLAB:

> The MathWorks, *The Student Edition of MATLAB,*
> *Version 4, User's Guide,* Prentice-Hall 1995
> *MATLAB, Reference Guide,* MathWorks, 1992
> *MATLAB, User's Guide,* MathWorks, 1992
> *MATLAB, Building a Graphical User Interface,* MathWorks, 1993

HOW TO OBTAIN M-FILES DISKETTE

All the scripts and functions developed in the present book are included in the
diskette available from MathWorks. Please mail the diskette request card inserted
at the end of this book. If the request card is missing, MathWorks' address appears
on the next page. The diskette includes the following files:

> (1) All M-files listed at the end of chapters.
> (2) All scripts illustrated in the book (except short ones).
> (3) Scripts to plot typical figures in the book.

SOLUTION KEYS

Solution keys for the problems at the end of chapters will be included in the M-Files
Diskette.

HOW TO OBTAIN MORE INFORMATION ABOUT MATLAB

Answers to frequently asked questions and Technical Notes on MATLAB are available directly from MathWorks via ftp. Its Internet address is `ftp.mathworks.com`
`(144.212.100.10)`. The FAQ and the Technical Notes can be found in the di-
rectories `/pub/doc/faq` and `/pub/tech-support/tech-notes` respectively.

You may also receive the following information free of charge:

* The MathWorks Newsletter (quarterly publication)
* The MATLAB News Digest (distributed via email)
* Technical Support

Send email to `subscribe@mathworks.com`. Include in the email your name, company/university, address, phone number, email address, and license or serial number, which can be found by entering "ver" at the MATLAB prompt.

For other communication with MathWorks, their address is: The MathWorks, Inc., 24 Prime Park Way, Natick, MA 01760, Phone: 508-653-1415, Fax: 508-653-2997.

LIST OF REVIEWERS

This book has been reviewed by:

Professor T. Aldemir, Nuclear Engineering,
The Ohio State University, Columbus, Ohio

Professor M. Darwish, Mechanical Engineering Department,
American University of Beirut, Beirut, Lebanon

The MathWorks Inc., Natick, Massachusetts

Professor J. K. Shultis, Nuclear Engineering,
Kansas State University, Manhattan, Kansas

Professor S. V. Sreenivasan, Department of Mechanical Engineering,
University of Texas, Austin, Texas

TRADE NAMES

Image Alchemy is a registered trademark of Handmade Software, Inc.
MATLAB is a registered trademark of MathWorks, Inc.
Qtake is a registered trademark of Apple, Inc.
Unix is a registered trademark of AT&T Bell Laboratories.
Windows is a registered trademark of Microsoft, Inc.

ACKNOWLEDGEMENTS

Editor Mary Franz originally suggested the idea of developing this book. Her initial suggestion was coincident with the time the author started teaching numerical methods with MATLAB. Without her continuous encouragement and administrative assistance, this book would have been impossible. The author is grateful for the full support of this book by MathWorks. Paul Costa, Allison Babb, and John Galenski of MathWorks have given the author substantial technical support. Cristina Palumbo's encouragement and administrative help have been indispensable.

Several university professors have provided useful example problems, which are acknowledged in the footnotes below the material. David Smith of The Ohio State University assisted the author to finish the appendix on graphical user interface with MATLAB. Special thanks are given to Keiji Yano of The Ohio State University, and Y. C. Su of Washington State University, who patiently proofread the whole manuscript. Many thanks are given to instructors who used the manuscript as text for a numerical methods course and to the students in the classes who used the manuscript as a text. Comments from the instructors and students were invaluable.

The author is grateful to the reviewers cited in a prior section. They provided the author with valuable suggestions and comments.

Manuscript for this book was written in LaTex. All figures except a few were created by MATLAB, saved in postscript form, and then were taken into LaTex manuscript files. Robert Chong of The Ohio State University typed a major part of the first draft in LaTex. The author owes much to Professor Shultis, who not only reviewed the manuscript, but also was helpful, along with his book *LaTex Notes* (Prentice-Hall 1994), in typesetting using LaTex.

Finally, the author sincerely hopes that the reader will enjoy the study of *Numerical Analysis and Graphic Visualization with MATLAB*.

S. Nakamura
Columbus, Ohio

Chapter 1

MATLAB Primer

This chapter will serve as a hands-on tutorial for beginners who are unfamiliar with MATLAB. We assume that readers have either the student edition of MATLAB 4 (on a PC or Macintosh) or a professional version 4.1 or higher. Before reading this chapter, the reader should set up the MATLAB software on the computer and open the command window. As commands are explained, try to write and execute each command.

Please understand that throughout this book `log` is $\log_e$. The log function to the base 10 will be specifically denoted as `log10`. Trigonometric functions use *radians* but not degrees; however, the angles in graphic views are in degrees.

The results of the computation may differ slightly among different computers because rounding errors among different computer models can vary.[1]

1.1 TUTORIALS ON COMMAND WINDOW

1.1.1 Before Starting Calculations

How to open MATLAB: On a Unix workstation, MATLAB can be opened by typing

```
> matlab
```

Once the prompt sign of MATLAB, such as >>, appears, type the commands that are explained throughout this section. To quit MATLAB, type

```
>> quit
```

On Macintosh or Windows, click the icon of MATLAB or STUDENT-MATLAB. The procedure of quitting MATLAB is similar to quitting any other software on Macintosh or Windows.

---

[1]The differences are normally negligibly small. Some problems, however, are sensitive to rounding errors and produce significantly different results on different computers. Such problems are often called ill-conditioned problems and usually are difficult to solve on any computer.

Help: When meaning of a command is not clear, type `help` and the command name in question. The `help` command will give you a concise but precise explanation of commands. It may not be useful for beginners, but will be one of the most frequently used commands. For example, the response for `help quit` and `help help`, respectively, are illustrated next:

```
>> help quit

QUIT    Terminate MATLAB.
        QUIT terminates MATLAB.

>> help help

HELP    On-line documentation.
        HELP, by itself, lists all primary help topics.  Each primary
        topic corresponds to a directory name on MATLABPATH.

        "HELP topic" gives help on the specified topic.  The topic
        can be a command name or a directory name.  If it is a command
        name, HELP displays information on that command.  If it is a
        directory name, HELP displays the Tabler Of Contents for the
        specified directory.

        It is not necessary to give the full pathname of the directory;
        the last component, or last several components, are sufficient.

        For example, "help general" and "help matlab/general" both list
        the Table Of Contents for the directory toolbox/matlab/general.

        LOOKFOR XYZ looks for the string XYZ in the first comment line
        of the HELP text in all M-files found on MATLABPATH.  For all
        files in which a match occurs, LOOKFOR displays the matching
        lines.

        MORE ON causes HELP to pause between screenfuls if the help
        text runs to several screens.

        See also LOOKFOR, WHAT, WHICH, DIR, MORE.
```

Version: The first thing you should know about the MATLAB software is what version you are using. To get this information, type `version`.

What: `what` will list M-, MAT-, and MEX-files in the current working directory.[2] The command `what dirname` lists the files in directory `dirname` on the `matlabpath`. It is not necessary to give the full pathname of the directory; the last component or last several components are sufficient. For example, `what general` and `what matlab/general` both list the M-files in directory

---

[2]M-file: a script or function file (its format is `filename.m`).
MAT-file: a file containing binary data (its format is `filename.mat`).
MEX-file: MATLAB executable file compiled from Fortran or C (`filename.mex`)

```
toolbox/matlab/general.
```

Who: who lists the variables in the current workspace. whos lists more information about each variable. who global and whos global list the variables in the global workspace.

Clock: The clock command prints out numbers like

```
ans =
     1.0e+03 *
     1.9950   0.0030   0.0050   0.0150   0.0140   0.0091
```

The first number 1.0e+03 is a multiplier. The numbers in the second line have the following meaning:

```
[year, month, day, hour, minute, second]
```

The same can be printed out in the integer form by fix(clock). The answer is

```
ans =
         1995     3     5    15    19    56
```

which says time was year 1995, 3rd month, 5th day, 15 hr, 19 min and 56 sec, approximately six minutes after the first example of clock was printed out. The elapsed time of an execution may be measured by clock. For example, set t_0=clock before a computation starts, and t_1=clock when completed. Then, t_1 - t_0 gives the time elapsed for the computation. One may also use tic and toc to measure the elapsed time.

The date command gives similar information, but in a more brief format:

```
ans =
        5-Mar-95
```

Path: path prints MATLAB's current search path. Command p = path returns a string p containing the path. Command path(p0) changes the path to p0, which is a string containing the new path. Command path(p1,p2) changes the path to the concatenation of the two path strings p1 and p2. Therefore, path(path, p3) appends a new directory p3 to the current path and path(p3, path) prepends a new path.

Getenv: getenv('MATLABPATH') will show current MATLAB paths.

Diary: diary on starts writing all keyboard input as well as most screen output to a file named diary, and diary off terminates writing. If file diary already exists, the screen output is appended to diary file. Filename other than diary may be specified by writing the intended filename after diary. Without on or off, `diary` itself toggles `diary on` and `diary off`. The file may be printed as a hard copy, or may be edited later.

Escape: ! mark is the operator to escape from MATLAB. With this mark, you have access to the directory by escaping from MATLAB. For example, suppose MATLAB has been opened from a Unix shell. Then, the Unix command can be issued from within MATLAB by writing the Unix command after the escape mark. For example, a text editing software like *vi* editor may be opened from within MATLAB by `!vi filename`. Escape may be used similarly on a PC for DOS commands, or even on a Mac for a limited number of commands. For example, formatting a diskette from MATLAB on a PC is possible by `!format a:`. Executing programs in this way, however, particularly graphic or communication software, may mess up the computing environment.

Demonstration: The `demo` command guides the user to numerous demonstrations selectable from a menu. The contents of demonstrations are not necessarily easy to understand immediately, but can be visited many times as interests occur.

1.1.2 How to Start Calculations

Calculation with single variables: When a command window is opened, a prompt sign >> is seen at the upper left corner of the window. Any command can be written after the prompt sign. In the explanation of the commands, however, the prompt signs will be omitted for simplicity.

As a simple example, let us evaluate:

$$\text{Volume} = \frac{4}{3}\pi r^3, \quad \text{with } r = 2$$

The commands to type on the screen are:

List 1.1a
```
r = 2;
vol = (4/3)*pi*r^3;
```

where `pi` $= \pi$ in MATLAB. Each line is typed after the prompt sign >> and the return key is hit when typing a line is over. Notice in the preceding script that each line is a command and completed by a semicolon. The karat ^ after `r` is the exponent operator.

When we work in the command window, the computer calculates the answer for each command immediately after the return key is hit. Therefore, the value of `vol` is already in the computer. How can we get the result printed out on the screen?

The quickest way of printing out the result is to type `vol` and hit return. Then the computer prints out

```
vol =
     33.510
```

Another way of printing out the value of `vol` is to omit the semicolon at the end of the second command:

List 1.1b

```
r = 2;
vol = (4/3)*pi*r^3
```

Without a semicolon, the result is printed out immediately after the computation. Because displaying every result is cumbersome, however, we generally place a semicolon after each command.

Multiple commands may be written in a single line separated by semicolons. If the results are to be printed out for each command executed, separate commands by commas, and the line is terminated with or without a comma. For example, if you write

```
r = 2,   vol = (4/3)*pi*r^3
```

the values of `r` and `vol` are printed out, but if you write

```
r = 2;   vol = (4/3)*pi*r^3;
```

no results are displayed.

A long command may be split into multiple lines. In Fortran, it is done by a continuation mark on column 6. In MATLAB, the continuation mark is ... and it is placed at the end of the line to be continued; for example,

List 1.2

```
r = 2;
vol = (4/3)*3.14159   ...
      *r^3;
```

The prompt sign will not appear for the line following the continuation mark.

Arithmetic operators: Arithmetic operators such as +, -, *, and / are the same as those in traditional programming languages such as Fortran and, respectively, *plus*, *minus*, *multiply*, and *divide*. MATLAB uses one untraditional operator \, which may be named *inverse division*. This operator yields the reciprocal of division, that is, `a\b` yields `b/a`. For example,

```
c = 3\1
c =
    0.3333
```

It is not recommended that readers use this operator in usual computations, but this operator will become important in Chapter 3 for linear algebra.

If statement: An if statement is always closed with an end statement; for example,

List 1.3
```
r = 2;
if  r>0,   vol = (4/3)*3.14159*r^3;
end
```

Notice also in writing the foregoing script that the prompt sign does not appear after if until end is typed. When the mathematical statement needs to use *equal* after if, use == as in the C language; for example,

List 1.4
```
r = 2;
if r==2, vol = (4/3)*pi*r^3;
end
```

The *not equal* operator is written as ~=; for example,

List 1.5
```
r = 2;
if r ~= 3, vol = (4/3)*pi*r^3;
end
```

The *greater than, less than, equal or greater than*, and *equal or less than* are, respectively,

```
>
<
>=
<=
```

The logical statements *and* and *or* are denoted by & and |, respectively. For example, the conditional equation,

$$\text{if } g > 3 \text{ or } g < 0, \text{ then } a = 6$$

is written as

```
if g>3 | g<0, a = 6; end
```

Also the conditional equation

$$\text{if } a > 3 \text{ and } c < 0, b = 19$$

is stated as

```
if a>3 & c<0, b=19; end
```

The & and | operators can be used in a clustered form, for example,

```
if ((a==2 | b==3) & c<5)   g=1; end
```

The `if` statement can be used with `else` or `elseif`; for example,

List 1.6
```
r=2;
if r > 3        b=1;
elseif r==3     b=2;
else            b=0;
end
```

Of course, `elseif` can be repeated as often as desired; however, `else` and `elseif` sometimes become tricky, particularly when the variables after the `elseif` statements involve array variables with different sizes. When `elseif` statements do not work, give up `elseif` and repeat simple `if` statements as many times as needed.

Disp: Command `disp` displays a number, vector, matrix, or a string on the command window without variable name. Therefore, it may be used to display messages or data on the screen. For example, `disp(pi)` and `disp pi` both print `3.14159` on the command screen. Try also `disp 'This is a test for disp.'`.

Variables and variable names: Variable names and their types do not have to be declared. This is because variable names in MATLAB make no distinction among integer, real, and complex variables. Any variable can take real, complex, and integer values. Even the size of an array does not have to be predeclared.

In principle, any name can be used as far as it is compatible in MATLAB. We should, however, be aware of two incompatible situations. The first is that the name is not accepted by MATLAB. The second is that the name is accepted but it destroys the original meaning of a reserved name. These conflicts can occur with the following types of names:

> (a) names for certain values
> (b) function (subroutine) names
> (c) command names

One method to examine compatibility of the variable name is to test it on the command screen. A valid statement such as `x=9` is responded to as

```
x =
   9
```

which means that the variable is accepted. If `end=4` (as a bad example) is attempted, however, it is ignored.

An example of the second conflict is as follows: If `sin` and `cos` are used (as poor examples of variables) with no relation to the trigonometric functions, for example,

```
sin = 3;
cos = sin^2;
```

the calculations proceed; however, `sin` and `cos` can never be used as trigonometric functions thereafter until variables are cleared by issuing the `clear` command or MATLAB is quitted. If any error message concerning a conflict appears, the reader should investigate the cause.

Traditionally, symbols i, j, k, l, m and n have been used as integer variables or indices. At the same time, i and j are used to denote unit imaginary value, or $\sqrt{-1}$. In MATLAB, i and j are reserved as unit imaginary. Therefore, if the computation involves complex variables, it is advisable to avoid i and j as user-defined variables if possible.

Table 1.1 lists samples of reserved variable names that have special meanings. If a variable or files exist it also may be checked by `exist` command.

Table 1.1 Special numbers and variable names

Variable name	Meaning	Value
eps	Machine epsilon	2.2204e-16
pi	π	3.14159...
i and j	Unit imaginary	$\sqrt{-1}$
inf	Infinity	∞
NaN	Not a number	
date	Date	
flops	Floating point operation count	
nargin	Number of function input arguments	
nargout	Same for output	

Loops: MATLAB has `for/end`, and `while/end` loops. To illustrate a `for/end` loop, let us calculate the volume of spheres for `r=1` through `5`. The commands for this can be written as

List 1.7
```
for r=1:5
    vol = (4/3)*pi*r^3;
    disp([r, vol])
end
```

The computation for the present loop will not start until `end` is typed and the return key is hit. The statement `disp([r, vol])` is to print the values of `r` and `vol` in a row each time `vol` is computed. No semicolon is necessary after each of `for r=1:5` and `end`.

An alternative way of writing a loop is to use the `while`/`end`; for example,

List 1.8

```
r = 0;
while r<5
    r = r+1;
    vol = (4/3)*pi*r^3;
    disp([r, vol])
end
```

The loop index can be decremented as

```
for r=5:-1:1
    vol = (4/3)*pi*r^3;
    disp([r, vol])
end
```

In this example, `-1` between two colon operators is the decrement of the parameter `r` after each cycle of the loop operation.

Double and triple loops can be written, for example, as

List 1.9

```
for r=1:5
  for s=1:r
    vol = (4/3)*pi*(r^3 - s^3);
    disp([r, vol])
  end
end
```

Format: Numbers displayed are five digit numbers by default:

```
pi
ans =
    3.1416
```

The same numbers, however, may be displayed with 16 digits after the command `format long`; for example,

```
format long
pi
ans =
    3.141592653589793
```

In order to return to the short format, use `format short`. Also, with `format short e` and `format short e`, respectively, short and long numbers are printed in floating-point format.

Break: The `break` terminates the execution of a `for` or `while` loop. When used in nested loops, only the immediate loop where `break` is located is terminated. In the next example, `break` terminates the inner loop as soon as `j>2*i` is satisfied once, but the loop for `i` is continued until `i=6`:

List 1.10

```
for i=1:6
   for j=1:20
      if j>2*i, break, end
   end
end
```

Another example is

List 1.11

```
r=0
while r<10
   r = input('Type radius (or -1 to stop): ');
   if  r< 0, break, end
   vol = (4/3)*pi*r^3;
   fprintf('Volume = %7.3f\n', vol)
end
```

In the foregoing loop, the radius r is typed through the keyboard. The `fprintf` statement is to print out `vol` with a format, `%7.3f`, which is equivalent to `F7.3` in Fortran. If $0 \leq r < 10$, `vol` is computed and printed out, but if $r < 0$ the loop is terminated. Also, if $r < 10$ is dissatisfied once, the `while` loop is terminated. More explanations for `input` and `fprintf` are given in later subsections.

In a programming language that has no break command, `goto` would be used to break a loop. MATLAB, on the other hand, has no `goto` statement.

Infinite loop: Sometimes a loop that can continue infinitely is used, which may be terminated when a certain condition is met. The following example shows an infinite loop that is broken only if the condition `x > xlimit` is met:

```
while 1
   .
   .
   .
   if x > xlimit, break; end
   .
   .
   .
end
```

How to clear variables: As you execute commands, MATLAB memorizes the variables used. Their values stay in memory until you quit MATLAB, or clear the variables. To clear all the variables, use the `clear` command. If only certain variables are to be cleared, name the variables after `clear`; for example,

```
clear x y z
```

How to clear the command window: If you wish to clear window, use the command,

```
clc
```

1.1.3 Reading and Writing

Passing data to and from MATLAB is possible in several different ways. The methods may be classified into three classes:

  (a) Interactive operation by keyboard or mouse

  (b) Reading from or writing to a data file

  (c) Using `save` or `load`

In the remainder of this subsection, only a minimal amount of information regarding reading and writing is introduced. More information can be found in Section 1.8.

Reading input from keyboard: MATLAB can take input data through the keyboard using the `input` command. To read a number, the synopsis would be

```
z = input('Type radius:')
```

The `Type radius:` is a prompting message to be printed out on the screen. As the value for radius is typed and return key is hit, the input is saved in z. A string input can be typed from the keyboard. The synopsis is

```
z = input('Your name please: ', 's')
```

The second argument `'s'` indicates that the input from the keyboard is a string. The variable z becomes an array variable (row vector) unless the string has only one character. A string input can be taken by `input` without `'s'` if the typed string is enclosed by single quote signs. In this case, a prompt message may be written as

```
z = input('Type your name (in single quote signs):')
```

Output format: Printing out formatted messages and numbers is possible using `fprintf`; for example,

```
fprintf('The volume of the sphere %12.5f.\n', vol)
```

Included between two single quote signs is a string to be printed out, the format for a number, and a new-line operator. The style of the format is familiar to those who know the C language: `The volume of the sphere` is the string to be printed out, `%12.5f` is the format and similar to `F12.5` in Fortran, `\n` is the new-line operator that advances the screen position by one line. The new-line operator can be placed anywhere within the string. Finally, `vol` is the variable to be printed out in accordance with the format `%12.5f`. If `\n` is omitted, the next print starts without advancing a line.

The command

```
fprintf('e_format: %12.5e\n', 12345.2)
```

will print out

```
e_format:   1.23452e+04
```

If two print statements are consecutively written without `\n` in the first statement, for example,

```
fprintf('e_format: %12.5e', 12345.2);
fprintf('f_format: %12.3f\n', 7.23462)
```

then all the output will be printed out in a single line as

```
e_format: 1.23452e+04   f_format: 7.235
```

An integer value can be typed using the same format, except 0 is placed after the decimal point; for example,

```
fprintf('f_format: %12.0f\n', 93)
```

yields

```
f_format: 93
```

When multiple numbers are to be printed on a single line, `fprintf` may be repeatedly used without `\n` except in the last statement.

Writing into a specific file: With the `fprintf` command, it is possible to write formatted output into a file. To do this, the filename is included in the argument; for example,

```
fprintf('file_x', 'Volume=  %12.5f\n', vol)
```

will write the output in the file named `file_x`. If no such file exists, a new file is created. If the file exists, the output is appended. If necessary, the existing file `file_x` can be deleted by `!rm file_x` on Unix, or `!erase file_x` on Windows.

Better control of files is possible by `fopen` and `fclose`. See the MATLAB User's Guide for more details.

1.2   ARRAY VARIABLES

One-dimensional array variables: One-dimensional array variables are in a column or a row form, and are closely related to vectors and matrices. In MATLAB, *row array* is synonymous with *row vector*, and *column array* is synonymous with *column vector*. The variable x can be defined as a row vector by specifying its elements; for example:

```
x = [0, 0.1, 0.2, 0.3, 0.4, 0.5];
```

To print a particular element, type x with its subscript. For example, typing $x(3)$ as a command will show

```
ans =
      0.2
```

An equivalent way of defining the same x is

```
for i=1:6
   x(i) = (i-1)*0.1;
end
```

The size of the vector does not have to be predeclared as it is adjusted automatically. The number of elements of x can be increased by defining additional elements, for example,

```
x(7) = 0.6;
```

A row array variable with a fixed increment or decrement may be equivalently written as

```
x = 2:-0.4:-2
```

It yields

```
x = 2.0000  1.6000  1.2000  0.8000  0.4000  -0.0000
```

Definition of a column array is similar to a row array except the elements are separated by semicolons; for example,

```
z = [0; 0.1; 0.2; 0.3; 0.4; 0.5];
```

An alternative way of defining the same is to put a prime after a row array:

```
z = [0, 0.1, 0.2, 0.3, 0.4, 0.5]';
```

The prime operator is the same as the transpose operator in the matrix and vector calculus, so it converts a column vector to a row vector and vice versa. Typing z as a command yields

```
z =
     0
     0.1
     0.2
     0.3
     0.4
     0.5
```

If a single element of an array c is defined, for example,

```
c(8) = 11;
```

$c(i) = 0$ is assumed for $i=1$ through 7. Therefore, typing c yields

```
c =
     0    0    0    0    0    0    0    11
```

When y and x have the same length and the same form (row or column), the vector y and x can be added, subtracted, multiplied, and divided using the array arithmetic operators as

```
z = x + y
z = x - y
z = x .* y
z = x ./ y
```

which are equivalent respectively to

List 1.12
```
for i=1:6;   z(i) = x(i) + y(i); end
for i=1:6;   z(i) = x(i) - y(i); end
for i=1:6;   z(i) = x(i)*y(i);   end
for i=1:6;   z(i) = x(i)/y(i);   end
```

The rules for addition and subtraction are the same as for vectors in linear algebra. However, .* and ./ are named array multiplication and array division operators, respectively, which are not the same as multiplication and division for matrices and vectors. If the period of .* or ./ is omitted, the meaning becomes entirely different (see Chapter 3 for more details).

The array power operator is illustrated by

```
g = z.^1.2;
```

where z is a vector of length 6, a period is placed before the ^ operator, and g becomes a vector of the same length. The foregoing statement is equivalent to

```
for i=1:6;   g(i) = z(i)^1.2; end
```

where no period is placed before the ^ operator.

The size of an array can be increased by appending an element or a vector (or vectors). As an example, assume

```
x =
    2    3
```

The following command appends 5 to x and makes its length 3:

```
x = [x, 5]
```

which returns

```
x =
    2    3    5
```

   A column vector may be appended with a number or a vector or vectors. Suppose y is a column vector,

```
y =
    2
    3
```

then

```
y = [y; 7]
```

yields

```
y =
    2
    3
    7
```

Here, 7 is appended to the end of the column vector. Notice that a semicolon is used to append to a column vector. An element can be prepended to a vector also, for example, x = [9,x] yields

```
x =
    9    2    3    5
```

where x on the right side was defined earlier. Similarly [-1;y] yields

```
y =
    -1
    2
    3
    7
```

   A reverse procedure is to extract a part of a vector. For the foregoing y,

```
w = y(3:4)
```

will define w that equals the 3rd and 4th elements of y, namely

```
w =
      3
      7
```

If you don't remember the size of a vector, ask the computer. For a vector

```
x =   [9,   2,   3,   5]
```

the inquiry

```
length(x)
```

is responded to by

```
ans =
      4
```

The answer is the same for a column array. Let us define $y = [9, 2, 3]'$. Then, `length(y)` returns `ans = 3`; however, when you want to know if the vector is a column or row type in addition to the length, use `size`. For example, `size(y)` will return

```
ans =
      3      1
```

where the first is the number of rows and the second the number of columns. From this answer, we learn that y is a 3-by-1 array, that is a column vector of length 3. For $z=[9,2,3,5]$, `size(z)` will return

```
ans =
      1      4
```

that is, z is a row vector of length 4.

String variables: String variables are arrays. For example, a string variable v defined by

```
v = 'glacier'
```

is equivalent to

```
v = ['g', 'l', 'a', 'c', 'i', 'e', 'r']
```

The variable v can be converted to a column string by

```
v = v'
```

which is

```
g
l
a
c
i
e
r
```

Two-dimensional array variables: A two-dimensional array, which is synonymous with a matrix in MATLAB, can be defined by specifying its elements. For example, a 3-by-3 array can be defined by

```
m = [0.1, 0.2, 0.3; 0.4, 0.5, 0.6; 0.7, 0.8, 0.9];
```

Notice that the elements for a row are terminated by a semicolon. Of course the number of elements in each row must be identical. Otherwise the definition will not be accepted. The statement is equivalent to writing

List 1.13
```
m(1,1)=0.1;
m(1,2)=0.2;
m(1,3)=0.3;
m(2,1)=0.4;
m(2,2)=0.5;
m(2,3)=0.6;
m(3,1)=0.7;
m(3,2)=0.8;
m(3,3)=0.9;
```

Typing m as a command yields

```
m =
    0.1000    0.2000    0.3000
    0.4000    0.5000    0.6000
    0.7000    0.8000    0.9000
```

A whole column or a row of a two-dimensional array can be expressed using a colon. For example, $m(1,:)$ and $m(:,3)$ are the first row of m and the third column of m, respectively, and treated as vectors. For example,

```
c(1,:) = m(3,:);
c(2,:) = m(2,:);
c(3,:) = m(1,:);
```

yield

```
c =
    0.7000    0.8000    0.9000
    0.4000    0.5000    0.6000
    0.1000    0.2000    0.3000
```

Two-dimensional arrays can be added, subtracted, multiplied and divided using the array arithmetic operators:

List 1.14a

```
c = a + b
c = a - b
c = a .* b
c = a ./ b
```

Here, a and b are two-dimensional arrays of the same size. The foregoing statements are equivalent to, respectively,

List 1.14b

```
for i=1:3
    for j=1:3
        c(i,j)   = a(i,j) + b(i,j);
    end
end

for i=1:3
    for j=1:3
        c(i,j)   = a(i,j) - b(i,j);
    end
end

for i=1:3
    for j=1:3
        c(i,j)   = a(i,j)*b(i,j);
    end
end

for i=1:3
    for j=1:3
        c(i,j)   = a(i,j)/b(i,j);
    end
end
```

Note that the expressions in List 1.14a are significantly more compact and clearer than the expressions in List 1.14b.

The statement with the array power operator,

```
g = a.^3
```

is equivalent to

```
for i=1:3
    for j=1:3
        g(i,j)   = a(i,j)^3;
    end
end
```

Column vectors and row vectors are both special cases of a matrix. Therefore, array operators work equally on vectors and matrices. There are two advantages in using the array arithmetic operators. First, programming becomes short. Second, computational efficiency of MATLAB is higher with the short form than writing the same using loops.

If **statements comparing arrays:** Array variables may be compared in an `if` statement. Assuming that `a` and `b` are matrices of the same size:

(a) `if  a==b` is satisfied only if `a(i,j)=b(i,j)` for all the elements.
(b) `if  a>=b` is satisfied only if `a(i,j)>=b(i,j)` for all the elements.
(c) `if  a~=b` is satisfied if `a(i,j)~=b(i,j)` for at least one element.

If two string variables of different lengths are compared by an `if` statement, an arithmetic error occurs because the two arrays must have the same length. In order to compare string variables in `if` statements, all the string variables must be adjusted to a predetermined length by appending blank spaces. For example, instead of

```
a = 'echinopsis'
b = 'thithle'
c = 'cirsium'
d = 'onopordon'
```

write as

```
a = 'echinopsis'
b = 'thithle   '
c = 'cirsium   '
d = 'onopordon '
```

Then, `a`, `b` and `c` may be compared in `if` statements.

This task may be more easily achieved, however, by `str2mat`. For example, suppose string variables have been given by

```
t1 = 'digitalis'
t2 = 'nicotiana'
t3 = 'basilicum'
t4 = 'lychnis'
t5 = 'chrysanthemum'
```

Then they may be organized in a single string matrix by

```
s = str2mat(t1,t2,t3,t4,t5)
```

The first row of `s` becomes `t1`, the second row `t2`, and so on, of an identical length because blank spaces are added to shorter strings.

1.3   UNIQUE ASPECT OF NUMBERS IN MATLAB

In ordinary programming languages, numbers are classified into several categories such as single, double, real, integer, and complex. In MATLAB, all variables are treated equally in double precision. There is no distinction between integer and real variables, nor between real and complex variables. How to assign a value to a variable is entirely up to the user. If a variable is to be used as an integer, just set the value as an integer. Integers are recognized as far as they are recognizable from the mantissa and exponents in the memory. No distinction between real and complex variables is unique to MATLAB, but provides great advantages. In Fortran, for example, real variables and complex variables cannot share the same subroutines.

As a simple example, consider roots of a quadratic polynomial

$$ax^2 + bx + c = 0$$

The solution may be written as

$$x = \frac{-b \pm \sqrt{b^2 - 4ac}}{2a}$$

In Fortran or C, one has to separate the solutions to two cases:

(i) $b^2 \geq 4ac$,

$$x = \frac{-b \pm \sqrt{b^2 - 4ac}}{2a}$$

(ii) $b^2 < 4ac$,

$$x = \frac{-b \pm i\sqrt{4ac - b^2}}{2a}$$

where i equals $\sqrt{-1}$, and the solutions in the second case are complex values. In MATLAB, however, no separation is necessary. Regardless of the sign of the value inside the square root, the roots are computed by

```
x1 = (-b + sqrt(b^2 - 4*a*c))/(2*a)
x2 = (-b - sqrt(b^2 - 4*a*c))/(2*a)
```

If the roots are complex, MATLAB treats the variables as complex automatically.

Accuracy of computations is affected by how numbers are recorded and processed. The key parameters that signify accuracy of the numbers in a programming language are

Smallest positive number: x_min
Largest positive number: x_max
Machine epsilon: *eps*

Table 1.2 Comparison of the range of numbers and machine epsilon

Software Precision	MATLAB (workstation)	Fortran(workstation) Single (Double)	Fortran(Cray)
x_min	4.5e-324	2.9e-39(same)	4.6e-2476
x_max	9.9e+307	1.7e+38(same)	5.4e+2465
eps	2.2e-16	1.2e-7(2.8e-17)	1.3e-29

In Table 1.2, these three numbers in MATLAB are compared to those in Fortran on a few typical computers.

Table 1.2 shows that the machine epsilon of MATLAB is equivalent to that of double precision in Fortran on typical workstations.[3] MATLAB treats all numbers in double precision. The x_min of MATLAB is significantly smaller than in Fortran on VAX and x_max is significantly larger. Indeed, x_min and x_max are next to those of Cray. The wide range of numbers on MATLAB is indeed a significant advantage when exponential functions or functions with singularities are computed.

If the reader would like to verify the x_min, x_max, and eps on the reader's own computer, run the following scripts (the last number appearing on the screen is the answer):

List 1.15
```
% To find x_min
x=1; while x>0, x=x/2, end
```

List 1.16
```
% To find x_max
x=1; while x<inf, x=x*2, end
```

List 1.17
```
% To find machine epsilon
x=1;   while x>0,    x=x/2; ex = x*0.98 + 1; ex=ex - 1;
          if ex > 0, ex, end
       end
```

If a value becomes greater than x_max, the number is treated (in MATLAB) as ∞, denoted by `inf`. If you type `inf` on the command window, the response is

```
ans =
      ∞
```

Typing `x = 1/inf` will yield

---

[3] 0.71 Nakamura, *Applied Numerical Methods in C*, Prentice-Hall, 1992

```
ans =
      0
```

Sometimes, however, the answer becomes `NaN`, which means *not a number*. For example, if you try to compute `i*inf`, the answer of MATLAB is

```
ans =
      NaN
```

1.4   MATHEMATICAL FUNCTIONS OF MATLAB

Like any other programming languages, MATLAB has numerous mathematical functions from elementary to high levels. Elementary functions may be classified in three categories:

(a) Trigonometric functions
(b) Other elementary functions
(c) Functions that do chores

Table 1.3 shows the functions in the first two categories. The functions in the third category are explained in Section 1.5.

Mathematical functions in MATLAB have two distinctive differences from those in other programming languages such as Fortran and C: (1) mathematical functions work for complex variables without any discrimination, (2) mathematical functions work for vector and matrix arguments.

Complex arguments: To show how the functions of MATLAB work for imaginary or complex variables, let us try

```
cos(2 + 3*i)
```

where `i` equals the unit imaginary number, or equivalently square root of -1. Then the answer is

```
ans =
      -4.1896 - 9.1092i
```

For another example, consider the arccosine function, which is the inverse of the cosine function defined by

$$y = \mathrm{acos}(x) = \cos^{-1}(x)$$

The command

```
acos(0.5)
```

yields

Table 1.3 Elementary mathematical functions

Trigonometric functions	Remarks
`sin(x)`	
`cos(x)`	
`tan(x)`	
`asin(x)`	
`acos(x)`	
`atan(x)`	$-\pi/2 \geq \mathrm{atan}(x) \geq \pi/2$
`atan2(y,x)`	Same as `atan(y/x)` (see manual)
	$-\pi \geq \mathrm{atan}(y,x) \geq \pi$
`sinh(x)`	
`cosh(x)`	
`tanh(x)`	
`asinh(x)`	
`acosh(x)`	
`atanh(x)`	

Other elementary mathematical functions	Remarks
`abs(x)`	Absolute value of x
`angle(x)`	Phase angle of complex value:
	If x = real, angle = 0
	If $x = \sqrt{-1}$, angle = $\pi/2$
`sqrt(x)`	Square root of x
`real(x)`	Real part of complex value x
`imag(x)`	Imaginary part of complex value x
`conj(x)`	Complex conjugate x
`round(x)`	Round to the nearest integer
`fix(x)`	Round a real value toward zero
`floor(x)`	Round toward $-\infty$
`ceil(x)`	Round x toward $+\infty$
`sign(x)`	+1 if $x > 0$; -1 if $x < 0$
`rem(x,y)`	Remainder upon division: $x - y*\mathrm{fix}(x/y)$
`exp(x)`	Exponential base e
`log(x)`	Log base e
`log10(x)`	Log base 10

```
    ans =
          1.0472
```

The argument x in acos(x) is ordinarily limited to the range $-1 \leq x \leq 1$ (this is the way `acos` function works in Fortran). In MATLAB, however, `acos` accepts any value in $-\infty < x < \infty$ because the values of acos(x) are not restricted to real values. Indeed, if we try

```
    acos(3)
```

then

```
ans =
      0 + 1.7627i
```

Array arguments: Most functions in MATLAB can take vectors and matrices as argument. For example, if

```
x =
      1       2       3
      9       8       7
```

then `sin(x)` will yield

```
ans =
      0.8415      0.9093      0.1411
      0.4121      0.9894      0.6570
```

which is a matrix of the same size as x. The computation performed here is equivalent to

List 1.18
```
for i=1:2
  for j=1:3
    x(i,j) = sin(x(i,j))
  end
end
```

If x is a column or row array, `sin(x)` becomes a column or row array accordingly.

1.5   FUNCTIONS THAT DO CHORES

Besides functions that compute straightforward mathematical functions listed in Table 1.3, there are several functions that do chores.

Sort: `sort` reorders elements of a vector to ascending order. This command is useful if data in a random order have to be reordered in ascending order. The argument x can be a row vector, column vector, or a matrix. If x is a matrix, reordering is performed for each column. A few examples are given next:

```
sort([2 1 5])
ans =
      1       2       5

sort([2 1 5]')
ans =
      1
      2
      5
```

```
sort([9 1 5; 2 8 4])
ans =
        2       1       4
        9       8       5
```

Sum: `sum(x)` computes the summation of the elements of a vector or matrix `x`. For both a column vector or a row vector, `sum` computes the total of the elements. If `x` is a matrix, sum of each column is computed and a row vector consisting of the summation of each column is returned. A few examples are given next:

```
sum([2 1 5])
ans =
        8

sum([2 1 5]')
ans =
        8

sum([2 1 5; 9 8 5])
ans =
       11       9      10
```

Maximum and minimum: `max(x)` finds the maximum in vector `x`, and `min(x)` finds the minimum. Argument `x` can be a row or column vector, or a matrix. If `x` is a matrix, the answer is a row vector containing the maximum or minimum of each column of `x`. (The rule is the same as that for `sort` and `sum`.)

Random numbers: Random numbers can be generated by `rand`. Its synopsis is `rand(n)`, where `n` specifies the size of matrix of random numbers to be returned. If `n = 1`, a single random number is returned, and for `n > 1`, a n-by-n matrix of random numbers is returned. Unless otherwise specified, the random numbers generated in this way are in $0 \leq x \leq 1$. If `rand` is called repeatedly, a sequence of random numbers is generated. The random number generator may be initialized by giving a seed number. The synopsis of initialization is

```
rand('seed', k)
```

where `k` is the seed number. When the seed number is the same, the sequence of the random numbers becomes the same. If, however, the sequence is desired to be different randomly whenever the random generator is started, a randomly chosen seed number must be given. It could be the pollen count of the day, or the time in seconds, or a number drawn at a state lottery during the week, although finding a truly random number from natural phenomena or our daily life is not easy (see Example 1.1). The seed number must be greater than unity.

1.6 DEVELOPING A PROGRAM AS AN M-FILE

Executing commands from a window is suitable only if the amount of typing is small, or if you want to explore ideas interactively. When commands are more than a few lines long, however, the user should write a script M-file, or a function M-file, because the M-files are saved to disk and can be corrected as many times as needed.[4] The M-file can include anything the user would write directly in the command window. Beginners should try to develop short M-files first and execute them.

MAC and Windows: To prepare a new M-file on Macintosh or Windows, click NEW in the File menu at the top of the command window; then a new window will pop up. For exercise, type the content of List 1.1b, for example, and save it as an M-file by clicking SAVE AS in the Edit menu. The name of the M-file would be sphere.m. The file can be executed from the command window by typing sphere as a command. It may even be executed from another M-file by sphere. Another way to execute the file from Macintosh is to click SAVE and GO in the File menu.

Unix Workstation: Open MATLAB from the working directory where M-files are to be saved.[5] Also open an editor from the same directory. Any editing software can be used, including *vi, emacs* and *jot*. A file can be edited on the editor window and saved without closing the editor window. The filename needs extension .m on Unix. When ready to execute the M-file just saved, move to the MATLAB window and execute it by typing the filename without extension. In case Unix commands have to be invoked from MATLAB environment, type ! first followed by the Unix command. An editor software such as *vi* or *emac* may be opened in this way.

Echo: When a script is executed, the statements in the M-file are not usually printed on the screen. After echo is turned on with the echo on command, however, the statements are printed out. By this, the user can see which part of the M-file is being executed. To turn off echo, type echo off.

Comment statements: The % sign in M-files indicates that any statements after this sign on the same line are comments and are to be ignored for computations. Comments added to M-files in this way can help explain the meaning of variables and statements.

---

[4]M-files are classified into two categories: script M-file and function M-file. Script corresponds to a main program in traditional programming languages, while function corresponds to subprogram, subroutine, or function in traditional languages.

[5]MATLAB can be opened from any directory; however, in order to access to user-defined M-files and data files, appropriate paths must have been set up.

Example 1.1

Random numbers may be used to play a game. The x=rand(1) command generates a random number between 0 and 1 randomly and sets x to that number. Consider 13 spade cards which have been well shuffled. The probability of picking up one particular card from the stack is 1/13. Write a program to simulate the action of picking up one spade card by a random number. The game is to be continued by returning the card to the stack and shuffling again after each game is over.

Solution

Since the probability that a random number falls in an interval of size dx equals dx, we assume that if the random number falls in $(n-1)/13 < x < n/13$ then the nth card is drawn; however, n can be found by multiplying x by 13 and rounding up to the nearest higher integer.

Of course, before using rand, we have to initialize rand with a seed number. If the same seed is used, an identical sequence of random numbers is generated. One way to pick up a seed number is to use clock command. For example, c=clock will set c to a row vector of length 6. The product of the second through the last numbers, namely c(2)*c(3)*c(4)*c(5)*c(6) has approximately 3e+7 combinations and changes every second through a year.

The following M-file determines a card every time it is executed. The game is repeated by answering the prompted question by r but is terminated by typing any letter other than r. This M-file is saved by List1_19.m, so it can be executed from the command window by typing List1_19.

List 1.19
```
c=clock;
k=c(2)*c(3)*c(4)*c(5)*c(6);
rand('seed', k)
for k=1:20
  n=ceil(13*rand(1));
  fprintf('Card number drawn:    %3.0f\n', n)
  disp(' ')
  disp('Type r and hit Return to repeat')
  r = input('or any letter to terminate   ','s');
  if r ~= 'r', break, end
end
```

One interesting but useful feature of M-files is that an M-file can call other M-files. The calling M-file is a parent M-file, while the called M-files are children M-files. This implies that one script may be broken into one parent M-file and multiple children M-files. The children M-files are similar to function M-files that are explained in the next section. The difference, however, is that the parent and children M-files can see all the variables among them while function M-files can see only those variables given through arguments.

1.7 HOW TO WRITE USER'S OWN FUNCTIONS

Functions in MATLAB, which are saved as separate M-files, are equivalent to subroutines and functions in other languages.

A function that returns only one variable: Let us consider a function M-file for the following equation:

$$f(x) = \frac{2x^3 + 7x^2 + 3x - 1}{x^2 - 3x + 5e^{-x}} \tag{1.7.1}$$

Assuming the M-file is saved as demof_.m, its script is illustrated by

List 1.20
```
function y = demof_(x)
y = (2*x.^3+7*x.^2+3*x-1)./(x.^2-3*x+5*exp(-x));
```

Notice that the name of the M-file is identical to the name of the function, which appears on the right side of the equality sign. In the M-file, the array arithmetic operators are used, so the argument x can be a scaler as well as a vector or matrix. Once demof_.m is saved as an M-file, it can be used from the command window or in another M-file. The command

```
y = demof_(3)
```

yields

```
y =
    502.1384
```

If the argument is a matrix, for example,

```
demof_([3,1; 0, -1])
```

the result becomes a matrix also:

```
ans =
   502.1384   -68.4920
    -0.2000     0.0568
```

Function that returns multiple variables: A function may return more than one variable. Suppose a function that evaluates mean and standard deviation of data. To return the two variables, a vector is used on the left side of the function statement, for example,

List 1.21
```
function [mean,stdv] = mean_st(x)
n=length(x);
mean = sum(x)/n;
stdv = sqrt(sum(x.^2)/n - mean.^2);
```

To use this function, the left side of the calling statement should also be a vector. The foregoing script is to be saved as mean_st.m. Then,

```
x = [ 1 5 3 4 6 5 8 9 2 4];
[m, s] = mean_st(x)
```

yield

```
m =
    4.7000
s =
    2.3685
```

Function that uses another function: The argument of a function may be the name of another function. For example, suppose a function that evaluates a weighted average of a function at three points as

$$f_{av} = \frac{f(a) + 2f(b) + f(c)}{4} \tag{1.7.2}$$

where $f(x)$ is the function to be named in the argument. The following script illustrates a MATLAB function f_av.m that computes Eq.(1.7.2):

List 1.22
```
function wa = f_av(f_name, a, b, c)
wa = (feval(f_name,a) + 2*feval(f_name,b) ...
                      + feval(f_name,c))/4;
```

In the foregoing script, f_name (a string variable) is the name of the function $f(x)$. If $f(x)$ is the sine function, f_name equals 'sin'. The feval(f_name,x) is a MATLAB command that evaluates the function named f_name for the argument x. For example, y = feval('sin',x) becomes equivalent to y=sin(x).

Example 1.2

Evaluate Eq.(1.7.2) for the function defined by Eq.(1.7.1) with $a = 1, b = 2$ and $c = 3$. Equation (1.7.1) has been programmed as demof_.m given in List 1.19.

Solution

We assume f_av.m (List 1.22) has been saved as an M-file. Then, the command

```
        A = f_av('demof_', 1, 2, 3)
```
yields
```
        89.8976
```

The number of input and output arguments of `feval` must agree with the format of the function `f_name`. For example, if the function `f_name` needs four input variables and returns three output variables, the statement to call `feval` would be:

```
    [p, q, s] = feval( f_name, u, v, w, z)
```

Debugging of function M-files: Debugging function M-files is more difficult than script M-files. One reason is that you cannot see the values of variables by typing the variable names unless debugging commands are used. The most basic but effective method of developing a function M-file is to comment out the function statement on the first line by placing `%` before `function`, and test the M-file as a script M-file. Put the function statement back after a thorough examination of the M-file.

Using debugging commands is recommended only for advanced MATLAB users.

1.8   SAVING AND LOADING OF DATA

Save and load: If `save` is used by itself, like

```
    save
```

all the variables are saved in default file `matlab.mat`. The `load` command is the inverse of `save` command and retrieves all the variables saved by `save`.

The filename may be specified by placing it after `save`; for example:

```
    save file_name
```

saves all the variables in the file named `file_name.mat`. When you wish to retrieve the variables, write

```
    load file_name
```

If only selected variables are to be saved, write the variable names after `file_name`; for example:

```
    save file_name a b c
```

In this example, `a`, `b` and `c` are saved in the file named `file_name`. Do not separate `file_name` and variables by comma. All the variables are saved in double precision binary. When you wish to load the data in `file_name.mat`, type

```
load file_name
```

without variable names. Then, all of a, b and c are retrieved.

Save and load in ASCII format: save can be used to write data in ASCII format. The save and load with the ASCII option are important because export and import of data from MATLAB are possible by this means.

To use the ASCII format, -ascii or /ascii is appended after the variable names; for example,

```
save data.tmp  x  -ascii
```

saves variable x in 8-digit ASCII to the file named data.tmp. The save command can save more than one variable; for example,

```
x = [1, 2, 3, 4 ]
y = [-1, -2, -3]'
save dat1.tmp  x  y  -ascii
```

If you open the dat1.tmp M-file, it looks like

```
 1.0000000e+00   2.0000000e+00   3.0000000e+00   4.0000000e+00
-1.0000000e+00
-2.0000000e+00
-3.0000000e+00
```

The load command is to read a data file into a variable, but loading a file in ASCII format is not quite the inverse of save in ASCII format. The reason is that while save in ASCII can write multiple variables, load reads the entire data file into only one variable. Furthermore, the filename becomes the variable's name. For example, if a file named y_dat.e is loaded by

```
load y_dat.e
```

the content is loaded to the variable named y_dat regardless of the extension name.

Therefore, the data file y_dat must be only in one of the following data formats:

(1) a single number

(2) a row vector

(3) a column vector

(4) a matrix

If multiple variables have to be loaded, each variable should be prepared in a separate ASCII data file.

Data files prepared by Fortran or C in ASCII (or text) format can be loaded by load as long as the data structure is one of the four forms. For more advanced methods of exporting and importing data files, consult the MATLAB User's Guide.

1.9 HOW TO MAKE HARD COPIES

One frequently asked question is how to make hard copies of the MATLAB output on the screen. To produce a record file of keyboard input and output from MATLAB, use `diary`, introduced in Section 1.1. If `diary` is used without a specific filename, the filename becomes `diary` in the directory. The file can be printed out as a text file. Graphic figures are not captured in `diary`.

PROBLEMS

In answering the problems that follow, always prepare your answers with MATLAB.

(1.1) Run the following statements:

```
a = [1 2 3; 4 5 6]'
b = [9;7;5;3;1]
c = b(2:4)
d = b(4:-1:1)
e = sort(b)
f = [3,b']
```

(1.2) Develop a function M-file, `fun_es(x)`, to compute the following function:

$$y = 0.5e^{x/3} - x^2 \sin x$$

The argument must accept a scaler as well as a vector. Test your function by typing on MATLAB

```
fun_es(3)
fun_es([1 2 3])
```

(1.3) Repeat the task of Problem (1.2) for the function:

$$y = \sin(x)\log(1 + x) - x^2, \quad x > 0$$

Denote the function `fun_lg(x)`.

(1.4) (a) Write a function M-file that calculates solution of

$$ax^2 + bx + c = 0$$

Its synopsis is `quad_rt(a,b,c)` where a, b and c are allowed to be vectors. (b) Test the function by `a=3, b=1, c=1, quad_rt(a,b,c)`. (c) Test the function for `a=[3 1 2],b=[1 -4 9],c=[1 3 -5]`.

(1.5) The reader is assumed to have completed `fun_es` and `fun_lg` developed for Problems 1.2 and 1.3. Now, develop a function, `f_es(x)` that:

- asks the name of the function to be evaluated,
- lets the user type the function name,
- evaluates the function by `feval` and returns the functional values, and
- stops if the choice is neither `fun_es` nor `fun_lg`.

Test your `f_es` by computing `fun_es(3)` and `fun_lg(3)`.

(1.6) Two variables `x` and `y` are saved in `out_asc.m` file:

```
x = 1:5
y = [-1:-1:-5]'
save out_asc x y -ascii
```

How does the file look when the file is opened as an M-file? Is it possible to read both `x` and `y` from the same file? If `x` and `y` have to be saved in ASCII format and also have to be read later, what should you do?

(1.7) Rewrite the following script without using `break`:

```
for p=7:8
  for q = 3:5
    for r = 1:2
      fprintf(' %3.0f,    %3.0f,    %3.0f\n', p, q, r)
    end
    if q==4, break; end
  end
end
```

(1.8) Rewrite the script in Problem (1.7) using `while` but not using `for`.

(1.9) A vector is given:

```
A = [1 2 3 4 5 6 7 8 9 0]
```

Write a script to print out the vector content using the `fprintf` command in a loop such that the printout becomes

```
Vector A is
[  1, 2, 3, 4, 5, 6, 7, 8, 9, 0]
Print completed.
```

In the output, place a comma and two blank spaces between two numbers. Elements of `A` should be printed as numbers but not as strings.

(1.10) Write a script for a dice function that asks the player to type 0 or 1. If 1, the software finds ten numbers randomly from 1 through 6. Print out the ten numbers found in a row vector form. If the player's input is 0, the program is stopped. Obtain a seed random number by `clock` as follows:

```
c = clock;
sdnum = c(1)*c(2)*c(3)*c(4)*c(5)*c(6);
```

(1.11) Develop a function M-file named `fun_xa` that evaluates the following series:

$$f(x) = 1 + x + \frac{x^2}{2!} + \frac{x^3}{3!} + .. + \frac{x^n}{n!}$$

The values of x and n are passed to the function through arguments. Test the function by comparing the result with hand calculations for $x = 1$ and $n = 4$. The foregoing series is a truncated Mclaurin expansion of e^x and converges for $-\infty < x < \infty$. Knowing this, test your function for selected x values such as $x = 0.5, 3.0$ and -1, with $n = 1, 2, 3, 5, 10$ and compare with e^x.

(1.12) Develop a function M-file named `fun_xb` that evaluates the following series:

$$f(x) = x - \frac{x^2}{2} + \frac{x^3}{3} - .. + (-1)^{n+1} \frac{x^n}{n}$$

The values of x and n are passed to the function through arguments. Test the function by comparing the result with hand calculations for $x = 1$ and $n = 4$. The foregoing series is a truncated Mclaurin expansion of $\log(1+x)$ and converges for $-1 < x < 1$. Knowing this, test your function for selected x values such as $x = -0.5$ and 0.5, with $n = 1, 2, 3, 5, 10, 20, 50$ and compare with $\log(1+x)$. (Convergence becomes increasingly difficult as x approaches -1 or 1.

Chapter 2

Graphics with MATLAB

Because most mathematical equations express complicated relations in one, two, three, or more dimensions, trying to understand them without graphics is almost the same as being blindfolded. The use of graphics is important from elementary to higher education as well as to professional engineers and scientists for the same reason. In professional presentations, almost all mathematical, scientific, and engineering analyses are presented with graphics.

During the past three decades, when Fortran dominated among computing languages, graphics were unfortunately quite dissociated from computations. Therefore, many Fortran users were forced to read the computed results in the form of a printout of numbers.

Graphics are now a natural part of the computing environment with MATLAB, and plotting the results of computation is possible with very few commands. Readers are encouraged to plot mathematical functions encountered and results of analyses. Trying to understand mathematical equations with graphics is an enjoyable and very efficient way of learning mathematics. This chapter is written to assist the reader to do this.

Before unfolding this chapter, there are a few words of caution. Some graphic commands remain effective even after the plotting is completed, and may interfere with later works. An erratic behavior of MATLAB may start after some commands such as `hold on` or `subplot` are used, or execution of a script is abruptly interrupted. Readers are advised to clear variables and graphic windows before any plotting work starts. If MATLAB nevertheless behaves in a strange way, quit MATLAB completely and then reopen.

2.1 SIMPLE PLOTTING

Plot: Suppose a set of data points, (x_i, y_i), $i = 1, 2, ...n$, is to be plotted. One needs to prepare x and y in an identical array form; namely, x and y are both row arrays or column arrays of the same length. The data are plotted using `plot`. For example, $y = \sin(x)\exp(-0.4x)$, $0 \le x \le 10$, is plotted by List 2.1.

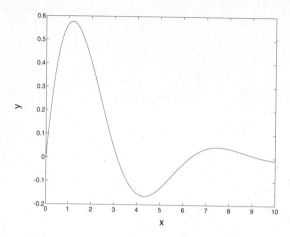

Figure 2.1 Plot by List 2.1 or 2.2

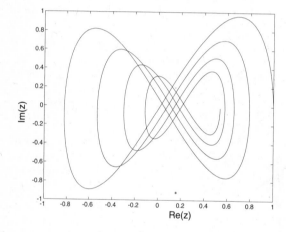

Figure 2.2 Plot by List 2.3

List 2.1
```
x = 0:0.05:10;
y=sin(x).*exp(-0.4*x);
plot(x,y)
xlabel('x'); ylabel('y')
```

Column vectors may also be used in the arguments of `plot`, as shown in the
following script:

List 2.2
```
x = (0:0.05:10)';
y=sin(x).*exp(-0.4*x);
plot(x,y)
xlabel('x'); ylabel('y')
```

The two foregoing scripts produce the same graph of Figure 2.1. The axis labels
are printed by `xlabel` and `ylabel` commands, which are explained in more detail
later. Figure 2.2 is plotted by List 2.3 connecting a series of points on a complex
plane.

List 2.3
```
p=0: 0.05: 8*pi;
z=(cos(p) + i*sin(2*p)).*exp(-0.05*p) + 0.01*p;
plot(real(z), imag(z))
xlabel('Re(z)'); ylabel('Im(z)')
```

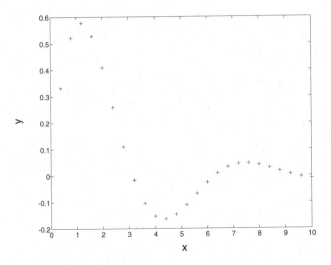

Figure 2.3 A graph plotted by marks only (List 2.4)

Plotting by marks only: Data can be plotted by marks only without being
connected by lines. Five types of marks or letters are available:

Mark type	Symbol
Point	.
Plus	+
Star	*
Circle	o
x-mark	x

To plot with one type of mark only, place the mark symbol as a string after the coordinates in the arguments of `plot`. The graph produced by List 2.4 is shown in Figure 2.3.

List 2.4
```
x = (0:0.4:10)';
y=sin(x).*exp(-0.4*x);
plot(x,y,'+')
xlabel('x'); ylabel('y')
```

To plot a function with both lines and a mark, plot twice: first time with lines and second time with marks only. To plot in this way, the last statement in List 2.4 is changed to `plot(x,y,x,y,'+')`. The `text` command may be used to plot with any mark or letter; however, the location of the mark may be somewhat offset from the actual location of the data point.

Line types and line colors: Four line types are available:

Line type	Symbol
solid	–
dash	– –
dotted	:
dashdot	–.

Default is the solid line type. To plot with a selected line type, specify the line mark after the coordinates, for example,

```
plot(x,y,'--')
```

The following colors are available:

Line color	Symbol
red	r
yellow	y
magenta	m
cyan	c
green	g
blue	b
white	w
black	k

Use the color symbol just like the line types in the argument of `plot`, for example:

```
plot(x,y,'g')
```

A combination of mark and color also is possible:

```
plot(x,y,'+g')
```

plots the data by + marks in green color.

Plotting a function by fplot: Another way to plot a single function is to use `fplot('f_name', [xmin,xmax])`, where `f_name` is the function name or function M-file to be plotted, and `xmin` and `xmax` are limits of the plot. Maximum and minimum of y-axis are determined by the actual maximum and minimum of the function. Limits of the graph, however, may be adjusted by `axis`; that is explained shortly.

Clearing plots: `clf` clears everything inside the graphic window, while `cla` clears the plotted curves and redraws the axes.

Implicit function: If a function is given implicitly, for example,

$$y^3 + \exp(y) = \tanh(x)$$

it cannot be expressed by x as a function of y nor y as a function of x. The curve can be be plotted, however, using `contour`. More details of this approach are discussed in Section 2.3.

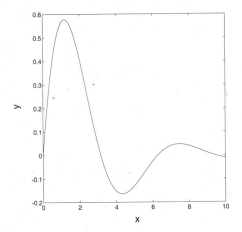

Figure 2.4 A plot with `axis('square')`

Axis: The minimum and maximum of the coordinates, tic marks, and the coordinate values at the tic marks are all determined automatically. The shape of the frame, and minimum and maximum of the coordinates, however, may be changed by `axis`. A figure can be reshaped to a square form by

```
axis('square')
```

(see Figure 2.4). The coordinate axis and tic marks can be removed by

```
axis('off')
```

This effect is canceled by `axis('on')`.

The maximum and minimum of the coordinates on the graph may be specified by

```
axis([x_min, x_max, y_min, y_max])
```

Any lines outside the limits will be clipped. This command is used after `plot` so view area can be changed as many times as desired. It is suggested that the reader append `axis([-2, 6, -0.7, 0.7])` to List 2.4 in order to see the effect of `axis` to limit the boundary of the figure.

Grid: A grid can be added to the graph by `grid on`. On the other hand, `grid off` removes the grid. Simply using `grid` multiple times turns on and off the grid. An example of using `grid on` is given in the following script:

List 2.5

```
x = (0:0.2:10)';
y=sin(x).*exp(-0.4*x);
plot(x,y)
grid on
xlabel('x'); ylabel('y')
```

(See Figure 2.5 produced by List 2.5.)

Polar plot: A function on a polar coordinate can be plotted by `polar`. Figure 2.6 is plotted by List 2.6.

List 2.6

```
t = 0:.05:pi+.01;
y = sin(3*t).*exp(-0.3*t);
polar(t,y)
title('Polar plot')
grid
```

Log and semilog plots: A function may be plotted on a log-log scale by `loglog`. (See List 2.7 and Figure 2.7.)

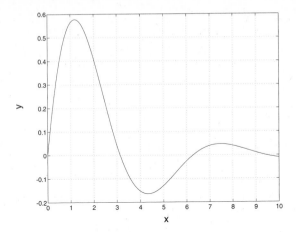

Figure 2.5 A figure with a grid (List 2.5)

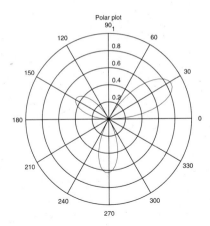

Figure 2.6 Polar plot (List 2.6)

List 2.7

```
t = .1:.1:3;
x = exp(t);
y = exp(t.*sinh(t));
loglog(x,y)
grid
xlabel('x');ylabel('y')
```

A semilog plot with the log scale for y is produced by List 2.8.

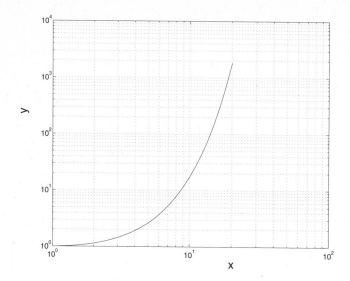

Figure 2.7 A log plot (List 2.7)

List 2.8
```
t = .1:.1:3;
semilogy(t,exp(t.*t))
grid
xlabel('t'); ylabel('exp(t.*t)');
```

Similarly, a semilog plot with log scale for x is produced by List 2.9.

List 2.9
```
t = .1:.1:3;
semilogx(t,exp(t.*t))
grid
xlabel('t'); ylabel('exp(t.*t)');
```

Multiple Curves: To plot two or more curves with a single `plot` command, write all the sets of coordinates repeatedly in the `plot` command:

List 2.10
```
x = 0:0.05:5;
y = sin(x);
z = cos(x);
plot(x,y,x,z)
```

Different line type or color is automatically selected for each curve by default. Line color, type or mark, however, may be specified after each pair of coordinates; for example,

```
plot(x,y,'--', x,z, '*')
plot(x,y,':', x,z, '*g')
plot(x,y,'r', x,z, 'y')
```

The following two lists show another way to plot multiple curves by one `plot` command:

List 2.11

```
x = 0:0.05:5;
y(1,:) = sin(x);
y(2,:) = cos(x);
plot(x,y)
```

List 2.12

```
x = (0:0.05:5)';
y(:,1) = sin(x);
y(:,2) = cos(x);
plot(x,y)
```

Hold on: Until now we plotted all the curves at once with a single `plot` command. It becomes often desirable, however, to add a curve to the graph that has been already plotted. Such additional plotting can be done using `hold on` (see Figure 2.8).

List 2.13

```
x = 0:0.05:5;
y = sin(x);
plot(x,y);
hold on
z = cos(x);
plot(x,z,'--')
xlabel('x');ylabel('y(-) and  z(--) ');
```

Once `hold on` command is issued, the graph stays on even when another script is run. Therefore, it is prudent to place a `hold off` command at both the beginning and end of the script; for example

List 2.14

```
clear; clf; hold off
x = 0: 0.05: 5;
y = sin(x);
plot(x,y)
hold on
z = cos(x)
plot(x,z)
hold off
```

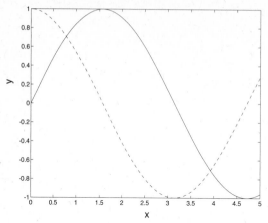

Figure 2.8 Two curves plotted with `hold on` command (List 2.13)

When multiple curves are plotted with `hold on`, it is desirable to specify minimums and maximums of the coordinates on the graphic domain by `axis` command. Otherwise, the limits are determined by default based on the first curve, which may cause other curves to be clipped.

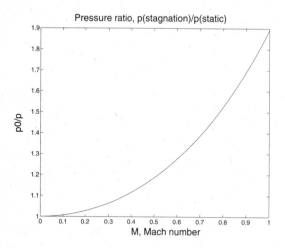

Figure 2.9 Application of `title` command (List 2.15A)

The `hold on` command also becomes very important when a time-consuming plot is undertaken, for the following reason: The command to change parameters for figures such as axis, color map, view angles, color axis, and other parameters can be changed after a figure is plotted, but each time a new command is issued, the whole figure is replotted. In order to save time, give all the parameter commands before plotting, hold with `hold on`, and then use `plot`.

Titles and labels: Coordinate labels and titles may be added to the graph using `xlabel`, `ylabel` and `title`. The following script uses all three commands:

List 2.15A

```
M = [0: 0.01: 1]';k=1.4;
p0_over_p = (1 + (k-1)/2*M.^2).^(k/(k-1));
plot(M,p0_over_p)
xlabel('M, Mach number')
ylabel('p0/p')
title('Pressure ratio, p(stagnation)/p(static)')
```

Figure 2.9 illustrates the graph produced by List 2.15A.

The argument of `xlabel`, `ylabel` and `text` can include more than one string, but they must be written in row vector form; for example,

```
title(['string1', 'string2', ...])
```

Conversion of number to string: In writing texts and labels, one may wish to include numerical values in the text. The commands `num2str` and `int2str`, which stand for *number to string* and *integer to string*, respectively, may be used for this purpose; for example,

```
st = num2str(pi)
```

defines `st` as a string containing `3.142`. By `int2str`, a real value is converted to a string containing only the integer part of the number. For example, by

```
st = int2str(pi)
```

`st` becomes a string variable containing 3. Once a number is converted to a string, it can be used in the arguments of `title`, `xlabel` and `ylabel`, or `text`; for example,

```
title([' Case: ', st, ' cm'])
```

Text in the graph: Text can be written in a graph by `text` or `gtext`. The former needs three parameters in the argument, namely `text(x, y, 'string')`. The first two are x and y values of the absolute coordinates where the string starts. The third is a string variable to be printed. The string variable can be a text enclosed by quote signs or a predefined string variable. An example of the command is

```
text( 2, 4, '+++ material')
```

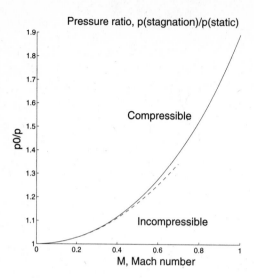

Figure 2.10 A graph with texts (List 2.15B)

The foregoing command prints `+++ material` starting at (2,4) on the current coordinate system.

List 2.15B illustrates the use of `text`, and its result is illustrated in Figure 2.10.

List 2.15B

```
% Pressure ratio vs. Mach number
clear; clf; hold off;
M = [0:0.01:1]';
k=1.4;
p0_over_p = (1 + (k-1)/2*M.^2).^(k/(k-1));
hold on
axis('square'); %makes graph square
plot(M,p0_over_p)
xlabel('Mach number, M')
ylabel('p0/p')
title('Pressure ratio, p(stagnation)/p(static)')
text(0.45, 1.55, 'Compressible')
Mb= [0: 0.01: 0.7]';
p0_over_pb = 1 + k/2*Mb.^2;
plot(Mb,p0_over_pb,'--')
text(0.5, 1.1, 'Incompressible')
```

If location of a text needs to be determined manually, `gtext('string')` is useful. When this command is executed, the program waits for mouse or key to be pressed while the mouse pointer is within the graphic screen. The text is written at any desired location pointed to by the mouse or cursor.

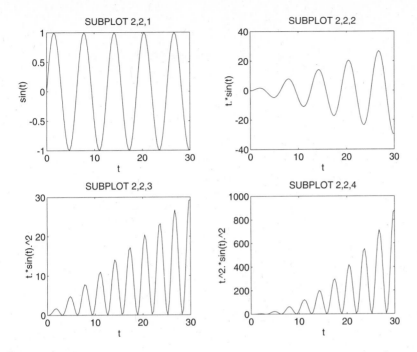

Figure 2.11 Illustration of subplots (List 2.16)

While `text` also works in three-dimensional axes, `gtext` works only in two-dimensional axes.

Color and font size of a text in the graph may be changed. For example,

```
text(0.3,0.2,'string','FontSize',[18],'Color','r')
```

will print `string` in red color with font size 18. If a default color is to be changed, write:

```
set(gcf,'DefaultTextColor','yellow')
```

Thereafter, the text will be printed in yellow. Color for text may be chosen from red, yellow, green, cyan, blue, and magenta, which can be abbreviated by 'r','y','g','c','b', and 'm', respectively. Color may be changed for another text in a similar way as many times as necessary. Availability of font sizes seem to vary depending on the MATLAB edition.

Greek symbols may be typed by `text` also; for example,

```
text(2,0,'abcdefg..', 'FontName','symbol')
```

will print $\alpha\beta\chi\delta\epsilon\phi\gamma$... The specifiers `'FontName'` and `'symbol'` in the arguments convert the alphabetic letters to Greek. The conversion of alphabetic letters to greek letters and symbols in MATLAB is shown in Table 2.1.

Table 2.1 Conversion of alphabetic letters to Greek letters and symbols

a	α	q	θ
b	β	r	ρ
c	χ	s	σ
d	δ	t	τ
e	ϵ	u	υ
f	ϕ	v	ϖ
g	γ	w	ω
h	η	x	ψ
i	ι	z	ζ
j	φ	D	Δ
k	κ	G	Γ
l	λ	S	Σ
m	μ	W	Ω
n	ν	X	Ψ
o	o	\$	$\exists$
p	π	?	$\forall$

The font size of the axis tic mark values may be changed by `set`; for example,

```
set(gca, 'FontSize',[18])
```

will change the font of axis to size 18. In case a text is improperly placed, there is no means to erase it. The only way to correct it is to redraw the whole figure after correcting the script.

Figure: Multiple graphic windows may be opened by `figure`. If only one window is used, this command is not necessary. When more graphic windows are necessary, however, `figure` will open additional graphic windows. When a graphic window previously opened needs to be reactivated, `figure(n)` will reactivate the n-th window, where n is the sequential figure number that is displayed on the top of the graphic window. Properties of figures, such as size, location, assigned colormap, and so on, may be changed. For more details, see MATLAB Reference Guide, or type `help figure`.

Subplot: With `subplot` one can plot m-by-n graphs in a single figure. The synopsis is

```
subplot(m,n,k)
```

where m, n, and k are integers. Here, the pair of m and n means a m-by-n array of graphs, and k is the sequential number of the graph. For example, `plot` following `subplot(3,2,1)` will plot the first graph in the 3-by-2 figures. The following script plots four graphs, as illustrated in Figure 2.11:

List 2.16

```
clear;clf
t=0:.3:30;
subplot(2,2,1), plot(t,sin(t)),title('SUBPLOT 2,2,1')
            xlabel('t'); ylabel('sin(t)')
subplot(2,2,2), plot(t,t.*sin(t)),title('SUBPLOT 2,2,2')
            xlabel('t'); ylabel('t.*sin(t)')
subplot(2,2,3), plot(t,t.*sin(t).^2),title('SUBPLOT 2,2,3')
            xlabel('t'); ylabel('t.*sin(t).^2')
subplot(2,2,4), plot(t,t.^2 .*sin(t).^2),title('SUBPLOT 2,2,4')
            xlabel('t'); ylabel('t.^2.*sin(t).^2')
```

A vertical stack of two graphs is plotted by

```
    subplot(2,1,1), plot( ..
    subplot(2,1,2), plot( ..
```

Likewise a row of two graphs is plotted by

```
    subplot(1,2,1), plot( ..
    subplot(1,2,2), plot( ..
```

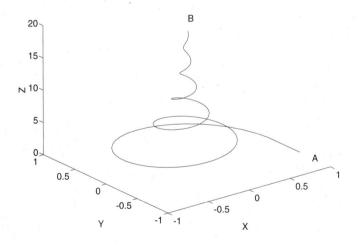

Figure 2.12 Illustration of 3D plot (List 2.17)

Axes: Advanced users of MATLAB may be interested in axes command, which is useful for plotting multiple graphs in one figure window like subplot.

However, `axes` provides more freedom with respect to locations and sizes of the plots. See Appendix E for more details of `axes`.

3D version of plot: `plot3` is the three-dimensional version of `plot`. All the rules and commands explained for `plot` apply to `plot3`. A spiral motion of a particle from point A to B in Figure 2.12 is plotted by List 2.17 using `plot3`. The view angle may be changed by `view`, as explained in Section 2.6. The `axis` command,

```
axis([x_min, x_max, y_min, y_max, z_min, z_max])
```

also may be used to define bounds of the three-dimensional space.

List 2.17
```
clear,clf
t=0:0.1:20;
r= exp(-0.2*t);
th=pi*t*0.5;
z=t;
x=r.*cos(th);
y=r.*sin(th);
plot3(x,y,z)
hold on
plot3([1,1], [-0.5,0], [0,0])
text( 1,-0.7,0, 'A')
n=length(x);
text( x(n),y(n),z(n)+2,'B')
xlabel('X'); ylabel('Y'); zlabel('Z');
```

2.2   HOW TO MAKE HARD COPY OF GRAPHS

There are two kinds of procedures for producing hard copies of figures. The first is direct printing on the current printer. The second is to create a file to be printed later by a designated printer.

The method of immediately printing out the figures of the screen on the current printer varies, depending on which computer you use.[1]

Macintosh: There is a print command in the menu window. Click it after the graph is plotted on the screen. A postscript graphic file may be created by `print f_name.ps`.

PC Windows: Same as Macintosh.

---

[1]For color postscript copying, see MATLAB User's Guide.

Unix Workstation: Command `print` sends the plot to the default printer of the system.

In order to create a file of the figure to be printed out later or on another computer, the type of printer must be specified. For example, to create a file to be printed by a postscript printer, the command is

    print -dps filename

or

    print filename.ps

This creates a postscript file `filename.ps` which can be printed out by a postscript printer.[2] For an HP DeskJet 500C printer with 1 bit/pixel color, as another example, the command is

    print -dcdeskjet filename

The foregoing command creates a file named `filename.jet`, which can be printed from any computer with the HP DeskJet 500C. To obtain more information for different situations, use `help print`.

2.3   CONTOUR OF TWO-DIMENSIONAL FUNCTIONS

Mesh: A two-dimensional function $z = z(x, y)$ may be defined with discrete points by

$$z_{i,j} = z(x_i, y_j) \qquad (2.3.1)$$

where $x_i, i = 1, 2, ...m$, and $y_j, j = 1, 2, ...n$, are points on x and y axes in increasing order. The intersections comprise a cartesian grid.

For illustration, let us consider the grid defined by

$$x_{i,j} = x_i = -2 + 0.2(i - 1), \quad 1 \le i \le 21$$
$$y_{i,j} = y_j = -2 + 0.2(j - 1), \quad 1 \le j \le 21$$

and functional values by

$$z_{i,j} = x_i \exp(-x_i^2 - y_j^2) \qquad (2.3.2)$$

The foregoing function is plotted in Figure 2.13 by List 2.18.

---

[2]Most figures in this book were created by MATLAB and saved as postscript files. LaTex, which was used to typeset the book, is capable of including the graphs from postscript files. To do this, the names of the postscript files are written in appropriate places in the LaTex manuscript.

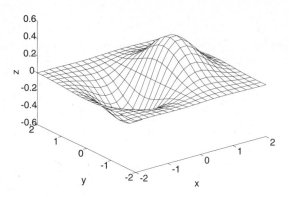

Figure 2.13 Mesh plot (List 2.18)

List 2.18
```
clear, clf
xa = -2:.2:2;
ya = -2:.2:2;
[x,y] = meshgrid(xa,ya);
z = x .* exp(-x.^2 - y.^2);
mesh(x,y,z)
title('This is a 3-D plot of  z = x * exp(-x^2 - y^2)')
xlabel('x'); ylabel('y'); zlabel('z');
```

In List 2.18, meshgrid is used to create two-dimensional arrays, x and y, where x is a two-dimensional array for the x coordinates of the grid, and y is an array of the y coordinates. These x and y are used in computing the two-dimensional array, z.

It is very important to recognize, however, how the two-dimensional arrays, namely x, y and z, correspond to $x_{i,j}$, $y_{i,j}$ and $z_{i,j}$, respectively. The fact is that x(j,i), y(j,i) and z(j,i) correspond to $x_{i,j}$, $y_{i,j}$ and $z_{i,j}$, respectively. In other words, the first index of x, y and z changes in the y direction while the second index changes in the x direction. This rule should be respected if elements of z(j,i) are computed using for/end loops.

The mesh command in the foregoing script may be replaced by mesh(z). The first index of z changes in the y direction while the second index in the x direction.

Contour: Contour of a function in a two-dimensional array can be plotted by contour. Its basic synopsis is

```
contour(x, y, z, level)
```

Here, z is the two-dimensional array of function, x and y are, respectively, x and y coordinates in two-dimesnional arrays, and `level` is a vector containing the levels of contour. The coordinates, x and y can also be one-dimensional arrays. The rule mentioned earlier, however, regarding the indices of z for `mesh` applies here again. That is, the first index of z changes in the direction of y while the second index in the direction of x. If the grid is equispaced, a simpler form is `contour(z)`. In this case, the first and second grid indices change in the y and x directions, respectively. Also, `level` may be replaced by an integer, m, which will be interpreted as the number of contour levels. The contour levels are determined by dividing the minimum and maximum values of z into m-1 intervals.

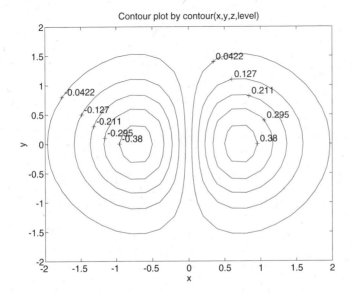

Figure 2.14 Contour plot (List 2.19)

Figure 2.14 shows a contour plot by List 2.19, where the function plotted is defined by Eq.(2.3.1) and the same as for Figure 2.13. The contour values in the figure were annotated by `clabel(h,'manual')` which allows the user to locate the position of the numbers by mouse. The contour levels may be automatically annotated by `clabel(h)`.

List 2.19

```
clear, clc, clf, axis('square')
xm=-2:.2:2; ym=-2:.2:2;
[x , y ] = meshgrid(xm,ym);
z = x .* exp(-x.^2 - y.^2);
zmax=max(max(z)); zmin=min(min(z));
```

```
dz = (zmax-zmin)/10;
level = zmin + 0.5*dz: dz: zmax;
h=contour(x,y,z,level); clabel(h,'manual')
title('Contour plot by contour(x,y,z,level)')
xlabel('x'); ylabel('y')
```

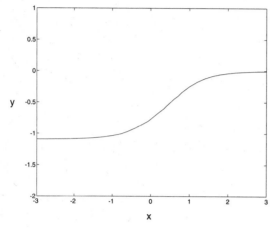

Figure 2.15 Plot of a curve specified by an implicit function

The `contour` command may be used to plot an implicit function such as

$$y^3 + \exp(y) = \tanh(x)$$

To plot the curve, we rewrite the equation to

$$f(x,y) = y^3 + \exp(y) - \tanh(x)$$

and plot contour for only one level corresponding to $f = 0$ (see Figure 2.15). The following script illustrates the plotting procedure:

List 2.20
```
clear, clf
xm = -3:0.2:3;   ym = -2:0.2:1;
[x, y] = meshgrid(xm, ym);
f = y.^3 + exp(y) - tanh(x);
contour(x,y,f,[0,0])
xlabel('x'); ylabel('y')
```

Notice in the foregoing script that the vector `[0,0]` in the arguments of `contour` is to specify the level of the contour. The only contour we are interested in is for level 0, but the contour levels must be in a vector form, so we repeat zero twice.

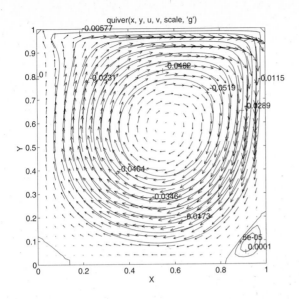

Figure 2.16 Contour and vectors

Vector plot: Quantities at grid points sometimes may be given as a vector form. For example, velocity distribution in a two-dimensional fluid flow may be expressed by velocity vectors at grid points. The vectors at grid points may be plotted by `quiver`. The vectors for the grid points need two components, one for the x direction and another for the y direction. Suppose these components are given by u and v, which are both matrices of the same size as x and y. Then, the vectors are plotted by

```
quiver(x,y,u,v,s)
```

where s is a scale factor that is a user parameter to adjust the lengths of the vectors. Figure 2.16 illustrates the plots of velocity vectors in a typical flow problem (called a driven cavity flow). The figure also shows plots of stream lines by `contour`. The following script illustrates essential parts of the script to plot Figure 2.16.

```
%   (Earlier part of the script to compute x,y,s,u, and v
%   are omitted.)
clf
L=[-0.00577:-0.00577:-0.054,  0, 0.0001, 0.00005];
c=contour(x,y,s,L);      % s=stream function
clabel(c)
title('stream function  Re=400 (grid 51x51)')
xlabel('x   direction')
ylabel('y   direction')
axis('square')
hold on                  % u and v comprise a vector.
```

```
quiver(x(1:2:ni,1:2:ni),y(1:2:ni,1:2:ni), ...
       u(1:2:ni,1:2:ni),v(1:2:ni,1:2:ni),4)
```

In the foregoing list, we assume that x, y, u, and v have been computed by an earlier part of the script which is not shown.

2.4   TRIANGULAR GRID AND CONTOURS

A triangular grid consists of triangular elements and is most often used in the finite element or finite volume analyses.

Plotting a triangular grid: To plot a triangular grid, the two data files denoted cell_da and point_da are necessary. The former includes the data of triangular elements, and the latter includes the coordinates of the nodal points. (More details of the files are explained in FM 2-1, page 76.)

When List 2.21 is executed, two questions are prompted. The first question is whether element numbers are to be annotated. Type 1 for yes, or 0 for no. The second question is whether point numbers are to be annotated. Type 1 for yes, or 0 for no. The first figure of Figure 2.17 shows the grid plotted.

List 2.21

```
%tri_grid_plot
clear,clf
load cell_da
load point_da
tri_grid(cell_da,point_da, 1.8)
```

Contour plot on triangular grid: For a discrete function defined at the nodal points on a triangular grid, contour may be plotted by tri_cont in FM 2-2 (page 79). To run this script, two data files cell_da and point_da (the same as used in tri_cont) and an additional function file f_da are necessary. The second figure in Figure 2.17 illustrates the contour plot by List 2.22 using tri_cont.

List 2.22

```
%Contour plot on triangular grid
clear,clf
load cell_da
load point_da
load f_da
tri_cont(cell_da,point_da,f_da, 1.8)
```

2.5   CURVILINEAR GRID AND CONTOURS

Suppose the functional values of $f(x, y)$ are given on grid points, $(x_{i,j}, y_{i,j})$, by

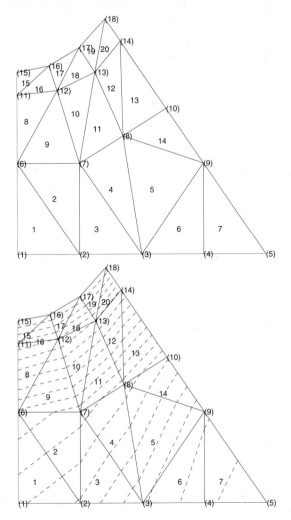

Figure 2.17 A triangular grid, and contour plot (printing element and point numbers are optional.)

$$f_{i,j} = f(x_{i,j}, y_{i,j})$$

where $i = 1, 2, ..., i_{max}$ and $j = 1, 2, ..., j_{max}$ are indices of points. The grid system is named a Cartesian grid if the grid lines are parallel to the axes of the Cartesian coordinates. When a complicated geometry is involved, however, the grid points fitted to curved boundaries, as illustrated in Figure 2.18, may be used. Such a grid is called a *curvilinear grid*.

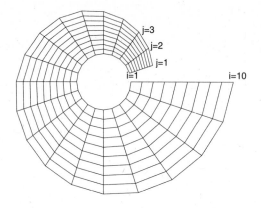

Figure 2.18 Plot of a curvilinear grid

Curvilinear grid and contour of $f_{i,j}$ on a curvilinear grid may be plotted by g_cont in FM 2.3 (page 81). Its synopsis is:

```
g_cont(x, y, f, level)
```

where

    x, y: the coordinates of the grid points.
    f : two-dimensional array of the functional values.
    level : contour levels in the vector form.

For demonstration purpose, the reader might run the following script:

List 2.23
```
clear, clf
[x, y ,f] = td_data;
f_max = max(max(f))
f_min = min(min(f))
kmax=20;
for k=1:kmax
    ELV(k)=(k-1)/kmax*(f_max-f_min)*0.9999 + f_min ;
end
g_cont(x, y, f, ELV)
0    % To automatically answer the question from g_cont
```

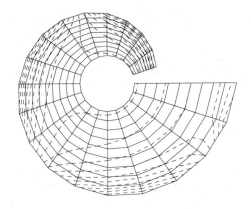

Figure 2.19 A sample of contour plot

```
1    % Ditto
axis([-10, 15, -15, 10])
axis('square')
axis('off')
```

In the foregoing script, td_data is a function M-file in FM 2.3 that generates the sample grid and function for demonstration. The contour plot plotted by List 2.23 is shown in Figure 2.19. The data f generated by td_data can be plotted by mesh as shown in Figure 2.20 or surf explained in Section 2.6, but contour cannot be used because the grid is not rectangular.

2.6   MESH AND SURFACE PLOTTING

In this section, we study three-dimensional graphics, which have been significantly enhanced in the new student edition and late professional versions of MATLAB. Although mesh has been already introduced, we revisit mesh for more details.

Mesh plot of a matrix: The simplest application of three-dimensional graphics is to plot a matrix. Consider an m-by-n matrix, z. The element, z(j,i), is considered to be the functional value at $y = j$ and $x = i$ on the two-dimensional plane. We define a sample matrix by

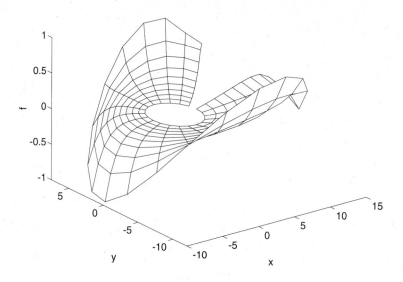

Figure 2.20 Mesh plot corresponding to Fig.2.19

List 2.24

```
clear,clf
for i=1:4     %  corresponds to x direction
    for j=1:7 %  corresponds to y direction
        z(j,i) = sqrt(i^2 + j^2);
    end
end
mesh(z)
xlabel('i')
ylabel('j')
zlabel('z')
```

Then,

```
mesh(z)
```

yields the mesh plot shown in Figure 2.21.

   Default color: On a color screen, the lines connecting the points are colored
by the default color map `hsv` (hue saturation value). Red is assigned for both the
lowest and highest values of $z(i,j)$. In between the lowest and highest, the color
is determined linearly in order of red, yellow, green, cyan, blue, magenta, red.

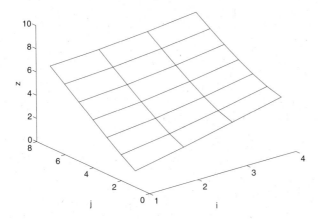

Figure 2.21 Mesh plot of a matrix

   The lines in Figure 2.21 at the highest elevation (if viewed on a color screen), however, are purple and at the lowest elevation are reddish yellow. This is because the color of a line is determined by the average of the z values of the two points connected. For the present mesh plot, the color value of a line at the highest elevation is somewhere close to magenta, while the color value of the line at the lowest elevation is close to yellow. If much finer mesh is plotted, then the highest and lowest lines both become red.

   Axis and labels: The limits of the three-dimensional space in the plot are determined automatically, but may be changed by axis[xmin, xmax, ymin, ymax, zmin, zmax] just like its use in two-dimensional plots. The labels for the x-, y-, and z-axes may be added by xlabel, ylabel and zlabel, respecively.

   View: The view angle of mesh plot may be changed by view([az, el]) or view([x, y, z]). Here, az is the azimuthal angle and el is the elevation angle. When az=0 and el=0, the viewer's eye position is at the reference view angle that is along the negative y-axis (see Figure 2.22). With this view, the plot becomes a two-dimensional x-z plane with the z-axis vertical and x-axis stretching horizontally to the right. The az rotates the eye position *counterclockwise* by az degrees about the z-axis from the reference angle (the same as rotating the plot about the z-axis clockwise by the same degrees). The el elevates the eye angle by el degrees from the x-y plane. The default values are az = -37.5 degrees and

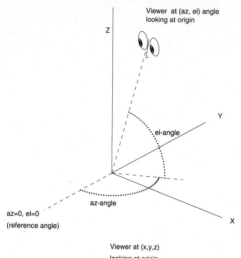

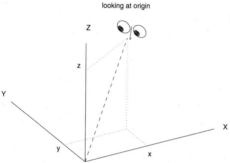

Figure 2.22 Eye position in angles.

Figure 2.23 Eye position at (x, y, z)

el=30 degrees.

When view is used with three-dimensional coordinates as view([x, y, z]), the viewer's eye is assumed to be along the vector [x, y, z] extended from the origin (see Figure 2.23). The view([0,-1,0]) is equivalent to view([0,0]) in angles. The relations between angles and triplets are given by

```
az = atan2(x,-y)*180/pi;
el = atan2(z,sqrt(x^2 + y^2))*180/pi
```

Figures 2.24 and 2.25 illustrate different views of a mesh. The mesh plots illustrated in Figure 2.24 are plotted by the following script:

List 2.25
```
clear, clf
yp=1:5;
xp=1:4;
```

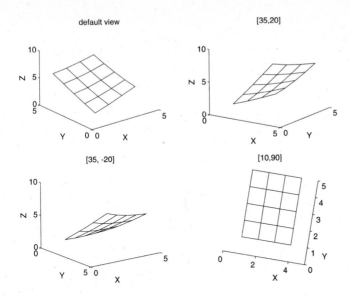

Figure 2.24 Mesh with different views

```
[x,y]=meshgrid(xp,yp);
z=sqrt(x.^2 + y.^2);
%
subplot(221)
mesh(x,y,z)
axis([0,5,0,5,0,10])
title('default view')
xlabel('X')
ylabel('Y')
zlabel('Z')
%
subplot(222)
mesh(x,y,z)
axis([0,5,0,5,0,10])
title('[35,20]')
view([35,20])
xlabel('X')
ylabel('Y')
zlabel('Z')
%
subplot(223)
mesh(x,y,z)
axis([0,5,0,5,0,10])
title('[35, -20]')
view([35, -20])
xlabel('X')
ylabel('Y')
```

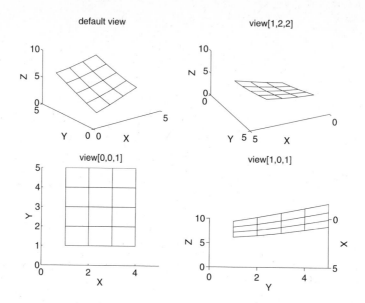

Figure 2.25 Mesh plot with different views

```
zlabel('Z')
%
subplot(224)
mesh(x,y,z)
axis([0,5,0,5,0,10])
title('[10,90]')
xlabel('X')
ylabel('Y')
zlabel('Z')
view([10,90])
axis('square')
```

Contour with mesh: The `meshc` plots contour of z on the x-y plane in addition to plots by `mesh(z)`. Figure 2.26 is plotted by the following script:

List 2.26

```
clear,clf,hold off
dth=pi/20;
j=1:21;
i=1:10;
x = log(i);
y = log(j);
[x,y] = meshgrid(x,y);
z=sqrt(0.1*((x-log(5)).^2 + (y-log(5)).^2))+1;
meshc(x,y,z)
```

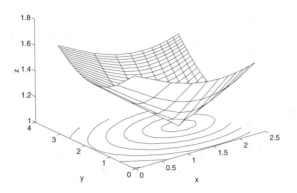

Figure 2.26 Mesh and contour of a matrix

```
xlabel('x')
ylabel('y')
zlabel('z')
```

Surface and contour: The `surf` and `surfc` commands produce similar plots as `mesh` and `meshc` except `surf` and `surfc` paint the inside of each mesh cell with color, so an image of surfaces is created. The color of the cell is determined by the average of z at four corner points.

Surface with lighting: The `surf` command can be replaced by `surfl`, but the latter creates a surface object with lighting. The direction of the light source can be also specified. For example, its basic synopsis is `surfl(x,y,z,s)` with a default lighting. However, a specifc lighting source direction may be specified by `surfl(x,y,z,s)`, where s is a directional vector for the light in the same form as the view angle in degrees. It is recommnded to use `surfl` with `colormap gray` and `shading flat` or `shading interp`. An example of a plot is illustrated in Appendix B (see Figure B4).

More control of lighting conditions:[3] More lighting control is possible using `surfnorm`, and `diffuse` or `specular` in conjunction with `surf`. The `[xn,yn,zn] = surfnorm(x,y,z)` command generates a vector set `[xn,yn,zn]` that represents the normal directions of the surface `(x, y, z)`. Command `r = specular(xn,yn,zn, L)` determines the intensity of light that come from the surface, where `L` is a directional vector or an angular vector in degrees that

---

[3]This is an advanced subject. Beginners are advised to skip this subject.

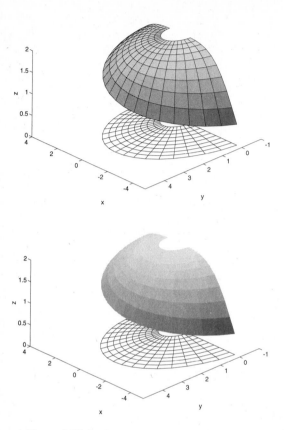

Figure 2.27 Surface on a curvilinear grid

defines the direction of the light. Therefore, using `r` in place of color vector
in `surf`, a diffuse lighting image is created. The `diffuse` may be replaced by
`specular(nxn,yn,zn, L,V)` where `V` is a directional vector or angular vector
that defines the viewer's direction. A sample script is illustrated next. Readers
are encouraged to investigate the effects of changing parameters in the script. An
example of surface plot with specular lighting is shown as a spiral pipe in the color
plates.

```
clear,clf
axis([-1.5, 1.5, -1.5 1.5, -1.3 1.3])
view([1 -0.5 0.31])
caxis([-0.8 1.5])
colormap hot
hold on
L=[0.5,0.3,0.7]; V=[1,1,1];
```

```
[x,y,z] = sphere(20);
[xn,yn,zn] = surfnorm(x,y,z);
% r = specular(xn,yn,zn, L,V);
  r = diffuse(xn,yn,zn, L);
surf(x,y,z,r)
shading interp
```

Mesh or surface on a curvilinear grid: For a surface on a curvilinear grid, order of i and j is of no concern as far as they are used consistently among all arrays involved. For a curvilinear grid, x is an n-by-m matrix and its element x(i,j) is the x-coordinate of point (i,j), while y is the y-coordinate. The first figure in Figure 2.27 displays the surface plot with the nonrectangular grid (see List 2.27).

List 2.27

```
clear,clf,hold off
dth=pi/20
for j=1:21
for i=1:10
r=0.5+0.2*i + j*0.01*i;
th = dth*(j-1);
x(i,j) = r*cos(th);
y(i,j)= r*sin(th);
z=cos(0.1*(x.^2 + y.^2))+1;
end
end
surf(x,y,z) % plotting a surface
xlabel('x')
ylabel('y')
zlabel('z')
axis([-5, 4, -1 , 5 ])
view([-135,40])
hold on
mesh(x,y,zeros(size(x))) % plotting a grid on x-y plane
colormap hot
caxis([-0.5,3])
hold off
% shading flat    % for the second plot of Fig 2.27
```

Contour cannot be plotted by meshc and surfc if the grid is not rectangular.

Color axis: Control of colors is possible by writing the fourth argument in mesh and surf commands; for example,

```
mesh(x,y,z,c)
```

The fourth argument c is a vector of the same size as z and specifies the color coordinate. When c is omitted, c is assumed to equal z, and the colors of lines and surfaces are determined by the values of z.

Unless `colormap` command has been used, the colormap is set to `colormap hsv` by default. Then, the red color is assigned to the point with the lowest value of `c(j,i)`, as well as to the point with the highest value of `c(j,i)`. The color for `c(j,i)` in between the lowest and highest is determined linearly in order of red, yellow, green, cyan, blue, magenta, and red. Different color values, however, can be assigned to the mesh points by `c` defined by the user. The command

```
caxis([0, 100])
```

sets red to 0 and 100. Therefore, if the color matrix elements in `c(j,i)` are all set near 0, the whole plot becomes reddish, while if the color matrix elements are around 50, the whole plot becomes bluish to purple.

Colormap: Definition of colors on the color axis may be changed by `colormap`. Alternative colormap definitions include `colormap(hot)`, `colormap (cold)`, and `colormap(jet)` to replace `colormap(hsv)`. Try these commands to alter the color scheme of a mesh or surface plot. More general aspects are described in Appendix A. The argument of `colormap` may be written without parentheses like `colormap hsv`.

Shading: The objects created by `surf` consist of quadrilateral tiles which are separated by black lines as illustrated in the second figure in Figure 2.27. This corresponds to the default option of `shading`, namely `shading faceted`. The border lines may be eliminated by `shading flat`. To both eliminate and make the surface smooth, use `shading interp`. The second figure in Figure 2.27 is plotted by adding the `shading interp` command. (See also Figure 5.14, Figure 9.11, and fan rotor blades in color plates as examples of using `shading interp`).

Hold on revisited: The `hold on` command becomes very important also when a time-consuming plot is undertaken for the following reason: The command to change graphic properties such as axis, color map, view angles, color axis, and other parameters can be specified after a figure is plotted; but each time a new command is issued, the whole figure is replotted. Time can be saved by giving all the property commands before plotting and hold with `hold on`.

2.7   MATLAB AS DRAWING TOOL

MATLAB can be used as a drawing board for pictures and diagrams. Unlike ordinary drawing software, mathematical functions may be used to define lines and curves. In this section, we first explain elements of drawing pictures and diagrams with MATLAB, and then introduce a set of drawing tools.

Simple picture: The first thing to do before drawing is to determine the area of the drawing on the x-y plane by `axis` followed by `hold on`. Then, lines and curves are plotted by `plot`. The following script draws a happy face as shown in the first picture in Figure 2.28.

List 2.28

```
clear, clf, hold off
dt = pi/20;
t=0:dt:2*pi;
x=cos(t); y=sin(t);
axis([-1 1 -1 1]), hold on
plot( x,y)          % face outline
hold on
for k=0.8:-0.05:0.05
    plot(k*0.1*x-0.3,k*0.15*y+0.1) % left eye
    plot(k*0.1*x+0.3,k*0.15*y+0.1) % right eye
end
s1 = 3*pi/2-1.1;
s2 = 3*pi/2+1.1;
s = s1:dt:s2;
xs = 0.5*cos(s); ys = 0.5*sin(s);
plot(xs,ys)          % mouth
hold off
```

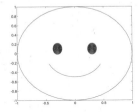 

Figure 2.28 Happy face

By `axis('square')` and `axis('off')`, the drawing is completed as the second picture in Figure 2.28.[4]

Mathematical functions are useful to draw creative figures and patterns. Figure 2.29 illustrates a soap bubble pattern created by randomly drawing circles. The locations and sizes of the bubbles are determined by `rand`. See List 2.29.

---

[4]If the figure does not become square even with `axis('square')`, one alternative is to multiply all the y-values by a scale factor to offset the distortion. Another way is to change the minimum and maximum of y in `axis`.

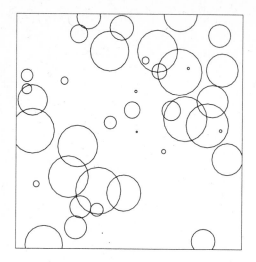

Figure 2.29 Soap bubbles

List 2.29

```
clear,clf, hold off
axis([-0. 1. -0. 1. ])
axis('square')
axis('off')
hold on
plot([0,1,1,0,0], [0,0,1,1,0])
h=pi/10;
t=0:h:pi*2;
xx = cos(t);
yy = sin(t);
for n=1:40
    r = rand(1)*0.1;
    xc = rand(1);
    yc = rand(1);
x = xx*r + xc;
y = yy*r + yc;
plot (x,y)
end
hold off
```

Figures may be expressed by connecting a series of points. For example, the wings and body of the insect in the first picture of Figure 2.30 are defined by points connected by lines. Function insect_(p1, p2) in FM 2.4 plots one insect placed between two points, p1 and p2, where p1 and p2 are coordinate pairs in vector forms. Function insect_ may be tested by executing insect_t listed after insect_.m. The second picture in Figure 2.30 is created by rotating and translating the insect by the algorithms explained next.

Figure 2.30 An insect and its random pattern

Rotation and translation: When one wishes to draw a complicated picture or diagram, a number of subfigures may be developed as function M-files. Each subfigure may be developed in a normalized domain such as $-1 \leq x \leq 1, -1 \leq y \leq 1$, or $0 \leq x \leq 1, 0 \leq y \leq 1$. Then, by translation, rotation and rescaling, they are placed at desired locations. Figure 2.31 illustrates a coil defined in a unit area, and its replacement after rotation and translation to a location in a larger figure.

In translation and rotation, we need to specify two reference points in the subfigure and two corresponding points in the whole picture. The coordinates of the two points in the subfigure will be denoted by (x_1, y_1) and (x_2, y_2), while the coordinates of the corresponding points in the whole figure are denoted by (X_1, Y_1) and (X_2, Y_2). In order to keep the shape of the figure the same after rotation and translation, the following relation must be satisfied between the coordinates (x, y) and (X, Y):

$$
\begin{aligned}
X &= cx - dy + f \\
Y &= dx + cy + g
\end{aligned}
\tag{2.7.1}
$$

where the coefficients c, d, f and g are determined by

Figure 2.31 Translation and rotation of a figure

$$X_1 = cx_1 - dy_1 + f$$
$$Y_1 = dx_1 + cy_1 + g$$
$$X_2 = cx_2 - dy_2 + f$$
$$Y_2 = dx_2 + cy_2 + g$$

(2.7.2)

Particularly if $x_1 = -1, x_2 = 1, y_1 = y_2 = 0$, the coefficients become

$$c = \frac{x_2 - x_1}{2}$$
$$d = \frac{y_2 - y_1}{2}$$
$$g = \frac{x_2 + x_1}{2}$$
$$f = \frac{y_2 + y_1}{2}$$

(2.7.3)

A subfigure originally developed in an arbitrarily chosen domain may be standardized by the inverse of the foregoing transformation. Suppose that the reference points of the original figures are given by (X_1, Y_1) and (X_2, Y_2). Then, the figure is transformed to the normalized domain of $(x_1 = -1, y_1 = 0)$ and $(x_2 = 1, y_2 = 0)$ by

$$x = CX - DY + F$$
$$y = DX + CY + G$$

(2.7.4)

where the coefficients C, D, F and G are determined by

$$x_1 = CX_1 - DY_1 + F = -1$$
$$y_1 = DX_1 + CY_1 + G = 0$$
$$x_2 = CX_2 - DY_2 + F = 1$$
$$y_2 = DX_2 + CY_2 + G = 0$$

(2.7.5)

The coefficients satisfying the foregoing equations are

$$C = \frac{-2(X_1 - X_2)}{(Y_1 - Y_2)^2 + (X_1 - X_2)^2}$$

$$D = \frac{2(Y_1 - Y_2)}{(Y_1 - Y_2)^2 + (X_1 - X_2)^2}$$

$$F = 1 - CX_2 + DY_2$$

$$G = -DX_2 - CY_2$$

(2.7.6)

Drawing diagrams: Table 2.1 is a list of subfigures that can be used to develop diagrams and pictures:

Table 2.1 Commands for component pictures and diagrams

```
f-name              Synopsis
capacit_            capacit_(u,w,p1,p2)
battery_            battery_(u,w,p1,p2)
circle_             circle_(r,x0,y0)
coil_b              coil_b(n,u,w,p1,p2)
coil_a              coil_a(n,u,w, p1,p2)
damper_             damper_(w,p0,p1)
line_               line_(p1,p2)
arrow_              arrow_(w, p1,p2)
arrow_dot           arrow_dot(w, p1,p2)
resist_             resist_(n,u,w,p1,p2)
spring_             spring_(n,u,w,p1,p2)
switch_             switch_(u,w,p1,p2)
box_                box_(w,p1,p2)
human_              human_(p1,p2, Body, ...
```

```
                              Rarm1,Rarm2,Larm1,Larm2, ...
                              Rleg1,Rleg2,Lleg1,Lleg2  )
       insect_                insect_(p1,p2)
       two_eyes               two_eyes(phi,eyeangle, x0,y0,z0,width)
       ellip_                 ellip_(x0,y0,rx,ry)
```

The meanings of arguments in the foregoing table are as follows:

    n: number of oscillations or windings
    u: relative length of the component
    w: relative width of the component
    p1: the x and y values of the left reference point (row vector)
    p2: the x and y values of the right reference point (row vector)
    r: radius of circle
    x0, y0: center of circle
    Body, Rarms1, etc: (see Figure 2.36)
    phi, eyeangle, etc: see FM-list 2.4 for two_eyes
    rx,ry: radii in x and y directions.

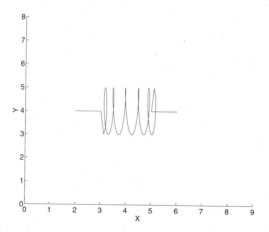

Figure 2.32 Illustration of coil

Each component can be placed at a desired location with a desired amount of rotation in the final drawing by appropriate definitions of p1 and p2. It is important to set axis and hold on before calling the functions. List 2.30 illustrates use of the components. The figure drawn by List 2.30 is shown in Figure 2.32. Notice that the coil starts at p1 ($x = 2, y = 4$) and ends at p2 ($x = 6$, $y = 4$).

Figures 2.33 and 2.34 illustrate pictures created by human_. Script of human_.m is found in FM 2-5.

List 2.30

```
clear,clf
axis([0,9,0,8])
hold on
p1=[2,4]; p2 = [6,4]
n = 6; u = 0.5, w=0.5;
coil_b(n,u,w, p1,p2)
hold off
```

Seven noisy kids are coming.

Figure 2.33 Picture 1

2.8 INTERACTIVE GRAPHICS

The most fundamental element of interactive graphics is the capability of a program to read the coordinates of the mouse pointer at any desired location. This is possible with `ginput` in one of the following formats:

```
[x,y] = ginput
[x,y,button] = ginput
[x,y,button] = ginput(n)
```

Suppose the mouse is clicked at a desired location within a graphic screen. Then, `[x,y] = ginput` gathers an unlimited number of points until the return key is hit, so x and y become vectors of the length equal to the number of points gathered. `[x,y,button] = ginput` is the same except the button numbers of the mouse are also recorded. The button number is 1, 2, or 3, respectively, counted from the left side of the mouse. `[x,y,button] = ginput(n)` gathers n points, but can be terminated by the return key.

They are going back.

Figure 2.34 Picture 2

List 2.31 illustrates use of ginput. When List 2.31 is executed, the program awaits mouse to be clicked. If the left button of mouse is clicked, a '+' mark in red is printed at the location of the pointer. Likewise, if the middle button or right button is clicked, a 'o' mark in yellow, or a '*' in green is printed, respectively. The execution is terminated if mouse is clicked with cursor inside the box at the left bottom corner of the screen. Figure 2.35 illustrates the marks plotted by List 2.31.

List 2.31
```
clear,clf,hold off
axis([0,10,0,10])
hold on
plot([1,2,2,1,1], [2,2,3,3,2])
text(1,1.6,'Click inside the box to terminate')
while 1
    [x,y,buttun] = ginput(1)
    if buttun==1, plot(x,y,'+r'), end
    if buttun==2, plot(x,y,'oy'), end
    if buttun==3, plot(x,y,'*g'), end
    if x>1 & x<2 & y>2 & y<3, break;end
end
hold off
```

2.9   M-FILES

FM 2-1 Triangular mesh plot
Purpose: to plot a triangular grid.

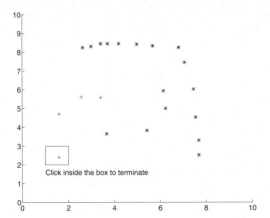

Figure 2.35 Illustration of interactive graphics

Synopsis: `tri_grid(data1, data2, y_scale)`

> `data1`: Name of the array that contains the vertex point numbers for each triangular element. Column 1 is the triangle number. Columns 2 through 4 are the vertex numbers for the triangle in the clockwise order. See the sample data file named `cell_da`.

> `data2`: Name of the array that contains coordinates of vertices. The first column is the sequential number of the points, and the next two columns are x and y values of the point. See the file `point_da`.

> `y_scale`: Scale factor for the y-coordinate. If a circle is plotted without adjustment, for example, it becomes an ellipse. An appropriate scale factor can be found by measuring how a square or a circle is distorted when this factor is set to unity.

Example: `tri_grid(cell_da, point_da, y_scale)`

tri_grid.m
```
function tri_grid(tri_d, xy_d, y_scale)
hold off
[n_tr,n] = size(tri_d);
[n_pt,n] = size(xy_d);
nmax=tri_d(1,1);
x=xy_d(:,2);
y=xy_d(:,3)*y_scale;
tri_num_prnt = input('Annotate element numbers ?  1 yes/ 0 no: ');
```

```
pnt_num_prnt = input('Annotate grid point numbers ? 1 yes/0 no: ');
xmin =min(x);   xmax =max(x); x_cen = 0.5*(xmin + xmax);
ymin =min(y);   ymax =max(y); y_cen = 0.5*(ymin + ymax);
Dx=xmax-xmin; Dy=ymax-ymin;
if Dx<Dy, xmin = x_cen-Dy/2; xmax = x_cen+Dy/2; end
if Dx>Dy, ymin = y_cen-Dx/2; ymax = y_cen+Dx/2; end
clf;  hold off;  clc;  %axis('square')
axis([xmin, xmax,ymin,ymax])
xlabel('Plot of triangular grid');    hold on
del_x = 0.1; del_y = 0.1;  % Adjust location of element no.
for k=1:n_tr
    for l=1:3
       p=tri_d(k,l+1);
       xx(l)=x(p);   yy(l)=y(p);
    end
    xx(4)=xx(1);   yy(4)=yy(1);
    plot(xx,yy)
    x_cen = sum(xx(1:3))/3;   y_cen = sum(yy(1:3))/3;
    if tri_num_prnt == 1 % if 0, elmnt numbers are not printed.
       text(x_cen - del_x, y_cen - del_y, int2str(k))
    end
end
%plot(x,y,'*')
if pnt_num_prnt == 1   % if 0, point numbers are not printed.
    for n=1:n_pt
    text(x(n), y(n), ['(',int2str(n),')'])
    end
end
axis('off')
```

cell_da

1	1	6	2
2	2	6	7
3	3	2	7
4	3	7	8
5	3	8	9
6	3	9	4
7	4	9	5
8	6	11	12
9	7	6	12
10	7	12	13
11	7	13	8
12	8	13	14
13	8	14	10
14	8	10	9
15	11	15	16
16	11	16	12
17	12	16	17
18	12	17	13
19	13	17	18
20	13	18	14

point_da

```
1   0.0     0.0
2   1.0     0.0
3   2.0     0.0
4   3.0     0.0
5   4.0     0.0
6   0.0     1.0
7   1.0     1.0
8   1.7     1.3
9   3.0     1.0
10  2.4     1.6
11  0.0     1.75
12  0.65    1.8
13  1.25    2.0
14  1.66    2.34
15  0.0     2.0
16  0.518   2.069
17  1.0     2.268
18  1.414   2.586
```

FM 2-2 Contour plotting on triangular grid

Purpose: to plot contour for a function defined on a triangular grid

Synopsis: `tri_cont(data1, data2, data3, y_scale)`

>   `data1`: see FM 2-1
>
>   `data2`: see FM 2-1
>
>   `data3`: functional values on the grid points. See data named `phi_da`
>
>   `scale`: see FM 2-1

Example: `tri_cont(cell_da, point_da, phi_da, y_scale)`

tri_cont.m

```
function dummy=tri_cont(tri_data,xy_data,f_data,ys)
[n_tr,n] = size(tri_data);
[n_pt,n] = size(xy_data);
nmax=tri_data(1,1);
x=xy_data(:,2);
y=xy_data(:,3);
f = f_data;
tri_num_prnt = input('Annotate element numbers ?  1 yes/ 0 no: ');
pnt_num_prnt = ...
        input('Annotate grid point numbers ? 1 yes/0 no: ');
xmin =min(x);   xmax =max(x); x_cen = 0.5*(xmin + xmax);
ymin =min(y*ys);ymax =max(y*ys);y_cen = 0.5*(ymin + ymax);
fmin =min(f)+0.01   fmax =max(f)-0.01;
Dx=xmax-xmin; Dy=ymax-ymin;
n_cont=20;
df = (fmax-fmin)/n_cont;kmax=n_cont;
s = fmin:df:fmax;
if Dx<Dy, xmin = x_cen-Dy/2, xmax = x_cen+Dy/2, end
if Dx>Dy, ymin = y_cen-Dx/2, ymax = y_cen+Dx/2, end
```

```
clf;   hold off;   clc;   %axis('square')
axis([xmin, xmax,ymin,ymax]); m=0;
title('Contour Plot');    hold on
del_x = 0.1; del_y = 0.1;  % Adjust location of element no.
for k=1:n_tr
  for j=1:3
    p=tri_data(k,j+1);
    xx(j)=x(p);  yy(j)=y(p);
    ff(j) = f(p);
  end
  xx(4)=xx(1);  yy(4)=yy(1);  ff(4)=ff(1);
  plot(xx,yy*ys)
  f_min = min([ff(1),  ff(2),  ff(3)]);
  f_max = max([ff(1),  ff(2),  ff(3)]);
  for kv = 1:kmax
    if f_min <= s(kv) & s(kv) <= f_max;
      m=0;
      for i=1:3
        if (s(kv) - ff(i)) * (s(kv) - ff(i+1))<= 0,
          m = m + 1;
          if f(i+1) == f(i),   alph=0.5;end
          if f(i+1) ~= f(i),
            alph = (s(kv)-ff(i))/(ff(i+1)-ff(i));
          end
          xp(m)= alph*xx(i+1) + (1-alph)*xx(i);
          yp(m)= alph*yy(i+1) + (1-alph)*yy(i);
        end
        if m == 2,
          plot([xp(1),xp(2)],[yp(1)*ys,yp(2)*ys],'--');
          break
        end
      end
    end
  end
  %==
  x_cen = sum(xx(1:3))/3;  y_cen = sum(yy(1:3))/3;
  if tri_num_prnt == 1 % if 0, elmnt numbers are not printed.
    text(x_cen - del_x, (y_cen - del_y)*ys, int2str(k))
  end
end
% plot(x,y*ys,'*')   % Use if points are to be marked by *.
%==================
if pnt_num_prnt == 1   % if 0, point numbers are not printed.
  for n=1:n_pt
  text(x(n), y(n)*ys, ['(',int2str(n),')'])
  end
end
axis('off')
```

phi_da

```
.3.3744378e+02    3.4924482e+02    3.7328341e+02    3.9020757e+02
```

```
4.0131868e+02    3.1453162e+02    3.2645937e+02    3.3443546e+02
3.8200298e+02    3.4679150e+02    2.5358725e+02    2.5990002e+02
2.6843571e+02    2.6889073e+02    2.2356239e+02    2.2439244e+02
2.2498863e+02    2.2577131e+02
```

FM 2-3 Contour plot on generalized curvilinear grid

Purpose: to plot curvilinear grid and contour on the curvilinear grid

Synopsis: g_cont(x, y, f, s)

      x: 2-dim. array of x-coordinates

      y: 2-dim. array of y-coordinates

      f: 2-dim. array of functional values

      s: 1-dim. array of contour levels

g_cont.m

```
function g_cont(x, y, f, s)
x_max=max(max(x));
x_min=min(min(x));
y_max=max(max(y));
y_min=min(min(y));
axis('square')
axis([x_min,x_max,y_min,y_max]); hold on
kmax=length(s);
m_plot=input('Do you wish to plot grid ? 1/0  ');
if m_plot == 1
   for j=1:nj
      plot(x(:,j),y(:,j))
   end
   for i=1:ni
      plot(x(i,:),y(i,:))
   end
else
   for j=1:nj-1:nj
      plot(x(:,j),y(:,j))
   end

   for i=1:ni-1:ni
      plot(x(i,:),y(i,:))
   end
end
for i = 1:ni-1
  for j=1:nj-1
    f_min = min([f(i,j), f(i+1,j), f(i,j+1), f(i+1,j+1)]);
    f_max = max([f(i,j), f(i+1,j), f(i,j+1), f(i+1,j+1)]);
    ip = i+1;
    jp = j+1;
    for k = 1:kmax
      if f_min <= s(k) & s(k) <= f_max
        l=0;
        if (s(k) - f(i,j)) * (s(k) - f(ip,j)) <= 0; l=l+1;
           [xp(l),yp(l)] = GC_interp(s(k),i,j,ip,j,x, y,f);
```

```
          end
          if (s(k) - f(ip,j)) * (s(k) - f(ip,jp)) <= 0,l=l+1;
             [xp(l),yp(l)] = GC_interp(s(k),ip,j,ip,jp,x, y,f);
          end
          if (s(k) - f(i,j)) * (s(k) - f(i,jp)) <= 0,l=l+1;
             [xp(l),yp(l)] = GC_interp(s(k),i,j,i,jp,x, y,f);
          end
          if (s(k) - f(i,jp)) * (s(k) - f(ip,jp)) <= 0,l=l+1;
      [xp(l),yp(l)] = GC_interp(s(k),i,jp,ip,jp,x, y,f);
          end
          if l >= 2, plot([xp(1),xp(2)], [yp(1),yp(2)], '--');
          end
          if l == 4 plot([xp(3),xp(4)], [yp(3),yp(4)], '--');
          end
       end
     end
   end
end
return
```

GC_interp.m

```
function [x_,y_] = GC_interp(s_lev,i1,j1,i2,j2,x_grid, y_grid,fun)
   if abs(fun(i1,j1) - s_lev) < 1.0e-5 &   ...
      abs(fun(i2,j2) - s_lev) < 1.0e-5
      x_ = (x_grid(i1,j1) + x_grid(i2,j2))/2;
      y_ = (y_grid(i1,j1) + y_grid(i2,j2))/2;
   else
      a  =  (fun(i2,j2) - s_lev)/(fun(i2,j2) - fun(i1,j1));
%    if  a<0 | a>1, a, end
      b  =  1-a;
      x_ =  x_grid(i1,j1)*a + x_grid(i2,j2)*b;
      y_ =  y_grid(i1,j1)*a + y_grid(i2,j2)*b;
   end
return
```

td_data.m

```
function [x,y,f] = td_data
ni= 10; nj=20;
   for j=1:nj
     for i=1:ni
       r = 3 + (5+j)*0.05*(i-1) ;
       th = j*pi/10;
       x(i,j) = r*cos(th) ;
       y(i,j) = r*sin(th);
     end
   end
   f=zeros(ni,nj);
   for j=2:nj-1
     f(ni,j)=sin(0.5*j);
   end
   for it = 1:20
     for i=2:ni-1
```

```
      f(i,nj) = f(i,nj-1);
      f(i,1) = f(i,2);
    end
    f(ni,nj) = 0.5*(f(ni-1,nj) + f(ni,nj-1));
    f(ni,1) = 0.5*(f(ni,2) + f(ni-1,1));
    for i=2:ni-1
      for j=2:nj-1
        f(i,j) = 0.375*(f(i-1,j)+f(i+1,j)+f(i,j-1)+f(i,j+1)) ...
                 - 0.5* f(i,j) ;
      end
    end
  end
```

FM 2-4 Subfigures of pictures and diagrams

Purpose: to draw a component of a picture or diagram at a desired location.
Synopsis: see Table 2.1. (It is important to set `axis` and `hold` on before calling
the picture and diagram functions listed here.)

capacit_.m

```
function y =  capacit_(u,w, p1,p2)
c = (p2(1)-p1(1))/2;   d = (p2(2)-p1(2))/2;
f = (p2(1)+p1(1))/2;   g = (p2(2)+p1(2))/2;
x1 =[-1,-u];  y1 = [0, 0];
x2 = [-u,-u]; y2 = [-1,1]*w;
x3 = [u,u];   y3 = [-1,1]*w;
x4 =[u,1];    y4 = [0, 0];
 xx1 = c*x1 - d*y1 + f;   yy1 = d*x1 + c*y1 + g;
 xx2 = c*x2 - d*y2 + f;   yy2 = d*x2 + c*y2 + g;
 xx3 = c*x3 - d*y3 + f;   yy3 = d*x3 + c*y3 + g;
 xx4 = c*x4 - d*y4 + f;   yy4 = d*x4 + c*y4 + g;
plot(xx1,yy1)
plot(xx2,yy2)
plot(xx3,yy3)
plot(xx4,yy4)
```

circle_.m

```
function y =  circle_(r,x0,y0)
delt = 2*pi/30;
t = 0:delt:2*pi;
x=r*cos(t)+x0;   y = r*sin(t)+y0;
plot(x,y)
```

coil_b.m

```
function dummy =  coil_b(n,u,w, p1,p2)
c = (p2(1)-p1(1))/2;   d = (p2(2)-p1(2))/2;
f = (p2(1)+p1(1))/2;   g = (p2(2)+p1(2))/2;
k = n*2;
Dx = 2/k/2;
x = -1:0.01:1;
z = k*acos(x);
y = w*sin(z);
```

```
x = x + 0.1*(1-cos(z)); %x = [-1,x,1];
x = [-1,-u, u*x,u,1];
y = [0,0,y,0,0];
xx = c*x - d*y + f;
 yy = d*x + c*y + g;
plot(xx,yy)
```

coil_a.m

```
function dummy =  coil_a(n,w, p1,p2)
c = (p2(1)-p1(1))/2;   d = (p2(2)-p1(2))/2;
f = (p2(1)+p1(1))/2;   g = (p2(2)+p1(2))/2;
x = -1:0.01:1;
t =(x+1)*pi*(n+0.5);
y = -w*sin(t);
x = x + 0.15*(1-cos(t)); a=x(1); b=x(length(x));
x = 2*(x-a)/(b-a) - 1;
xx = c*x - d*y + f;
yy = d*x + c*y + g;
plot(xx,yy)
```

damper_.m

```
function y =  damper_(w,p0,p1)
c = (p1(1)-p0(1))/2;   d = (p1(2)-p0(2))/2;
f = (p1(1)+p0(1))/2;   g = (p1(2)+p0(2))/2;
s = 0.25;
x1 =[-1,-s];   y1 = [0, 0];
x2 = [-s,-s];  y2 = [-1.2,1.2]*w;
x3 = [s,s];    y3 = [-0.7,0.7]*w;
x4 =[s,1];     y4 = [0, 0];
 tx1 = c*x1 - d*y1 + f;    ty1 = d*x1 + c*y1 + g;
 tx2 = c*x2 - d*y2 + f;    ty2 = d*x2 + c*y2 + g;
 tx3 = c*x3 - d*y3 + f;    ty3 = d*x3 + c*y3 + g;
 tx4 = c*x4 - d*y4 + f;    ty4 = d*x4 + c*y4 + g;
plot( tx1, ty1)
plot( tx2, ty2)
plot( tx3, ty3)
plot( tx4, ty4)
x=[-s, 2*s]; y = [1.2,1.2]*w
 tx = c*x - d*y + f;    ty = d*x + c*y + g;
plot( tx, ty)
x=[-s, 2*s]; y = [-1.2,-1.2]*w
 tx = c*x - d*y + f;    ty = d*x + c*y + g;
plot( tx, ty)
```

line_.m

```
function dummy = line_(p1,p2)
plot([p1(1),p2(1)],[p1(2),p2(2)])
```

resistor_.m

```
function dummy =  resist_(n,u,w, p1,p2)
% n: # of turns
% u: length
% w: width
```

```
% p1: coordinate pair for srating point
% p2: same for ending point
% Example>> p1 =[1,0]; p2=[2,0]; resist_(5, 0.4, 0.1, p1,p2)
c = (p2(1)-p1(1))/2;   d = (p2(2)-p1(2))/2;
f = (p2(1)+p1(1))/2;   g = (p2(2)+p1(2))/2;
 Dx = 1/(2*n);
x =u*[-1+Dx:2*Dx:1];
[m1,n1]=size(1:length(x));
y = w*[0, (-ones(1,n1-2)).^(1:n1-2),0];
x=[-1,x,1];
y=[0,y,0];
 xx = c*x - d*y + f;
 yy = d*x + c*y + g;
plot(xx,yy)
```

spring_.m

```
function dummy =  spring_(n,u,w, p1,p2)
% n: # of winding
% u: length of spring
% w: width of spring
% p1: coordinate pair for srating point
% p2: same for ending point
% Example>> p1 =[1,0];   p2=[2,0];
%              spring_(5,0.4, 0.2, p1,p2)
c = (p2(1)-p1(1))/2;   d = (p2(2)-p1(2))/2;
f = (p2(1)+p1(1))/2;   g = (p2(2)+p1(2))/2;
k = 2*n;
x = -1:0.02:1;
z=k*x*2;
y = w*cos(z).*cos(-x*pi/2);
x = x - 0.2*sin(z);
x=[-1,u*x,1]; y=[0,y,0];
xx = c*x - d*y + f;
yy = d*x + c*y + g;
plot(xx,yy)
```

switch_.m

```
function y =  switch_(u, w, p1,p2)
% u: switch size
% w: relative height of switch
% p1: coordinate pair for srating point
% p2: same for ending point
% Example>>
%        p1 =[1,0]; p2=[2,0]; switch_(0.4, 1.2, p1,p2)
c = (p2(1)-p1(1))/2;   d = (p2(2)-p1(2))/2;
f = (p2(1)+p1(1))/2;   g = (p2(2)+p1(2))/2;
x1 =[-1,-0.5*u, 0.5*u];
y1 = w*[0, 0, 0.5*u];
x2 = [0.5*u, 1];
y2 = [0,0];
 x1 = c*x1 - d*y1 + f;
 y1 = d*x1 + c*y1 + g;
 x2 = c*x2 - d*y2 + f;
```

```
  y2 = d*x2 + c*y2 + g;
plot( x1, y1)
plot( x2, y2)
```

box_.m

```
function dummy =  box_(hi, p1,p2)
% hi=height of box; p1 and p2 are coordinates of center point
% of the left side of box wall, and p2 the same for the right.
% Example >> p1 = [0,0]; p2 =[1,0]; box_(0.5,p1,p2)
%
c = (p2(1)-p1(1))/2;   d = (p2(2)-p1(2))/2;
f = (p2(1)+p1(1))/2;   g = (p2(2)+p1(2))/2;
x = [-1 1 1 -1 -1]; y = hi*[-1 -1 1 1 -1];
 xx1 = c*x - d*y + f;   yy1 = d*x + c*y + g;
plot(xx1,yy1)
```

human_.m

```
function y =  human_(p1,p2, Body,    ...
Rarm1,Rarm2,Larm1,Larm2, ...
Rleg1,Rleg2,Lleg1,Lleg2   )
%10,10,30,30,90 30 90 90 20
x0=p1(1);
y0=p1(2);
x1=p2(1);
y1=p2(2);
c = (x1-x0)/2;   d = (y1 - y0)/2;
f = (x1+x0)/2;   g = (y1 + y0)/2;
M = [c,-d; d,c]/3; F = [f,g]';
  thb = Body/180*pi;% body angle
  thrh1=Rarm1/180*pi;% right arm theta-1
  thrh2=Rarm2/180*pi;% right arm theta-2
  thlh1=Larm1/180*pi;% left arm theta-1
  thlh2=Larm2/180*pi;% left arm theta-2
  thrg1=Rleg1/180*pi;% right leg theta-1
  thrg2=Rleg2/180*pi;% right leg theta-2
  thlg1=Lleg1/180*pi;% left leg theta-1
  thlg2=Lleg2/180*pi;% left leg theta-2
  t = 0:0.25:6.3;
% body
  b1=[0,0]';
  b2=b1 + 1.5*[sin(thb), cos(thb)]';
  b3=b1 + 2*[sin(thb), cos(thb)]';
  b=[b1,b2,b3];
  [m,n]=size(b); w=ones(1,n); b = M*b+[f*w;g*w];
  plot(b(1,:), b(2,:))
% head
  b4=b3+1.*[sin(thb), cos(thb)]';
  xHd= 1.*cos(t)+b4(1);
  yHd= 1.*sin(t)+b4(2);
  b = [xHd; yHd];
  w=ones(1,n);
  [m,n]=size(b); w=ones(1,n); b = M*b+[f*w;g*w];
  plot(b(1,:), b(2,:))
```

```
%right arm/hand
  rh1=b2;
  rh2=rh1 + 1.5*[cos(thrh1), sin(thrh1)]';
  rh3=rh2 + 1.5*[cos(thrh2), sin(thrh2)]';
  rh4=rh3 + 0.2*[cos(thrh2), sin(thrh2)]';
  b=[rh1,rh2,rh3];
  w=ones(1,n);
  [m,n]=size(b); w=ones(1,n); b = M*b+[f*w;g*w];
  plot(b(1,:), b(2,:))
  xrp= 0.2*cos(t)+rh4(1);
  yrp= 0.2*sin(t)+rh4(2);
  b=[xrp;yrp];
  w=ones(1,n);
  [m,n]=size(b); w=ones(1,n); b = M*b+[f*w;g*w];
  plot(b(1,:), b(2,:))
%left arm/hand
  lh1=b2;
  lh2=lh1 + 1.5*[-cos(thlh1), sin(thlh1)]';
  lh3=lh2 + 1.5*[-cos(thlh2), sin(thlh2)]';
  lh4=lh3 + 0.2*[-cos(thlh2), sin(thlh2)]';
  b=[lh1,lh2,lh3];
w=ones(1,n);
  [m,n]=size(b); w=ones(1,n); b = M*b+[f*w;g*w] ;
  plot(b(1,:), b(2,:))
  xlp= 0.2*cos(t)+lh4(1);
  ylp= 0.2*sin(t)+lh4(2);
b = [xlp;ylp];
 w=ones(1,n);
  [m,n]=size(b); w=ones(1,n); b = M*b+[f*w;g*w] ;
  plot(b(1,:), b(2,:))
%right leg/foot
  rg1=b1;
  rg2=rg1 + 1*[cos(thrg1), -sin(thrg1)]';
  rg3=rg2 + 1.5*[cos(thrg2), -sin(thrg2)]';
  rg4=rg3 + 0.2*[cos(thrg2), -sin(thrg2)]';
  b=[rg1,rg2,rg3];
  w=ones(1,n);
  [m,n]=size(b); w=ones(1,n); b = M*b+[f*w;g*w];
  plot(b(1,:), b(2,:))
  xrf= 0.2*cos(t)+rg4(1);
  yrf= 0.2*sin(t)+rg4(2);
  b=[ xrf; yrf];
  w=ones(1,n);
  [m,n]=size(b); w=ones(1,n); b = M*b+[f*w;g*w];
  plot(b(1,:), b(2,:))
%left leg/foot
  lg1=b1;
  lg2=lg1 + 1.*[-cos(thlg1), -sin(thlg1)]';
  lg3=lg2 + 1.5*[-cos(thlg2), -sin(thlg2)]';
  lg4=lg3 + 0.2*[-cos(thlg2), -sin(thlg2)]';
  b=[lg1,lg2,lg3];
  w=ones(1,n);
  [m,n]=size(b); w=ones(1,n); b = M*b+[f*w;g*w];
```

```
    plot(b(1,:), b(2,:))
    xlf= 0.2*cos(t)+lg4(1);
    ylf= 0.2*sin(t)+lg4(2);
    b=[xlf;ylf];
    [m,n]=size(b); w=ones(1,n); b = M*b+[f*w;g*w]  ;
    plot(b(1,:), b(2,:))
```

two_eyes.m

```
function f=two_eyes(phi,eyeangle, x0,y0,z0,width)
% Sample call statement:
%         clf;hold on; Two_eyes(120,45,0,0,0,0.2);view(120,30)
%         axis([-1 1 -1 1 -1 1]); ylabel('y'); hold off
%  phi : direction of face. Degrees.
%         If 0 the face is on the x-z plane toward positive y.
%  eyeangle:  direction of eye balls.  Degree.
eyr = 0.2;
angle0=eyeangle;
x=[-1,0,1,0,-1]; z=[0, 0.3,0,-0.3, 0]; y=[0,0,0,0,0];
dth=pi/10;  th=0:dth:2*pi;
zc=cos(th)*eyr; xc=sin(th)*eyr; yc=zeros(size(xc));
th=0:dth:10*pi;
ze=cos(th)*eyr.*(1.0- 0.03*th);     %eye ball
xe=sin(th)*eyr.*(1.0- 0.03*th);
angle = angle0/180*pi;
xd=xe/2 + eyr*cos(angle)/2;
zd=ze/2 + eyr*sin(angle)/2;
b = eyr^2 - xd.^2 - zd.^2;
yd=sqrt((eyr+0.01)^2 - xd.^2 - zd.^2);
xcL=xc-0.25; xcR=xc+0.25;
yc=yc;  zc=zc;
xdL=xd-0.25;  xdR=xd+0.25;
yd=yd*0.2; zd=zd;  xdR=xd+0.25;
xns=[0,0,0];  yns=[0, 0.1,0];  zns=[0.1,-0.3,-0.3]; % nose
S=width/0.2/2;  %scale factor
[x1,y1,z1]=rotz_(xcL,yc,zc, phi);
plot3(x1*S+x0,y1*S+y0,z1*S+z0);
[x2,y2,z2]=rotz_(xcR,yc,zc, phi);
plot3(x2*S+x0,y2*S+y0,z2*S+z0);
[x3,y3,z3]=rotz_(xdL,yd,zd, phi);
plot3(x3*S+x0,y3*S+y0,z3*S+z0);
[x4,y4,z4]=rotz_(xdR,yd,zd, phi);
plot3(x4*S+x0,y4*S+y0,z4*S+z0);
[x5,y5,z5]=rotz_(xns,yns,zns, phi);
plot3(x5*S+x0,y5*S+y0,z5*S+z0);
axis('off')
```

arrow_.m

```
function dummy =  arrow_(w, p1,p2)
%   w width of arrow
%   p1 and p2:  starting and ending point coordinate pairs
c = (p2(1)-p1(1))/2;   d = (p2(2)-p1(2))/2;
f = (p2(1)+p1(1))/2;   g = (p2(2)+p1(2))/2;
x = [-1 1]; y = [0,0];
```

```
xx1 = c*x - d*y + f;    yy1 = d*x + c*y + g;
plot(xx1,yy1)
x = [0.5, 1]; y = w*[0.5,0];
xx1 = c*x - d*y + f;    yy1 = d*x + c*y + g;
plot(xx1,yy1)
x = [0.5, 1]; y = w*[-0.5,0];
xx1 = c*x - d*y + f;    yy1 = d*x + c*y + g;
plot(xx1,yy1)
```

arrow_dot.m

```
function dummy =  arrow_dot(w, p1,p2)
%   w width of arrow
%   p1 and p2:  starting and ending point coordinate pairs
c = (p2(1)-p1(1))/2;   d = (p2(2)-p1(2))/2;
f = (p2(1)+p1(1))/2;   g = (p2(2)+p1(2))/2;
x = [-1 1]; y = [0,0];
xx1 = c*x - d*y + f;    yy1 = d*x + c*y + g;
plot(xx1,yy1,':')
x = [0.5, 1]; y = w*[0.5,0];
xx1 = c*x - d*y + f;   yy1 = d*x + c*y + g;
plot(xx1,yy1,':')
x = [0.5, 1]; y = w*[-0.5,0];
xx1 = c*x - d*y + f;   yy1 = d*x + c*y + g;
plot(xx1,yy1,':')
```

insect_.m

```
function y = insect_(p1,p2)
hold on
x0 = p1(1); y0=p1(2);
x1 = p2(1); y1=p2(2);
c = (x1-x0)/2;   d = (y1 - y0)/2;
f = (x1+x0)/2;   g = (y1 + y0)/2;
xwL = [-13   -18 -20 -20 -18 -13 -8 -6 0 0 -6 -13]/50;
ywL = [13 0 -10 -40 -47 -50 -45 -38 -17 -10 2 13]/50;
xx = c*xwL - d*ywL + f;
yy = d*xwL + c*ywL + g;
xxb = -c*xwL - d*ywL + f;
yyb = -d*xwL + c*ywL + g;
plot(xx,yy); plot( xxb,yyb)
xneck = [-13   0   13]/50;
yneck = [13   14   13]/50;
xx = c*xneck - d*yneck + f;
yy = d*xneck + c*yneck + g;
plot(xx,yy)
xhL = [ -13 -12.5 -10]/50;
yhL = [13 20 27]/50;
xx = c*xhL - d*yhL + f;
yy = d*xhL + c*yhL + g;  plot(xx,yy)
xx = -c*xhL - d*yhL + f;
yy = -d*xhL + c*yhL + g;  plot(xx,yy)
xtop = [-5 0 7]/50;
```

```
ytop = [30 32 30]/50;
xx = c*xtop - d*ytop + f;
yy = d*xtop + c*ytop + g;   plot(xx,yy)
t = 0:0.5:pi*2;
xeyeL =( -.08 + .03*cos(t))*2;
yeyeL =( .29 + .03*sin(t))*2;
xx = c*xeyeL - d*yeyeL + f;
yy = d*xeyeL + c*yeyeL + g;   plot(xx,yy)
xeyeR = (.10 + .03*cos(t))*2;
yeyeR = (.30 + .03*sin(t))*2;
xx = c*xeyeR - d*yeyeR + f;
yy = d*xeyeR + c*yeyeR + g;   plot(xx,yy)
plot (xeyeR, yeyeR)
xantL=[-10 -15 -18 -21]/50;
yantL=[27 31 37 38]/50;
xx = c*xantL - d*yantL + f;
yy = d*xantL + c*yantL + g;   plot(xx,yy)
xantR=[25 19 13]/50;
yantR=[41 39 27]/50;
xx = c*xantR - d*yantR + f;
yy = d*xantR + c*yantR + g;   plot(xx,yy)
hold off
```

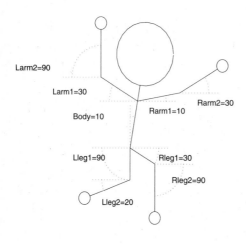

Legend.

Figure 2.36 Explanation of arguments in human

FM 2-5 Illustration of picture drawing
Purpose: to draw Figure 2.33.
Synopsis: `kids1`

kids1.m

```
hold off, clear, clf
axis([-5 14 -5 14])
hold on
axis('square')
axis('off')
x0=-1;x1=2;y0=2;y1=2;
Body=10 ;                    % body angle.  See Figure 2.36.
Rarm1=10; Rarm2=30;
Larm1=30;  Larm2=90;
Rleg1=30;  Rleg2=90;
Lleg1=90;  Lleg2=20;
human_([x0,y0],[x1,y1], Body, Rarm1,Rarm2,Larm1,Larm2, ...
                        Rleg1,Rleg2,Lleg1,Lleg2  )
human_([2,0],[5,1], Body, Rarm1,Rarm2,Larm1,Larm2, ...
                        Rleg1,Rleg2,Lleg1,Lleg2  )
human_([3,1],[6,1], -Body, Rarm1,Rarm2,Larm1,Larm2, ...
                        Rleg1,Rleg2,Lleg1,Lleg2  )
human_([-3,1],[-1.,1], Body*1.1,-Rarm1,Rarm2,Larm1,Larm2, ...
                        Rleg1,Rleg2,Lleg1,Lleg2  )
human_([-4,4],[-2.,4], Body, Rarm1,Rarm2,Larm1,Larm2, ...
                        Rleg1,Rleg2,Lleg1,Lleg2  )
human_([7,0.5],[10.5,0.5], Body, -Rarm1,Rarm2*2,Larm1,Larm2, ...
human_([9.5,-2],[13,-2], 2*Body, -Rarm1,-Rarm2,Larm1,Larm2, ...
                        Rleg1,Rleg2,Lleg1,Lleg2  )
xlabel('Seven noisy kids are coming.')
```

FM 2-6 Demonstration of insect drawing
Purpose: to illustrate drawing insect patterns
Synopsis: insect_t

insect_t.m
```
%insect_test
clear, clf, hold on
axis([-0, 10, -0, 10])
axis('square')
for k=1:20
  r  = rand(size(1:6));
  r(1:4)=r(1:4)*10;
  p1 = [r(1),  r(2)];
  p2 = [r(1)+(2*r(5)-1)*2,  r(2)+(2*r(6)-1)*2];
  insect_(p1,p2)*2;
end
axis('off')
```

PROBLEMS

In the following assignments of plotting figures, print axis labels, legends to explain the meaning of each curve if there are multiple curves. You should also print title of the figure in each graph you produce. Use `labelx`, `labely`, `title`, `text`, `gtext`, **but do not finish your figures by adding hand writing.**

(2.1) Plot the following functions in the indicated domain:

$$y = \frac{\sin(x)}{1 + \cos(x)}, \quad 0 \le x \le 4\pi$$

$$y = \frac{1}{1 + (x - 2)^2}, \quad 0 \le x \le 4$$

$$y = \exp(-x)x^2, \quad 0 \le x \le 10$$

(2.2) Plot $y = \tan(x)$ in the graphic domain, $0 \le x \le 10, -10 \le y \le 10$, as accurately as possible. Explain what special effort is necessary to do this.

(2.3) Plot the following two functions on the same graph by a single use of `plot`:

$$y = \frac{(x - 1)(x - 2)(x - 4)(x - 5)}{(3 - 1)(3 - 2)(3 - 4)(3 - 5)}, \quad 0 \le x \le 6$$

$$y = \frac{(x - 2)(x - 3)(x - 4)(x - 5)}{(1 - 2)(1 - 3)(1 - 4)(1 - 5)}, \quad 0 \le x \le 6$$

Repeat the same by `plot` command two times and `hold on`.

(2.4) Plot $y = \cos(m \cos^{-1}(x))$ named Chebyshev polynomials for each of m = 1, 2, ... 8 in $-1 \le x \le 1$ in two sets of four graphs using `subplot`.

(2.5) The following functions have singularities. Plot each of the following functions separately in the indicated domain:

$$y = \tan(x)/x^{0.3}, \quad 0 < x \le 5$$
$$y = \frac{\exp x}{\sqrt{1 - x^2}}, \quad 0 < x \le 1$$
$$y = x^{-x}, \quad 0 < x \le 2$$

(2.6) A curve is expressed by

$$x = \sin(-t) + t, \quad y = 1 - \cos(-t)$$

Plot the curve on the x-y plane for $0 \le t \le 4\pi$.

(2.7) Suppose $z = x + iy$ is a line on the complex domain, where $i = \sqrt{-1}$. Show graphically that $w = 1/z$ becomes a circle for any line. Hint: Plot w for $y = ax + b$ with three sets of values of a and b:

$$a = 0, b = 1$$
$$a = 1, b = 1$$
$$a = 100, b = 0$$

(**2.8**) Plot the following function by `mesh`:

$$f(x, y) = 0.2 \cos x + y \exp(-x^2 - y^2), \quad -3 \le x \le 3, -3 \le y \le 3$$

(**2.9**) Using `contour`, plot the implicit function $f(x, y) = 0$ where

$$f(x, y) = y^2 + x \exp(y) - \tanh(x), \quad 0 \le x \le 5$$

(**2.10**) Two design parameters are bounded by $0 < x < 5$, and $0 < y < 5$. The cost of the product is

$$f = x^2 - 8x + y^2 - 6y - 0.1xy + 50$$

Using the mesh plot, find approximately the optimum parameters to minimize the cost, and the minimum cost.

(**2.11**) Repeat Problem (2.10) by contour plot.

(**2.12**) Draw your own happy face with nose and hair.

(**2.13**) Using the commands in Table 2.1, draw an electrical diagram of Figure 10.1 or Figure 10.6.

(**2.14**) Draw a random pattern of ten insects by `insect_` with heads up.

(**2.15**) Draw two persons playing boxing by `human_`.

(**2.16**) Draw a bicycle with a rider by `human_`.

(**2.17**) Develop an interactive graphic program by modifying the script in List 2.31 such that: (a) multiple points are collected by clicking the left mouse button until the middle button is hit, and (b) as points are collected they are marked on the screen by 'x' marks and connected by lines. The graph is shown until mouse is clicked inside the box at the left bottom corner.

Chapter 3

Linear Algebra

There are two primary reasons why it is advantageous to learn linear algebra at this early stage of the numerical methods study. First, linear algebra is fundamental in numerical methods, so the sooner we learn it the easier the remainder of study of numerical methods will be. Second, MATLAB capabilities are built upon the matrix and vector operations. Therefore, proficiency on MATLAB will be significantly enhanced by learning linear algebra.

The objective of this chapter is to understand the fundamentals of linear algebra and become able to solve linear equations, particularly with MATLAB. This, however, requires at least four areas of study. First, we have to understand how to express linear equations and basic operations of equations in matrix and vector notations. Second, we have to understand MATLAB commands to operate linear equations in the matrix notations. Third, we have to understand problems that are difficult or impossible to solve. The fourth area includes additional topics that enhance understanding as well as help apply linear algebra.

3.1 MATRICES AND VECTORS

In mathematical notation, matrices are enclosed in a pair of parentheses or square brackets, and follow certain mathematical rules. In MATLAB, however, matrices are printed out without parentheses or brackets. Although *matrix* and *array* are synonymous in MATLAB, one should be aware of whether an array is being used for a matrix in mathematics, or simply as an array variable. In the present chapter, we discuss matrices and vectors in the former sense.

A matrix is a rectangular array of numbers enclosed in a pair of brackets or parentheses:

$$\begin{bmatrix} b_{1,1} & b_{1,2} & . & b_{1,n} \\ b_{2,1} & b_{2,2} & . & b_{2,n} \\ . & . & . & . \\ b_{m,1} & b_{m,2} & . & b_{m,n} \end{bmatrix} \tag{3.1.1}$$

The foregoing matrix is called an m-by-n matrix. Notice that the first subscript in a matrix changes in the vertical direction and the second subscript changes in the horizontal direction. A matrix is represented by a symbol; for example,

$$B = \begin{bmatrix} b_{1,1} & b_{1,2} & . & b_{1,n} \\ b_{2,1} & b_{2,2} & . & b_{2,n} \\ . & . & . & . \\ b_{m,1} & b_{m,2} & . & b_{m,n} \end{bmatrix} \tag{3.1.2}$$

Once B is defined as Eq.(3.1.2), mathematical equations can be expressed in terms of B rather than writing the whole matrix. The definition may be abbreviated by

$$B = [b_{i,j}]$$

Vectors are special forms of matrices. If $m>1$ but $n=1$, B becomes

$$B = \begin{bmatrix} b_{1,1} \\ b_{2,1} \\ . \\ b_{m,1} \end{bmatrix}$$

with only one column, which is called a column vector. On the other hand, if $m=1$ and $n>1$, the matrix becomes

$$B = \begin{bmatrix} b_{1,1} & b_{1,2} & . & b_{1,n} \end{bmatrix}$$

which has only one row, and is called a row vector. When the number of columns or rows is only one, it is not necessary to use two subscripts. Indeed, the second index of the elements in the column vector, and the first subscript of the elements in the row vector are omitted, so the column and row vectors are written as

$$B = \begin{bmatrix} b_1 \\ b_2 \\ . \\ b_m \end{bmatrix} \tag{3.1.3}$$

and

$$B = \begin{bmatrix} b_1 & b_2 & . & b_n \end{bmatrix} \tag{3.1.4}$$

respectively.

In another special case of $m = n = 1$, B is a 1-by-1 matrix and may be written as

$$B = [b_{1,1}]$$

or simply

$$B = [b]$$

The 1-by-1 matrix B is called a scalar, and the same as $B = b$.

Names of some special matrices and vectors are defined next:

SQUARE MATRIX: a matrix with $m = n$.

NULL MATRIX: elements of the null matrix are all zero:

$$A = \begin{bmatrix} 0 & 0 & 0 \\ 0 & 0 & 0 \\ 0 & 0 & 0 \end{bmatrix} \tag{3.1.5}$$

A null matrix is defined in MATLAB by `zeros`. By `A = zeros(m,n)`, A becomes an m-by-n null matrix. An n-by-n null matrix is returned by `A = zeros(n)`.

IDENTITY MATRIX: square matrix in which all the diagonal elements are unity but all other elements are zero. An identity matrix is denoted by I, namely

$$I = \begin{bmatrix} 1 & 0 & 0 \\ 0 & 1 & 0 \\ 0 & 0 & 1 \end{bmatrix} \tag{3.1.6}$$

The MATLAB command to define an identity matrix is `eye`. By `A = eye(n)`, A becomes an n-by-n identity matrix.

TRANSPOSED MATRIX: the transpose of matrix $A = [a_{i,j}]$ is $A^t = [a_{j,i}]$ (i and j are interchanged). For example:

$$A = \begin{bmatrix} 2 & 3 \\ 0 & 5 \end{bmatrix}, \qquad A^t = \begin{bmatrix} 2 & 0 \\ 3 & 5 \end{bmatrix} \tag{3.1.7}$$

$$B = \begin{bmatrix} 1 \\ 7 \end{bmatrix}, \qquad B^t = \begin{bmatrix} 1 & 7 \end{bmatrix} \tag{3.1.8}$$

Transpose of a matrix is defined in MATLAB with the prime operator.

PERMUTATION MATRIX: matrix that is obtained by exchanging rows of an identity matrix. For example, by exchanging the first and third rows of Eq.(3.1.6), a permutation matrix is obtained:

$$A = \begin{bmatrix} 0 & 0 & 1 \\ 0 & 1 & 0 \\ 1 & 0 & 0 \end{bmatrix} \tag{3.1.9}$$

Addition and subtraction of matrices: A matrix may be added to or subtracted from another matrix if the matrices have the same size (same numbers of columns and rows). Because vectors are a special form of matrices, the same rules apply to vectors. Addition and subtraction of two matrices

$$A = [a_{i,j}], \quad B = [b_{i,j}]$$

of the same size are defined by

$$C = A \pm B \qquad\qquad (3.1.10)$$

where $C = [c_{i,j}]$ is a matrix with

$$c_{i,j} = a_{i,j} \pm b_{i,j}$$

Example 3.1

Two square matrices and two vectors are defined by

$$A = \begin{bmatrix} 1 & 2 & 4 \\ 3 & 1 & 2 \\ 4 & 1 & 3 \end{bmatrix}, \quad B = \begin{bmatrix} 7 & 3 & 1 \\ 2 & 3 & 5 \\ 8 & 1 & 6 \end{bmatrix}$$

$$x = \begin{bmatrix} 1 \\ 4 \\ 2 \end{bmatrix}, \quad y = \begin{bmatrix} 3 \\ 9 \\ 4 \end{bmatrix}$$

Calculate $A + B$, $B - A$, $x + y$, and $x - y$.

Solution

The calculations are shown next:

$$A + B = \begin{bmatrix} 1+7 & 2+3 & 4+1 \\ 3+2 & 1+3 & 2+5 \\ 4+8 & 1+1 & 3+6 \end{bmatrix} = \begin{bmatrix} 8 & 5 & 5 \\ 5 & 4 & 7 \\ 12 & 2 & 9 \end{bmatrix}$$

$$A - B = \begin{bmatrix} 1-7 & 2-3 & 4-1 \\ 3-2 & 1-3 & 2-5 \\ 4-8 & 1-1 & 3-6 \end{bmatrix} = \begin{bmatrix} -6 & -1 & 3 \\ 1 & -2 & -3 \\ -4 & 0 & -3 \end{bmatrix}$$

$$x + y = \begin{bmatrix} 1+3 \\ 4+9 \\ 2+4 \end{bmatrix} = \begin{bmatrix} 4 \\ 13 \\ 6 \end{bmatrix}$$

$$x - y = \begin{bmatrix} 1 - 3 \\ 4 - 9 \\ 2 - 4 \end{bmatrix} = \begin{bmatrix} -2 \\ -5 \\ -2 \end{bmatrix}$$

Multiplication: Suppose B and C are matrices. When the number of columns of A and the number of rows of B are identical, they can be multiplied as

$$C = AB$$

where $C = [c_{i,j}]$ is a matrix representing the result of the multiplication. The elements of C are related to those of A and B by

$$c_{i,j} = \sum_k a_{i,k} b_{k,j} \tag{3.1.11}$$

The number of rows of C equals that of A, and the number of columns of C equals that of B. In other words, if A is a p-by-q matrix and B is a q-by-r matrix, then C is a p-by-r matrix. Obviously, if A and B are square matrices of the same size, then C also becomes a square matrix of the same size.

The product AB is not equal to BA in general. If $AB = BA$, then matrices A and B are said to commute.

Division: Division of one matrix by another matrix is related to finding the solution of a linear equation in a matrix form. More details are explained in Section 3.4.

Example 3.2

Calculate the following products:

(a)

$$\begin{bmatrix} 1 & 2 \\ 4 & 3 \\ 0 & 2 \end{bmatrix} \begin{bmatrix} 5 \\ 1 \end{bmatrix}$$

(b)

$$\begin{bmatrix} 2 & 1 & 7 \end{bmatrix} \begin{bmatrix} 1 & 2 \\ 4 & 3 \\ 0 & 2 \end{bmatrix}$$

(c)

$$\begin{bmatrix} 8 & 1 & 3 \\ 1 & 5 & 2 \end{bmatrix} \begin{bmatrix} 1 & 2 \\ 4 & 3 \\ 0 & 2 \end{bmatrix}$$

(d)

$$\begin{bmatrix} 1 & 2 \\ 4 & 3 \\ 0 & 2 \end{bmatrix} \begin{bmatrix} 8 & 1 & 3 \\ 1 & 5 & 2 \end{bmatrix}$$

Solution

(a)

$$\begin{bmatrix} 1 & 2 \\ 4 & 3 \\ 0 & 2 \end{bmatrix} \begin{bmatrix} 5 \\ 1 \end{bmatrix} = \begin{bmatrix} 1 \times 5 + 2 \times 1 \\ 4 \times 5 + 3 \times 1 \\ 0 \times 5 + 2 \times 1 \end{bmatrix} = \begin{bmatrix} 7 \\ 23 \\ 2 \end{bmatrix}$$

(b)

$$\begin{bmatrix} 2 & 1 & 7 \end{bmatrix} \begin{bmatrix} 1 & 2 \\ 4 & 3 \\ 0 & 2 \end{bmatrix} = \begin{bmatrix} 2 \times 1 + 1 \times 4 + 7 \times 0 & 2 \times 2 + 1 \times 3 + 7 \times 2 \end{bmatrix}$$

$$= \begin{bmatrix} 6 & 21 \end{bmatrix}$$

(c)

$$\begin{bmatrix} 8 & 1 & 3 \\ 1 & 5 & 2 \end{bmatrix} \begin{bmatrix} 1 & 2 \\ 4 & 3 \\ 0 & 2 \end{bmatrix} = \begin{bmatrix} 8 \times 1 + 1 \times 4 + 3 \times 0 & 8 \times 2 + 1 \times 3 + 3 \times 2 \\ 1 \times 1 + 5 \times 4 + 2 \times 0 & 1 \times 2 + 5 \times 3 + 2 \times 2 \end{bmatrix}$$

$$= \begin{bmatrix} 12 & 25 \\ 21 & 21 \end{bmatrix}$$

(d)

$$\begin{bmatrix} 1 & 2 \\ 4 & 3 \\ 0 & 2 \end{bmatrix} \begin{bmatrix} 8 & 1 & 3 \\ 1 & 5 & 2 \end{bmatrix} = \begin{bmatrix} 1 \times 8 + 2 \times 1 & 1 \times 1 + 2 \times 5 & 1 \times 3 + 2 \times 2 \\ 4 \times 8 + 3 \times 1 & 4 \times 1 + 3 \times 5 & 4 \times 3 + 3 \times 2 \\ 0 \times 8 + 2 \times 1 & 0 \times 1 + 2 \times 5 & 0 \times 3 + 2 \times 2 \end{bmatrix}$$

$$= \begin{bmatrix} 10 & 11 & 7 \\ 35 & 19 & 18 \\ 2 & 10 & 4 \end{bmatrix}$$

Example 3.3

Calculate Ax, AB, BA, and $x^t A^t$, using the definitions of the matrices and vectors given in Example 3.2.

Solution

The calculations are shown next:

$$
AB = \begin{bmatrix} 1 & 2 & 4 \\ 3 & 1 & 2 \\ 4 & 1 & 3 \end{bmatrix} \begin{bmatrix} 7 & 3 & 1 \\ 2 & 3 & 5 \\ 8 & 1 & 6 \end{bmatrix}
$$

$$
= \begin{bmatrix} 1\times7+2\times2+4\times8 & 1\times3+2\times3+4\times1 & 1\times1+2\times5+4\times6 \\ 3\times7+1\times2+2\times8 & 3\times3+1\times3+2\times1 & 3\times1+1\times5+2\times6 \\ 4\times7+1\times2+3\times8 & 4\times3+1\times3+3\times1 & 4\times1+1\times5+3\times6 \end{bmatrix}
$$

$$
= \begin{bmatrix} 43 & 13 & 35 \\ 39 & 14 & 20 \\ 54 & 18 & 27 \end{bmatrix}
$$

(3.1.12)

$$
BA = \begin{bmatrix} 7 & 3 & 1 \\ 2 & 3 & 5 \\ 8 & 1 & 6 \end{bmatrix} \begin{bmatrix} 1 & 2 & 4 \\ 3 & 1 & 2 \\ 4 & 1 & 3 \end{bmatrix} = \begin{bmatrix} 20 & 18 & 37 \\ 31 & 12 & 29 \\ 35 & 23 & 52 \end{bmatrix}
$$

(Notice that AB is not equal to BA.)

$$
Ax = \begin{bmatrix} 1 & 2 & 4 \\ 3 & 1 & 2 \\ 4 & 1 & 3 \end{bmatrix} \begin{bmatrix} 1 \\ 4 \\ 2 \end{bmatrix} = \begin{bmatrix} 1\times1+2\times4+4\times2 \\ 3\times1+1\times4+2\times2 \\ 4\times1+1\times4+3\times2 \end{bmatrix} = \begin{bmatrix} 17 \\ 11 \\ 11 \end{bmatrix}
$$

$$
x^t A^t = \begin{bmatrix} 1 & 4 & 2 \end{bmatrix} \begin{bmatrix} 1 & 3 & 4 \\ 2 & 1 & 1 \\ 4 & 2 & 3 \end{bmatrix}
$$

$$
= \begin{bmatrix} 1\times1+4\times2+2\times4 & 1\times3+4\times1+2\times2 & 1\times4+4\times1+2\times3 \end{bmatrix}
$$

$$
= \begin{bmatrix} 17 & 11 & 11 \end{bmatrix}
$$

Transpose of a product of matrices: Transpose of a product of matrices becomes product of transpose of each matrix in the reversed order. For example, $(AB)^t = B^t A^t$, and $(AB..G)^t = G^t..B^t A^t$.

3.2   MATRIX AND VECTOR OPERATIONS IN MATLAB

In MATLAB, matrix, column vector, and row vector are entered by the same rule as arrays, as already explained in Chapter 1. For example, the matrix

$$
b = \begin{bmatrix} 1 & 6 \\ 5 & 2 \end{bmatrix}
$$

is entered into MATLAB by

```
b = [1, 6; 5, 2];
```

A column or a row vector may be defined as a matrix of one column or one row, respectively; for example,

```
c = [1, 2]; (row vector)
d = [1; 7]; (column vector)
```

A matrix may be transposed in MATLAB by placing a prime after the matrix; for example, by

```
e = b'
```

matrix e becomes the transpose of matrix b.

An m-by-m identity matrix is generated by

```
s = eye(m)
```

Similarly, An m-by-m null matrix is

```
s = zeros(m)
```

An m-by-n square null matrix is generated by s = zeros(m,n). An m-by-n matrix consisting of unity only is written as

```
w = ones(m,n)
```

If a is an already existing matrix, zeros(size(a)) and ones(size(a)) becomes, respectively, the null matrix and the unity matrix of the same size as a. An m-by-n random matrix is generated by rand(m,n) (see more details of random numbers in Section 1.5). A special matrix named *Hilbert matrix* is generated by hilb(m) (see Example 3.6).

Multiplication of matrices in MATLAB is expressed by multiplication operator; for example,

```
b = [1 2; 4 3; 0 2];
d = [5; 1];
g = b*d
```

yield

```
g =
    7
   23
    2
```

which corresponds to (a) in Example 3.2. Additions and subtractions of matrices are the same as for two-dimensional arrays.

3.3 INVERSE MATRIX

Having learned how to multiply matrices by both hand calculations and MATLAB, we can study the concept of inverse matrices. When two square matrices A and B satisfy

$$AB = I \text{ or } BA = I \qquad (3.3.1)$$

where I is the identity matrix, then A and B are in the inverse relation. That is, A is the inverse of B, and B is the inverse of A; for example,

$$A = \begin{bmatrix} 1 & 6 \\ 5 & 2 \end{bmatrix}, \ B = \begin{bmatrix} -0.0714 & 0.2143 \\ 0.1786 & -0.0357 \end{bmatrix}$$

are in the inverse relation to each other, that is

$$AB = \begin{bmatrix} 1 & 6 \\ 5 & 2 \end{bmatrix} \begin{bmatrix} -0.0714 & 0.2143 \\ 0.1786 & -0.0357 \end{bmatrix} = \begin{bmatrix} 1 & 0 \\ 0 & 1 \end{bmatrix}$$

and

$$BA = \begin{bmatrix} -0.0714 & 0.2143 \\ 0.1786 & -0.0357 \end{bmatrix} \begin{bmatrix} 1 & 6 \\ 5 & 2 \end{bmatrix} = \begin{bmatrix} 1 & 0 \\ 0 & 1 \end{bmatrix}$$

The inverse of a matrix M is written as M^{-1}. Therefore, the foregoing relation between A and B may be written as $A = B^{-1}$ and $B = A^{-1}$. Thus, Eq.(3.3.1) may be written as

$$AA^{-1} = I \text{ and } A^{-1}A = I \qquad (3.3.2)$$

Inverse exists only for square matrices.

The inverse of a product of matrices is equal to the product of the inverse of the matrices in the reversed order. For example, if $W = ABC...G$ where A, B, ... G are square matrices, then

$$W^{-1} = G^{-1}...C^{-1}B^{-1}A^{-1} \qquad (3.3.3)$$

In MATLAB, the inverse of M is computed by `inv(M)`. For example, let

```
A = [1 6; 5 2]
```

then,

```
B = inv(A)
```

yields

```
B =
    -0.0714     0.2143
     0.1786    -0.0357
```

To make sure B is the inverse of A, we compute both AB and BA as follows:

```
A*B
ans =

     1.0000     0.0000
     0.0000     1.0000

B*A
ans =
     1.0000     0.0
     0.0000     1.0000
```

The `inv` command will compute the inverse of any square matrix except when it is singular. If MATLAB refuses to compute inverse, we find that the matrix is singular. It is worthwhile, however, to learn how to make an example of a singular matrix. A singular matrix is such that at least one row (or column) can be expressed by subtracting or adding other rows (or columns). Therefore, in order to make a 3-by-3 singular matrix, write the first and second rows by arbitrarily choosing numbers, but write the third row as a constant times the first row, plus another constant times the second row. Then, the matrix is singular. If no row (or column) can be expressed by adding or subtracting other rows (or columns), all the rows (or columns) are linearly independent and the matrix is nonsingular.

3.4 LINEAR EQUATIONS

We consider a set of m equations with n unknowns given by

$$a_{1,1}x_1 + a_{1,2}x_2 + a_{1,3}x_3 + \cdots + a_{1,n}x_n = y_1$$
$$a_{2,1}x_1 + a_{2,2}x_2 + a_{2,3}x_3 + \cdots + a_{2,n}x_n = y_2$$
$$\cdots \quad\quad (3.4.1)$$
$$a_{m,1}x_1 + a_{m,2}x_2 + a_{m,3}x_3 + \cdots + a_{m,n}x_n = y_m$$

where $a_{i,j}$ are known coefficients, x_i are unknowns, and y_i are known terms which are named inhomogeneous terms (or source terms).

The foregoing linear equations may be expressed compactly by

$$Ax = y \quad\quad (3.4.2)$$

where A, x and y are respectively defined by

$$A = \begin{bmatrix} a_{1,1} & .. & a_{1,n} \\ . & & \\ . & & \\ a_{m,1} & & a_{m,n} \end{bmatrix}$$

$$x = \begin{bmatrix} x_1 \\ . \\ . \\ x_n \end{bmatrix}$$

$$y = \begin{bmatrix} y_1 \\ . \\ . \\ y_n \end{bmatrix}$$

Eq.(3.4.2) may also be expressed in the form,

$$x^t A^t = y^t \tag{3.4.3}$$

where A^t is an n-by-m matrix, and x^t and y^t are row vectors.

Linear equations expressed by Eq.(3.4.2) may be classified into the following three cases:

Case 1: $m=n$
Case 2: $m<n$ (under-determined equation)
Case 3: $m>n$ (over-determined equation)

Case 1 is the most usual case in that the number of equations is equal to the number of unknowns. In Case 2, the number of equations is less than the number of unknowns, which is called an under-determined problem. In Case 3, the number of equations is greater than the number of unknowns, which is called an over-determined problem. This occurs in curve fitting and will be discussed in Chapter 8.

In Case 1, the matrix is square. To find the solution by MATLAB, write

```
x = A\y
```

An equivalent way also is

```
x = inv(A)*y
```

The former, however, is more efficient computationally (the computational time in MATLAB for the latter is approximately 50 percent longer than that for the former).

When the equation is written in the form of Eq.(3.4.3), the MATLAB solution is obtained by

```
z = y'/A'
```

where y' is a row vector and z becomes also a row vector. The following expressions all yield the same result:

```
inv(A)*y
A^(-1)*y
y'*inv(A')
```

The results of the first two are in the column vector form while that of the last is in the row vector form.

Example 3.4

Using MATLAB, find the solution of

$$Ax = y$$

where

$$A = \begin{bmatrix} 3 & 2 \\ 1 & -1 \end{bmatrix}, \quad y = \begin{bmatrix} -1 \\ 1 \end{bmatrix}$$

Solution

Set

```
A = [ 3    2;   1  -1];
y = [-1,   1]';
```

Then,

```
x = A\y
```

yields

```
x =
     0.2000
    -0.8000
```

Also if we write

```
z = y'/A'
```

the same answer comes back in a row vector form as

```
z =
     0.2000    -0.8000
```

Example 3.5

Shown in Figure 3.1(i) is an electric network connected to three terminals with known voltages. Find the voltages of the nodes a, b, and c.

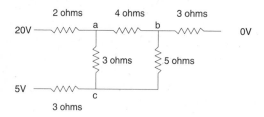

(i) An electric network of resistors

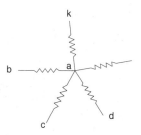

(ii) A node connected to resistors

Figure 3.1 Electric networks

Solution

We first refer to a hypothetical node a that is connected to b, c, $\cdots$, k shown in Figure 3.1(ii). The electric current i from node a to b, denoted by i_{ab}, is related to voltages by

$$i_{ab} = \frac{e_a - e_b}{r_{ab}} \tag{A}$$

where r_{ab} is the resistance between a and b, and e_a and e_b are voltages. The total of the currents leaving node a must be zero:

$$\sum_{j=b,c,..k} i_{aj} = 0 \tag{B}$$

or equivalently, by introducing the relations between current and voltages like Eq.(A),

$$\left(\sum_{j=b,c,..k} \frac{e_a - e_j}{r_{aj}} \right) = 0 \qquad\qquad (C)$$

The foregoing equation applies to each node of an unknown voltage. For the network of Figure 3.1(i), three equations are written as

$$\frac{e_a - 20}{2} + \frac{e_a - e_b}{4} + \frac{e_a - e_c}{3} = 0$$

$$\frac{e_b - e_a}{4} + \frac{e_b - 0}{3} + \frac{e_b - e_c}{5} = 0$$

$$\frac{e_c - 5}{3} + \frac{e_c - e_a}{3} + \frac{e_c - e_b}{5} = 0$$

or equivalently

$$\left(\frac{1}{2} + \frac{1}{4} + \frac{1}{3} \right) e_a - \frac{1}{4} e_b - \frac{1}{3} e_c = \frac{20}{2}$$

$$-\frac{1}{4} e_a + \left(\frac{1}{4} + \frac{1}{3} + \frac{1}{5} \right) e_b - \frac{1}{5} e_c = 0$$

$$-\frac{1}{3} e_a - \frac{1}{5} e_b + \left(\frac{1}{3} + \frac{1}{3} + \frac{1}{5} \right) e_c = \frac{5}{3}$$

The MATLAB solution of the equations is as follows:

List 3.1
```
clear
a(1,1)  = 1/2 + 1/4 + 1/3;  a(1,2)  = -1/4;  a(1,3)= -1/3;
a(2,1)  = a(1,2);  a(2,2)  = 1/4 + 1/3 + 1/5;  a(2,3)  = -1/5;
a(3,1)  = a(1,3);  a(3,2)  = a(2,3);  a(3,3)  = 1/3 + 1/3 + 1/5;
y(1)  = 20/2;  y(2)  = 0;  y(3)  = 5/3;
x = a\y';
x' =
   13.3453     6.4401     8.5420
```

In the foregoing results, the values are, respectively, e_a, e_b and e_c in voltages.

3.5 UNSOLVABLE PROBLEMS

A set of linear equations is not always numerically solvable. The following three sets of equations are simple but important examples:

Case(A):

$$-x + y = 1$$
$$-2x + 2y = 2$$

(3.5.1)

Case (B):

$$-x + y = 1$$
$$-x + y = 0$$

(3.5.2)

Case (C):

$$x + 2y = -2$$
$$-x + y = 1$$
$$2x - y = 0$$

(3.5.3)

The equations in each set are plotted in Figure 3.2.

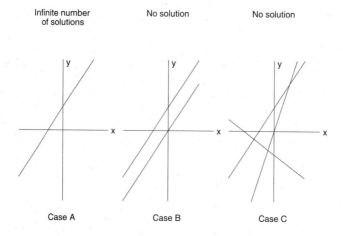

Figure 3.2 Three unsolvable sets of linear equations

In Case (A), the second equation is 2 times the first equation, so they are mathematically identical. Any point (x, y) satisfying one equation also is a solution of the other. Therefore, the number of solutions is infinite. In more general terms, if one equation is a multiple of another or can be obtained by adding or subtracting other equations, that equation is said to be linearly dependent. If none of the equations is linearly dependent, the equations are linearly independent.

In Case (B), the two equations are parallel lines which never intersect, so there is no solution. Such a system is called an "inconsistent system". A set of equations is inconsistent if the left side of at least one equation can be completely eliminated by adding or subtracting other equations, while the right side still remains nonzero.

In Case (C), there are three independent equations for two unknowns. As seen in Figure 3.2, these three equations can never be simultaneously satisfied.

Let us apply MATLAB to these cases any way to see what happens:

Case (A): MATLAB command to get solution is

```
[-1, 1; -2, 2]\[1;2]
```

The MATLAB response is

```
Warning: Matrix is singular to working precision.
ans =
        ∞   ∞
```

If we try, however, to solve only the first equation by

```
[-1, 1]\[1]
```

then the MATLAB response is

```
ans =
        -1
         0
```

Case (B): MATLAB command is

```
[-1, 1; -1, 1]\[1;0]
```

then the MATLAB response is

```
Warning: Matrix is singular to working precision.
ans =
        ∞   ∞
```

which is the same as for Case (A).

Case (C): MATLAB command is

```
[1, 2; -1, 1; 2, -1]\[-2; 1; 0]
```

which is responded to without any complaints by

```
ans =
        -0.6
        -0.6
```

Notice, however, the foregoing solution does not satisfy any of the equations in (C). How can this be true?

We now review what happened to the MATLAB answers. The answer for Eq.(3.5.1) is reasonable and consistent to what we pointed out. That is, Case (A) has an infinite number of solutions but no unique solution. MATLAB, however, determines that the coefficient matrix is singular, so the problem cannot be solved. The solution printed out, $x_1 = x_2 = \infty$, is a trivial solution with no practical meaning. It is interesting that if only one equation is solved, MATLAB finds a solution. The solution $x_1 = -1$ and $x_2 = 0$ is a solution among an infinite number of possible solutions. MATLAB finds one answer of an under-determined equation if equations are linearly independent. The answer for Case (B) is exactly the same as for Case (A). MATLAB does not comment on the inconsistency of the equations. Case (C) needs serious attention because, as we wrote earlier, there is no solution, but MATLAB prints out a solution. What happened is that MATLAB solves Case (C) as over-determined equations and prints out the solution of

$$A^t A x = A^t y \qquad (3.5.4)$$

The foregoing equation may be derived by the least-square method. The solution does not exactly satisfy the original equation when over-determined, but the total of square of the residual of each equation, namely,

$$R \equiv (x_1 + 2x_2 + 2)^2 + (-x_1 + x_2 - 1)^2 + (2x_1 - x_2)^2 \qquad (3.5.5)$$

is minimized (residual is the left side minus the right side of each equation). Equation (3.5.4) is obtained by

$$\frac{\partial R}{\partial x_1} = 0, \ \frac{\partial R}{\partial x_2} = 0 \qquad (3.5.6)$$

3.6 DETERMINANT

The determinant is an important quantity associated with a square matrix. Indeed, an inhomogeneous set of linear equations cannot be uniquely solved if the determinant of the coefficient matrix is zero. This is because, if at least one equation in a set of linear equations is not linearly independent, the determinant becomes zero.[1] If the value of the determinant is extremely small or large, it is indicative of large errors

---

[1] If the determinant is zero, the matrix is said to be a singular matrix. For a singular matrix, there is no inverse. Remember that we wrote earlier how to write an example of a singular matrix.

in the solution of the equations. The determinant of a matrix plays an important role also when eigenvalues of a matrix are computed.

The determinant of matrix A is expressed by $\det(A)$ or $|A|$. For a 2x2 matrix, the determinant of matrix A is calculated as

$$\det(A) = \begin{bmatrix} a_{1,1} & a_{1,2} \\ a_{2,1} & a_{2,2} \end{bmatrix} = a_{1,1}a_{2,2} - a_{2,1}a_{1,2} \tag{3.6.1}$$

For a 3×3 matrix, the determinant is

$$\det(A) = \det \begin{bmatrix} a_{1,1} & a_{1,2} & a_{1,3} \\ a_{2,1} & a_{2,2} & a_{2,3} \\ a_{3,1} & a_{3,2} & a_{3,3} \end{bmatrix}$$
$$= a_{1,1}a_{2,2}a_{3,3} + a_{2,1}a_{3,2}a_{1,3} + a_{3,1}a_{1,2}a_{2,3}$$
$$- a_{1,1}a_{3,2}a_{2,3} - a_{2,1}a_{1,2}a_{3,3} - a_{3,1}a_{2,2}a_{1,3} \tag{3.6.2}$$

We may easily memorize the rule for a 3-by-3 matrix as the *spaghetti rule*. In Figure 3.3, each of three solid lines connects three numbers. The products along the solid lines have positive signs in Eq.(3.6.2). The products of three numbers along dotted lines have negative signs in Eq.(3.6.2). The spaghetti rule can't be extended to a matrix of 4-by-4 or greater, however.

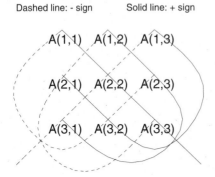

Dashed line: - sign   Solid line: + sign

Figure 3.3 Spaghetti rule to calculate determinant of a 3-by-3 matrix

A formal definition of the determinant of a matrix A of order n is given by

$$\det(A) = \sum_{(i,j,k \,\ldots\, r)} (\pm)a_{i,1}a_{j,2}\,a_{k,3}\ldots a_{r,n} \tag{3.6.3}$$

where the summation is extended over all permutations of the first subscript of a, and ($\pm$) takes $+$ if the permutation is even and $-$ if it is odd.[2] Equations (3.6.1) and (3.6.2) are in accordance with Eq.(3.6.3).

In case the matrix is a lower triangular matrix, or a upper triangular matrix, or a diagonal matrix, the computation of Eq.(3.6.3) becomes very simple. The lower triangular matrix is a matrix in which all the elements above the diagonal line are zero. The upper triangular matrix is a matrix in which all the elements below pivots are zero. The diagonal matrix is a special case of the upper triangular or lower triangular matrix. For these matrices, Eq.(3.6.3) reduces to

$$\det(A) = a_{1,1} a_{2,2}\, a_{3,3} ... a_{n,n} \tag{3.6.4}$$

that is, the determinant equals the product of all the pivots. For example,

$$\det \begin{bmatrix} 1 & 5 & 3 \\ 0 & 4 & 6 \\ 0 & 0 & 2 \end{bmatrix} = (1)(4)(2) = 8 \tag{3.6.5}$$

$$\det \begin{bmatrix} -9 & 0 & 0 \\ 1 & 7 & 0 \\ 6 & 2 & 3 \end{bmatrix} = (-9)(7)(3) = -189 \tag{3.6.6}$$

$$\det \begin{bmatrix} 4 & 0 & 0 \\ 0 & 1 & 0 \\ 0 & 0 & -4 \end{bmatrix} = (4)(1)(-4) = -16 \tag{3.6.7}$$

If a matrix is expressed as a product of matrices like $M = ABC...K$, the determinant of M equals the product of determinants of the matrices, namely

$$\det(M) = \det(A)\det(B)\det(C)...\det(K) \tag{3.6.8}$$

Therefore, when the determinant of a matrix needs to be evaluated, often the matrix is transformed to a product of the matrices for which the evaluation of the determinant is easy. For example, if a matrix M is decomposed to the product of L and U, where L is a lower triangular matrix and U is an upper triangular matrix, $\det(A)$ equals $\det(L)\det(U)$. More details of the L and U matrices are described in Section 3.10.

---

[2]The sequence of the first subscript $(i, j, k, \cdots, r)$ and called "permutation". A permutation is odd or even if $(i, j, k, \cdots, r)$ is obtained by changing the order of any two consecutive numbers in $(1,2,3,...,n)$ an odd or even number of times, respectively. For example, $(3,2,1,4,...,n)$ is obtained through exchanges of the first three numbers as 123 -> 213 -> 231 -> 321, (namely three times). So, the permutation of $(3,2,1,4,...,n)$ is odd. It turns out, however, that the exchanges of two numbers do not have to be between two consecutive numbers, but can be done between any pair of numbers. In the present example, $(3,2,1,4,...,n)$ is obtained by exchanging 1 and 3 in $(1,2,3,...,n)$. The number of exchanges is one, so the permutation $(3,2,1,4,...,n)$ is odd.

Another alternative of computing determinant of a matrix is to use the forward elimination of the Gauss elimination. More details are described in Section 3.8.

To compute determinant in MATLAB, use `det(A)` where `A` is a square matrix. The following illustration shows calculation of the determinant of a 3-by-3 matrix:

```
A = [3, 4, 1; 0, 2, 7; 5, -1, 2];
d = det(A)
d =
     163
```

3.7 ILL-CONDITIONED PROBLEMS

There are a number of linear equations that are solvable but yet solutions become very inaccurate because of severe rounding errors. Problems of this type are named ill-conditioned problems.

Small rounding errors during computation or small changes in coefficients can cause significant errors in solving an ill-conditioned problem. The effect of rounding errors can be illustrated with two equations:

$$(A) \quad 0.12065x + 0.98775y = 2.01045$$

$$(3.7.1)$$

$$(B) \quad 0.12032x + 0.98755y = 2.00555$$

where the two equations are very close to each other. The solution will be denoted by (x_1, y_1), which is

$$x_1 = 14.7403$$
$$y_1 = 0.23942$$

To illustrate the effect of an error in the coefficients, we artificially increase the inhomogeneous term of the first equation (line A) by 0.001, so Eq.(3.7.1) is now altered to

$$(C) \quad 0.12065x + 0.98775y = 2.01145$$

$$(3.7.2)$$

$$(B) \quad 0.12032x + 0.98755y = 2.00555$$

The solution of Eq.(3.7.2) denoted by (x_2, y_2) becomes

$$x_2 = 17.9756$$
$$y_2 = -0.15928$$

The amounts of differences between (x_1, y_1) and (x_2, y_2) are significant, particularly when compared to the amount of the change made in the inhomogeneous term of the first equation. Small changes in other coefficients can cause similar effects. Errors in the coefficients can occur unintentionally by rounding in the process of solving the equation.

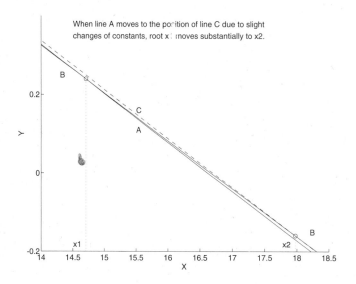

Figure 3.4 Ill-conditioned problem

In Figure 3.4, the two equations in Eq.(3.7.1) and the first equation in Eq.(3.7.2) are shown as A, B, and C, respectively. Line A intersects with B at a very acute angle (a characteristic symptom of the ill-conditioned problem). Line C is parallel to A but slightly higher than A. Since gradients of Line A and B are very close, any small change in the gradient or height of one of the lines causes a serious shift in the location of the intersection of the two lines. Although a set of only two equations is used in the preceding illustration, similar effects occur for a larger set of ill-conditioned equations. The reader might graphically explain how the solution of an ill-conditioned set of three linear equations can be affected by errors in the coefficients. The effect of rounding errors becomes more pronounced as the number of equations increases.

In the remainder of this section, we study two ways of finding whether a matrix is ill-conditioned. The first way is to use the *condition number*; however, to understand the condition number, we have to start the definition of *2-norm*. The 2-norm of matrix A is defined by

$$||A|| = \left(\sum_{i,j} |A_{i,j}|^2 \right)^{1/2} \qquad (3.7.3)$$

The condition number of matrix A, denoted by $\text{Cond}(A)$, is defined by

$$\text{Cond}(A) = ||A|| \times ||A^{-1}||$$

The condition number always satisfies

$$\text{Cond}(A) \geq 1$$

The condition number tends to be large when the matrix is ill-conditioned. The condition number, however, does not give a direct measure of the error of the solution. In MATLAB, the condition number can be calculated by

```
cond(A)
```

For example, the condition number for Eq.(3.7.1) is calculated as

```
cond([0.12065, 0.98775; 0.12032, 0.98755])
ans =
          6.5598e+3
```

In order to compute accurately the solution of an ill-conditioned problem, the precision of the computing should be high. For mildly ill-conditioned problems, double precision solves the difficulty. Severely ill-conditioned problems may need much higher precision, such as quadruple precision.[3]

Computed inverse and determinant both become inaccurate if the matrix is ill-conditioned. Therefore, a direct measure of errors in solving an ill-conditioned problem may be obtained from one of the following symptoms:

- Computed $\det(A)\det(A^{-1})$ deviates from 1.

- Computed $(A^{-1})^{-1}$ becomes different from A.

- Computed AA^{-1} deviates from the identity matrix.

- Computed $A^{-1}(A^{-1})^{-1}$ deviates from the identity matrix more significantly than AA^{-1}.

Severeness of the symptoms also depends on the precision of the computing environment. For example, if one of the symptoms above is found to be serious with single precision, it may disappear with double precision. If it appears even in

---

[3]Not possible with MATLAB.

double precision, however, it indicates that the computed inverse, determinant and, more significantly, the solution of the linear equation can be seriously inaccurate even in double precision.

Example 3.6

Hilbert matrices are notoriously ill-conditioned. They are defined by

$$A = [a_{i,j}]$$

where

$$a_{i,j} = \frac{1}{i + j - 1}$$

Compute the condition number and $\det(A)\det(A^{-1})$ for the 5-by-5 through 14-by-14 Hilbert matrices.

Solution

Both answers are computed by the following script:

List 3.2
```
clear
for n=5:14
    for i=1:n
        for j=1:n
            a(i,j) = 1/(i+j-1);
        end
    end
    c = cond(a);
    d = det(a)*det(a^(-1));
    fprintf('n=%3.0f  cond(a)= %e det*det= %e\n', n,c,d)
end
```

The output is:
```
n=  5    cond(a)  = 4.76e+05    det*det  = 1.000000
n=  6    cond(a)  = 1.49e+07    det*det  = 1.000000
n=  7    cond(a)  = 4.75e+08    det*det  = 1.000000
n=  8    cond(a)  = 1.52e+10    det*det  = 1.000000
n=  9    cond(a)  = 4.93e+11    det*det  = 1.000000
n= 10    cond(a)  = 1.60e+13    det*det  = 1.000016
n= 11    cond(a)  = 5.22e+14    det*det  = 0.999657
n= 12    cond(a)  = 1.71e+16    det*det  = 0.993415
n= 13    cond(a)  = 7.32e+17    det*det  = 1.027812
n= 14    cond(a)  = 2.48e+17    det*det  = 2.245038
```

During the execution, a message similar to the following is printed out for each of $n = 11$ through $n = 14$:

```
Warning: Matrix is close to singular or badly scaled.
         Results may be inaccurate. RCOND = 2.48e-17
```

The condition number is already huge for $n = 5$, but it even increases rapidly with increase in n. The values of det*det are sensitive to the rounding errors that are dependent on the computer used. Therefore, the reader may not get exactly the same values as above. In other words, a deviation of det*det from unity indicates that the inverse of the matrix is not accurate in the current computing environment.

Example 3.7

Compute AA^{-1} and print out the product where A is the 11-by-11 Hilbert matrix.

Solution

The product of the matrices is computed by the following script:

List 3.3
```
clear
for n=11:11
    for i=1:n
        for j=1:n
            a(i,j) = 1/(i+j-1);
        end
    end
    a_inv = a*inv(a);
    for j=1:n;
        for i=1:n
        fprintf(' %7.4f', a_inv(i,j))
        end
        fprintf(' \n')
    end
end
```

The product of the matrices must become exactly an identity matrix if computation is precise. The output shown next, however, demonstrates a significant deviation from the identity matrix:

```
 0.9998 -0.0001 -0.0001 -0.0001 -0.0001 -0.0001 -0.0001 -0.0001 -0.0001 -0.0001 -0.0001
-0.0001  0.9999 -0.0001 -0.0001 -0.0000 -0.0000 -0.0000 -0.0000 -0.0000 -0.0000 -0.0000
 0.0014  0.0012  1.0010  0.0009  0.0008  0.0008  0.0007  0.0006  0.0006  0.0006  0.0005
-0.0006 -0.0005 -0.0004  0.9997 -0.0003 -0.0003 -0.0002 -0.0002 -0.0002 -0.0002 -0.0002
 0.0029  0.0022  0.0016  0.0014  1.0012  0.0011  0.0009  0.0008  0.0007  0.0006  0.0006
-0.0103 -0.0072 -0.0059 -0.0049 -0.0039  0.9962 -0.0030 -0.0028 -0.0024 -0.0025 -0.0018
 0.0241  0.0176  0.0140  0.0118  0.0093  0.0089  1.0074  0.0075  0.0062  0.0053  0.0043
-0.0354 -0.0269 -0.0226 -0.0186 -0.0155 -0.0135 -0.0114  0.9890 -0.0101 -0.0094 -0.0080
 0.0291  0.0224  0.0166  0.0151  0.0117  0.0112  0.0090  0.0091  1.0077  0.0072  0.0061
-0.0129 -0.0096 -0.0074 -0.0062 -0.0052 -0.0049 -0.0037 -0.0038 -0.0031  0.9969 -0.0023
 0.0020  0.0013  0.0010  0.0008  0.0006  0.0005  0.0004  0.0004  0.0003  0.0003  1.0002
```

3.8   GAUSS ELIMINATION

Gauss elimination consists of (i) forward elimination, and (ii) backward substitution. For Eq.(3.4.1) with $m = n$, the forward elimination proceeds as follows: The first equation times $a_{2,1}/a_{1,1}$ is subtracted from the second equation to eliminate the first term of the second equation. Likewise, the first term of every equation thereafter, $i>2$, is eliminated by subtracting the first equation times $a_{i,1}/a_{1,1}$. Then, the equations should look like

$$a_{1,1}x_1 + a_{1,2}x_2 + a_{1,3}x_3 + \cdots + a_{1,n}x_n = y_1$$
$$a'_{2,2}x_2 + a'_{2,3}x_3 + \cdots + a'_{2,n}x_n = y'_2$$
$$\cdots$$
$$a'_{n,2}x_2 + a'_{n,3}x_3 + \cdots + a'_{n,n}x_n = y'_n \qquad (3.8.1)$$

where

$$a'_{i,j} = a_{i,j} - (a_{i,1}/a_{1,1})a_{1,j}$$
$$y'_i = y_i - (a_{i,1}/a_{1,1})y_1$$

Notice that the first equation is unchanged.

Next, the leading term of every equation in the third through the last equation, $i>2$, is eliminated by subtracting the second equation times $a'_{i,2}/a'_{2,2}$. After this step is completed, the leading terms of the fourth through the last equations are eliminated. When the forward elimination process is finished, the set of the equations will be in the form

$$a_{1,1}x_1 + a_{1,2}x_2 + a_{1,3}x_3 + \cdots + a_{1,n}x_n = y_1$$
$$a'_{2,2}x_2 + a'_{2,3}x_3 + \cdots + a'_{2,n}x_n = y'_2$$
$$a''_{3,3}x_3 + \cdots + a''_{3,n}x_n = y''_3 \qquad (3.8.2)$$
$$\cdots$$
$$a^{(n-1)}_{n,n}x_n = y^{(n-1)}_n$$

The leading term in each equation in Eq.(3.8.2) is called pivot. Each equation could have been normalized by dividing through by the leading coefficient, but no normalization is used in Gauss elimination. The primary reason is that normalization of the equations increases the overall computing time, but also the computation of determinant during Gauss elimination is easier without nomalization.

The backward substitution procedure starts with the last equation. The solution for x_n is obtained from the last equation by

$$x_n = y^{(n-1)}_n / a^{(n-1)}_{n,n} \qquad (3.8.3)$$

Subsequently,

$$x_{n-1} = \left(y_{n-1}^{(n-2)} - a_{n-1,n}^{(n-2)} x_n \right) / a_{n-1,n-1}^{(n-2)} \qquad (3.8.4)$$

$$\cdots$$

$$x_1 = \left(y_1 - \sum_{i=2}^{n} a_{1,i} x_i \right) / a_{1,1} \qquad (3.8.5)$$

Thus, Gauss elimination is completed.

So far we assumed an ideally simple situation that no pivot (or diagonal coefficient), $a_{i,i}$, becomes zero. If any pivot becomes zero in the process of solution, however, the forward elimination process cannot proceed. Pivoting is to prevent this, but it helps increase accuracy of the solution even when the diagonal coefficients are all nonzero.

Pivoting is to exchange order of equations so the pivot coefficient $a_{i,i}$ becomes larger in magnitude than any other coefficients which are below in the same column and are to be eliminated. For example, look at Eq.(3.4.1) before elimination starts, assuming $m = n$. The first pivot $a_{1,1}$ is compared with leading coefficients of each equation below it. If $|a_{1,1}| \geq |a_{i,1}|$, $i>1$, no pivoting is necessary. Otherwise, the first equation is exchanged with the one with the largest $|a_{i,1}|$. The second pivoting may take place before the second elimination process starts, when the equation is in the form of Eq.(3.8.1). That is, $|a'_{2,2}|$ is compared with $|a'_{i,2}|$ of each equation below it. If $|a'_{2,2}| \geq |a'_{i,2}|$ is not satisfied, then the equation is exchanged so the pivot becomes the largest in magnitude before elimination starts. The same is repeated for every pivot until the forward elimination is completed. Gauss elimination with pivoting is illustrated in Example 3.8, and the effect of pivoting on accuracy of the solution is illustrated in Example 3.9.

Example 3.8

Solve the following equation by Gauss elimination step-by-step on MAT-LAB:

$$\begin{bmatrix} -0.04 & 0.04 & 0.12 \\ 0.56 & -1.56 & 0.32 \\ -0.24 & 1.24 & -0.28 \end{bmatrix} \begin{bmatrix} x_1 \\ x_2 \\ x_3 \end{bmatrix} = \begin{bmatrix} 3 \\ 1 \\ 0 \end{bmatrix} \qquad (A)$$

Solution

We define an augmented matrix by

```
a = [-0.04   0.04   0.12    3;  ...
      0.56  -1.56   0.32    1;  ...
     -0.24   1.24  -0.28    0]
```

where the first three columns are the coefficient matrix and the last column is the right side of Eq.(A).

First pivoting (rows 1 and 2 are exchanged):

```
tempo = a(2,:);  a(2,:) = a(1,:);  a(1,:) = tempo;
```

Then,

```
a =
    0.5600    -1.5600     0.3200     1.0000
   -0.0400     0.0400     0.1200     3.0000
   -0.2400     1.2400    -0.2800          0
```

Elimination of numbers below the first pivot by

```
a(2,:) = a(2,:) - a(1,:)*a(2,1)/a(1,1);
a(3,:) = a(3,:) - a(1,:)*a(3,1)/a(1,1);
```

yields

```
a =
    0.5600    -1.5600     0.3200     1.0000
         0    -0.0714     0.1429     3.0714
         0     0.5714    -0.1429     0.4286
```

Since the absolute value of the second pivot is less than that of the number below, second pivoting is necessary:

```
tempo = a(3,:);  a(3,:) = a(2,:);  a(2,:) = tempo;
```

Then,

```
a =
    0.5600    -1.5600     0.3200     1.0000
         0     0.5714    -0.1429     0.4286
         0    -0.0714     0.1429     3.0714
```

Eliminating the number below the second pivot by

```
a(3,:) = a(3,:) - a(2,:)*a(3,2)/a(2,2);
```

yields

```
a =
    0.5600    -1.5600     0.3200     1.0000
         0     0.5714    -0.1429     0.4286
         0          0     0.1250     3.1250
```

The forward elimination is completed. Backward substitution is

```
x(3) = a(3,4)/a(3,3);
x(2) = (a(2,4) - a(2,3)*x(3))/a(2,2);
x(1) = (a(1,4) - a(1,2:3)*x(2:3))/a(1,1);
```

The solution becomes

```
x =
    7.0000
    7.0000
   25.0000
```

The entire script for the foregoing computation is shown next:

List 3.4
```
clear
a = [-0.04 0.04 0.12 3; 0.56 -1.56 0.32 1; -0.24 1.24 -0.28 0]
x = [0,0,0]';  % x is initialized as a column vector
% First pivoting (Rows 1 and 2 are exchanged)
tempo = a(2,:);   a(2,:) = a(1,:); a(1,:)=tempo;a
% Elimination of elements below the first pivot.
a(2,:) = a(2,:) - a(1,:)*a(2,1)/a(1,1);
a(3,:) = a(3,:) - a(1,:)*a(3,1)/a(1,1);a
% Second pivoting (Rows 2 and 3 are exchanged)
tempo = a(3,:);   a(3,:) = a(2,:); a(2,:)=tempo;a
% Eliminating the elements below the second pivot.
a(3,:) = a(3,:) - a(2,:)*a(3,2)/a(2,2);a
x(3) = a(3,4)/a(3,3);
x(2) = (a(2,4) - a(2,3)*x(3))/a(2,2);
x(1) = (a(1,4) - a(1,2:3)*x(2:3))/a(1,1);x
```

Example 3.9

The following array represents a linear equation set with four equations and four unknowns. The exact solution is unity for all the unknowns, because each inhomogeneous term (last column) equals summation of the coefficients on the same line:

```
1.334-4   4.123+1   7.912+2   -1.544+3   -711.5698662
1.777     2.367-5   2.070+1   -9.035+1   -67.87297633
9.188     0         -1.015+1   1.988-4   -0.961801200
1.002+2   1.442+4  -7.014+2    5.321       13824.12100
```

(a) Solve the equations without pivoting, and then with pivoting, using single precision in Fortran or C.

(b) Repeat using double precision.

(c) Repeat by MATLAB.

Solution

The solutions for (a) and (b) were obtained by Fortran.[4]

(a) Single precision:

i	Without Pivoting x_i	With Pivoting x_i
1	0.95506	0.99998
2	1.00816	1
3	0.96741	1
4	0.98352	1

---

[4]See Nakamura, *Applied Numerical Methods with Software*, Prentice-Hall 1991.

The results in single precision without pivoting are very poor, but pivoting improves accuracy significantly.

(b) Double precision:

i	Without Pivoting x_i	With Pivoting x_i
1	0.9999 9999 9861 473	1.0000 0000 0000 002
2	1.0000 0000 0000 784	1.0000 0000 0000 000
3	0.9999 9999 9984 678	1.0000 0000 0000 000
4	0.9999 9999 9921 696	1.0000 0000 0000 000

Double precision improves the accuracy significantly, but the best result is obtained when both double precision and pivoting are applied.

(c) MATLAB:
Solution was obtained by the script shown next:

List 3.5
```
clear
a = [ 1.3340e-04   4.1230e+01   7.9120e+02  -1.5440e+03;
      1.7770e+00   2.3670e-05   2.0700e+01  -9.0350e+01;
      9.1880e+00            0  -1.0150e+01   1.9880e-04;
      1.0020e+02   1.4420e+04  -7.0140e+02   5.3210e+00]
y=sum(a')';
format long e
x=a\y
```

The results are

```
x =
      1.0000 0000 0000 007
      1.0000 0000 0000 000
      1.0000 0000 0000 000
      1.0000 0000 0000 000
```

The result of MATLAB is equivalent to the solution with Fortran or C in double precision on an IBM PC or a workstation.

Using Gauss elimination, the determinant of the matrix may be easily and efficiently computed. Indeed, when the forward elimination of Gauss elimination is completed, the determinant equals the product of all the pivots (terms along the diagonal line), times 1 or -1, depending upon whether the number of pivoting operations is even or odd, respectively.

3.9   GAUSS-JORDAN ELIMINATION AND MATRIX INVERSION

Gauss-Jordan elimination is a variation of Gauss elimination. The Gauss-Jordan elimination eliminates the numbers above and below a pivot without distinguishing the forward elimination and backward substitution separately. Pivoting is necessary, however, for the same reason as for Gauss elimination.

In the present section, we first illustrate solution of a linear equation by Gauss-Jordan elimination, and then apply it to inversion of a matrix. A benefit of Gauss-Jordan elimination is that explanation of the algorithm to compute inverse of a matrix becomes simple.

Example 3.10

Solve the same problem of Example 3.8 by Gauss-Jordan elimination.

Solution

We start with the same augmented matrix as in Example 3.8. The procedure for the first pivoting is the same as in Example 3.8. After the first pivoting, however, the first row is normalized by dividing through by the pivot:

```
a =
    1.0000   -2.7857    0.5714    1.7857
   -0.0400    0.0400    0.1200    3.0000
   -0.2400    1.2400   -0.2800         0
```

All the elements below the first pivot are then eliminated by subtracting (or adding) a multiple of the first row:

```
a =
    1.0000   -2.7857    0.5714    1.7857
         0   -0.0714    0.1429    3.0714
         0    0.5714   -0.1429    0.4286
```

The second pivot is compared with the elements below it. Since the second pivot is smaller in magnitude than the element below, pivoting is necessary. Then, the second row is divided by its own pivot:

```
a =
    1.0000   -2.7857    0.5714    1.7857
         0    1.0000   -0.2500    0.7500
         0   -0.0714    0.1429    3.0714
```

All the elements above and below the second pivot are eliminated by subtracting (or adding) a multiple of the second row:

```
a =
    1.0000         0   -0.1250    3.8750
         0    1.0000   -0.2500    0.7500
         0         0    0.1250    3.1250
```

The third row is now normalized by dividing by its own pivot:

```
a =
    1.0000         0   -0.1250    3.8750
         0    1.0000   -0.2500    0.7500
         0         0    1.0000   25.0000
```

The elements above the third pivot are eliminated by subtracting (or adding) the third row times the number to be eliminated. Now, the augmented matrix is

```
a =
        1.0000           0           0      7.0000
             0      1.0000           0      7.0000
             0           0      1.0000     25.0000
```

Here, the first three columns comprise an identity matrix, while the last column is the solution.

Example 3.11

Find inverse of the matrix in Example 3.10.

Solution

As mentioned earlier, Gauss-Jordan elimination may be used to find the inverse of a matrix. To do this, an augmented matrix is written, in which the first three columns are the original matrix A, and the next three columns are the identity matrix:

```
a =
     -0.0400    0.0400    0.1200    1.0000         0         0
      0.5600   -1.5600    0.3200         0    1.0000         0
     -0.2400    1.2400   -0.2800         0         0    1.0000
```

The remainder of the operation is exactly the same as in Example 3.10. After the pivoting, the first row is normalized.

```
a =
      1.0000   -2.7857    0.5714         0    1.7857         0
     -0.0400    0.0400    0.1200    1.0000         0         0
     -0.2400    1.2400   -0.2800         0         0    1.0000
```

The elements below the first pivot are eliminated by subtracting the first row times the number to be eliminated:

```
a =
      1.0000   -2.7857    0.5714         0    1.7857         0
              -0.0714    0.1429    1.0000    0.0714         0
           0    0.5714   -0.1429         0    0.4286    1.0000
```

Second pivoting yields

```
      1.0000   -2.7857    0.5714         0    1.7857         0
           0    0.5714   -0.1429         0    0.4286    1.0000
           0   -0.0714    0.1429    1.0000    0.0714         0
```

The second row is normalized by dividing by its own pivot:

```
a =
      1.0000   -2.7857    0.5714         0    1.7857         0
           0    1.0000   -0.2500         0    0.7500    1.7500
           0   -0.0714    0.1429    1.0000    0.0714         0
```

The elements above and below the second pivot are eliminated by sub-tracting the second row times the number to be eliminated:

```
a =
    1.0000         0 -0.1250         0  3.8750  4.8750
         0  1.0000 -0.2500         0  0.7500  1.7500
         0         0  0.1250  1.0000  0.1250  0.1250
```

The third row is normalized and then the numbers above the third pivot are eliminated by subtracting the third row times the number to be eliminated:

```
a =
    1.0000         0         0  1.0000  4.0000  5.0000
         0  1.0000         0  2.0000  1.0000  2.0000
         0         0  1.0000  8.0000  1.0000  1.0000
```

Now, the first three columns are an identity matrix, and the last three columns are the inverse of A. We denote the inverse by A_inv:

```
A_inv =
    1.0000  4.0000  5.0000
    2.0000  1.0000  2.0000
    8.0000  1.0000  1.0000
```

To check, we calculate A*A_inv and find

```
A*A_inv
ans =

    1.0000  0.0000  0.0000
   -0.0000  1.0000 -0.0000
   -0.0000 -0.0000  1.0000
```

A script to perform the foregoing computation is shown next:

List 3.6
```
clear
A = [-0.04 0.04 0.12 ; 0.56 -1.56 0.32 ...
; -0.24 1.24 -0.28]
a=[A,eye(3)];
% First pivoting (Rows 1 and 3 are exchanged)
tempo = a(2,:);  a(2,:) = a(1,:); a(1,:)=tempo;
% Fist row is divided by its pivot:
a(1,:) = a(1,:)/a(1,1)
% The elements below a(1,1) are all eliminated.
for i=2:3;  a(i,:)=a(i,:) - a(i,1)*a(1,:);  end;a
% Eliminates all the elements above and
%                          below the second pivot.
% Second pivoting
tempo = a(3,:);  a(3,:) = a(2,:); a(2,:)=tempo;a
% Normalization of second row
a(2,:)=a(2,:)/a(2,2);a
for i=1:3; if i~=2, a(i,:)=a(i,:)-a(i,2)*a(2,:); end;
end;a
% Eliminate all the elements above the third pivot.
```

```
a(3,:)=a(3,:)/a(3,3)
for i=1:3; if i~=3, a(i,:)=a(i,:)-a(i,3)*a(3,:); end;
end;a
A_inv = a(:,4:6)
A*A_inv
```

3.10 LU DECOMPOSITION

The LU decomposition scheme transforms a matrix A to a product of two matrices,

$$A = LU \tag{3.10.1}$$

where L is a lower triangular matrix and U is an upper triangular matrix. With $A = LU$, the equation $Ax = y$ is written equivalently as

$$LUx = y \tag{3.10.2}$$

The foregoing equation is solved as follows. By setting

$$Ux = z \tag{3.10.3}$$

Eq.(3.10.2) becomes

$$Lz = y \tag{3.10.4}$$

Solution of the foregoing equation for z is easy because of the triangular form of L. Once z is obtained, Eq.(3.10.3) is solved for x.

When one has to solve a number of linear equation sets with the same coefficient matrix but different inhomogeneous (right-side) terms, solving the equations using the LU decomposition is significantly more efficient than solving each equation individually by Gauss elimination.

Example 3.12

By LU decomposition, solve the linear equation

$$Ax = y$$

where

$$A = \begin{bmatrix} 2 & 1 & -3 \\ -1 & 3 & 2 \\ 3 & 1 & -3 \end{bmatrix}, \quad y = \begin{bmatrix} 2 \\ 0 \\ 1 \end{bmatrix}$$

and $A = LU$ with

$$L = \begin{bmatrix} 1 & 0 & 0 \\ -0.5 & 1 & 0 \\ 1.5 & -0.1428 & 1 \end{bmatrix}, \quad U = \begin{bmatrix} 2 & 1 & -3 \\ 0 & 3.5 & 0.5 \\ 0 & 0 & 1.5714 \end{bmatrix}$$

Solution

We first solve $Lz = y$ for z, or

$$\begin{bmatrix} 1 & 0 & 0 \\ -0.5 & 1 & 0 \\ 1.5 & -0.1428 & 1 \end{bmatrix} \begin{bmatrix} z_1 \\ z_2 \\ z_3 \end{bmatrix} = \begin{bmatrix} 2 \\ 0 \\ 1 \end{bmatrix}$$

The solution is $z_1 = 2$, $z_2 = 0 - 2(-0.5) = 1$ and $z_3 = 1 - 2(1.5) - (-0.1428) = -1.8572$. Then, $Ux = z$ becomes

$$\begin{bmatrix} 2 & 1 & -3 \\ 0 & 3.5 & 0.5 \\ 0 & 0 & 1.5714 \end{bmatrix} \begin{bmatrix} x_1 \\ x_2 \\ x_3 \end{bmatrix} = \begin{bmatrix} 2 \\ 1 \\ -1.8572 \end{bmatrix}$$

The solution is

$$x_3 = -1.8572/1.5714 = -1.1818$$
$$x_2 = (1 - 0.5x_3)/3.5 = 0.4545$$
$$x_1 = (2 - x_2 + 3x_3)/2 = -1$$

A matrix may be decomposed to L and U using Gauss elimination. Indeed, the matrix after the forward elimination is the U matrix. We first assume that no pivoting is necessary. The forward elimination may be regarded as a transformation of matrix A to U, and the transformation is represented equivalently by premultiplication of a matrix F:

$$FA = U \tag{3.10.5}$$

The matrix F can be found if we apply the same operation of the forward elimination to an identity matrix. To illustrate the point, we first write matrix A of Example 3.12 and an identity matrix together:

$$\begin{bmatrix} 2 & 1 & -3 \\ -1 & 3 & 2 \\ 3 & 1 & -3 \end{bmatrix}, \quad \begin{bmatrix} 1 & 0 & 0 \\ 0 & 1 & 0 \\ 0 & 0 & 1 \end{bmatrix} \tag{3.10.6}$$

If we apply the forward elimination to the first matrix and perform the same operation to the identity matrix, the results are

$$\begin{bmatrix} 2 & 1 & -3 \\ 0 & 3.5 & 0.5 \\ 0 & 0 & 1.5714 \end{bmatrix}, \begin{bmatrix} 1 & 0 & 0 \\ 0.5 & 1 & 0 \\ -1.4286 & 0.1428 & 1 \end{bmatrix} \qquad (3.10.7)$$

The first matrix is $FA = U$. The second matrix is the result of F times an identity matrix, I, which equals F itself. By comparing

$$A = F^{-1}U \qquad (3.10.8)$$

to Eq.(3.10.1), F must equal the inverse of L, namely $F = L^{-1}$. Therefore, L can be obtained by taking the inverse of F. Inverse of a triangular matrix is easy and fast. Inverse of a lower triangular matrix is always a lower triangular matrix.

We now ask how pivoting affects L and U matrices. Remember that in Gauss elimination, the order of rows is changed by pivoting. If the changes of the order is known prior to Gauss elimination, we can express the effects of changes by an operator P, where P is a unitary matrix. Premultiplying the original equation $Ax = y$ by P yields

$$PAx = Py$$

or equivalently

$$\tilde{A}x = \tilde{y} \qquad (3.10.9)$$

where $\tilde{A} = PA$ and $\tilde{y} = Py$. If we apply Gauss elimination to the foregoing $\tilde{A}$, no pivoting will be necessary. Likewise, if $\tilde{A}$ is decomposed to L and U, no pivoting will be necessary. In Gauss elimination with pivoting, the matrix after the forward elimination is the U matrix for $\tilde{A}$. The P matrix may be obtained by applying the pivoting to an identity matrix in the same way as performed in the Gauss elimination.

The LU decomposition may be performed by `lu` in MATLAB. There are two formats in writing the command. The first format is

```
[l,u,p] = lu(A)
```

where A is the matrix to be decomposed; l, u and p respectively correspond to L, U and P in the foregoing discussions. For example, if we write:

```
A = [2 1 -3; -1 3 2; 3 1 -3];
[l, u, p] = lu(A)
```

then the answer is

```
l =
      1.0000            0            0
     -0.3333       1.0000            0
      0.6667       0.1000       1.0000


u =
      3.0000       1.0000      -3.0000
           0       3.3333       1.0000
           0            0      -1.1000


p =
        0         0         1
        0         1         0
        1         0         0
```

Here, l is the lower triangular matrix, u is the upper triangular matrix, and p is the unitary matrix representing the pivoting. The L and U matrices thus obtained satisfy

$$PA = LU \qquad (3.10.10)$$

That is, LU is the decomposition of PA rather than A. Therefore, the original linear equation is written first as

$$PAx = Py \qquad (3.10.11)$$

and then

$$LUx = Py \qquad (3.10.12)$$

The original matrix A may be recovered from L, U and P by $P^{-1}LU$. In MATLAB, we type

```
p^(-1)*l*u
```

then the response is

```
ans =
        2         1        -3
       -1         3         2
        3         1        -3
```

The second format is

```
[l,u] = lu(A)
```

which yields

```
l =
      0.6667      0.1000      1.0000
     -0.3333      1.0000           0
      1.0000           0           0

u =
      3.0000      1.0000     -3.0000
           0      3.3333      1.0000
           0           0     -1.1000
```

where l equals $P^{-1}L$ and u equals U, so $(P^{-1}L)U = A$.

3.11   ITERATIVE SOLUTION

Iterative solution of linear equations is not applicable to every problem, but it is useful to solve certain types of problems. When the number of unknowns is very large but the coefficient matrix is sparse, Gauss elimination becomes inefficient, and sometimes inapplicable if the memory requirement exceeds the limit. For such problems, iterative methods are preferred. Additional advantages of iterative methods include (1) programming is simple, and (2) it is easily applicable when coefficients are nonlinear. Although there are many versions of iterative schemes, we introduce three iterative methods, Jacobi iterative, Gauss-Seidel, and successive-over-relaxation (SOR) methods. Consider a linear equation,

$$Ax = y \tag{3.11.1}$$

where A is a square matrix, x is an unknown vector, and y is the source term. All iterative schemes need an initial guess for iteration to get started, which will be denoted by $x^{(0)}$. The initial guess can be any arbitrary vector. If a good guess is available, convergence of the iterative solution becomes fast; however, if not, the initial guess may be set to a null vector (all elements are zero).

A sufficient condition for the iterative solution to converge is:[5]

$$|a_{i,i}| > \sum_{j=1, j \neq i}^{n} |a_{i,j}|, \quad \text{for all } i \tag{3.11.2}$$

If A is irreducible, however, (that is, if no part of the equation can be solved independently of the rest), a sufficient condition is

$$|a_{i,i}| \geq \sum_{j=1, j \neq i}^{n} |a_{i,j}|, \quad \text{for all } i \tag{3.11.3}$$

---

[5]For a nonsingular matrix, the iterative solution described in this section unconditionally converges if applied after premultiplying the equation $Ax = y$ by A^t.

with strict inequality for at least one i.

The linear equations arising from (but not limited to) the following problems are known to satisfy one or both of the foregoing conditions:

(a) Electric network consisting of resistors
(b) Heat-conduction problems
(c) Particle diffusion
(d) Certain stress-strain problems
(e) Fluid, magnetic, or electric potential

The Jacobi iterative method is written as

$$x_i^{(t)} = \left(y_i - \sum_{j=1, j \neq i}^{n} a_{i,j} x_j^{(t-1)} \right) / a_{i,i} \qquad (3.11.4)$$

where superscript t is the iteration count. When $t = 1$ in the foregoing equation, x on the right side has superscript 0, which means that the value is an initial guess. In each iteration cycle, x_i is evaluated in increasing order of i.

The Gauss-Seidel method is slightly different from the Jacobi iterative scheme and is written as

$$x_i^{(t)} = \left(y_i - \sum_{j=1}^{i-1} a_{i,j} x_j^{(t)} - \sum_{j=i+1}^{n} a_{i,j} x_j^{(t-1)} \right) / a_{i,i} \qquad (3.11.5)$$

This scheme is related to the Jacobi iterative method as follows: In Eq.(3.11.5), x_j for $j < i$ has superscript (t) rather than $(t - 1)$. That is, whenever updated values of iterative are available, they are used. This helps accelerate convergence and also simplifies programming because whenever a new value is obtained it can be written over the old values.

The successive-over-relaxation (SOR) is a further improvement of the Gauss-Seidel scheme, and is written as

$$x_i^{(t)} = \omega \left(y_i - \sum_{j=1}^{i-1} a_{i,j} x_j^{(t)} - \sum_{j=i+1}^{n} a_{i,j} x_j^{(t-1)} \right) / a_{i,i} + (1 - \omega) x_i^{(t-1)} \quad (3.11.6)$$

where ω is an over-relaxation parameter satisfying

$$1 \leq \omega < 2$$

As a rule of thumb, ω may be set to a value between 1.2 and 1.7.[6]

---

[6]An algorithm to determine an optimum ω is described in Nakamura, *Applied Numerical Methods in C*, Prentice-Hall, 1992.

Example 3.13

Solve the linear equation in Example 3.5 by SOR.

Solution

A script to solve the equation by SOR is given next:

List 3.7
```
clear
a(1,1) = 1/2 + 1/4 + 1/3; a(1,2) = -1/4; a(1,3) = -1/3;
a(2,1) = a(1,2); a(2,2) = 1/4 + 1/3 + 1/5; a(2,3) = -1/5;
a(3,1) = a(1,3); a(3,2) = a(2,3); a(3,3) = 1/3 + 1/5 + 1/3;
y(1) = 20/2; y(2) = 0; y(3) = 5/3;
x = zeros(1,3);
w=1.2;
for it=1:50
    error = 0;
    for i=1:3
        s=0; xb = x(i);
        for j=1:3
            if i~=j, s = s + a(i,j)*x(j); end
        end
        x(i) = w*(y(i) -s)/a(i,i) + (1-w)*x(i);
        error = error + abs(x(i) - xb);
    end
    fprintf(' It. no. = %3.0f, error = %7.2e\n', ...
            it, error)
    if error/3 < 0.0001, break; end
end
x
```

The result is:
```
It. no. =    1, error = 2.39e+01
It. no. =    2, error = 4.75e+00
It. no. =    3, error = 7.24e-01
It. no. =    4, error = 2.64e-01
It. no. =    5, error = 5.03e-02
It. no. =    6, error = 1.36e-02
It. no. =    7, error = 4.39e-03
It. no. =    8, error = 1.16e-03
It. no. =    9, error = 3.03e-04
It. no. =   10, error = 8.55e-05

x =
   13.3453     6.4401     8.5420
```

3.12   MATRIX EIGENVALUES

Suppose A is an n-by-n matrix. Then, the function defined by

$$f(\lambda) = \det[A - \lambda I] \qquad (3.12.1)$$

is called the characteristic polynomial of matrix A. The function $f(\lambda)$ is a polynomial of λ of order n. For example, for

$$A = \begin{bmatrix} 1 & 3 \\ -1 & 2 \end{bmatrix} \qquad (3.12.2)$$

$f(x)$ becomes

$$\det[A - \lambda I] = (1 - \lambda)(2 - \lambda) + 3$$
$$= \lambda^2 - 3\lambda + 5 \qquad (3.12.3)$$

Therefore, Eq.(3.12.1) is reduced to

$$f(\lambda) = \lambda^2 - 3\lambda + 5 \qquad (3.12.4)$$

The solutions of $f(\lambda) = 0$ are called characteristic values and are the same as the eigenvalues of matrix A.

In MATLAB, the coefficients of the characteristic polynomial are computed by

```
c = poly(A)
```

where A is the matrix and c is an array of polynomial coefficients. The characteristic values are then computed by

```
roots(c)
```

Eigenvalues of matrix A may be more directly computed by

```
eig(A)
```

Of course, the answers of `roots(c)` and `eig(A)` are identical.

Example 3.14

Matrix A is given by

$$A = \begin{bmatrix} 3 & 4 & -2 \\ 3 & -1 & 1 \\ 2 & 0 & 5 \end{bmatrix} \qquad (A)$$

Find eigenvalues directly by `eig`, expand A into its characteristic polynomial, and find the roots of the characteristic polynomial.

Solution

Matrix A is entered by

```
A = [3 4 -2;  3 -1 1;  2 0 5]
```

Then, eigenvalues are computed as

```
eig(A)
ans =
  -2.7503
   4.8751 + 1.4314i
   4.8751 - 1.4314i
```

The command, `poly(A)`, will compute coefficients of the characteristic polynomial:

```
ans =
    1.0000   -7.0000   -1.0000   71.0000
```

which indicates that the characteristic equation is

$$f(\lambda) = \det(A - \lambda I) = \lambda^3 - 7\lambda^3 - \lambda + 71 \qquad (B)$$

The roots of a polynomial can be computed by `root`. Therefore, once the characteristic polynomial coefficients are obtained, its roots may be computed by

```
c = poly(A)
c =
    1.0000   -7.0000   -1.0000   71.0000
roots(c)
ans =
   4.8751 + 1.4314i
   4.8751 - 1.4314i
  -2.7503
```

The roots of the characteristic equations are identical to the eigenvalues computed directly by `eig` command.

Example 3.15

Consider a system consisting of masses and springs as shown in Figure 3.5. The equations for the displacements are given by

$$m_1 \frac{d^2}{dt^2} y_1(t) = -(k_{01} + k_{12})y_1 + k_{12}y_2$$

$$m_2 \frac{d^2}{dt^2} y_2(t) = k_{12}y_1 - k_{12}y_2 \qquad (A)$$

where y_1 and y_2 are displacements of m_1 and m_2 (downward positive), respectively, and

$$k_{01} = 0.3 \text{ N/m}, \quad k_{12} = 0.1 \text{ N/m} \quad \text{(spring constants)}$$
$$m_1 = 0.1 \text{ kg}, \quad m_2 = 0.2 \text{ kg} \quad \text{(masses)}$$

Find the frequencies of harmonic oscillations.

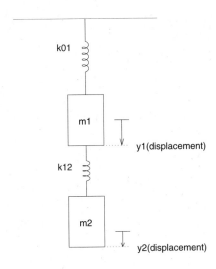

Figure 3.5 A spring-mass system

Solution

For a harmonic oscillations, the solution may be written as

$$y_k(t) = e^{2\pi j \lambda t} f_k, \quad k = 1, 2 \tag{B}$$

where λ is the frequency and $j = \sqrt{-1}$. Introducing Eq.(B) into Eq.(A) yields

$$-\gamma f_1 = -(\frac{k_{01} + k_{12}}{m_1}) f_1 + \frac{k_{12}}{m_1} f_2$$

$$-\gamma f_2 = \frac{k_{12}}{m_2} f_1 - \frac{k_{12}}{m_2} f_2 \tag{C}$$

where $\gamma = (2\pi\lambda)^2$. The foregoing two equations may be written in a matrix form as

$$A f = \gamma f \tag{D}$$

with

$$A = \begin{bmatrix} (k_{01} + k_{12})/m_1 & -k_{12}/m_1 \\ -k_{12}/m_2 & k_{12}/m_2 \end{bmatrix}$$
$$= \begin{bmatrix} (0.3 + 0.1)/0.1 & -0.1/0.1 \\ -0.1/0.2 & 0.1/0.2 \end{bmatrix} = \begin{bmatrix} 4 & -1 \\ -0.5 & 0.5 \end{bmatrix}$$
$$f = \begin{bmatrix} y_1 \\ y_2 \end{bmatrix}$$

We now find eigenvalues of A by

```
eig([4, -1; -0.5, 0.5])
```

which yields

```
ans =
    4.1375
    0.3625
```

Using the earlier definition, $\gamma = (2\pi\lambda)^2$, the frequencies are $\lambda = \sqrt{\gamma}/(2\pi) = 0.3237$ and 0.0958 Hz.

PROBLEMS

(3.1) Calculate $C = A + B$, $D = A - B$, $E = AB$, where

$$A = \begin{bmatrix} 1 & 2 & 3 \\ 0 & 1 & 4 \\ 3 & 0 & 2 \end{bmatrix}, \quad B = \begin{bmatrix} 4 & 1 & 2 \\ 3 & 2 & 1 \\ 0 & 1 & 2 \end{bmatrix}.$$

(3.2) Calculate $B^t A^t$ and $(AB)^t$ where A and B are defined in the previous problem and show that the results are identical.

(3.3) Calculate $E = AB$, where

$$A = \begin{bmatrix} 1 & 2 & 3 \\ 0 & 1 & 4 \\ 3 & 0 & 2 \end{bmatrix}$$

$$B = \begin{bmatrix} 3 \\ 5 \\ 1 \end{bmatrix}$$

(3.4) Calculate $D = A + E$, $E = A - E$, $F = AB$, $G = BA$, and $H = BC$ where

$$A = \begin{bmatrix} 1 & 2 & 3 & 1 \\ 0 & 1 & 4 & 2 \\ 3 & 0 & 2 & 3 \end{bmatrix}, \quad E = \begin{bmatrix} 2 & 3 & 0 & 1 \\ 0 & 1 & 0 & 1 \\ 2 & 1 & 5 & 0 \end{bmatrix}$$

$$B = \begin{bmatrix} 4 & 1 & 2 \\ 3 & 2 & 1 \\ 0 & 1 & 2 \\ 3 & 1 & 0 \end{bmatrix}$$

$$C = \begin{bmatrix} 7 \\ 1 \\ 4 \end{bmatrix}$$

(3.5) Compute $E = B + CD$, where

$$B = \begin{bmatrix} 3 & 2 & 1 \\ 0 & 4 & 3 \\ 0 & 0 & 6 \end{bmatrix}, \quad C = \begin{bmatrix} 1 & 0 & 2 \\ -1 & 1 & 0 \\ 0 & 3 & 2 \end{bmatrix}, \quad D = \begin{bmatrix} 1 & 0 & 0 \\ -2 & 1 & 0 \\ 5 & 2 & 7 \end{bmatrix}$$

(3.6) Solve the following set of equations by MATLAB and verify the results by hand calculations.

(a)

$$\begin{bmatrix} 2 & 1 & -3 \\ -1 & 3 & 2 \\ 3 & 1 & -3 \end{bmatrix} \begin{bmatrix} x_1 \\ x_2 \\ x_3 \end{bmatrix} = \begin{bmatrix} -1 \\ 12 \\ 0 \end{bmatrix}$$

(b)

$$\begin{bmatrix} 0.1 & -0.6 & 1 \\ -2 & 8 & 0.3 \\ 1 & 6 & 4 \end{bmatrix} \begin{bmatrix} x_1 \\ x_2 \\ x_3 \end{bmatrix} = \begin{bmatrix} 0 \\ 1 \\ 2 \end{bmatrix}$$

(3.7) Solve the following sets of equations by Gauss-Jordan elimination:

(a)

$$\begin{bmatrix} 4 & 1 & -1 \\ 3 & 2 & -6 \\ 1 & -5 & 3 \end{bmatrix} \begin{bmatrix} x_1 \\ x_2 \\ x_3 \end{bmatrix} = \begin{bmatrix} 9 \\ -2 \\ 1 \end{bmatrix}$$

(b)

$$\begin{bmatrix} 1 & 1 & 0 \\ -1 & 2 & -1 \\ 0 & -1 & 1.1 \end{bmatrix} \begin{bmatrix} x_1 \\ x_2 \\ x_3 \end{bmatrix} = \begin{bmatrix} 0 \\ 1 \\ 0 \end{bmatrix}$$

(3.8) The following sets of linear equations have common coefficients but different right-side terms:

(a)

$$\begin{bmatrix} 1 & 1 & 1 \\ 2 & -1 & 3 \\ 3 & 2 & -2 \end{bmatrix} \begin{bmatrix} x_1 \\ x_2 \\ x_3 \end{bmatrix} = \begin{bmatrix} 1 \\ 4 \\ -2 \end{bmatrix}$$

(b)

$$\begin{bmatrix} 1 & 1 & 1 \\ 2 & -1 & 3 \\ 3 & 2 & -2 \end{bmatrix} \begin{bmatrix} x_1 \\ x_2 \\ x_3 \end{bmatrix} = \begin{bmatrix} -2 \\ 5 \\ 1 \end{bmatrix}$$

(c)

$$\begin{bmatrix} 1 & 1 & 1 \\ 2 & -1 & 3 \\ 3 & 2 & -2 \end{bmatrix} \begin{bmatrix} x_1 \\ x_2 \\ x_3 \end{bmatrix} = \begin{bmatrix} 2 \\ -1 \\ 4 \end{bmatrix}$$

The coefficients and the three sets of right-side terms may be combined into an array

$$\begin{bmatrix} 1 & 1 & 1 & 1 & -2 & 2 \\ 2 & -1 & 3 & 4 & 5 & -1 \\ 3 & 2 & -2 & -2 & 1 & 4 \end{bmatrix}$$

If we apply the Gauss-Jordan scheme to the foregoing array and reduce the first three columns to the unit matrix form, then the solutions for the three problems are automatically obtained in the fourth, fifth, and sixth columns when the elimination is completed. Calculate the solution step-by-step in this way by MATLAB.

(3.9) Calculate the inverse of

$$A = \begin{bmatrix} 7 & 1 \\ 4 & 5 \end{bmatrix}$$

by MATLAB, and then verify that $AA^{-1} = I$ and $A^{-1}A = I$.

(3.10) By MATLAB, calculate the inverse of

$$A = \begin{bmatrix} 1 & -1 & 0 & 0 \\ -1 & 2 & -1 & 0 \\ 0 & -1 & 2 & -1 \\ 0 & 0 & -1 & 2 \end{bmatrix}$$

$$B = \begin{bmatrix} 1 & 4 & 5 \\ 2 & 1 & 2 \\ 8 & 1 & 1 \end{bmatrix}$$

(3.11) By MATLAB find the inverse of

$$M = \begin{bmatrix} 3 & 1 & 0 \\ 1 & 2 & 1 \\ 0 & 1 & 1 \end{bmatrix}$$

(3.12) Find the inverse of

$$M = \begin{bmatrix} 0 & 5 & 1 \\ -1 & 6 & 3 \\ 3 & -9 & 5 \end{bmatrix}$$

by the Gauss-Jordan method on MATLAB. Use pivoting.

(3.13) (i) Decompose the following matrices into L and U matrices step-by-step by MATLAB; (ii) verify the decomposition by calculating the product LU.

(a)

$$A = \begin{bmatrix} 2 & -1 & 0 \\ -1 & 2 & -1 \\ 0 & -1 & 2 \end{bmatrix}$$

(b)

$$B = \begin{bmatrix} 2 & -1 & 0 \\ -3 & 4 & -1 \\ 0 & -1 & 2 \end{bmatrix}$$

(3.14) Solve the following equations using LU decomposition:

(a)

$$\begin{bmatrix} 2 & -1 & 0 \\ -1 & 2 & -1 \\ 0 & -1 & 2 \end{bmatrix} \begin{bmatrix} x_1 \\ x_2 \\ x_3 \end{bmatrix} = \begin{bmatrix} 1 \\ 2 \\ 3 \end{bmatrix}$$

(b)

$$\begin{bmatrix} 2 & -1 & 1 \\ -3 & 4 & -1 \\ 1 & -1 & 1 \end{bmatrix} \begin{bmatrix} x_1 \\ x_2 \\ x_3 \end{bmatrix} = \begin{bmatrix} 4 \\ 5 \\ 6 \end{bmatrix}$$

(3.15) Find the determinant of the following matrices by forward elimination of the Gauss elimination method:

$$A = \begin{bmatrix} 1 & 4 \\ 3 & 2 \end{bmatrix}$$

$$B = \begin{bmatrix} 3 & 2 \\ 1 & 3 \end{bmatrix}$$

$$C = \begin{bmatrix} 4 & -1 & 2 \\ 1 & 2 & -3 \\ 0 & 3 & 1 \end{bmatrix}$$

$$D = \begin{bmatrix} -1 & 1 & 2 & -3 \\ 2 & -1 & 3 & 2 \\ 0 & 2 & 4 & 1 \\ 5 & 1 & 1 & -1 \end{bmatrix}$$

(3.16) Calculate the determinant of

$$A = \begin{bmatrix} 8 & 2 & 1 & 1 \\ 1 & 9 & 3 & 0 \\ 3 & -1 & 2 & 6 \\ 2 & -2 & -1 & 4 \end{bmatrix}$$

which may be decomposed to the product of

$$L = \begin{bmatrix} 8 & 0 & 0 & 0 \\ 1 & 8.75 & 0 & 0 \\ 3 & -1.75 & 2.2 & 0 \\ 2 & -2.5 & -0.4285 & 4.8052 \end{bmatrix}$$

$$U = \begin{bmatrix} 1 & 0.25 & 0.125 & 0.125 \\ 0 & 1 & 0.238 & -0.0143 \\ 0 & 0 & 1 & 2.545 \\ 0 & 0 & 0 & 1 \end{bmatrix}$$

(3.17) (i) Develop an example of 3-by-3 matrix which is singular; (ii) Try to find the inverse of the matrix. Try to find the determinant of the matrix. Try to decompose the matrix to L and U matrices.

(3.18) Evaluate the determinant of A^{-1} where

$$A = BCD$$

and

$$B = \begin{bmatrix} 3 & 2 & 1 \\ 0 & 4 & 3 \\ 0 & 0 & 6 \end{bmatrix}, \quad C = \begin{bmatrix} 1 & 0 & 2 \\ -1 & 1 & 0 \\ 0 & 3 & 2 \end{bmatrix}, \quad D = \begin{bmatrix} 1 & 0 & 0 \\ -2 & 1 & 0 \\ 5 & 2 & 7 \end{bmatrix}$$

(3.19) Evaluate the determinant of the transpose of the matrices of the previous problem and show that the determinant of A equals the determinant of A^t. Do this first by hand calculation, and then verify by MATLAB.

(3.20) Matrix A is the 12-×-12 Hilbert matrix given by

$$A = [a_{i,j}]$$

where $a_{i,j} = 1/(i + j - 1)$. Compute (i) A^{-1}, (ii) $A^{-1}A$, (iii) $(A^{-1})^{-1}A^{-1}$

(3.21) Develop your own script to solve a linear equation of any size (square matrix) by the Gauss elimination. The script should include computation of the determinant.

(3.22) Develop your own script to compute the inverse of any square matrix by the Gauss-Jordan method.

(3.23) Expand the determinant of the following matrix into a polynomial form:

$$A = \begin{bmatrix} 2 - s & 4 & 6 \\ 1 & -1 - s & 5 \\ 2 & 0 & 1 - s \end{bmatrix}$$

Chapter 4

Polynomials and Interpolation

The main purpose of interpolation is to interpolate data known at discrete points so the functional values between these data points can be estimated. This basic purpose, however, is extended and used in many different ways in deriving other numerical methods. For example, numerical integration schemes are derived by integrating interpolation polynomials. Finite difference approximations are derivatives of interpolation polynomials. For this reason, it is essential to study expressions of interpolation polynomials, their accuracy, and the effects of selecting data points. Although there are alternative ways of expressing the interpolation polynomials, we focus on power series and Lagrange interpolation forms. We also study differentiation and integration of interpolation polynomials. Interpolation polynomials using nonequispaced points are introduced in conjunction with Chebyshev points. For two dimensions, double Lagrange interpolation and transfinite interpolation are introduced.

4.1   MATLAB COMMANDS FOR POLYNOMIALS

We express the power series form of a polynomial by

$$y = c_1 x^n + c_2 x^{n-1} + ... + c_n x + c_{n+1} \qquad (4.1.1)$$

where n is the order of the polynomial and c_is are coefficients. The polynomial may be expressed also in the clustered form

$$y = ((..((c_1 x + c_2)x + c_3)x... + c_n)x + c_{n+1}) \qquad (4.1.2)$$

or in the factorized form

$$y = c_1(x - r_1)(x - r_2)...(x - r_n) \qquad (4.1.3)$$

where r_is are roots of the polynomial. For example, the polynomial

$$y = x^4 + 2x^3 - 7x^2 - 8x + 12 \qquad (4.1.4)$$

may be written equivalently as

$$y = ((((x + 2)x - 7)x - 8)x + 12) \qquad (4.1.5)$$

or

$$y = (x - 1)(x - 2)(x + 2)(x + 3) \qquad (4.1.6)$$

A polynomial of order n has n roots, some of which may be multiple or complex values. If all the coefficients are real, all the complex roots are found in complex conjugate pairs.

Power coefficients: In MATLAB, a polynomial is represented by a row vector containing the coefficients of powers in descending order. For example, the polynomial

$$y = 2x^3 + x^2 + 4x + 5 \qquad (4.1.7)$$

is represented by

```
p = [2  1  4  5]
```

Roots: The roots of a polynomial are found by the `roots` command. For example, for the polynomial given by Eq.(4.1.7),

```
r = roots(p)
```

yields

```
r =
    0.2500 + 1.5612i
    0.2500 - 1.5612i
   -1.0000
```

Here the roots are given in a column vector form.

When all the roots are known, the coefficients can be recomputed by the `poly` command. For example,

```
poly(r)
```

yields

```
ans =
    1.0000  0.5000  2.0000  2.5000
```

Notice, however, that all the coefficients are half the original coefficients of Eq.(4.1.7). This occurs because a polynomial determined with only the roots is still arbitrary by a constant multiplier. In order to determine a polynomial of order n, $n + 1$ data points are necessary, but the number of roots of a polynomial is just n. Therefore, the coefficients are normalized in MATLAB so the leading coefficient becomes unity.

Although conversions from coefficients to roots and back from roots to coefficients are easy with MATLAB, one should be cautious about the accuracy of the computations. The conversion tends to be less accurate if there are multiple roots. For an example of poor accuracy, consider

$$y = (x - 1)^6$$
$$= x^6 - 6x^5 + 15x^4 - 20x^3 + 15x^2 - 6x + 1 \qquad (4.1.8)$$

which has a sextuple root of $x = 1$. If we try to compute the roots by `roots`, the answers are

```
r = roots([1 -6 15 -20 15 -6 1])
r =
   1.0035 + 0.0020i
   1.0035 - 0.0020i
   1.0000 + 0.0040i
   1.0000 - 0.0040i
   0.9965 + 0.0020i
   0.9965 - 0.0020i
```

which deviate from unity. The discrepancy of each root from unity is due to rounding errors in computation, and depends on the computer used. On a different computer, the discrepancies may be different.[1]

Evaluation of polynomial: Polynomials can be evaluated by the `polyval` command. As an example, for the polynomial

$$y = 3x^4 - 7x^3 + 2x^2 + x + 1 \qquad (4.1.9)$$

the following commands compute the value of $y(2.5)$:

```
c = [3, -7, 2, 1, 1];
xi = 2.5;
yi = polyval(c, xi)
```

If `xi` is a vector containing multiple values of abscissa, `yi` becomes a vector of the answers with the same length as `xi`.

----

[1]Finding a highly multiple root is one of the most difficult problems for numerical methods.

Polynomial fitting: A polynomial of order n is determined uniquely if $n + 1$ points are given. In other words, the polynomial of order n fitted to $n + 1$ data points, (x_i, y_i), $i = 1, 2, ..., n + 1$, is unique. The coefficients of the polynomial can be determined easily by `polyfit`. Suppose a data set is given by

```
x = [1.1,    2.3,    3.9,    5.1]
y = [3.887, 4.276, 4.651, 2.117]
```

Then

```
a = polyfit(x,y,length(x)-1)
```

yields

```
a =
    -0.2015    1.4385    -2.7477    5.4370
```

which is a vector of the coefficients of the polynomial. The third argument in `polyfit` is important, which is set to `length(x)-1` because the order of the polynomial equals the number of data points minus one. The polynomial determined here is

$$y = -0.2015x^3 + 1.4385x^2 - 2.7477x + 5.4370 \qquad (4.1.10)$$

In order to evaluate the foregoing polynomial for a vector of abscissas `xi`, write

```
yi = polyval(a,xi)
```

Differentiation and integration: Integration of the polynomial given by Eq.(4.1.1) is

$$Y = \int y\,dx = \frac{c_1}{n+1}x^{n+1} + \frac{c_2}{n}x^n + ... + \frac{c_n}{2}x^2 + c_{n+1}x + c_{n+2} \qquad (4.1.11)$$

where c_{n+2} is an integrating constant. If the coefficients of Eq.(4.1.11) are given by a row vector c, the coefficients of Y may be computed by the `poly_itg` listed in FM 4.1. Its synopsis is as follows:

```
d = poly_itg(c)
```

where c is the coefficient vector of the polynomial y and d is the coefficient vector after integration, which equals

$$[\frac{c_1}{n+1}, \frac{c_2}{n}, ...c_{n+1}] \qquad (4.1.12)$$

Notice, however, the integrating constant c_{n+2} is not included.

The first derivative of Eq.(4.1.1) is

$$y' = nc_1 x^{n-1} + (n-1)c_2 x^{n-2} + ... + c_n \qquad (4.1.13)$$

The coefficients of the first derivative may be computed by `polyder`. Its synopsis is

```
b = polyder(c)
```

where c is the same as before, while b is the coefficient vector that equals

$$[nc_1, (n-1)c_2, ...c_n] \qquad (4.1.14)$$

We define two polynomials:

$$y_a = a_1x^m + a_2x^{m-1} + ... + a_mx + a_{m+1}$$
$$y_b = b_1x^n + b_2x^{n-1} + ... + b_nx + b_{n+1}$$

and assume that their coefficient vectors are a and b, respectively. The synopsis is

```
c = poly_add(a,b)
```

For subtraction of polynomial b from a:

```
c = poly_add(a,-b)
```

The product of two polynomials, one is of order m and the other is of order n, becomes a polynomial of order $d = m + n$:

$$y_c = y_ay_b = c_1x^d + c_2x^{d-1} + ... + c_dx + c_{d+1} \qquad (4.1.15)$$

The MATLAB command to find the coefficients of y_c is

```
c = conv(a,b)
```

Division of a polynomial y_a by another polynomial y_b satisfies

$$y_a = y_qy_b + y_r$$

where y_q is the quotient and y_r is the remainder upon division. The polynomials y_q and y_r are computed by deconv as

```
[q,r] = deconv[a,b]
```

where q and r represent coefficients of y_q and y_r, respectively.

4.2 LINEAR INTERPOLATION

Linear interpolation is a basis for many numerical schemes. For example, by integrating the linear interpolation, the integration scheme called the trapezoidal rule is derived. As another example, the gradient of the linear interpolation is used as an approximation for the first derivative of the function.

The linear interpolation is a line fitted to two data points (see Figure 4.1) and is given by

$$g(x) = \frac{b - x}{b - a} \, f(a) \; + \; \frac{x - a}{b - a} \, f(b) \qquad (4.2.1)$$

or equivalently

$$g(x) = \frac{f(b) - f(a)}{b - a}(x - a) + f(a)$$

where $f(a)$ and $f(b)$ are known values of $f(x)$ at $x = a$ and $x = b$ respectively.

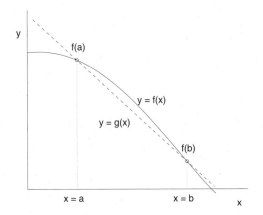

Figure 4.1 Linear interpolation

Error of the linear interpolation may be expressed in the form

$$e(x) = 0.5(x - a)(x - b) \, f''(\xi), \quad a \le x \le b, \; a \le \xi \le b \qquad (4.2.2)$$

where ξ (pronounced "xi") is dependent on x but somewhere between a and b.[2] Equation (4.2.2) is an awkward function because we have no means to evaluate ξ exactly. From Eq.(4.2.2), however, we can say that $|e(x)|$ is bounded by

$$|e(x)| \; \le \; 0.5 \, |(x - a)(x - b)| \max_{a \le x \le b} |f''(\xi)| \qquad (4.2.3)$$

It is seen that the error is a function of x, which vanishes at $x = a$ and $x = b$. The peak of the error occurs approximately at the midpoint, $x_m = 0.5(a + b)$. When $f''(x)$ is nearly constant in the interval, $f''(\xi)$ in Eq.(4.2.2) may be approximated by $f''(x_m)$.

---

[2]See Nakamura, *Applied Numerical Methods in C*, Prentice-Hall 1992)

A command for linear interpolation is available in MATLAB. The `interp1` command determines the functional value for a specified abscissa denoted by `xi` by linearly interpolating from the function table. In `interp1`, linear interpolation is applied to each data interval. The `xi` may also be a vector of specified x values. Its synopsis is

```
yi = interp1(x, y, xi)
```

Here, `x` is a column array of the x values of the data; `y` is a column array of the y values of the data. Both arrays, `x` and `y`, must have the same number of rows; however, `y` can have more than one column. `xi` is a scalar or an array of x values for which y values are to be evaluated by linear interpolation. Alternatively, `interp1` may be written as

```
yi = interp1(x, y, xi, 'linear')
yi = interp1(x, y, xi, 'spline')
yi = interp1(x, y, xi, 'cubic')
```

In the second format, the method of interpolation can be chosen from (i) linear interpolation, (ii) cubic spline, and (iii) cubic interpolation. All the methods require that `x` be monotonic. The cubic interpolation requires that `x` be equispaced. More details of cubic and spline interpolation are described in Chapter 9.

Example 4.1

Two material properties of carbon monoxide gas are given by the following table:

```
T     Beta     Alpha
300   3.33e3   0.2128e4
400   2.50e3   0.3605e4
500   2.00e3   0.5324e4
600   1.67e3   0.7190e4
```

where T is temperature in Kelvin, Beta is thermal expansion coefficient (1/K), and `Alpha` is thermal diffusivity (m^2/s). Find by MATLAB the properties for T= 321, 440, and 571, respectively.

Solution

The following script will answer the question:

```
Temp = [300, 400, 500, 600]';
Beta = 1000*[3.33, 2.50, 2.00, 1.67]';
Alpha= 10000*[ 0.2128, 0.3605, 0.5324, 0.7190]';
Ti=[321, 440, 571]';
Propty = interp1(Temp, [Beta, Alpha], Ti, 'linear');
[Ti, Propty]
```

The results are

```
ans =
     1.0e+03  *
      0.3210      3.1557      2.4382
      0.4400      2.3000      4.2926
      0.5710      1.7657      6.6489
```

where the first column is temperature, the second is Beta and the third is Alpha.

Example 4.2

Suppose a functional relation $y = y(x)$ is given in a tabular form as

```
x     y
0     0.9162
0.25  0.8109
0.50  0.6931
0.75  0.5596
1.00  0.4055
```

where $y(x)$ is a monotonically decreasing function of x. Find the values of x that satisfy $y = 0.9, 0.7, 0.6$ and 0.5, respectively, by MATLAB.

Solution

This is an inverse problem; that is, x is considered to be a function of y, namely $x = f(y)$. The solution is computed by the following script:

```
x = [0.0, 0.25, 0.5, 0.75, 1.0]';
y = [0.9162, 0.8109, 0.6931, 0.5596, 0.4055]';
yi = [0.9, 0.7, 0.6, 0.5]';
xi = interp1(y, x, yi, 'linear');
[yi, xi]
```

The results are

```
ans =
      0.9000      0.0385
      0.7000      0.4854
      0.6000      0.6743
      0.5000      0.8467
```

where the first column is for y values, and the second, x values.

4.3 POLYNOMIAL INTERPOLATION WITH POWER SERIES FORM

Although we studied how to fit a polynomial to a set of data points by `polyfit`, we revisit the subject from a more fundamental point of view in this section.

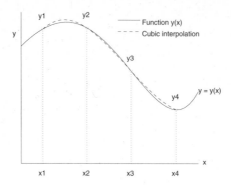

Figure 4.2 Plot of data set

An interpolation polynomial may be expressed in various alternative forms, which can be transformed from one to another. Among them are power series, Lagrange interpolation, Newton forward interpolation, and Newton backward interpolation. Regardless of the formula of expression, all polynomial interpolation formulas fitted to the same data are mathematically equivalent.

Suppose $n + 1$ data points are given as

$$
\begin{array}{cccc}
x_1 & x_2 & \cdots & x_{n+1} \\
y_1 & y_2 & \cdots & y_{n+1}
\end{array}
$$

where x_1, x_2 ... are abscissas of the data points and assumed to be in increasing order. The increment between two consecutive x values is arbitrary. The polynomial of order n passing through the $n + 1$ data points may be written in a power series as

$$g(x) = c_1 x^n + c_2 x^{n-1} + \ldots + c_{n+1} \tag{4.3.1}$$

where c_is are coefficients. Setting $g(x_i) = y_i$ for each of $n + 1$ data points yields $n + 1$ linear equations, which are expressed in matrix notation by

$$Ac = y \tag{4.3.2}$$

where

$$
A = \begin{bmatrix}
x_1^n & x_1^{n-1} & \cdots & x_1 & 1 \\
x_2^n & x_2^{n-1} & \cdots & x_2 & 1 \\
\cdot & \cdot & \cdots & \cdot & 1 \\
x_{n+1}^n & x_{n+1}^{n-1} & \cdots & x_{n+1} & 1
\end{bmatrix},
\ c = \begin{bmatrix}
c_1 \\
c_2 \\
\cdot \\
c_{n+1}
\end{bmatrix},
\ y = \begin{bmatrix}
y_1 \\
y_2 \\
\cdot \\
y_{n+1}
\end{bmatrix} \tag{4.3.3}
$$

By solving Eq.(4.3.2), the coefficients are determined. The coefficients can also be determined by `polyfit(x,y,n)`, as described in Section 4.1. Figure 4.2 illustrates a polynomial fitted to four data points taken from a function $y(x)$.

Example 4.3

Determine the polynomial that passes through the three data points: (0, 1), (1, 0.75) and (2, 0), where the first number in the parentheses is x value and the second is y value of each data point.

Solution

The order of a polynomial that fits to three data points is 2, so we first write the second-order polynomial as

$$g(x) = c_1 x^2 + c_2 x + c_3$$

By setting the polynomial to each data point, we get

$$c_1(0)^2 + c_2(0) + c_3 = 1$$
$$c_1(1)^2 + c_2(1) + c_3 = 0.75$$
$$c_1(2)^2 + c_2(2) + c_3 = 0$$

From the first equation, we get $c_3 = 1$. From the second and third equations, we find $c_2 = 0$ and $c_1 = -0.25$. Finally, the polynomial is

$$g(x) = -0.25x^2 + 1$$

Example 4.4

A set of four data points is given by

```
x = [1.1,    2.3,    3.9,    5.1]
y = [3.887,  4.276,  4.651,  2.117]
```

Find the coefficients of the interpolation polynomial fitted to the data set by solving Eq.(4.3.2), and then determine the value of y for $x = 2.101$ and 4.234 by the interpolation formula. Plot the polynomial along with the data points.

Solution

A MATLAB script is shown next:

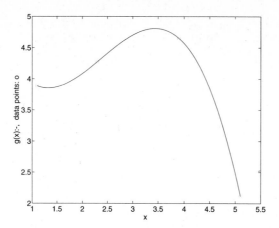

Figure 4.3 Plot of the interpolation polynomial

List 4.1
```
clear,clf,hold off
x = [1.1,    2.3,    3.9,    5.1]';
y = [3.887, 4.276, 4.651, 2.117]' ;
n=length(x)-1 ;
a(:,n+1)=ones(x);
a(:,n)=x;
for j=n-1:-1:1
   a(:,j)=a(:,j+1).*x;
end
coeff=a\y      %Solution of linear equation.
xi=[2.101, 4.234];
yi=zeros(size(xi))
for k=1:n+1
   yi = yi + coeff(k)*xi.^(n+1-k)
end
yi
%   plotting
xp=1.1:0.05:5.1;
yp=zeros(size(xp));
for k=1:n+1
   yp = yp + coeff(k)*xp.^(n+1-k);
end
plot(xp,yp,  x,y,'o')
xlabel('x')
ylabel('g(x):-,  data points: o')
```

The answer is

```
    coef =
        -0.2015    1.4385    -2.7477    5.4370
```

```
ans =
     4.1457     4.3007
```

The interpolation polynomial determined is plotted in Figure 4.3.

Comment: The foregoing script may be much more compactly written using `polyfit` and `polyval` or `Lagran_`.

The uniqueness of the interpolation polynomial of order n fitted to $n + 1$ data points may be proved as follows: Assume the contrary by hypothesis that the interpolation $g(x)$ is not unique. If so, there must be another polynomial $k(x)$ of order n that passes through the same $n + 1$ data points. The difference between the interpolation polynomials $g(x)$ and $k(x)$ is defined by

$$r(x) = g(x) - k(x)$$

must be a polynomial of order n or less because $g(x)$ and $k(x)$ are both polynomials of order n. On the other hand, since $g(x)$ and $k(x)$ both agree at the $n + 1$ data points, $r(x)$ must become zero at the $n + 1$ data points. It means that $r(x)$ has $n + 1$ zeros, so $r(x)$ must be a polynomial of order $n + 1$. This is contradictory to the hypothesis that $r(x)$ is a polynomial of order n or less, and proves that the hypothesis is incorrect.

4.4   LAGRANGE INTERPOLATION POLYNOMIAL

The Lagrange interpolation formula is an alternative to the power series form of an interpolation polynomial. It has the following two major advantages: (1) with the Lagrange interpolation formula, there is no need to solve linear equations, and (2) the Lagrange interpolation formulas allow interpolation even when functional values are expressed by symbols but no numerical values are known. Because of the first advantage, computational efficiency of Lagrange interpolation is higher than the power series form, particularly when the number of data points is large. Furthermore, it is less susceptible to the rounding error effects. Because of the second advantage, it becomes possible to express a polynomial in terms of undetermined ordinates of data points.

We consider a polynomial interpolation formula that passes through the data points:

x_1	x_2	...	x_{n+1}
y_1	y_2	...	y_{n+1}

To introduce the basic principle of the Lagrange formula, consider the product of factors

$$u_1(x) = (x - x_2)(x - x_3)...(x - x_{n+1}) \qquad (4.4.1)$$

which is related to the $n+1$ data points shown in the previous section. The function u_1 is an n-th order polynomial of x, and becomes zero at $x = x_2, x_3, ..., x_{n+1}$ but not zero for $x = x_1$. If we divide $u_1(x)$ by $u_1(x_1)$, the resulting function

$$v_1(x) = \frac{u_1(x)}{u_1(x_1)} = \frac{(x - x_2)(x - x_3)...(x - x_{n+1})}{(x_1 - x_2)(x_1 - x_3)...(x_1 - x_{n+1})} \qquad (4.4.2)$$

satisfies $v_1(x_1) = 1$ and $v_1(x_i) = 0$ for $i = 2, 3, ..., n + 1$. Similarly,

$$v_2(x) = \frac{u_2(x)}{u_2(x_2)} = \frac{(x - x_1)(x - x_3)...(x - x_{n+1})}{(x_2 - x_1)(x_2 - x_3)...(x_2 - x_{n+1})}$$

satisfies $v_2(x_2) = 1$, and $v_2(x_i) = 0$ for all i except for $i = 2$. In more general terms, we can write v_i by

$$v_i(x) = \frac{u_i(x)}{u_i(x_i)} = \prod_{j=1, j \neq i}^{n+1} \frac{(x - x_j)}{(x_i - x_j)} \qquad (4.4.3)$$

The function $v_i(x)$ is an n-th order polynomial which satisfies $v_i(x_i) = 1$ and $v_i(x_j) = 0$ for all $j \neq i$. We call $v_i(x)$ a coefficient polynomial or shape function. The shape functions are illustrated in Figure 4.4, where $n = 7$ and spacing of the abscissas is assumed to be unity.

If we multiply $v_1(x)$, $v_2(x)$, $...v_{n+1}(x)$ by y_1, y_2, ..., y_{n+1}, respectively, and add them together, the summation becomes a polynomial of order n again, and equals y_i for each $x = x_i$. The $v_i(x)$ functions are illustrated in Figure 4.4. The Lagrange interpolation formula of order n is written by

$$g(x) = \sum_{i=1}^{n+1} v_i(x)y_i \qquad (4.4.4)$$

For $n = 3$ as example, the foregoing equation is written more explicitly as

$$g(x) = \frac{(x - x_2)(x - x_3)(x - x_4)}{(x_1 - x_2)(x_1 - x_3)(x_1 - x_4)}y_1$$
$$+ \frac{(x - x_1)(x - x_3)(x - x_4)}{(x_2 - x_1)(x_2 - x_3)(x_2 - x_4)}y_2$$
$$+ \frac{(x - x_1)(x - x_2)(x - x_4)}{(x_3 - x_1)(x_3 - x_2)(x_3 - x_4)}y_3$$
$$+ \frac{(x - x_1)(x - x_2)(x - x_3)}{(x_4 - x_1)(x_4 - x_2)(x_4 - x_3)}y_4$$

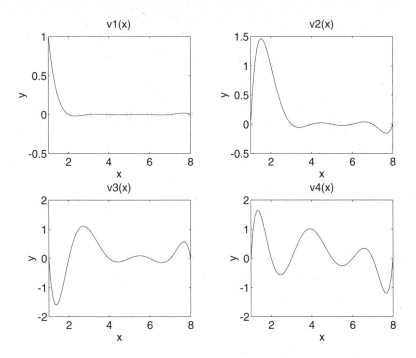

Figure 4.4 Illustration of shape functions

Example 4.5

(a) Densities of sodium for three temperatures are given as follows:

i	Temperature T_i	Density ρ_i
1	94°C	929 kg/m^3
2	205	902
3	371	860

Write the Lagrange interpolation formula that fits the three data points.
(b) Find the density for $T = 251$°C by the Lagrange interpolation.

Solution

(a) Since the number of data points is 3, the order of the Lagrange interpolation formula is 2. The Lagrange interpolation becomes

$$\rho(T) = \frac{(T-205)(T-371)}{(94-205)(94-371)}(929) + \frac{(T-94)(T-371)}{(205-94)(205-371)}(902) + \frac{(T-94)(T-205)}{(371-94)(371-205)}(860)$$

(b) By setting $T = 251$ in the equation above, we obtain

$$g(251) = 890.5 \ \text{kg/m}^3$$

The function `Lagran_` in FM 4.4 performs Lagrange interpolation. Its synopsis is

```
yi = Lagran_(x, y, xi)
```

where x and y are, respectively, vectors of abscissas and ordinates of the data set, xi is the vector of x values for which y values are to be evaluated by interpolation, and yi is the result of interpolation. List 4.2 illustrates application of the `Lagran_` function with the data in Example 4.4.

List 4.2
```
clear
x = [1.1, 2.3, 3.9, 5.1];
y=[3.887, 4.276, 4.651, 2.117];
xi = [2.101, 4.234];
yi = Lagran_(x, y, xi)
```

The results are:

```
yi =
    4.1457    4.3007
```

4.5   ERROR OF INTERPOLATION POLYNOMIALS

To show how error occurs in polynomial interpolation, let us write an interpolation approximation of $y = \sin(x)$ in $0 \le x \le \pi$ with five equispaced points. The interpolation polynomial is a fourth-order polynomial passing through the data points given by

$$x = [0, \ \frac{\pi}{4}, \ \frac{\pi}{2}, \ \frac{3\pi}{4}, \ \pi]$$

$$y = [0, \ \sin(\frac{\pi}{4}), \ \sin(\frac{\pi}{2}), \ \sin(\frac{3\pi}{4}), \ \sin(\pi)]$$

The error is defined by

$$e(x) = \sin(x) - g(x)$$

where g is the interpolation polynomial fitted to the five data points. The error times 100 and the $\sin(x)$ function are plotted in Figure 4.5. We can observe that the error oscillates and its magnitude becomes greatest in the intervals near the end points. This behavior of the error is typical of any polynomial interpolation with equispaced points, although the actual shape of the error distribution changes depending on the function being interpolated and the size of the interpolation range, $|b - a|$.

In order to analyze the error of interpolations, we need to express it in a more systematic form. Indeed, the error of a polynomial interpolation formula (for both power series and Lagrange interpolation forms) is given by

$$e(x) = f(x) - g(x) = L(x)f^{(n+1)}(\xi) \tag{4.5.1}$$

$$x_1 = a \le \xi \le b = x_{n+1} \tag{4.5.2}$$

where $n + 1$ is the number of data points, $f^{(n+1)}$ is the $(n+1)$th derivative of $f(x)$ and

$$L(x) = \frac{(x - x_1)(x - x_2)...(x - x_n)(x - x_{n+1})}{(n+1)!} \tag{4.5.3}$$

In Eq.(4.5.1) ξ depends on x but it is between a and b. If $f(x)$ is a polynomial of order n or less, the $(n+1)$th derivative of $f(x)$ vanishes, so the error becomes zero. When the error does not vanish, we have the same difficulty as we had for

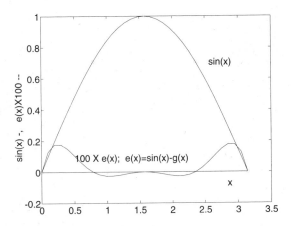

Figure 4.5 Interpolating approximation of sine function

Eq.(4.2.2) because ξ is dependent on x but not known. From Eq.(4.5.1), however, we can write

$$|e(x)| \leq |L(x)| \max_{a \leq \xi \leq b} |f^{(n+1)}(\xi)| \qquad (4.5.4)$$

The right side of Eq.(4.5.4) gives an upper estimate of the error at any value of x. The second term is a constant for the whole domain, so the distribution of the right side is determined by $L(x)$. Figure 4.6a shows a plot of $L(x)$ for the interpolation with five equispaced points. By comparison of Figure 4.6a to Figure 4.5, we can find that the peaks of errors in the intervals near the end points (in Figure 4.5) are due to local peaks of $|L(x)|$ near the end points.

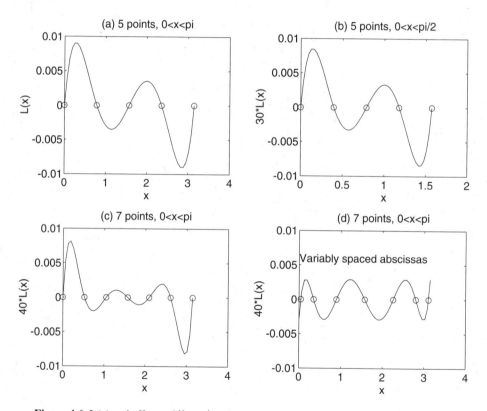

Figure 4.6 L(x) and effects of $|b - a|$ and number of points

Naturally, we are curious how the errors of interpolation polynomials can be decreased. Two immediate answers can be drawn from an analysis of $L(x)$. The first is to decrease the domain of interpolation, namely $b - a$. For example, if we interpolate $\sin(x)$ in $0 \leq x \leq 0.5\pi$, $L(x)$ becomes approximately 1/30, as plotted

in Figure 4.6b. The second is to increase the number of points. Figure 4.6c shows
a plot of $L(x)$ with 7 points for the original range of $0 \leq x \leq \pi$. Compared to
Figure 4.6a, the error has decreased to approximately 1/40. An additional means of
reducing errors of interpolation is to use variably spaced data points, as illustrated
in Figure 4.6d, where the Chebyshev points described in more detail in Section 4.7
are used.

Although reduction of errors by an increase in the number of data points
is remarkable, as shown in the preceding paragraph, it should not be overdone.
The reason for this precaution is that, if the ordinates of data points have errors
or uncertainties, the error of the interpolation polynomial becomes large, and it
increases rapidly as the number of points increases. In other words, if the data
have errors, accuracy becomes worse as the number of points increases. The errors
of data can come from many different sources, including human errors, rounding
errors, and experimental errors.

We will show how the errors of data affect. Suppose the data is expressed by

$$f_i = f_{i,exact} + e_i$$

where $f_{i,exact}$ is the exact value of f_i and e_i is an error. Then the error of the
Lagrange interpolation due to the data error is given by

$$e_d(x) = \sum_{i=1}^{n+1} v_i(x)e_i \qquad (4.5.5)$$

which is in the same form as Eq.(4.4.4) except g is replaced by e_d and f_i is replaced
by e_i. For illustration purposes, we consider interpolation of the $\sin(x)$ function
in $0 \leq x \leq \pi$ as before, with various numbers of points. Suppose all the data
are exact except that the midpoint in each data set has 1 percent error, namely
$e_i = 0$ except $e_m = 1$ percent error, where m is the index of the midpoint. Then
Eq.(4.5.5) becomes

$$e_d(x) = v_m(x) \quad \% \qquad (4.5.6)$$

Figure 4.7 shows plot of the foregoing equation. The errors with 5 and 7 points
(see Figure 4.7a and b) are comparable to the error at the midpoint. The error with
11 points, however, (see Figure 4.7c) is amplified by a factor of approximately 5
in the first and last intervals, and that with 21 points (see Figure 4.7d) is amplified
by a factor of approximately 1250.

To summarize, (1) the use of interpolation polynomial is recommended in as
small a domain as possible, (2) the accuracy of interpolation increases with an
increase in the number of data points only up to a certain number.

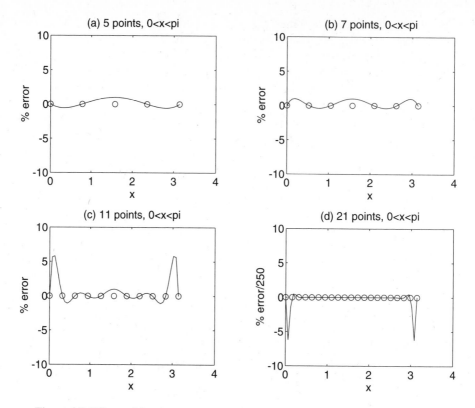

Figure 4.7 Effects of data error

4.6 DIFFERENTIATION AND INTEGRATION OF LAGRANGE INTERPOLATION FORMULA

While a function is approximated by an interpolation polynomial, derivative and integration of the function also may be approximated by the derivative and integration, respectively, of the interpolation polynomial. Indeed, this is the basic principle in deriving numerical differentiation and integration methods. In this section, we do not look into details of the numerical differentiation or integration, for these are the subjects of Chapters 5 and 6, respectively. We do discuss, however, how to evaluate derivative and integration of an interpolation polynomial, particularly, the Lagrange interpolation formula.

By differentiating Eq.(4.4.4), the first derivative of the Lagrange interpolation is written as

$$g'(x) = \sum_{i=1}^{n+1} v'_i(x) y_i \qquad (4.6.1)$$

The shape function v_i is given by Eq.(4.4.3) in a factorized form. In order to evaluate v_i' we express it in a power series form first.

Recognize that v_1 in Eq.(4.4.3) is a polynomial of order n fitted to the data points:

$$x = [x_1, x_2, ...x_{n+1}]$$
$$y = [1, 0, ..., 0]$$

Similarly, v_2 is for

$$x = [x_1, x_2, ..., x_{n+1}]$$
$$y = [0, 1, 0, .., 0]$$

and, in more general terms, v_i is for

$$x = [x_j]$$
$$y = [y_j], \text{ with } y_j = 0 \text{ except } y_i = 1$$

Therefore, the polynomial v_i may be expressed in a power series form by fitting a polynomial of order n to the data.

The power series form of $v_i(x)$ for all i may be computed by `shape_pw` listed in FM 4.6. Its synopsis is

```
p = shape_pw(x):
```

where x is a vector of abscissa points, and `p` is a matrix in which the i-th row represents the power coefficients for $v_i(x)$.

To verify `shape_pw`, a script to evaluate the Lagrange interpolation for x_i is shown in List 4.3:

List 4.3
```
clear
x = [1.1,    2.3,    3.9,    5.1];
y = [3.887, 4.276, 4.651, 2.117];
xi = [2.101 ,4.234];
np = length(x)
p=shape_pw(x)
for inp=1:2
  for i=1:np
    Temp = polyval(p(i,:),xi(inp))
    v(i) = Temp
  end
  yi(inp)=v*y';
end
yi
```

The answer is:

```
yi =
       4.1457      4.3007
```

The solution above agrees with that of Example 4.4.

To compute the first derivative of the Lagrange interpolation polynomial, each row of p is converted to the vector of coefficients of the first derivative using polyder. The following script shows computation of the first derivative at the abscissa points of the data set in Example 4.4:

List 4.4
```
clear
x = [1.1,    2.3,    3.9,    5.1];
y = [3.887, 4.276, 4.651, 2.117];
xi = [2.101 ,4.234];
np = length(x);
p=shape_pw(x);
for i=1:np
   pd(i,:) = polyder(p(i,:));
end
for inp=1:length(xi)
  for i=1:np
     vd(i) = polyval(pd(i,:),xi(inp));
  end
  yi(inp)=vd*y';
end
yi
```

The answer is:
```
yi =
     0.6292     -1.4004
```

In the foregoing script, $p(i,:)$ is the i-th row of p and the power coefficients of $v_i(x)$, and $pd(i,:)$ are the power coefficients of $v_i'(x)$. The values of yi are the first derivative values of the Lagrange interpolation evaluated for $x = 2.101$ and 4.234, respectively.[3]

4.7 INTERPOLATION WITH CHEBYSHEV AND LEGENDRE POINTS

From Figure 4.6a-c, we learned that local peaks of errors of the Lagrange interpolation using equispaced points become smallest in the middle, but increase toward the edges of the domain. The question is how to reduce the maximum

---

[3]An alternative way to get the former is to find the element before the last of the vector returned by c=polyfit(x-4.234, y, length(x)-1). Likewise, the latter is the same for c=polyfit(x-2.101, y, length(x)-1). For more details, see Section 6.1.

error of an interpolation. The answer is to redistribute the points by increasing the interval size in the middle, but decreasing the interval size toward the end points. The optimal distribution of points, however, depends on the purpose of the interpolation polynomial.

If the interpolation is to approximate a function, the points determined by a Chebyshev polynomial is optimal, because the $L(x)$ distribution becomes most evenly distributed. Another advantage is that errors in data are not spread nor amplified as with equispaced points.

Another subject of this section is Legendre points, which are similar to Chebyshev points but are used particularly for numerical integration. When the interpolation is used as an intermediate means to derive a numerical integration formula, the points determined by the Legendre polynomial are optimal, because error of the integration formula becomes minimal.

Chebyshev polynomials and Chebyshev points: Chebyshev polynomials are given by

$$T_0(x) = 1$$
$$T_1(x) = x - 1$$
$$T_2(x) = 2x^2 - 1$$
$$T_3(x) = 4x^3 - 3x$$
$$\cdots$$
$$T_k(x) = 2xT_{k-1}(x) - T_{k-2}(x) \tag{4.7.1}$$

The Chebyshev polynomials are plotted in Figure 4.8 for $n = 0, 1, 2, 3, 5$, and 8.

The coefficients of a Chebyshev polynomial in power series form may be computed by function `Cheby_pw` listed in FM 4.5. Its synopsis is

```
p = Cheby_pw(n)
```

where n is the order of the Chebyshev polynomial, and p is a row array of the coefficients.

Chebyshev roots may be computed by

```
sort(roots(Cheby_pw(n)))
```

`sort` is used to list the roots in ascending order. If $n = 5$, for example, the foregoing command yields:

```
sort(roots(Cheby_pw(5)))

ans =
    -1.446744735887175e+00
    -8.105119796664001e-01
```

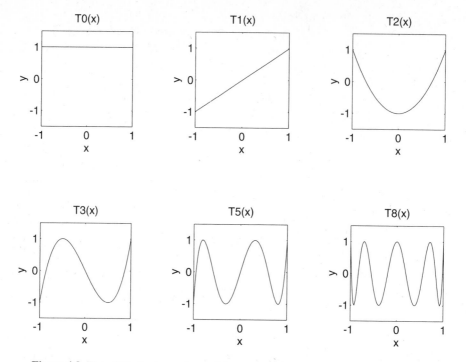

Figure 4.8 Plot of Chebyshev polynomials

```
                         0
      8.105119796664000e-01
      1.446744735887175e+00
```
The Chebyshev polynomial of order k alternatively can be written by

$$T_k(x) = \cos(k\cos^{-1}(x)), \ -1 \le x \le 1 \tag{4.7.2}$$

Equation (4.7.2) has k roots, all of which are in $[-1, 1]$. The roots can also be computed by

$$x_i = \cos(\frac{k + 0.5 - i}{k}\pi), \ i = 1, 2, ...k \tag{4.7.3}$$

which yields identical results as `roots(Cheby_pw(n))`. If the range of interpolation is $[a, b]$, the roots given by Eq.(4.7.3) are mapped to the range $[a, b]$ by

$$x_i = \frac{1}{2}[(b - a)\cos(\frac{k + 0.5 - i}{k}\pi) + a + b], \ i = 1, 2, ...k \tag{4.7.4}$$

Figure 4.9 shows the distribution of $L(x)$ with nine Chebyshev points and the same with equispaced points for the range of interpolation, $0 \le x \le 5$. The heights of local peaks of $L(x)$ are uniform, and the maximum value of $|L(x)|$ is approximately one fifth of that with the equispaced points.

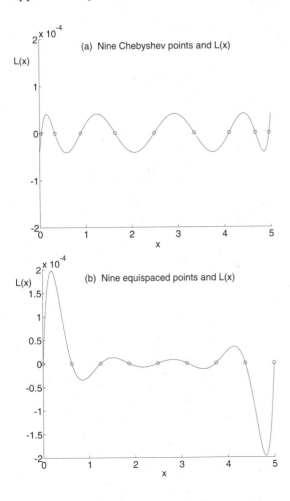

Figure 4.9 $L(x)$ of Chebyshev points

Besides reduction of the peak error by the Chebyshev points, another significant advantage is that the data error is not amplified, as with the equispaced points. In Figure 4.10, we plot the percentage error of the interpolation due to the data error of 1 percent at the middle data point. Comparing Figure 4.10 to each part of Figure 4.7, we can see that the influence of the data error is confined in the vicinity of that data point. Although we illustrated the effect of data error at the center point, the same conclusion can be drawn for data errors at different points.

Lobatto points: Lobatto points are roots of the first derivative of a Chebyshev

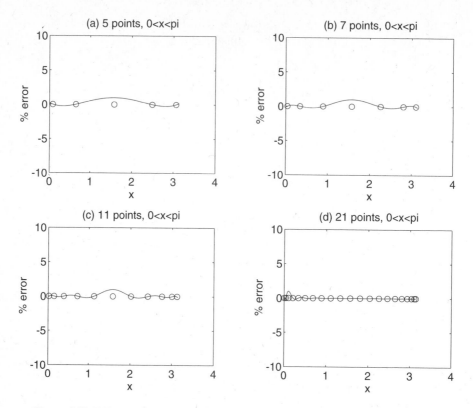

Figure 4.10 Effects of data error with Chebyshev points

polynomial plus $x = -1$ and $x = 1$. For an interval $[a, b]$, the Chebyshev polynomial of order k generates $k + 1$ Lobatto points, namely

$$x_i = \frac{1}{2}[(b - a)\cos(\frac{k - i}{k}\pi) + a + b], \; i = 0, 1, ...k \qquad (4.7.5)$$

Lobatto points, and $L(x)$ based on them, are plotted in Figure 4.11. The peak value of $L(x)$ in Figure 4.11 is higher than with the Chebyshev points in Figure 4.9a but significantly smaller than with equispaced points as in Figure 4.9b.

Legendre points: The Legendre points are seldom used merely for interpolation purposes, but they are important because the numerical integration method, named *Gauss-Legendre* quadrature (see Section 5.3), is based on integration of the interpolation polynomial using the Legendre points.

The Legendre polynomials are given by

$$P_0(x) = 1$$

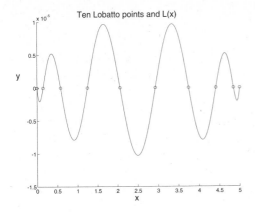

Figure 4.11 $L(x)$ with Lobatto points

$$P_1(x) = x$$

$$P_2(x) = \frac{1}{2}(3x^2 - 1)$$

$$P_3(x) = \frac{1}{2}(5x^3 - 3x)$$

$$\cdots$$

$$P_j(x) = \frac{1}{j}\left[(2j - 1)xP_{j-1}(x) - (j - 1)P_{j-2}(x)\right]$$

The coefficients of the Legendre polynomial of order n may be computed by Legen_pw; for example,

```
p = Legen_pw(6)
```

yields

```
p =
    14.4375, 0, -19.6875, 0, 6.5625, 0, -0.3121
```

The roots of a Legendre polynomial may be computed using roots. For $n = 6$ as an example:

```
sort(roots(Legen_pw(6)))
ans =
    -9.324695142031516e-01
    -6.612093864662646e-01
    -2.386191860831969e-01
     2.386191860831969e-01
     6.612093864662645e-01
     9.324695142031515e-01
```

where sort is used to list the points in ascending order.

4.8   CUBIC HERMITE INTERPOLATION

A polynomial can be fitted not only to functional values but also to derivatives. The polynomials fitted to both functional and derivative values are named *Hermite interpolation* polynomials or *osculating* polynomials. We consider here the cubic Hermite polynomial,

$$f(s) = c_1 s^3 + c_2 s^2 + c_3 s + c_4 \tag{4.8.1}$$

which is fitted to two functional values and two derivatives. Consider the interval between two points, s_1, s_2, and assume the functional values and first derivatives are specified at points 1 and 2 (see Figure 4.12). The four equations are written as

$$f(s_1) = c_1 s_1^3 + c_2 s_1^2 + c_3 s_1 + c_4 = f_1$$
$$f'(s_1) = 3c_1 s_1^2 + 2c_2 s_1 + c_3 = f_1'$$
$$f(s_2) = c_1 s_2^3 + c_2 s_2^2 + c_3 s_2 + c_4 = f_2 \tag{4.8.2}$$
$$f'(s_2) = 3c_1 s_2^2 + 2c_2 s_2 + c_3 = f_2'$$

Equation (4.8.2) has four linear equations with four coefficients to be determined.

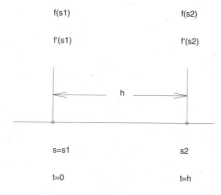

Figure 4.12 Interval for cubic Hermite interpolation

Example 4.6

Determine a curve that passes through point A and point B on the x-y coordinates (see Figure 4.13) with the following conditions:

A: $x = 1, y = 1, dy/dx = 0$

B: $x = 4, y = 2, dx/dy = 0$

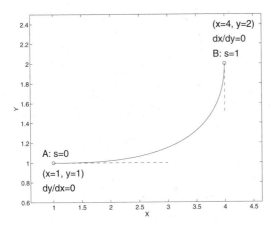

Figure 4.13 Conditions for the curve desired

Solution

Because both $y(x)$ and $x(y)$ become singular at one of the end points, it is not possible to fit y as a function of x, or x as a function of y. In fitting a geometric curve, as in this example, it is common to introduce a parameter s, and express each of x and y as $x(s)$ and $y(s)$. We assume $s = 0$ at point A and $s = 1$ at point B. Each of x and y will be expressed as a cubic polynomial of s as

$$x = x(s) = c_1 s^3 + c_2 s^2 + c_3 s + c_4 \tag{A}$$

$$y = y(s) = d_1 s^3 + d_2 s^2 + d_3 s + d_4 \tag{B}$$

The boundary conditions for $x(s)$ and $y(s)$ may be written as

$$s = 0: \quad x(0) = 1, dx/ds = a; \quad y(0) = 1, dy/ds = 0 \tag{C}$$

$$s = 1: \quad x(1) = 4, dx/ds = 0; \quad y(1) = 2, dy/ds = b \tag{D}$$

where a and b are arbitrary parameters. By eliminating ds, the original end conditions

$$s = 0: dy/dx = 0$$

$$s = 1: dx/dy = 0$$

are satisfied.

Introducing Eqs.(A) and (B) into (C) and (D), respectively, yields

$$c_4 = 1$$
$$c_3 = a$$
$$c_1 + c_2 + c_3 + c_4 = 4$$
$$3c_1 + 2c_2 + c_3 = 0$$

$$d_4 = 1$$
$$d_3 = 0$$
$$d_1 + d_2 + d_3 + d_4 = 2$$
$$3d_1 + 2d_2 + d_3 = b$$

The constants a and b are arbitrary, but they affect the shape of the curve to some extent. After a few trials, we choose the following values: $a = b = 3$. A script to determine the coefficients by solving the foregoing equations is

```
a = 3;
b = 3;
c = [0,0,0,1; 0,0,1,0; 1,1,1,1; 3,2,1,0]\[1; a; 4; 0]
d = [0,0,0,1; 0,0,1,0; 1,1,1,1; 3,2,1,0]\[1; 0; 2; b]
s = 0:0.01:1;
x = polyval(c,s); y = polyval(d,s);   plot(x,y)
```

The result is

```
c =
    -3.0000
     3.0000
     3.0000
     1.0000

d =
     1
     0
     0
     1
```

A plot of the cubic Hermite interpolation curve is shown in Figure 4.14.

Implementation of cubic Hermite interpolation can be simplified if the derivative boundary conditions are approximated by a finite difference formula, because then the Hermite interpolation can be implemented by means of the Lagrange interpolation. This approach is only an approximation, but the amount of error, practically, can be negligible. The boundary conditions given by Eq.(4.8.2) may be approximated by

$$f(s_1) = f_1$$
$$f(s_1 + \zeta) \approx f_1 + \zeta f_1'$$
$$f(s_2) = f_2 \tag{4.8.3}$$
$$f(s_2 - \zeta) \approx f_2 - \zeta f_2'$$

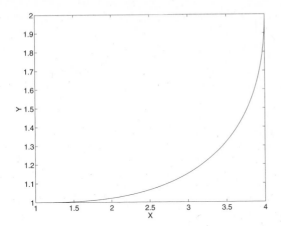

Figure 4.14 Curve determined by Hermite interpolation

where ζ is an arbitrarily chosen parameter satisfying $\zeta \ll s_2 - s_1$. Then, a third-order polynomial can be determined to fit to the conditions of Eq.(4.8.3) by the Lagrange interpolation.

Example 4.7

Repeat the task of Example 4.6 by `polyfit`.

Solution

By applying Eq.(4.8.3), we set four data points as follows:

$$
\begin{aligned}
s = 0 : & \quad x = 1, \ y = 1 \\
s = \zeta : & \quad x = 1 + a\zeta, \ y = 0 \\
s = 1 - b\zeta : & \quad x = 4, \ y = 2 - b\zeta \\
s = 1 : & \quad x = 4, \ y = 2
\end{aligned}
$$

The value ζ is an arbitrarily small positive quantity, so we set to $\zeta = 0.01$. If it is too small, however, rounding errors occur in determining the coefficients. The parameters a and b in the foregoing equations have similar roles to those they have in Example 4.6.

List 4.5 is a script to determine coefficients of cubic polynomials.

List 4.5
```
clear,clf,hold off
z=0.01; a=3; b=3;
s(1) = 0;          x(1) = 1;       y(1) = 1;
s(2) = z;          x(2) = 1+z*a;   y(2) = 1;
s(3) = 1 - z;      x(3) = 4;       y(3) = 2 - z*b;
s(4) = 1;          x(4) = 4;       y(4) = 2;
c=polyfit(s,x,length(s)-1)
d=polyfit(s,y,length(s)-1)
ss=0:0.1:1;
xp = polyval(c,ss);
yp = polyval(d,ss);
plot(xp,yp)
```

The result is:
```
c =
    -3.0921     3.1231      2.9691      1.0000
d =
     1.0307    -0.0309      0.0002      1.0000
```

where values are similar to the coefficients determined in Example 4.6. The plot of the curve shown in Figure 4.15 agrees well with that of Figure 4.14.

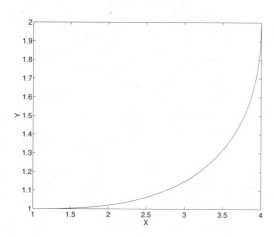

Figure 4.15 Hermite curve determined approximately by Lagrange interpolation

4.9 TWO-DIMENSIONAL INTERPOLATION

Bilinear interpolation: Data in a two-dimensional function table can be interpolated using linear interpolation twice.

The two-dimensional function table is an array of functional values $f_{i,j} = f(x_i, y_j)$ on a rectangular grid, (x_i, y_j). Suppose we have to estimate the functional value at a point located in a rectangular domain defined by $x_{i-1} \le x \le x_i$ and $y_{j-1} \le y \le y_j$, as shown in Figure 4.16. By linear interpolation in the y-direction, the values at E and F are found, respectively, as

$$f_E = \frac{y_j - y}{y_j - y_{j-1}} f_{i-1,j-1} + \frac{y - y_{j-1}}{y_j - y_{j-1}} f_{i-1,j}$$

$$(4.9.1)$$

$$f_F = \frac{y_j - y}{y_j - y_{j-1}} f_{i,j-1} + \frac{y - y_{j-1}}{y_j - y_{j-1}} f_{i,j}$$

Then, linear interpolation of f_E and f_F yields

$$g(x, y) = \frac{x_i - x}{x_i - x_{i-1}} f_E + \frac{x - x_{i-1}}{x_i - x_{i-1}} f_F \qquad (4.9.2)$$

Combining the two steps into one equation, the bilinear interpolation can be written as

$$g(x, y) = \frac{1}{(x_i - x_{i-1})(y_j - y_{j-1})} \times$$
$$[(x_i - x)(y_j - y)f_{i-1,j-1} + (x_i - x)(y - y_{j-1})f_{i-1,j}$$
$$+ (x - x_{i-1})(y_j - y)f_{i,j-1} + (x - x_{i-1})(y - y_{j-1})f_{i,j}] \quad (4.9.3)$$

In MATLAB, bilinear interpolation is performed by `table2`. Its synopsis is as follows:

```
f =table2(tab,x,y)
```

Here, `f` equals $g(x, y)$ of Eq.(4.9.3); `tab` is a two-dimensional data table. The first column of `tab` is the array of x_i values and the first row is the array of y_j values, both in increasing order. The remainder of columns and rows are occupied by $f_{i,j}$. The x and y are coordinates for which the interpolation is to be evaluated, and can be scalar, vector, or matrix.

Double Lagrange interpolation: Double Lagrange interpolation is to apply the Lagrange interpolation method twice in two dimensions. Therefore, the interpolation formula can use all the data points in the table. Suppose the function table has M columns and N rows. The coordinates of the points are denoted by (x_m, y_n), and the functional values by $F(x_m, y_n)$. Then, double Lagrange interpolation is given by

$$F(x, y) = \sum_{m=1}^{M} \sum_{n=1}^{N} \phi_m(x) \psi_n(y) F(x_m, y_n) \qquad (4.9.4)$$

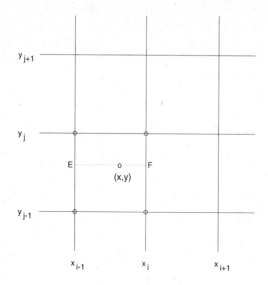

Figure 4.16 Bilinear interpolation in a two-dimensional domain

where ϕ_m and ψ_n are shape functions given by

$$\phi_m(x) = \prod_{k=1,k\neq m}^{M} \frac{x - x_k}{x_m - x_k}$$

(4.9.5)

$$\psi_n(y) = \prod_{k=1,k\neq n}^{N} \frac{y - y_k}{y_n - y_k}$$

Recognize that $\phi_m(x)\psi_n(y)$ is a two-dimensional shape function that becomes zero at all the data points except at (x_m, y_n). When $M = N = 2$, Eq.(4.9.4) reduces to the bilinear interpolation, Eq.(4.9.3). The Chebyshev or Lobatto points may be used to select x_m and y_n.

4.10 TRANSFINITE INTERPOLATION

Transfinite interpolation is an interpolation method for a two-dimensional space where the functional values along the external boundaries, as well as along the vertical and horizontal lines inside the boundaries, are known. The double-interpolation method of Section 4.9 applies when functional values are known only at the intersections of vertical and horizontal lines. In contrast to the double interpolation, transfinite interpolation fits to continuous functions specified along the horizontal and vertical lines.

To illustrate an application of transfinite interpolation, imagine an architect designing a curved roof on a rectangular building, the top view of which satisfies

$$x_1 \le x \le x_2, \; y_1 \le y \le y_2$$

His client has specified the shape of the roof line along the four edges, which are four analytical functions expressing the height of the roof along the edges. These four functions are continuous through the corners, so no sudden change of height occurs at any corner of the roof. The architect needs to create a smooth surface that fits the edge heights of his client.

The task can be restated as follows: Determine a smooth function $F(x, y)$ that satisfies the boundary conditions given by

$$\begin{aligned}
F(x_1, y) &= f_W(y) \\
F(x_2, y) &= f_E(y) \\
F(x, y_1) &= f_S(x) \\
F(x, y_2) &= f_N(x)
\end{aligned} \tag{4.10.1}$$

where the right side of each equation is an analytical function that the client has given to the architect. We recognize that no unique solution exists to this problem since there is no unique way of interpolating given data. There are several possible ways to find such a function, however, among which are (1) to solve a Laplace equation

$$\nabla^2 F(x, y) = 0 \tag{4.10.2}$$

with the boundary conditions, and (2) the transfinite interpolation.

The transfinite interpolation for this problem can be written as

$$F(x, y) = \sum_{m=1}^{2} \phi_m(x) F(x_m, y) + \sum_{n=1}^{2} \psi_n(y) F(x, y_n)$$
$$- \sum_{m=1}^{2} \sum_{n=1}^{2} \phi_m(x) \psi_n(y) F(x_m, y_n) \tag{4.10.3}$$

where

$$\phi_1(x) = \frac{x_2 - x}{x_2 - x_1}$$

$$\phi_2(x) = \frac{x - x_1}{x_2 - x_1}$$

$$\psi_1(y) = \frac{y_2 - y}{y_2 - y_1}$$

$$\psi_2(y) = \frac{y - y_1}{y_2 - y_1}$$

The transfinite interpolation is smooth and satisfies the boundary conditions.

The foregoing transfinite interpolation can be generalized to include the functions specified along multiple lines. Consider a rectangular domain divided by vertical and horizontal lines, as shown in Figure 4.17. The leftmost vertical line is the left boundary and the rightmost vertical line is the right boundary. The vertical lines are indexed by m, where the leftmost vertical lines are indexed by $m = 1$, while the last one is indexed by $m = M$. Likewise, the horizontal lines are indexed by n, where $n = 1$ is the bottom boundary and $n = N$ is the top boundary. Suppose the values of $F(x, y)$ are known along all the horizontal and vertical lines. The function given along the m-th vertical line, $F(x_m, y)$, is set to the known function; that along the n-th horizontal line, $F(x, y_n)$, is also set to the corresponding known function.

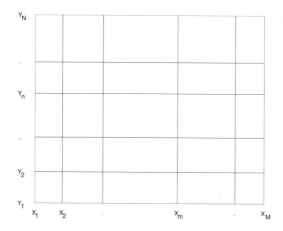

Figure 4.17 Domain for transfinite interpolations

Then, finding $F(x, y)$ satisfying these conditions along the vertical and horizontal lines is the task. This problem can be restated as: find a smooth function $F(x, y)$ that satisfies

$$F(x, y) = F(x_m, y), \quad \text{along } x = x_m \quad (m-\text{th vertical line})$$

$$F(x, y) = F(x, y_n), \quad \text{along } y = y_n \quad (n-\text{th horizontal line})$$

(4.10.4)

The transfinite interpolation satisfying the given conditions is

$$F(x, y) = \sum_{m=1}^{M} \phi_m(x) F(x_m, y) + \sum_{n=1}^{N} \psi_n(y) F(x, y_n)$$

$$- \sum_{m=1}^{M} \sum_{n=1}^{N} \phi_m(x) \psi_n(y) F(x_m, y_n)$$

(4.10.5)

where

$$\phi_m(x) = \prod_{k=1, k \neq m}^{M} \frac{x - x_k}{x_m - x_k}$$

(4.10.6)

$$\psi_n(y) = \prod_{k=1, k \neq n}^{N} \frac{y - y_k}{y_n - y_k}$$

One can see that the first term of Eq.(4.10.5) is the Lagrange interpolation on the x-coordinate of the vertical lines, while the second term is the Lagrange interpolation on the y-coordinate of the functions given along the horizontal lines. The third term is a double Lagrange interpolation given by Eq.(4.9.4). The transfinite interpolation satisfies all the boundary conditions at the external boundaries as well as along the internal boundaries.

To analyze the relation between the transfinite interpolation method and the double Lagrange interpolation more clearly, assume that F values are known only at intersections (m, n). In this case, $F(x, y_n)$ and $F(x_m, y)$ can be expressed by Lagrange interpolation as follows:

$$F(x, y_n) = \sum_{m=1}^{M} \phi_m(x) F(x_m, y_n)$$

$$F(x_m, y) = \sum_{n=0}^{N} \psi_n(y) F(x_m, y_n)$$

(4.10.7)

When the foregoing equations are introduced into Eq.(4.10.5), all three terms on the right side become identical except for signs, so two of them cancel and the transfinite interpolation reduces to the double Lagrange interpolation given by Eq.(4.9.4).

Although we have assumed that the functions along the vertical and horizontal lines are analytical functions, these can be applied to a discretely defined function, as illustrated in Example 4.8.

Example 4.8

In Table 4.1, the functional values are given along certain columns and rows. Fill the blank by the transfinite interpolation.

Table 4.1 A data table given for $F(x_i, y_j)$

j	$i=1$	2	3	4	5	6	7	8	9	10	11
1	0.2955	0.3894	0.4794	0.5646	0.6442	0.7174	0.7833	0.8415	0.8912	0.9320	0.9636
2	0.4794					0.8415					0.9975
3	0.6442					0.9320					0.9917
4	0.7833	0.8415	0.8912	0.9320	0.9636	0.9854	0.9975	0.9996	0.9917	0.9738	0.9463
5	0.8912					0.9996					0.8632
6	0.9636					0.9738					0.7457
7	0.9975	0.9996	0.9917	0.9738	0.9463	0.9093	0.8632	0.8085	0.7457	0.6755	0.5985

Solution

The table filled with the transfinite interpolation is shown in Table 4.2.

Table 4.2 Results of transfinite interpolation, $A(i, j)$

j	$i=1$	2	3	4	5	6	7	8	9	10	11
1	0.2955	0.3894	0.4794	0.5646	0.6442	0.7174	0.7833	0.8415	0.8912	0.9320	0.9636
2	0.4794	0.5647	0.6443	0.7174	0.7834	0.8415	0.8912	0.9320	0.9635	0.9854	0.9975
3	0.6442	0.7174	0.7834	0.8415	0.8912	0.9320	0.9635	0.9854	0.9974	0.9995	0.9917
4	0.7833	0.8415	0.8912	0.9320	0.9636	0.9854	0.9975	0.9996	0.9917	0.9738	0.9463
5	0.8912	0.9320	0.9635	0.9854	0.9975	0.9996	0.9917	0.9739	0.9464	0.9094	0.8632
6	0.9636	0.9854	0.9974	0.9995	0.9916	0.9738	0.9464	0.9094	0.8633	0.8086	0.7457
7	0.9975	0.9996	0.9917	0.9738	0.9463	0.9093	0.8632	0.8085	0.7457	0.6755	0.5985

4.11   M-FILES

FM 4.1 Integration of a polynomial
Purpose: finding the coefficients of the polynomial integrated.
Synopsis: `py = poly_itg(p)`
  p: coefficients of the polynomial to be integrated.
  py: coefficients of the polynomial after integration.

poly_itg.m

```
function py = poly_itg(p)
n=length(p)
py = [p.*[n:-1:1].^(-1),0]
```

FM 4.2 Adding two polynomials

Purpose: adding two polynomials.

Synopsis: b = poly_add(p1,p2)

        p1, p2: arrays of coefficients of the two polynomials.

        b : array of coefficients after addition.

poly_add.m

```
function p3 = poly_add(p1,p2)
n1=length(p1); n2 = length(p2);
if n1==n2 p3 = p1 + p2; end
if n1>n2  p3 = p1 + [zeros(1,n1-n2) ,p2];end
if n1<n2  p3 = [zeros(1,n2-n1) ,p1] + p2; end
```

FM 4.3 Lagrange interpolation

Purpose: to interpolate data by Lagrange interpolation.

Synopsis: yi = Lagran_(x,y,xi)

        x, y: data table in array form.

        xi : array of abscissas for which y values are to be computed.

        yi : array of y values computed by Lagrange interpolation.

Lagran_.m

```
function fi = Lagran_(x, f, xi)
fi=zeros(size(xi));
np1=length(f);
for i=1:np1
  z=ones(size(xi));
  for j=1:np1
    if i~=j, z = z.*(xi - x(j))/(x(i)-x(j));end
  end
  fi=fi+z*f(i);
end
return
```

FM 4.4 Shape function in power series form

Purpose: to expand Lagrange interpolation into power series.

Synopsis: c = shape_pw(x)

        c: power coefficients of all the shape functions. The j-th row

           becomes the power coefficients of the j-th shape function.

        x: abscissas of data table in array form.

shape_pw.m

```
function p = shape_pw(x)
np = length(x);
for j=1:np
   y = zeros(1,np); y(j) = 1;
   p(j,:)=polyfit(x,y,np-1);
end
```

FM 4.5 Chebyshev polynomial in power series form

Purpose: to expand the power coefficients of Chebyshev polynomial.

Synopsis: c = Cheby_pw

   c: power coefficients in array form.

   n: order of Chebyshev polynomial.

Cheby_pw.m

```
function pn = Cheby_pw(n)
pbb=[1];  if n==0, pn=pbb; break; end
pb=[1 0]; if n==1, pn=pb;  break; end
for i=2:n;
   pn=   2*[pb,0] - [0, 0, pbb] ;
   pbb=pb; pb=pn;
end
```

FM 4.6 Legendre polynomial in power series form

Purpose: to find power coefficients of Legendre polynomial.

Synopsis: c = Legen_pw(n)

   c: power coefficients in array form.

   n: order of Chebyshev polynomial.

Legen_pw.m

```
function pn = Legen_pw(n)
pbb=[1];  if n==0, pn=pbb; break; end
pb=[1 0]; if n==1, pn=pb;  break; end
for i=2:n;
   pn=   ( (2*i-1)*[pb,0] - (i-1)*[0, 0, pbb] )/i;
   pbb=pb; pb=pn;
end
```

PROBLEMS

(4.1) Rewrite the following polynomials into clustered form:

$$y = x^4 - 3x^3 + 2x^2 + x + 2$$
$$y = 3x^5 + 2x^3 + x^2 + 7$$

(4.2) Rewrite the polynomials of Problem 4.1 into factorized form.

(4.3) Rewrite the following polynomials into power series form using (i) `poly`, and (ii) `polyfit`:

$$y = 5(x - 3)(x - 4)(x + 1)(x + 3)$$
$$y = 4x(x - 2)(x - 1)(x + 3)(x + 5)$$

(4.4) (a) Find the polynomial fitted to data points 2, 3, 4, and 5 of the following data:

k	x_k	$f(x_k)$
1	0	0.9162
2	0.25	0.8109
3	0.5	0.6931
4	0.75	0.5596
5	1.0	0.4055

(b) Transform the polynomial to clustered form. (c) Transform the polynomial to factorized form.

(4.5) Convert the following polynomial to power series using `polyfit`:

$$v(x) = \frac{(x - 1)(x - 2.5)(x - 4)(x - 6.1)(x - 7.2)(x - 10)}{(5 - 1)(5 - 2.5)(5 - 4)(5 - 6.1)(5 - 7.2)(5 - 10)}$$

(4.6) Repeat Problem 4.5 using `poly`.

(4.7) A polynomial has three roots: -2, 1 and 2. If the polynomial y becomes $y(0) = 1$, determine the polynomial in power series form.

(4.8) Determine the polynomial in the power series form that passes through each of the following data sets:

   (a)   (0,1), (2,0)

   (b)   (1,1), (2,0), (4,2)

   (c)   (−1,2), (0,2.5), (1,1), (2,−1)

First, work with Eq.(4.3.3). Then verify the results by `polyfit`.

(4.9) Determine the polynomial in the power series form that passes through each of the following data sets:

   (a)   (−1,1), (1,4)

   (b)   (−2,2), (0,−1), (2,1)

   (c)   (−1,−1), (0,0), (1,2), (2,5)

Work with Eq.(4.3.3) first, and then verify the results by `polyfit`.

(4.10) Write a linear interpolation formula that approximates $\sin(x)$ in the interval of $0 \leq x \leq \pi/4$ using the values at $x = 0$ and $x = \pi/4$. Find the maximum error of the interpolation and at what x it occurs by plotting the error.

(4.11) Knowing that $\max|f''| \approx -0.3827$ in $0 \leq x \leq \pi/4$, predict the maximum possible error of the linear interpolation determined in Problem 4.10, using Eq.(4.2.3).

(4.12) (a) Find the polynomial in power series form fitted to the data points, $k = 2$, 3, and 4, given in the following table:

k	x_k	$f(x_k)$
1	0	0.9162
2	0.25	0.8109
3	0.5	0.6931
4	0.75	0.5596
5	1.0	0.4055

(b) Evaluate the polynomial for $x = 0.6$.

(4.13) Find the polynomial fitted to data points 2, 3, 4, and 5 of Problem 4.12 in power series form.

(4.14) Using the data table given in Problem 4.12, estimate the x values that satisfy $f(x)$ = 0.4137, 0.7233, and 0.8501, using `interp1` for linear interpolations.

(4.15) (a) Write the polynomial $y(x)$ in the power series fitted to the following data points:

k	x_k	$f(x_k)$
1	0	1.21
2	0.5	1.32
3	2.0	1.05
4	2.5	0.97

(b) Evaluate the derivative of the polynomial at $x = 1.75$.

(4.16) (a) Write the Lagrange interpolation that passes through the following data points:

x	0	0.4	0.8	1.2
f	1.0	1.491	2.225	3.320

(b) Knowing $f''''(0.6) = 1.822$, estimate the error at $x = 0.2$, 0.6, and 1.0 by Eq.(4.5.4) with $\xi_i = x_m$. (In case f'''' is not known, an approximation for f'''' may be calculated by a difference approximation if one more data point is available from the functional table.)

(c) Given the fact that the data table has been obtained from $f(x) = \exp(x)$, evaluate error of the interpolation formula at $x = 0.2$, 0.6, and 1.0 by $e(x) = f(x) - g(x) = \exp(x) - g(x)$.

(4.17) Repeat Problem 4.15 by the Lagrange interpolation fitted to all the data points.

(4.18) Fit $x \sin(x)$ in $0 \leq x \leq \pi/2$ with the Lagrange interpolation polynomial of order 4, using equispaced points. Calculate the error of each interpolation formula at every increment of $\pi/16$, and plot.

(4.19) (a) Write a program to evaluate the Lagrange interpolation for $y = x \cos(x)$ in $0 \leq x \leq 2$ with six equally spaced grid points with $h = 0.4$.

(b) Calculate the error of the interpolating polynomial at each increment of 0.1 of x. Plot the error distribution.

(4.20) Fit $\sin(x)$ in $0 \leq x \leq 2\pi$ by the Lagrange interpolation polynomial of order 4 and 8 using equispaced points (5 and 9 points, respectively). Plot the interpolating polynomials together with $\sin(x)$, and the error distributions.

(4.21) (a) Write the Lagrange interpolation formula fitted to:

x	0.5	1.0	1.5	2.0
y	y_1	y_2	y_3	y_4

where y_k are unknown values. (b) Convert the interpolation formula to power series form. (c) Derive the first derivative of the polynomial.

(4.22) Approximate

$$y = \frac{1+x}{1+2x+3x^2}$$

in $0 \leq x \leq 5$ by the Lagrange interpolation of order 4, and evaluate the error by $e(x) = y - g(x)$. Work according to the following steps: (a) determine the points, (b) write the Lagrange interpolation, (c) calculate the error for each increment of 0.2 in x, and (d) plot the error distribution.

(4.23) If a Lagrange interpolation is fitted to four data points at $x_i = 1, 2, 3$, and 4, the following cubic polynomials appear in the Lagrange interpolation formula:

$$\frac{(x-2)(x-3)(x-4)}{(1-2)(1-3)(1-4)}$$
$$\frac{(x-1)(x-3)(x-4)}{(2-1)(2-3)(2-4)}$$
$$\frac{(x-1)(x-2)(x-4)}{(3-1)(3-2)(3-4)}$$
$$\frac{(x-1)(x-2)(x-3)}{(4-1)(4-2)(4-3)}$$

Plot the four functions above and discuss implications of the shape of each.

(4.24) The Lagrange interpolation of order N fitted to $N + 1$ points of a function $f(x)$ becomes exact if $f(x)$ is a polynomial of order N or less. Explain the reason in two different ways.

(4.25) Using Eq.(4.7.1), derive the following Chebyshev polynomials and plot: T_4, T_5, T_6.

(4.26) (a) Develop a Lagrange interpolation approximation for $\log_e(x)$ in $1 \leq x \leq 2$ using four Chebyshev points. (b) Calculate actual error by $e(x) = \log_e(x) - g(x)$ and plot for $x = 1, 1.2, 1.3,... 1.9,$ and 2.0.

(4.27) The Legendre polynomials satisfy the orthogonality relation:

$$\int_{-1}^{1} P_m(x)P_n(x)dx = \left\{ \begin{array}{l} 0, \quad \text{if } m \neq n \\ \frac{2}{2n+1}, \text{if } m = n \end{array} \right\}$$

Verify the foregoing relation by computing

$$a_{m,n} = \int_{-1}^{1} P_m(x)P_n(x)dx$$

for $m = 1$ through 5 and n=1 through 5. Hint : use `poly_itg` explained in Section 4.1.

Chapter 5

Numerical Integration

Numerical integration schemes allow integration of functions that are analytically defined or given in tabular form. The basic principle of numerical integration schemes is to fit a polynomial to functional data points and then integrate it. Therefore, by changing the distribution of the abscissas of the data points, many different integration schemes can be derived. In this chapter, we will start with two simple but most frequently used methods, named trapezoidal and Simpson's rules, followed by more general derivation of the Newton-Cotes closed formulas, and Gauss quadrature. We will also study numerical computations of improper integrals and double integrals.

5.1 TRAPEZOIDAL RULE

The trapezoidal rule is a numerical integration method derived by integrating the linear interpolation formula. Suppose we evaluate

$$I = \int_a^b f(x)dx \qquad (5.1.1)$$

We approximate $f(x)$ by a linear interpolation

$$g(x) = \frac{b-x}{b-a}f_1 + \frac{x-a}{b-a}f_2 \qquad (5.1.2)$$

where

$$f_1 = f(a)$$
$$f_2 = f(b)$$

Then, Eq.(5.1.1) becomes

$$I = \int_a^b f(x)dx \approx \int_a^b g(x)dx = \frac{h}{2}(f_1 + f_2) \qquad (5.1.3)$$

with

$$h = b - a \qquad (5.1.4)$$

Equation (5.1.3) is the trapezoidal rule. We can rewrite it as

$$I = \int_a^b f(x)dx = \frac{h}{2}(f_1 + f_2) + E \qquad (5.1.5)$$

where E represents the truncation error. The trapezoidal rule is graphically illustrated in Figure 5.1. The area under the line interpolation, $g(x)$, equals the integral computed by the trapezoidal rule, while the area under $y = f(x)$ is the exact value. The error of Eq.(5.1.3), therefore, is equal to the area between $g(x)$ and $f(x)$, and is approximately,

$$E \approx -\frac{1}{12}h^3 f'' \qquad (5.1.6)$$

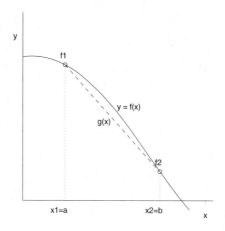

Figure 5.1 Trapezoidal rule

The foregoing error term may be verified easily as follows: First, expand $f(x)$ into the Taylor expansion about a selected point, say $x = a$. By integrating the Taylor expansion, the exact integral is expressed in power series form. On the other hand, the result of the trapezoidal rule may also be expressed in power series form by expanding f_2 into a Taylor series about the same point $x = a$. By subtracting the latter from the former, and keeping the leading term, Eq.(5.1.6) is obtained.

Equation (5.1.5) can be extended to multiple intervals. If the function integrated is represented by $n + 1$ data points with equally spaced abscissa points, Eq.(5.1.5) may be applied repeatedly to each interval. The equation thus obtained is the extended trapezoidal rule and is written as

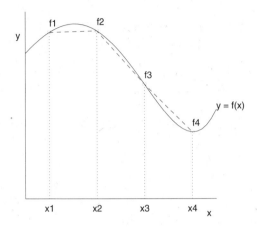

Figure 5.2 Extended trapezoidal rule

$$I = \int_a^b f(x)dx = \frac{h}{2}(f_1 + 2f_2 + \dots + 2f_n + f_{n+1}) + E \qquad (5.1.7)$$

with

$$h = (b - a)/n$$
$$x_i = a + (i - 1)h$$
$$f_i = f(x_i)$$
$$i = 1, 2, .., n + 1$$

The error term of the extended trapezoidal rule is given by

$$E \approx -\frac{b - a}{12}h^2\overline{f''} \qquad (5.1.8)$$

or equivalently

$$E \approx -\frac{(b - a)^3}{12n^2}\overline{f''} \qquad (5.1.9)$$

where $\overline{f''}$ is the average of $f''(x)$ in $a < x < b$. The foregoing equation indicates that the error is inversely proportional to n^2.

Suppose f is an array of f_i for equispaced abscissa points with an interval size h. The extended trapezoidal rule may be written in MATLAB as

```
I = h*(sum(f) - 0.5*(f(1) + f(length(f))))
```

A more convenient way of applying the trapezoidal rule is to use trapez_v, trapez_n or trapez_g listed in Section 5.7. Synopsis of trapez_v is

```
I = trapez_v(f, h)
```

where f is a vector of the ordinates of the integrand and h is the interval size. Synopses of trapez_n and trapez_g are

```
I = trapez_n('f_name', a, b, n)
I = trapez_g('f_name', a, b, n)
```

where f_name is the name of the function to be integrated, a and b are limits of integration, and n is the number of intervals used in the extended trapezoidal rule. A user-defined function M-file may be used for f_name.

Example 5.1

An automobile of mass M = 2000 kg is cruising at a speed of 30 m/s. The engine is suddenly disengaged at $t = 0$ s. Assume that the equation of cruising after $t = 0$ is given by

$$2000 \, u\frac{du}{dx} = -8.1u^2 - 1200 \qquad \text{(A)}$$

where u is the velocity and x is the linear distance of the car measured from the location at $t = 0$. The left side is the force of acceleration, the first term on the right side is the aerodynamic resistance, and the second term is the rolling resistance. Calculate how far the car moves before the speed reduces to 15 m/s.

Solution

We rewrite Eq.(A) to

$$\frac{2000 \, udu}{-8.1u^2 - 1200} = dx$$

Integrating yields

$$\int_{15}^{30} \frac{2000 \, udu}{8.1u^2 + 1200} = \int_{0}^{x} dx' = x \qquad \text{(B)}$$

where the sign on the left side of Eq.(B) has been changed by switching the limits of integration. To evaluate the integral on the left side we use the extended trapezoidal rule. If we use 15 intervals (or 16 data points), u_i is first set to

$$u_i = 15 + (i-1)\Delta u, \quad i = 1, 2, ..., 16$$

where $\Delta u = (30 - 15)/15 = 1$. By defining

$$f_i = \frac{200\ u_i}{8.1\ u_i^2 + 1200}$$

and applying the trapezoidal integration, Eq.(A) becomes

$$x \approx \Delta u \left[\sum_{i=1}^{16} f_i - 0.5(f_1 + f_{16}) \right]$$

A script to compute the foregoing equation follows:

List 5.1
```
clear
n_points=16 ; i = 1:n_points;
h=(30-15)/(n_points-1); u = 15 + (i-1)*h;
f = 2000*u./(8.1*u.^2 + 1200);
x = trapez_v(f,h)
```

The result is

```
x =
    127.50
```

Compare this to the exact solution, 127.51 m (the error is 0.005%).

Example 5.2

Knowing that the exact answer is $I = 4.006994$, analyze the effect of the number of intervals, n, on the errors of the trapezoidal rule applied to the following integral:

$$I = \int_0^2 \sqrt{1 + \exp(x)}\,dx$$

Solution

The following script is written to answer the question:

List 5.2
```
clear;    Iexact = 4.006994;
a = 0; b=2;
fprintf('\n Extended Trapezoidal Rule\n');
fprintf('\n    n           I                    Error\n');
n = 1;
for k=1:6
    n = 2*n;
    h = (b-a)/n;    i = 1:n+1;
    x = a + (i-1)*h;    f = sqrt(1 + exp(x));
    I =   trapez_v(f,h);
    fprintf('     %3.0f    %10.5f    %10.5f\n', ...
                     n,     I,    Iexact - I);
end
```

The result is:

```
Extended Trapezoidal Rule

    n    I              Error
    2    4.08358        0.07659
    4    4.02619        0.01919
    8    4.01180        0.00480
   16    4.00819        0.00120
   32    4.00729        0.00030
   64    4.00707        0.00008
```

As n is doubled, the error decreases by a factor of 4 (see Eq.(5.1.9)).

Example 5.2 indicates that errors of the extended trapezoidal rule decrease to approximately one fourth whenever the number of intervals is doubled. The trend can be verified by Eq.(5.1.9). Knowing this behavior of the errors, we can eliminate at least a major part of the errors. If we denote the result of the extended trapezoidal rule with n intervals by I_n and that with $2n$ by I_{2n}, then $I_n - I_{2n}$ must equal approximately three times the error of I_{2n}. Subtracting the error thus estimated, the result should become significantly more accurate. The formula based on this principle is named Romberg integration, and written as

$$I = I_{2n} - \frac{1}{3}(I_n - I_{2n}) \qquad (5.1.10)$$

The result, however, becomes identical to the Simpson's 1/3 rule using $2n$ intervals (see Section 5.2).

5.2   SIMPSON'S RULES

There are two Simpson's rules; namely, the 1/3 and 3/8 rules, which are complementary to each other. Considering evaluation of Eq.(5.1.1) again, a quadratic (second order) interpolation polynomial may be determined with three data points at $x_1 = a$, $x_2 = (a+b)/2$ and $x_3 = b$. We denote the functional values at the data points by f_1, f_2 and f_3. Simpson's 1/3 rule is derived by substituting this quadratic polynomial to $f(x)$ in Eq.(5.1.1):

$$I \approx \frac{h}{3}(f_1 + 4f_2 + f_3) \qquad (5.2.1)$$

where

$$h = (b - a)/2$$

Including the error term, Eq.(5.2.1) may be written as

$$I = \frac{h}{3}(f_1 + 4f_2 + f_3) + E \qquad (5.2.2)$$

where E is the error term given by

$$E \approx -\frac{h^5}{90}f'''' \qquad (5.2.3)$$

which indicates that the error is proportional to h^5. The error vanishes if $f(x)$ is a polynomial of order 3 or less. Equation (5.2.3) may be verified as follows. The exact integral may be expressed in a power series form by integrating the Taylor expansion of $f(x)$ about $x = a$. On the other hand, f_2 and f_3 in Eq.(5.2.1) may be expanded into Taylor series about $x = a$. After expressing both the exact integral and Simpson's 1/3 rule in power series forms, we subtract the latter from the former, and keep only the leading term.

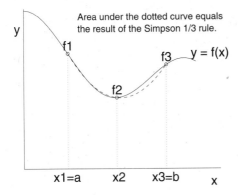

Figure 5.3 Simpson's 1/3 rule uses three points fitted by a quadratic polynomial

The extended Simpson's 1/3 rule is a repeated application of Eq.(5.2.1) for a domain divided into an even number of intervals. Denoting the total number of intervals by n(even), the extended Simpson's 1/3 rule is written as

$$I = \int_a^b f(x)dx$$

$$= \frac{h}{3}(f_1 + 4f_2 + 2f_3 + 4f_4 + \ldots + 2f_{n-1} + 4f_n + f_{n+1}) + E \quad (5.2.4)$$

where

$$f_i = f(a + (i-1)h) \qquad (5.2.5)$$

with

$$h = (b - a)/n \qquad (5.2.6)$$

The error term is given by

$$E \approx -(b - a)\frac{h^4}{180}\overline{f''''} \qquad (5.2.7)$$

where $\overline{f''''}$ is the average of f'''' in $a < x < b$.

Example 5.3

Evaluate the integral in Example 5.2 again by the extended Simpson's 1/3 rule with $n = 2, 4, 8,$ and 16.

Solution

The question is answered by the following script:

List 5.3
```
clear
Iexact = 4.006994;
a = 0; b=2;
fprintf('\n Extended Simpson 1/3 Rule\n');
fprintf('n                I             Error\n');
n = 1;
for k=1:4,    n = 2*n;
  h = (b-a)/n;    i = 1:n+1;
  x = a + (i-1)*h;    f = sqrt(1 + exp(x));
  I =   (h/3)*( f(1)+ 4*sum(f(2:2:n))  + f(n+1));
  if n>2, I = I+ (h/3)*2*sum(f(3:2:n));  end
  fprintf('%3.0f %10.5f    %10.5f\n', n,I,Iexact-I);
end
```

The results are:

```
Extended Simpson 1/3 Rule
   n        I              Error
   2     4.00791          0.00092
   4     4.00705          0.00006
   8     4.00700          0.00000
  16     4.00699          0.00000
```

The Simpson's 3/8 rule is based on the 3rd-order interpolation polynomial and is given by

$$I = \frac{3h}{8}(f_1 + 3f_2 + 3f_3 + f_4) + E \qquad (5.2.8)$$

where $h = (b-a)/3$, $f_i = f(a + (i-1)h)$, and E represents the error. The error term is given by

$$E \approx -\frac{3h^5}{80} f'''' \qquad (5.2.9)$$

The foregoing expression for the error can be derived by the Taylor expansion in a manner similar to that described for the Simpson's 1/3 rule.

When integration of data on equispaced points is attempted, the extended Simpson's 1/3 rule is not applicable if the number of intervals is odd. In this case the 3/8 rule is applied to the first or last three intervals, and then the extended 1/3 rule is applied to the remainder of intervals. Since the order of error of the 3/8 rule is the same as that of the 1/3 rule, the two rules blend naturally without losing order of accuracy.[1]

Two functions, Simps_v and Simps_n, may be used to integrate a function. The synopsis of the former is

```
I = Simps_v(f,h)
```

where f is the vector containing the ordinates of the integrand with an equispaced interval size h. The number of intervals is arbitrary, except that it must be at least 2. If the number of intervals is odd, the 3/8 rule is applied first, and then the 1/3 rule is applied to the remainder of intervals, as explained in the preceding paragraphs. The synopsis of Simps_n is

```
I = Simps_n('f_name', a, b, n)
```

where f_name is the name of the function (or function M-file for the integrand), a and b are limits of integration, and n is the number of intervals used in the extended trapezoidal rule. More details of the functions are explained in Section 5.7.

---

[1]If Simpson's rule is blended with the trapezoidal rule, the order of accuracy of the combined scheme is determined by that of the trapezoidal rule.

Example 5.4

A spherical water reservoir of radius 5 m is full to the top. Water is to be drained from the hole of radius $b = 0.1$ m at the bottom, starting at $t = 0$ s. If there is no friction, how much time does it take to drain the water until the water level reaches 0.5 m, measured from the bottom?

Solution

The velocity of the water draining from the hole is determined by the energy equation:

$$g(z + R) = \frac{u^2}{2} \qquad (A)$$

where u is the velocity, z is the level of water measured from the spherical center, R is the radius of the tank, and g is the gravity acceleration that equals 9.81 m/s^2. Consider the change of the water level dz during time interval dt. The volume of water in dz equals $\pi x^2 dz$, where x is the radius of the circular water surface at elevation z. The flow continuity relation can be written:

$$u A dt = -\pi x^2 dz \qquad (B)$$

where A is the cross-sectional area of the exit hole that equals

$$A = \pi b^2 \qquad (C)$$

The radius of the water surface x is related to z by

$$R^2 = z^2 + x^2 \qquad (D)$$

Eliminating u, x, and A from Eq.(B) by Eqs.(A), (C), and (D) yields

$$dt = -\frac{R^2 - z^2}{b^2 \sqrt{2g(z + R)}} dz$$

Notice that the level of water at the top of the tank is $z = R$, while that at 0.5 m from the bottom is $z = 0.9R$. By integrating from $z = R$ to $-0.9R$, we get

$$t = -\int_R^{-0.9R} \frac{R^2 - z^2}{b^2 \sqrt{2g(z + R)}} dz$$

or after interchanging the lower and upper limits of integration,

$$t = \int_{-0.9R}^R \frac{R^2 - z^2}{b^2 \sqrt{2g(z + R)}} dz$$

Now we integrate the foregoing equation by the extended Simpson's rule:

```
clear
R = 5;   g= 9.81;   b = 0.1;
z1=-R*0.90;  z2 = R;   h = (z2 - z1)/20;
z= z1:h:z2;
f = (R^2 - z.^2)./( b^2*sqrt(2*g*(z+R)));
I = Simps_v(f,h)/60/60
```

The result is

```
0.5145   hour
```

5.3 OTHER QUADRATURES

As we pointed out previously, many other numerical quadratures are derived by integrating different interpolation polynomials in the Lagrange interpolation form. We explain a few of them.

Newton-Cotes closed formulas: The Newton-Cotes closed formula of order n uses $n + 1$ data points with equispaced intervals. The abscissas of data points are

$$x_i = \frac{b - a}{n}(i - 1) + a, \quad i = 1, 2, ..., n + 1 \tag{5.3.1}$$

and ordinates of the data points are $f_i = f(x_i)$. Then, the Newton-Cotes closed formulas may be written in general form as

$$I = \int_a^b f(x)dx \approx h \sum_{i=1}^{n+1} w_i f_i \tag{5.3.2}$$

where $n + 1$ is the total number of points, w_is are weights given in Table 5.1, and

$$h = \frac{b - a}{n}$$

For $n = 1$, 2, and 3, Eq.(5.3.2) becomes the trapezoidal rule, Simpson's 1/3 rule, and Simpson's 3/8 rules, respectively.

To show how to derive Eq.(5.3.2), we write the Lagrange interpolation formula fitted to $f(x)$ in $a \leq x \leq b$ with equispaced points x_i as

$$g(x) = \sum_{i=1}^{n+1} v_i(x) f_i \tag{5.3.3}$$

where

Table 5.1 Weights of Newton-Cotes Closed Formulas

n					
n=1	i: w:	0 0.5000,0000	1 0.5000,0000		
n=2	i: w:	0 0.3333,3333	1 1.3333,3333	2 0.3333,3333	
n=3	i: w:	0 0.3750,0000	1 1.1250,0000	2 1.1250,0000	3 0.3750,0000
n=4	i: w:	0 4 0.3111,1111 0.3111,1111	1 1.4222,2222	2 0.5333,3333	3 1.4222,2222
n=5	i: w:	0 4 0.3298,6111 1.3020,8333	1 5 1.3020,8333 0.3298,6111	2 0.8680,5555	3 0.8680,5555
n=6	i: w:	0 4 0.2928,5714 0.1928,5714	1 5 1.5428,5714 1.5428,5714	2 6 0.1928,5714 0.2928,5714	3 1.9428,5714
n=7	i: w:	0 4 0.3042,2453 1.2108,2175	1 5 1.4490,1620 0.5359,3749	2 6 0.5359,3749 1.4490,1620	3 7 1.2108,2175 0.3042,2453
n=8	i: w:	0 4 8 0.2790,8289 -1.2811,2874 0.2790,8289	1 5 1.6615,1675 2.9618,3421	2 6 -0.2618,6948 -0.2618,6948	3 7 2.9618,3421 1.6615,1675

$$v_i(x) = \prod_{j=1, j \neq i}^{n+1} \frac{(x - x_j)}{(x_i - x_j)} \tag{5.3.4}$$

Approximating $f(x)$ by $g(x)$ in Eq.(5.1.1) yields

$$I = \int_a^b f(x)dx \approx \int_a^b g(x)dx = \sum_{i=1}^{n+1} \gamma_i f_i \tag{5.3.5}$$

where

$$\gamma_i = \int_a^b v_i(x)dx = \int_a^b \prod_{j=1, j \neq i}^{n+1} \frac{(x - x_j)}{(x_i - x_j)} dx \tag{5.3.6}$$

Equation (5.3.6) may be evaluated as follows: We define a new variable by

$$s = \frac{x - a}{b - a} n + 1 \tag{5.3.7}$$

Notice that, for $x = x_i$, Eq.(5.3.7) becomes $s_i = i$, where Eq.(5.3.1) is used. In terms of s, Eq.(5.3.6) becomes

$$\gamma_i = h \int_1^{n+1} \prod_{j=1, j \neq i}^{n+1} \frac{(s-j)}{(i-j)} ds \qquad (5.3.8)$$

or equivalently

$$\gamma_i = h w_i \qquad (5.3.9)$$

with

$$w_i = \int_1^{n+1} \prod_{j=1, j \neq i}^{n+1} \frac{(s-j)}{(i-j)} ds \qquad (5.3.10)$$

Notice in Eq.(5.3.10) that w_i is determined by i and n only. We convert the integrand of Eq.(5.3.10) to a power series form,

$$\prod_{j=1, j \neq i}^{n+1} \frac{(s-j)}{(i-j)} = \sum_{k=1}^{n+1} a_{i,k} s^{n+1-k} \qquad (5.3.11)$$

The left side of Eq.(5.3.11) is a polynomial passing through the points

$$s = [1, 2, 3, ..., n+1]$$
$$y = [0, 0, ...1, ...0]$$

where the elements of y are all zero except that the i-th element is unity. The power coefficients, $a_{i,k}$s are obtained by polyfit as

```
s = 1:n+1;
y = eye(n+1);
for i=1:n+1
    a(i,:) = polyfit(s,y(i,:))
end
```

where the i-th row of a contains the power coefficients, $a_{i,j}$s, for $i = 1, 2, ..n+1$. Introducing Eq.(5.3.11) into Eq.(5.3.10) yields

$$w_i = \int_1^{n+1} \left(\sum_{k=1}^{n+1} a_{i,k} s^{n+1-k} \right) ds$$

$$= \sum_{k=1}^{n+1} a_{i,k} \int_1^{n+1} s^{n+1-k} ds$$

$$= \sum_{k=1}^{n+1} a_{i,k} \left[\frac{s^{n+2-k}}{n+2-k} \right]_{s=1}^{s=n+1}$$

$$= \sum_{k=1}^{n+1} a_{i,k} \frac{(n+1)^{n+2-k} - 1}{n+2-k} \qquad (5.3.12)$$

Thus, the weights of the Newton-Cotes quadrature listed in Table 5.1 are computed by Eq.(5.3.12).

An analytical function may be integrated by `Newt_itg`. Its synopsis is

```
I = Newt_itg('f_name', a, b, n)
```

where `f_name` is the name of a function M-file that defines the integrand; `a` and `b` are lower and upper limits, respectively; `n` is the number of equispaced intervals between the two integrating limits.

Gauss-Legendre quadrature: Accuracy of integration can be significantly increased using nonequispaced points. The Gauss-Legendre quadrature uses roots of a Legendre polynomial. Its order of accuracy becomes twice as high as the Newton-Cotes formula using the same number of points.

The Legendre polynomials are given by

$$P_0(x) = 1$$
$$P_1(x) = x$$
$$P_2(x) = \frac{1}{2}(3x^2 - 1)$$
$$P_3(x) = \frac{1}{2}(5x^3 - 3x) \qquad (5.3.13)$$
$$\cdots$$
$$P_n(x) = \frac{2n-1}{n} x P_{n-1}(x) - \frac{n-1}{n} P_{n-2}(x)$$

The coefficients of a Legendre polynomial in the power form,

$$P_n(x) = c_1 x^n + c_2 x^{n-1} + \ldots + c_{n+1} \qquad (5.3.14)$$

can be obtained by `Legen_pw(n)` (listed in FM 5-5), which will return the coefficients in an array where n is the order of the Legendre polynomial. The roots of the Legendre polynomial of order n has n roots that are all between -1 and 1 as illustrated in Figure 5.4 for $n = 7$. Notice that no roots are located at the end points, and that the interval size decreases toward the edges.

We will first consider evaluation of the integral extended from $x = -1$ to $x = 1$:

$$I = \int_{-1}^{1} f(x) dx \qquad (5.3.15)$$

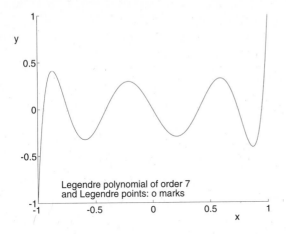

Figure 5.4 Legendre polynomial of order 7 and its roots

The Gauss-Legendre quadrature of order n to evaluate Eq.(5.3.15) may be stated as follows: The integrand is approximated by an interpolation polynomial fitted at the roots of the n-th order Legendre polynomial, which is then integrated. The Gauss-Legendre quadrature is written as

$$I \approx \int_{-1}^{1} g(x)dx = \sum_{i=1}^{n} \gamma_i f(x_i) \tag{5.3.16}$$

with

$$\gamma_i = \int_{-1}^{1} v_i(x)dx = \int_{-1}^{1} \prod_{j=1,j\neq i}^{n} \frac{(x - x_j)}{(x_i - x_j)}dx \tag{5.3.17}$$

where x_is are the roots of the Legendre polynomial of order n. The values of γ_i and x_i are tabulated in Table 5.2.

When the integrating limits are not -1 and 1, the roots between -1 and 1 are mapped between the actual limits, a and b, by a coordinate transformation. For an integral,

$$I = \int_{a}^{b} f(z)dz \tag{5.3.18}$$

the Gauss-Legendre quadrature is written as

$$I \approx \frac{b-a}{2} \sum_{i=1}^{n} \gamma_i f(z_i) \tag{5.3.19}$$

where z_i is given by the transformation:

$$z_i = \frac{(b-a)x_i + a + b}{2}$$

(5.3.20)

and satisfies $a < z_i < b$.

The roots of a Legendre polynomial of order n may be found by `roots(Legen_pw(n))`. The Gauss-Legendre quadrature may be applied by `Gauss_q`. Its synopsis is

```
Gauss_q('f_name', a, b, n_points)
```

where `f_name` is the name of a function M-file that defines the integrand; `a` and `b` are lower and upper limits, respectively; `n_points` is the number of points that equals the order of the Legendre polynomial.

Table 5.2 Weights of Gauss-Legendre Quadrature

n=2	x:	-0.5773,5027	0.5773,5027		
	w:	1.0000,0000	1.0000,0000		
n=3	x:	-0.7745,9667	0.0000,0000	0.7745,9667	
	w:	0.5555,5556	0.8888,8889	0.5555,5556	
n=4	x:	-0.8611,3631	-0.3399,8104	0.3399,8104	0.8611,3631
	w:	0.3478,5485	0.6521,4515	0.6521,4515	0.3478,5485
n=5	x:	-0.9061,7985 0.9061,7985	-0.5384,6931	0.0000,0000	0.5384,6931
	w:	0.2369,2689 0.2369,2689	0.4786,2867	0.5688,8889	0.4786,2867
n=6	x:	-0.9324,6951 0.6612,0939	-0.6612,0939 0.9324,6951	-0.2386,1919	0.2386,1919
	w:	0.1713,2449 0.3607,6157	0.3607,6157 0.1713,2449	0.4679,1393	0.4679,1393
n=7	x:	-0.9491,0791 0.4058,4515	-0.7415,3119 0.7415,3119	-0.4058,4515 0.9491,0791	0.0000,0000
	w:	0.1294,8497 0.3818,3005	0.2797,0539 0.2797,0539	0.3818,3005 0.1294,8497	0.4179,5918
n=8	x:	-0.9602,8986 0.1834,3464	-0.7966,6648 0.5255,3241	-0.5255,3241 0.7966,6648	-0.1834,3464 0.9602,8986
	w:	0.1012,2854 0.3626,8378	0.2223,8103 0.3137,0665	0.3137,0665 0.2223,8103	0.3626,8378 0.1012,2854
n=9	x:	-0.9681,6024 0.0000,0000 0.9681,6024	0.8360,3111 0.3242,5342	0.6133,7143 0.6133,7143	-0.3242,5342 0.8360,3111
	w:	0.0812,7439 0.3302,3936 0.0812,7439	0.1806,4816 0.3123,4708	0.2606,1070 0.2606,1070	0.3123,4708 0.1806,4816

5.4 NUMERICAL INTEGRATION WITH INFINITE LIMITS OR SINGULARITIES

In this section, we study two kinds of integral that need special attention; for example,

$$I = \int_{-\infty}^{\infty} \exp(-x^2)dx \tag{5.4.1}$$

$$I = \int_0^1 \frac{1}{\sqrt{x}(\exp(x) + 1)}dx \tag{5.4.2}$$

$$I = \int_0^1 x^{0.7} \cos(x)dx \tag{5.4.3}$$

The integration of Eq.(5.4.1) is extended over an infinite domain. Equations (5.4.2) and (5.4.3) involve a singularity of the integrand at $x = 0$ (the function approaches infinity as x approaches 0). Equation (5.4.3) does not seem difficult at a glance, but it is not a trivial problem for any numerical integration method described in the earlier sections. Indeed, if the extended trapezoidal rule or Simpson's rule is applied, the answer keeps changing as the number of intervals is doubled. Romberg integration does not work for this equation. The reason is that the function is not analytic at $x = 0$.

A function is integrable in an infinite or semi-infinite domain only if the function is significantly different from zero in a small domain, while the function approaches zero as x approaches ∞ or $-\infty$. The first step of evaluating

$$I = \int_{-\infty}^{\infty} f(x)dx \tag{5.4.4}$$

is to replace the infinite limits by finite limits as

$$I = \int_{-X}^{X} f(x)dx \tag{5.4.5}$$

where X is a sufficiently large value that the contribution from outside of $-X < x < X$ is negligibly small (see Figure 5.5).

5.4.1 Use of the Extended Trapezoidal Rule

The most efficient method for numerical integration for Eq.(5.4.5) has been found to be the extended trapezoidal rule, which can be written as

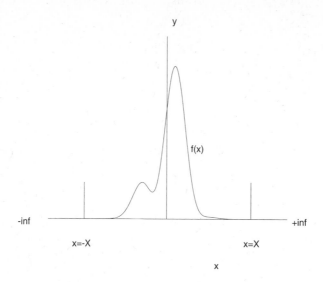

Figure 5.5 Sketch of a function integrable from $-\infty$ to ∞, and artificial limits for numerical integration

$$I \approx h \left(\sum_{i=-n}^{n} g_i - 0.5(g_{-n} + g_n) \right) \qquad (5.4.6)$$

where $x_i = ih$ and $nh = X$. Indeed, the following example shows that the extended trapezoidal rule gives highly accurate results with a relatively small number of points:

Example 5.5

Evaluate

$$I = \frac{1}{\sqrt{\pi}} \int_{-\infty}^{\infty} \exp(-x^2) dx$$

by the extended trapezoidal rule.

Solution

We replace the limits of integration by -10 and 10 as sufficiently large values for the present problem:

$$I = \frac{1}{\sqrt{\pi}} \int_{-10}^{10} \exp(-x^2)dx$$

The foregoing integral evaluated by `trapez_v`, with $n = 10$ and 20, for example, become

h	n	I
1	10	1.00010344
0.5	20	1.00000000

The exact value is 1, so the agreement is perfect to the eighth decimal place.

Until now, we assumed we knew an appropriate value for X. In general, however, it is not known a priori, so a few trials to find X are necessary. If X is too large, not only the computational time is wasted, but there also is a danger of causing overflow or underflow in the computations. On the other hand, if X is too small, the result of integration will be inaccurate. An optimum value of X is such that I will be affected if X is decreased by a factor of say 1.5, but will not change if X is increased. In order to determine an appropriate value for X, first fix h at a reasonable value. Then, evaluate Eq.(5.4.6) with varying values of n; increase by approximately a factor of 1.5 after each trial. When the computed value of I does not increase for the increased n, set $X = n \times h$. After X is fixed, the sensitivity of I on h should be examined by computing Eq.(5.4.6), by halving the value of h until I does not change any longer. Although determining both X and h by trials may seem cumbersome, the whole procedure does not take more than ten trials.

5.4.2 Exponential Transformation

Next, we consider integrating a function that is singular at one or both of finite limits (see Eqs.(5.4.2) and (5.4.3), for example). The finite domain of integration, say $[a, b]$, can be transformed to $[-\infty, \infty]$ by a coordinate transformation. Once it is reduced to the form of Eq.(5.4.4), the extended trapezoidal rule is applied.

Consider

$$I = \int_a^b f(x)dx \qquad (5.4.7)$$

where a and b are finite limits. The mapping may be written by

$$z = z(x)$$

or equivalently

$$x = x(z) \qquad (5.4.8)$$

such that

$$z(a) = -\infty, \ z(b) = \infty$$

Equation (5.4.7) can be then written as

$$I = \int_{-\infty}^{\infty} f(x(z)) \frac{dx}{dz} dz \tag{5.4.9}$$

An example for such transformation is the exponential transformation given by

$$x = \frac{a + b + (b - a)\tanh(z)}{2} \tag{5.4.10}$$

or equivalently

$$z = \tanh^{-1}(\frac{2x - a - b}{b - a}) \tag{5.4.11}$$

The first derivative of Eq.(5.4.10) is given by

$$\frac{dx}{dz} = \frac{b - a}{2\cosh^2(z)} \tag{5.4.12}$$

Example 5.6

(1) Evaluate

$$I = \int_0^1 f(x)dx \tag{A}$$

where

$$f(x) = \frac{\exp(-x^2)}{\sqrt{1 - x^2}}$$

by the extended trapezoidal rule after the exponential transformation using Eq.(5.4.10). Set the limits of integration on the z axis to ± 6 and $h = 0.1$.

(2) Graphically illustrate the transformation between the x and z coordinates.

(3) Plot the integrand $f(x)$ on the x-y coordinates with the data points used in the numerical integration.

(4) Plot the integrand, $g(z) = f(x)dx/dz$, on the z-x domain.

Solution:

With $a = 0$ and $b = 1$, the transformation Eq.(5.4.10) becomes

$$x = \frac{1 + \tanh(z)}{2}$$

(1) By dividing the domain, $-6 \leq z \leq 6$, into equispaced intervals of $h = 0.2$, the z values of the points are

$$z_i = ih, \qquad i = -30, .., 30 \tag{B}$$

We now approximate Eq.(A) by

$$I = \int_0^1 f(x)dx = \int_{-\infty}^{+\infty} f(x)\frac{dx}{dz}dz \approx \int_{-6}^{+6} g(z)dz \approx h\sum_{i=-30}^{30} g(z_i) \tag{C}$$

with

$$g(z) = f(x(z))\frac{dx}{dz} \tag{D}$$

The g_i values on the equispaced data points are computed by

$$g_i = \frac{\exp(-x_i^2)}{\sqrt{1 - x_i^2}}\frac{1}{2\cosh^2(z_i)} \tag{E}$$

where x_i are the points corresponding to z_i given by

$$x_i = \frac{1 + \tanh(z_i)}{2} \tag{F}$$

Then, the numerical result becomes

$$I \approx h\left(\sum_{i=-30}^{30} g_i - 0.5(g_{-30} + g_{30})\right) = 1.0120$$

The foregoing computation may be evaluated by `trapez_v`.

(2), (3), and (4): Figure 5.6 shows the transformation of the equispaced points onto the x axis. Figure 5.7 shows the data points along the integrand. Figure 5.8 shows the distribution of $g(z)$ and the data points used in the trapezoidal rule computation.

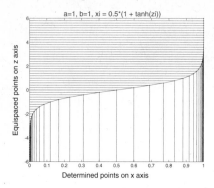

Figure 5.6 Transformation of equispaced points on the z axis to the x axis

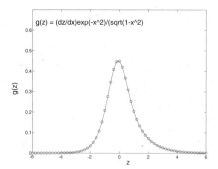

Figure 5.7 Integrand and data points along the x-axis

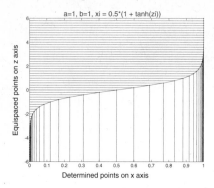

Figure 5.8 Integrand and data points on the z domain

5.4.3 Double-Exponential Transformation

Accuracy of the numerical integration is affected by the choice of the transformation. The double-exponential transformation given by

$$x = \frac{a + b + (b - a)\tanh(\frac{\pi}{2}\sinh(z))}{2} \tag{5.4.13}$$

has been proposed as a better choice than Eq.(5.4.10). With this choice dx/dz becomes

$$\frac{dx}{dz} = \frac{\pi}{4}\frac{(b-a)\cosh(z)}{\cosh^2\left(\frac{\pi}{2}\sinh(z)\right)} \tag{5.4.14}$$

We introduce Eqs.(5.4.13) and (5.4.14) into Eq.(5.4.9) and apply the extended trapezoidal rule. Here, the infinite limits in Eq.(5.4.9) are replaced by finite limits $-Z$ and Z. Then, the extended trapezoidal rule is applied:

$$I = h\sum_{k=-n}^{n} f(x_k)\left(\frac{dx}{dz}\right)_k \tag{5.4.15}$$

where $h = Z/n$, and

$$-Z \le z_k = kh \le Z \tag{5.4.16}$$

$$x_k = \frac{1}{2}\left[a + b + (b - a)\tanh\left(\frac{\pi}{2}\sinh(z_k)\right)\right] \tag{5.4.17}$$

$$\left(\frac{dx}{dz}\right)_k = \frac{\pi}{4}\frac{(b-a)\cosh(z_k)}{\cosh^2\left(\frac{\pi}{2}\sinh(z_k)\right)} \tag{5.4.18}$$

In Eq.(5.4.16), the question is how large the value of Z should be, which may be answered by examining the denominator of Eq.(5.4.18). When z_k increases, it approaches

$$\cosh^2(\frac{\pi}{2}\sinh(z_k)) \longrightarrow \frac{1}{4}\exp[\frac{\pi}{2}\exp(z_k)] \tag{5.4.19}$$

This term increases double-exponentially, and may cause an overflow. With single precision in Fortran or C on typical workstations, it occurs when

$$\frac{1}{4}\exp\left(\frac{\pi}{2}\exp(z_k)\right) > 2 \times 10^{38} \tag{5.4.20}$$

or equivalently if z_k is greater than approximately 4.0. This criterion determines the maximum possible Z. That is

$$Z = nh < 4 \tag{5.4.21}$$

In MATLAB, the highest floating value is approximately $+9.9\mathrm{e}307$, so that the criterion for Z is

$$Z = nh < 6.1 \tag{5.4.22}$$

Another problem is the rounding error in Eq.(5.4.17) that occurs when the hyperbolic tangent term becomes very close to -1 or 1. To avoid this, we first recognize that the hyperbolic tangent term can be written as

$$\tanh(p) = (s - 1/s) \, / \, (s + 1/s) \tag{5.4.23}$$

where $s = \exp(p)$. Using Eq.(4.2.23), Eq.(5.4.17) is written as

$$x_k = \left(b s_k + \frac{a}{s_k} \right) \, / \, \left(s_k + \frac{1}{s_k} \right) \tag{5.4.24}$$

where

$$s_k = \exp\left(\frac{\pi}{2} \sinh(z_k) \right)$$

Since Eq.(5.4.24) has no subtraction operation, a major source of rounding error has been eliminated.

The numerical scheme with the double-exponential transformation is implemented in `double_exp`. Its synopsis is

```
I = dbl_exp('f_name', a, b, n)
```

where arguments have the same meanings as for `Gauss_q`. See Section 5.7 for more details.

Example 5.7

The length of the curve of $y = g(x)$, $a < x < b$, can be computed by

$$I = \int_a^b \sqrt{1 + (g'(x))^2} \, dx \tag{A}$$

Calculate the length of the parabolic arc, $y^2 = 4x$, satisfying $0 < x < 2$.

Solution

Since $g(x) = 2\sqrt{x}$, its derivative is $g'(x) = 1/\sqrt{x}$. The integral becomes

$$I = \int_0^2 \sqrt{1 + \frac{1}{x}}\, dx \tag{B}$$

The integrand in the foregoing equation is singular at $x = 0$.

The computation is performed by dbl_exp. The limits of integration on the transformed coordinate are set to $Z = -4$ and $Z = 4$. The computed results are:

n	I
10	3.600710
20	3.595706
30	3.595706

5.5   MATLAB COMMANDS FOR INTEGRATIONS

MATLAB toolbox has quad and quad8. Function quad uses a recursive Simpson's rule, and quad8 uses a recursive Newton-Cotes quadrature of order 8. Synopsis of quad includes the following three forms:

```
quad('f_name', a, b)
quad('f_name', a, b, tol)
quad('f_name', a, b, tol, trace)
```

In the first form, the tolerance tol is set to a default value, 0.001. The quadrature computation is iterated until the tolerance is satisfied. If the third form is used with a nonzero value for trace, a graph showing progress of integration is plotted on the screen. The synopsis of quad8 is the same except that quad is replaced by quad8.

5.6   NUMERICAL INTEGRATION ON A TWO-DIMENSIONAL DOMAIN

Let us consider a domain illustrated in Figure 5.9, where the left and right boundaries are vertical lines, and the top and bottom boundaries are given by analytical functions. The integral of $f(x, y)$ extended over this domain is written as

$$I = \int_a^b \int_{c(x)}^{d(x)} f(x, y)\, dy\, dx \tag{5.6.1}$$

Equation (5.6.1) often is written in a different form, such as

$$I = \int_a^b dx \int_{c(x)}^{d(x)} dy\, f(x, y)$$

or

$$I = \int\!\!\int_A f(x, y)\, dx\, dy$$

where A is meant by the domain. In any case, the problem should be rewritten in the form of Eq.(5.6.1) before proceeding with numerical integrations. Exchange x and y if necessary.

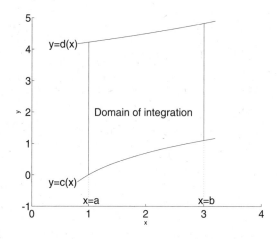

Figure 5.9 A two-dimensional domain for double integration

The general principle of numerical integration of Eq.(5.6.1) is to reduce it to a combination of one-dimensional problems. If we define

$$G(x) = \int_{c(x)}^{d(x)} f(x, y)\, dy \tag{5.6.2}$$

then, Eq.(5.6.1) becomes

$$I = \int_a^b G(x)\, dx \tag{5.6.3}$$

for which any numerical integration method described earlier is applicable. A numerical approximation for Eq.(5.6.3) may be written in the form:

$$I \approx \sum_{i=1}^{n+1} w_i G(x_i) \qquad (5.6.4)$$

where w_is are weights and x_is are points of the particular method chosen. Setting $x = x_i$, Eq.(5.6.2) becomes

$$G(x_i) = \int_{c(x_i)}^{d(x_i)} f(x_i, y)\, dy \qquad (5.6.5)$$

which is a one-dimensional problem because the only variable of the integrand is y. Equation (5.6.5) is evaluated also by a numerical integration scheme.

Example 5.8

By the Simpson's 1/3 rule, evaluate the double integral

$$I = \int_a^b \left(\int_{c(x)}^{d(x)} \sin(x + y) dy \right) dx \qquad (A)$$

where the limits of integrations are
$$a = 1$$
$$b = 3$$
$$c(x) = \ln(x)$$
$$d(x) = 3 + \exp(x/5)$$

Solution

For the Simpson's 1/3 rule, the grid points on the x-axis are

$$x_1 = 1, x_2 = 2, \text{ and } x_3 = 3$$

See Figure 5.10 for the domain of integration and points. Applying the Simpson's 1/3 rule to the first integral yields

$$I \approx \frac{h_x}{3}[G(x_1) + 4G(x_2) + G(x_3)] \qquad (B)$$

where
$$h_x = (b - a)/2 = 1$$

and

$$G(x_i) = \int_{\ln(x_i)}^{3+\exp(x_i/5)} \sin(x_i + y)\, dy \qquad (C)$$

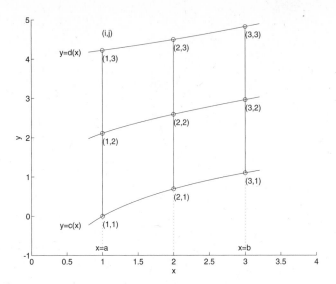

Figure 5.10 A grid for double integration

The whole procedure may be written more explicitly as

$$I = \int_1^3 \left(\int_{\ln(x)}^{3+\exp(x/5)} \sin(x+y)\, dy \right) dx$$

$$\approx \frac{h_x}{3} \left[\int_{\ln(1)}^{3+\exp(1/5)} \sin(1+y)\, dy + 4 \int_{\ln(2)}^{3+\exp(2/5)} \sin(2+y)\, dy \right.$$

$$\left. + \int_{\ln(3)}^{3+\exp(3/5)} \sin(3+y)\, dy \right] \qquad\qquad \text{(D)}$$

$$= \frac{h_x}{3} \left[\int_0^{4.2214} \sin(1+y)dy + 4 \int_{0.6931}^{4.4918} \sin(2+y)\, dy \right.$$

$$\left. + \int_{1.0986}^{4.8221} \sin(3+y)\, dy \right]$$

With the Simpson's 1/3 rule, the first integral in the previous line becomes

$$\int_0^{4.2214} \sin(1 + y)\, dy$$

$$\approx \frac{2.11070}{3} \left[\sin(1 + 0) + 4\sin(1 + 2.11070) + \sin(1 + 4.2214) \right]$$

$$= (2.11070/3)\left[0.84147 + (4)(0.03088) + (-0.87322) \right] = 0.064581$$

(E)

Similar computations yield

$$\int_{0.6931}^{4.4918} \sin(2 + y)\, dy \approx -2.1086$$

$$\int_{1.0986}^{4.8221} \sin(3 + y)\, dy \approx -0.67454$$

Thus, the final value of the double integration becomes

$$I \approx (1/3)[0.064581 + (4)(-2.1086) - 0.67454] = -0.30148$$

The double integration scheme is implemented in dbl_itg. Its synopsis is as follows:

```
I = dbl_itg('f_name', 'lower_limit', ...
              'upper_limit', a, b, m, n)
```

where f_name is the function M-file name of the integrand, lower_limit is the function M-file name that define $c(x)$, upper_limit is the function M-file name that defines $d(x)$, a and b are lower and upper limits of x, and m and n are the number of intervals in the x and y directions, respectively. Function dbl_itg calls Simps_v so the number of intervals can be any number that equals 2 or greater.

The boundaries for some domains, such as Figure 5.11, may not be expressed by two curves and two vertical lines. For such a domain, a coordinate transformation is necessary. New coordinates (ξ, η) are related to (x, y) by

$$x = x(\xi, \eta)$$
$$y = y(\xi, \eta)$$

(5.6.6)

Then, the double integral on the (x, y) domain becomes

$$\int\int_D f(x, y)\, dy dx = \int\int_\Gamma f(\xi, \eta) J d\eta d\xi$$

(5.6.7)

where Γ is the domain of integration on the ξ, η plane, and

$$J = \frac{\partial(x, y)}{\partial(\xi, \eta)} = x_\xi y_\eta - x_\eta y_\xi \qquad (5.6.8)$$

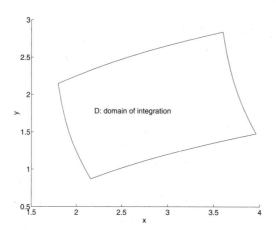

Figure 5.11 A domain of integration

Suppose the domain is covered by a curvilinear grid, as illustrated in Figure 5.12. If the domain is simple, a curvilinear grid may be easily generated. Otherwise, a numerical grid generation method[2] may be used. With a coordinate transformation, the curved geometry is mapped onto a rectangular domain on the ξ-η coordinates. The grid lines are denoted by indices i and j (see Figure 5.12). The grid line i corresponds to $\xi = i$, and the grid line j corresponds to $\eta = j$ on the domain illustrated in Figure 5.13. The grid on the ξ-η domain is rectangular and equispaced.

On the rectangular ξ-η domain, Eq.(5.6.7) becomes

$$\int\int_D f(x, y)dydx = \int_1^m \int_1^n G(\xi, \eta)d\eta d\xi \qquad (5.6.9)$$

where

$$G(\xi, \eta) = f(\xi, \eta)J \qquad (5.6.10)$$

---

[2]See the following references: [1] J.F. Thompson, "Grid Generation" in *Handbook of Numerical Heat Transfer*, W.J. Minkowycz, et al. ed., Wiley Interscience, 1988. [2] S. Nakamura, "Coordinate Transformation and Structured Grid Generation," in *Handbook of Fluid and Fluid Machinery*, J. A. Schetz, et al. ed., John Wiley, forthcoming. [3] P. Knupp and S. Stenberg, *Fundamentals of Grid Generation*, CRC Press, 1993.

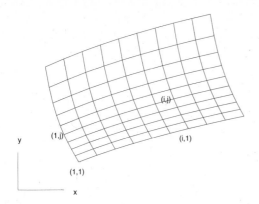

Figure 5.12 Grid on the domain of integration

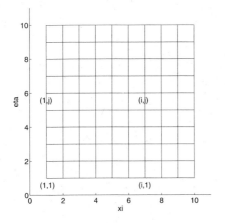

Figure 5.13 Grid on the computational domain

Numerical integration on the right side of Eq.(5.6.9) is performed using the grid on the ξ-η domain illustrated in Figure 5.13. The principle of numerical integration on the ξ-η coordinates is the same as for the double integration on the x-y coordinates. The values of $G_{i,j}$ are computed by

$$G_{i,j} = G(\xi_i, \eta_j) = f(\xi_i, \eta_j)J_{i,j} \qquad (5.6.11)$$

The partial derivatives of x at the grid points are evaluated by the following difference approximations:

$$(x_\xi)_{1,j} = (-x_{3,j} + 4x_{2,j} - 3x_{1,j})/2$$

$$(x_\xi)_{i,j} = (x_{i+1,j} - x_{i-1,j})/2, \quad 1 < i < m$$

$$(x_\xi)_{m,j} = (3x_{m,j} - 4x_{m-1,j} + x_{m-2,j})/2$$

$$(x_\eta)_{i,1} = (-x_{i,3} + 4x_{i,2} - 3x_{i,1})/2 \tag{5.6.12}$$

$$(x_\eta)_{i,j} = (x_{i,j+1} - x_{i,j-1})/2, \quad 1 < j < n$$

$$(x_\eta)_{i,n} = (3x_{i,n} - 4x_{i,n-1} + x_{i,n-2})/2$$

where m and n are maximum values of i and j respectively. The partial derivatives of y are same as Eq.(5.6.12) except x is replaced by y.

5.7   M-FILES

FM 5-1. Extended trapezoidal rule (1)
Purpose: Integration of a function by the extended trapezoidal rule.
Synopsis: I = trapez_v(f,h)
       f: array of the data on equispaced points. Vector length of f
        is arbitrary, but must be greater than 1.
       h: interval size
Example: x=0:0.1:5; y=sin(x);I = trapez_v(y,0.1)

trapez_v.m

```
function I = trapez_v(f, h)
I = h*(sum(f) - (f(1) + f(length(f)))/2);
```

FM 5-2. Extended trapezoidal rule (2)
Purpose: Integration of a function by extended trapezoidal rule. Function trapez_n uses the extended trapezoidal integration but does not plot any graph, while trapez_g does plotting.
Synopsis: trapez_n('f_name', a, b, n) or trapez_g('f_name', a, b, n)
       f_name: function M-file name of the integrand, $f(x)$
       a: lower limit of x
       b: upper limit of x
       n: number of intervals
Example: trapez_n('sin', 0, pi, 20)

trapez_n.m
```
function I = trapez_n(f_name, a, b, n)
h = (b-a)/n;
x = a+(0:n)*h;   f = feval(f_name, x);
I =  trapez_v(f,h)
```

trapez_g.m
```
function I = trapez_g(f_name, a, b, n)
n=n;hold off
h = (b-a)/n;
x = a+(0:n)*h;   f = feval(f_name, x);
I = h/2*(f(1) + f(n+1));
if n>1 I = I +  h*sum(f(2:n));end
h2 = (b-a)/100;
xc = a+(0:100)*h2;   fc = feval(f_name, xc);
plot(xc,fc,'r');  hold on
title('Trapezoidal Rule'); xlabel('x');ylabel('y');
plot(x,f);
plot(x,zeros(size(x)))
for i=1:n; plot([x(i),x(i)], [0,f(i)]); end
```

FM 5-3 Extended Simpson's rule
Purpose: Integration of a function in a tabular form by the extended Simpson's rule.

Synopsis: I = Simps_v(f,h) or I = Simps_n('f_name', a, b, n)

  f_name: function M-file name of the integrand, $f(x)$

  f: functional data on equispaced abscissa. Number of data points
      is arbitrary, but must be greater than 3

  h: interval size of the abscissa

Simps_v.m
```
function I = Simps_v(f,h)
n=length(f)-1;
if n==1, ...
  fprintf('Data has only one interval'),return;
  end
if n==2, ...
  I = h/3*(f(1) + 4*f(2) + f(3));
  return;end
if n==3, ...
  I = 3/8*h*(f(1) + 3*f(2) + 3*f(3) + f(4));
  return;end
I=0;
if  2*floor(n/2)~=n,
   I = 3/8*h*(f(n -2) + 3*f(n -1)   ...
       + 3*f(n) + f(n+1));
   m=n -3
else
   m=n;
end
```

```
I = I+ (h/3)*( f(1)+ 4*sum(f(2:2:m)) + f(m+1));
if m>2, I = I+ (h/3)*2*sum(f(3:2:m));
end
```

Simps_n.m

```
function I = Simps_n(f_name, a, b, n)
   h = (b-a)/n;
   x = a+(0:n)*h;   f = feval(f_name, x);
   I =  Simps_v(f,h)
```

FM 5-4 Newton-Cotes closed formula

Purpose: Integration of a function by the Newton-Cotes closed formula. The weights are automatically computed.

Synopsis: Newt_itg('f_name', a, b, n)

f_name: name of a function M-file that defines the integrand.

a, b: lower and upper limits, respectively.

n: number of equispaced intervals between the two integrating limits

Example: Newt_itg('sin', 0, pi, 4)

Newt_itg.m

```
function I = Newt_itg(f_name, a, b, n)
npt=n+1;
if npt<0, break; end
en = npt:-1:1;
x = 1:npt;
for i=1:npt
     power_2(i)  = npt^en(i); power_1(i) = 1^en(i);
end
for j=1:npt
     z = zeros(1,npt) ; z(j)=1;
     a1 = polyfit(x, z,npt-1);
     w(j) = sum(a1.*(power_2 - power_1)./en);
%      fprintf(' j=%3.0f       w=%12.8f\n', j, w)
end
x=a:(b-a)/(npt-1):b;
y=feval(f_name,x);
I = sum(w.*y)*(b-a)/(npt-1);
fprintf('\n    x                y              w \n')
for j=1:npt
fprintf('%e %e %e\n', x(j),y(j), w(j))
end
```

FM 5-5 Gauss-Legendre quadrature

Purpose: Integration of a function by the Gauss-Legendere quadrature. The Legendre points and weights are automatically computed.

Synopsis: Gauss_q('f_name', a, b, n)

f_name: function M-file name of the integrand, $f(x)$

> a: lower limit of x
> b: upper limit of x
> n: number of Legendre points

Example: `Gauss_q('sin', 0, pi, 8)`

Gauss_q.m

```
function I = Gauss_q(f_name, a, b, n)
p=Legen_pw(n);
x = roots(p)';x = sort(x);
for j=1:n
   y = zeros(1,n); y(j)=1;
   p = polyfit(x,y,n-1);
   P = poly_itg(p);
   w(j) = polyval(P,1) - polyval(P,-1);
end
x = 0.5*((b-a)*x + a + b);
y=feval(f_name, x);
I = sum(w.*y)*(b-a)/2;
fprintf('\n        x              y            w \n')
for j=1:n
fprintf('%e %e %e\n', x(j),y(j), w(j))
end
```

Legen_pw.m

```
function pn = Legen_p(n)
pbb=[1];  if n==0, pn=pbb; break; end
pb=[1 0]; if n==1, pn=pb;  break; end
for i=2:n;
   pn=  ( (2*i-1)*[pb,0] - (i-1)*[0, 0, pbb] )/i;
   pbb=pb; pb=pn;
end
```

Integration by double-exponential transformation

Purpose: Integration of a function by double-exponential transformation

Synopsis: `dbl_exp('f_name',a,b,n)`

> fun_name: function M-file name of the integrand, $f(x)$
> a: lower limit of x
> b: upper limit of x
> n: number of intervals

Example: `dbl_exp('fun_dbx',0, 2)`

dbl_exp.m

```
function I=dbl_exp(f_name,a,b,n)
%           a : lower limit of integration
%           b : upper limit of integration
%           h : grid interval
%           n : number of intervals
%           dxdz : dx/dz
```

```
%                   hcos : hyperbolic cosine
%                   hsin : hyperbolic sine
%                      I : result of integration
zmax=3.; h = 2*zmax/n;
z = -zmax:h:zmax;  exz = exp( z ); exzi=exz.^(-1);
hcos = (exz + exzi)/2.;   hsin = (exz - exzi)/2.;
s = exp( pi*0.5*hsin ); si=s.^(-1);
x = (b*s + a*si).*(s + si).^(-1);
p = pi*hsin/2;   w = exp( p );
dxdz = (b - a)*pi*hcos.*((w + w.^(-1))/2.0).^(-2)/4;
g = feval(f_name,x).*dxdz;
I = trapez_v(g,h);
```

fun_dbx.m
```
function y = fun_dbx(x)
y = sin(x)/sqrt(x);
```

Double integration

Purpose: Double integration of a two-dimensional function, $f(x, y)$

Synopsis:`dbl_itg('fun_name','c_lo','c_hi',a,b,m,n)`

        fun_name: function M-file name of the integrand, $f(x, y)$

        c_lo: function M-file name of the lower limit of y, $c(x)$

        c_hi: function M-file name of the upper limit of y, $d(x)$

        a: lower limit of x

        b: upper limit of x

        m: number of intervals in the x direction (must be even)

        n: number of intervals in the y direction (must be even) Example:

`dbl_itg('fun_dbl','low_lim','upp_lim',1,3,6,6)`

The function M-files samples are listed after `dbl_itg` in the following list.

dbl_itg.m
```
function I=dbl_itg(f_name,c_lo,c_hi,a,b,m,n)
%       Double Integration by Simpson's Rule
%        a :lower limit of integration over x
%        b :upper limit of integration over x
%     c_lo :function name for lower bound curve
%            (function of x),c(x)
%     d_hi :   function name for upper bound curve
%            (function of x), d(x)
% f_name : function name for integrand
% hx, hy : interval sizes
%        I : result of integration
%       m,n: number of intervals in x and y directions, resp.
if   m<2  | n<2
     fprintf( 'Number of intervals invalid \n' ); return
end
mpt=m+1;npt=n+1;     %number of intervals
hx = (b - a)/m ; x =a+(0:m)*hx;
for i=1:mpt
    ylo= feval(c_lo,x(i));
```

```
    yhi = feval(c_hi, x(i));
    hy=(yhi-ylo)/n;
    y(i,:)=ylo+ (0:n)*hy;
    f(i,:)=feval(f_name,x(i),y(i,:));
    G(i) = Simps_v(f(i,:),hy);
end
I = Simps_v(G,hx);
```

fun_dbl.m
```
function y= fun_dbl( x, y)
y = sin( x + y );
```

low_lim.m
```
function y =low_lim( x)
y = log( x );
```

upp_lim.m
```
function y = upp_lim( x)
  y = 3 + exp( x/5 );
```

PROBLEMS

(5.1) Evaluate the following integral by the extended trapezoidal rule with $n = 2, 4, 8,$ and 16 intervals:

(a) $\int_0^{\pi/4} \tan(x)\, dx$

(b) $\int_0^1 \exp(x)\, dx$

(c) $\int_0^1 \frac{1}{2+x}\, dx$

(5.2) Evaluate

$$\int_0^{\pi/2} \sin(x)\, dx$$

by the extended trapezoidal rule with $n = 2, 4, 8, 25,$ and 100 intervals. Then, find the error of the numerical results by comparison to the exact value.

(5.3) A spherical water reservoir of radius 20 m is located 40 m above the ground. A straight vertical drain pipe of radius $b = 0.2$ m and length 40 m is connected to the bottom of the tank to drain the water to ground level. The friction factor of the pipe is $f = 0.0016$. The tank is full to the top and draining starts at $t = 0$. How much time is needed to drain the water?

Hint: The energy equation to determine the velocity of the water in the pipe is given by

$$gz = \frac{u^2}{2} + f\frac{L}{2b}\frac{u^2}{2}$$

where the first term on the right side is the kinetic energy of water leaving the pipe and the second term is the friction loss effect. Use 20 intervals.

(5.4) The bottom of a circular cylinder has a radius of 0.5 m and is perpendicular to the axis, but the top is at 45 degrees to the axis, as shown in Figure 5.14. Find the volume by the trapezoidal rule with 20 intervals.

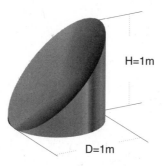

Figure 5.14 A cylinder

(5.5) With the function table given below, evaluate

$$\int_0^{0.8} f(x)\, dx$$

by the extended trapezoidal rule with $h = 0.4$, $h = 0.2$ and $h = 0.1$.

x	f(x)
0.0	0
0.1	2.1220
0.2	3.0244
0.3	3.2568
0.4	3.1399
0.5	2.8579
0.6	2.5140
0.7	2.1639
0.8	1.8358

(5.6) By applying the Romberg integral to the results of the trapezoidal rule with $h = 0.1$ and $h = 0.2$ for Problem 5.5, estimate a more accurate integral.

(5.7) A function table is given below.

i	x_i	$f(x_i)$
1	0	0.9162
2	0.25	0.8109
3	0.5	0.6931
4	0.75	0.5596
5	1.0	0.4055

(a) Calculate

$$I = \int_0^1 f(x)\, dx$$

by the extended trapezoidal rule with $h = 0.25$ and $h = 0.5$.

(b) By Romberg integration to the results for question (a), estimate a more accurate value of I.

(5.8) Consider three data points, $(-1, f_1), (0, f_2), (1, f_3)$. Fit the data set by the Lagrange interpolation formula. By integrating the Lagrange interpolation formula, show that the Simpson's 1/3 rule is obtained.

Hint: Transform the shape functions to power series by `polyfit`. Once the power coefficients are obtained, integrate the polynomial by `poly_itg`.

(5.9) The Simpson's 1/3 rule is exact if a polynomial of order 3 or less is integrated. Verify this by integrating

$$I = \int_0^3 x^3 dx$$

by Simpson's 1/3 rule and analytically. Repeat the same for the Simpson's 3/8 rule.

(5.10) Repeat Problem (5.1) using the Simpson's 1/3 method.

(5.11) Evaluate the following integrals by the extended Simpson's 1/3 rule using $n = 2, 4, 8, 16$, and 32:

(a) $\displaystyle\int_0^\pi \frac{dx}{2 + \cos(x)}$

(b) $\displaystyle\int_1^2 \frac{\log(1 + x)}{x} dx$

(c) $\displaystyle\int_0^{\frac{\pi}{2}} \frac{dx}{1 + \sin^2(x)}$

(5.12) Evaluate the following integral by the extended Simpson's 1/3 rule using $n = 2, 4,$ 8, 16, and 32:

(a) $\displaystyle\int_0^1 x \exp(2x)dx$

(b) $\displaystyle\int_0^1 x^{-x}\,dx$

(c) $\displaystyle\int_0^{2\pi} \exp(2x)\sin^2(x)dx$

(5.13) Suppose you are an architect and planning to use a large arch of the parabolic shape given by

$$y = 0.1x(30 - x) \text{ meters}$$

where y is the height above the ground and x is in meters. Calculate the total length of the arch by the extended Simpson's rule. (Divide the domain from $x = 0$ to $x = 30$ m into 10 equally spaced intervals.)

$$L = \int_0^{30} \sqrt{1 + \left(\frac{dy}{dx}\right)^2}\,dx$$

(5.14) An automobile of mass $M = 5400$ kg is cruising at a speed of 30 m/s. The engine is disengaged suddenly at $t = 0$ s. Assume that the equation of coasting after $t = 0$ is given by

$$5400\,\frac{dv}{dx} = -8.276v^2 - 2000$$

where $v = v(t)$ is the speed (m/s) of the car at t. The left side represents $Mv(dv/dx)$. The first term on the right side is the aerodynamic drag, and the second term is the rolling resistance of the tires. Calculate how far the car travels until the speed reduces to 15 m/s.

Hint: The equation of motion may be integrated as

$$\int_{15}^{30} \frac{5400}{8.276v^2 + 2000}v\,dv = \int_0^x dx' = x$$

Evaluate the equation above using the Simpson's 1/3 rule.

(5.15) (a) If $f(x)$ is a polynomial of order n or less, the Newton-Cotes closed formula of order n (using $n + 1$ points) becomes exact. Explain the reason. (b) Newton-Cotes closed formula of an even order n becomes exact if f is of order $n + 1$. Explain why.

(5.16) The length of a curve defined by $x = \phi(t)$, $y = \psi(t)$, $a < t < b$, is given by

$$s = \int_a^b \sqrt{[\phi'(t)]^2 + [\psi'(t)]^2} \, dt$$

Using the Gauss quadrature with $n=2$, 4 and 6, find the length of the cycloid defined by

$$x = 3[t - \sin(t)], \quad y = 2 - 2\cos(t), \quad 0 < t < 2\pi$$

(5.17) Repeat Problem (5.1) by Gauss quadrature of n= 2, 3, 4, 6 and 8 points.

(5.18) If $f(x)$ is a polynomial of order $2n - 1$ or less, the Gauss quadrature using n Legendre points becomes exact. Verify this by computing the following integral by the Gauss quadrature of order 3 (3 Legendre points):

$$y = x^5 + 3x^2$$

(5.19) Evaluate the following improper integral accurately up to the sixth decimal place by the extended trapezoidal rule:

$$\int_{-\infty}^{\infty} \frac{\exp(-x^2)}{1 + x^2} \, dx$$

(5.20) Calculate the following integrals by the Gauss quadrature of $n = 6$ points:

(a) $\displaystyle \int_0^\pi \frac{1}{2 + \cos(x)} \, dx$

(b) $\displaystyle \int_1^2 \frac{\log(1 + x)}{x} \, dx$

(c) $\displaystyle \int_0^1 x \exp(2x) \, dx$

(d) $\displaystyle \int_0^1 \cos(x) \log(x) \, dx$

(d) $\displaystyle \int_0^2 \log(x) \, dx$

(5.21) Evaluate the following improper integrals accurately up to the sixth decimal place by the extended trapezoidal rule, with the exponential transformation given by Eq.(5.4.10):

(a) $\displaystyle \int_0^1 \frac{\tan(x)}{x^{0.7}} \, dx$

(b) $\displaystyle \int_0^1 \frac{\exp(x)}{\sqrt{1 - x^2}}$

(5.22) Calculate the following integral by the extended trapezoidal rule for each axis:

$$I = \int_1^2 \int_0^1 \sin(x + y) \, dy dx$$

(Use only two intervals for each axis; the sine function is in radians.)

(5.23) Evaluate the following integral by the Simpson's 1/3 rule:

$$I = \int_0^1 \int_0^x \sqrt{x + y} \, dy dx$$

(5.24) The area of a unit circle is π. Accuracy of a numerical scheme for double integration may be tested by the problem:

$$I = \int \int_D dy dx$$

where D means that the integration is extended over the interior of

$$x^2 + y^2 \leq 2x$$

which is a unit circle. Perform the numerical evaluation of the preceding double integration by the extended Simpson's rule in both directions with 2×2, 4×4, 8×8, 16×16, 32×32, and 64×64 intervals.

(5.25) Repeat Problem (5.24) using the double-exponential transformation.

(5.26) By the extended Simpson's rule with 10 intervals in each direction, evaluate the double integral

$$I = \int_0^\pi \int_0^{\sin(x)} \exp(-x^2 - y^2) dy dx$$

(5.27) Evaluate the following double integral by the Simpson's 1/3 rule:

$$I = \int_1^2 \int_0^{2-0.5x} \sqrt{x + y} \, dy dx$$

(5.28) Repeat the problem in Example 5.6 by the Gauss-quadrature of $n = 3$.

(5.29) The Chebyshev polynomials satisfy the orthogonality relation:

$$\int_{-1}^1 T_{m-1}(x) T_{n-1}(x) \frac{dx}{\sqrt{1 - x^2}} = \left\{ \begin{array}{ll} 0, & \text{if } m \neq n \\ \pi/2, & \text{if } m = n > 1 \\ \pi, & \text{if } m = n = 0 \end{array} \right\}$$

Verify the foregoing relation for the combination of $m = 1$ through 7, and $n = 1$ through 7 by calculating the 7-by-7 matrix $A = [a_{m,n}]$ where

$$a_{m,n} = \int_{-1}^{1} T_{m-1}(x) T_{n-1}(x) \frac{dx}{\sqrt{1-x^2}}$$

Use the double-exponential transformation for integration.

Chapter 6

Numerical Differentiation

Numerical differentiation, or difference approximation, is a method used to evaluate derivatives of a function using the functional values at discrete data points. If the functional values are known at discrete points, the function can be expressed approximately by an interpolation polynomial. Then, by differentiating the interpolation polynomial, we can evaluate the derivatives.

6.1 DERIVATIVES OF INTERPOLATION POLYNOMIALS

Suppose a set of data points,

$$(x_i, y_i), i = 1, 2, ... n + 1$$

is fitted by an interpolation polynomial in power series as described in Chapter 4, and given by

$$g(x) = c_1 x^n + c_2 x^{n-1} + ... + c_n x + c_{n+1} \tag{6.1.1}$$

In order to find the first derivative of $g(x)$ for $x = 0$, we differentiate $g(x)$ and set $x = 0$. The result is $g'(0) = c_n$. Likewise, the second derivative for $x = 0$ is $g'' = 2c_{n-1}$ and, in more general terms, the k-th derivative is

$$g^{(k)}(0) = c_{n+1-k} k!, \quad k = 0, 1, 2, ... n \tag{6.1.2}$$

If we eliminate c_i in Eq.(6.1.1) by Eq.(6.1.2) and reverse the order of terms, we get

$$g(x) = g(0) + g'(0)x + \frac{g''(0)}{2}x^2 + \frac{g'''(0)}{3!}x^3 + ... + \frac{g^{(n)}(0)}{n!}x^n \tag{6.1.3}$$

This is the Taylor expansion of Eq.(6.1.1) about $x = 0$, or equivalently, Mclaurin expansion.

The foregoing relations may be applied to computation of derivatives for any value of x. Suppose derivatives of $g(x)$ at $x = a$ is desired. Then, with the coordinate transformation,

$$z = x - a$$

$g(x)$ may be written in terms of z as

$$g(x) = \bar{g}(z) = d_1 z^n + d_2 z^{n-1} + ... d_n z + d_{n+1} \qquad (6.1.4)$$

Therefore, derivatives $g^{(k)}(a)$ are given by

$$\left[\left(\frac{d}{dz} \right)^k \bar{g}(z) \right]_{z=0} = k! d_{n+1-k}, \quad k = 0, 1, 2, ... n \qquad (6.1.5)$$

Coefficients d_is need not be computed from c_i. Indeed, d_i may be obtained directly by fitting $\bar{g}(z)$ to data set $(x_i - a, y_i), i = 1, 2, .. n + 1$; by MATLAB, it is

```
d = polyfit(x-a, y, length(xd)-1)
```

where x is a vector of $x_i, i = 1, 2, .. n + 1$ and y is a vector of $y_i, i = 1, 2, .. n + 1$. All the derivatives of an interpolation polynomial fitted to a data set may be computed by `poly_drv` listed as FM 6-3 in Section 6.7.

Example 6.1

A data set is given by

```
xd: 0        0.2000   0.4000   0.6000   0.8000   1.0000
yd: 0.3927   0.5672   0.6982   0.7941   0.8614   0.9053
```

Estimate all the derivatives for $x = a = 0.3$ by `poly_drv`, and then by `polyfit` as described in this section.

Solution

We transform x-coordinate to z by $z = x - a$, where $a = 3$. Because there are six data points, a fifth-order polynomial will be used. The power coefficients of the interpolation polynomial are obtained by

```
xd = [0        0.2000   0.4000   0.6000   0.8000   1.0000]
yd = [0.3927   0.5672   0.6982   0.7941   0.8614   0.9053]
a=0.3;
d = poly_drv(xd,yd,a)
```

The results are, in increasing derivative order,

```
0.6533     -0.9710     1.0406     -1.3750     1.8750
```

The foregoing computations may be equivalently performed by

```
c0 = polyfit(xd-a,yd,length(xd)-1);
c1 = polyder(c0);  polyval(c1,0)
c2 = polyder(c1);  polyval(c2,0)
c3 = polyder(c2);  polyval(c3,0)
c4 = polyder(c3);  polyval(c4,0)
c5 = polyder(c4);  polyval(c5,0)
```

or, also equivalently,

```
c0 = polyfit(xd,yd,length(xd)-1);
c1 = polyder(c0); polyval(c1,a)
c2 = polyder(c1); polyval(c2,a)
c3 = polyder(c2); polyval(c3,a)
c4 = polyder(c3); polyval(c4,a)
c5 = polyder(c4); polyval(c5,a)
```

6.2   DIFFERENCE APPROXIMATIONS

In the preceding section, we showed that all derivatives of a polynomial fitted to a data set can be easily evaluated. In usual practical numerical analyses, however, not all derivatives are necessary, but rather one or two derivatives of a low order are most frequently required. The formulas to approximate derivatives are named difference approximations. In the present section, we derive difference approximations by polynomial interpolation.

To illustrate derivation of difference approximations, we consider a function $f(x)$ as depicted in Figure 6.1, and assume that the first derivative of $f(x)$ at $x = x_0$ is to be evaluated. If the values of $f_{-1} = f(x_0 - h)$, $f_0 = f(x_0)$ and $f_1 = f(x_0 + h)$ are given, where h is an interval between two consecutive points on the x-axis, then $f_0' = f'(x_0)$ may be approximated by the gradient of linear interpolation A, B, or C depicted in Figure 6.1. These three approximations using

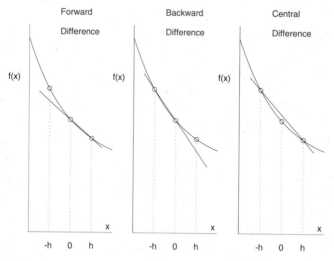

Figure 6.1   Graphical explanation of difference approximations for $f'(x_0)$

the gradient of the lines A, B, and C are called, respectively, forward, backward, and central difference approximations. The mathematical formulas of them are as follows:

(a) Approximation using A (forward difference approximation)

$$f_0' \approx \frac{f_1 - f_0}{h} \tag{6.2.1}$$

(b) Approximation using B (backward difference approximation)

$$f_0' \approx \frac{f_0 - f_{-1}}{h} \tag{6.2.2}$$

(c) Approximation using C (central difference approximation)

$$f_0' \approx \frac{f_1 - f_{-1}}{2h} \tag{6.2.3}$$

Difference approximations are closely related to interpolation polynomials. Let us consider $p+1$ abscissa points, $x_a, x_b, \ldots x_g$, and the corresponding ordinates, f_a, $f_b, \ldots f_g$. The interpolation polynomial fitted to these data points can be expressed by the Lagrange interpolation. The interpolation polynomial fitted to $p+1$ points is of order p at most. Therefore, up to the p-th order derivative can be evaluated. The derivative of the interpolation polynomial at points $a, b, \ldots g$ are named difference approximations. Depending on which of $x_a, x_b, \ldots x_g$ the derivative is evaluated for and order of the derivative, many different approximation formulas can be obtained.

Example 6.2

(a) Write the Lagrange interpolation polynomial that passes through data points $x_0 = 0$, $x_1 = h$ and $x_2 = 2h$, with ordinates f_0, f_1, and f_2, respectively. Derive the difference approximation for $f'(0)$ by differentiating the interpolation formula once and setting $x = 0$. Derive also the difference approximation for $f''(0)$ by differentiating the interpolation formula twice and setting $x = 0$.

(b) Write the Lagrange interpolation polynomial that passes through $x_{-1} = -h$, $x_0 = 0$ and $x_1 = h$ with ordinates f_{-1}, f_0 and f_1, respectively. By differentiating the interpolation formula, derive the difference approximation for $f_0' = f'(x_0)$. Derive also the difference approximation for $f_0'' = f''(x_0)$.

(c) Repeat the same for the points x_{-2}, x_{-1}, and x_0.

Solution

(a) We approximate $f(x)$ by the Lagrange interpolation polynomial passing through points $i = 0$, 1 and 2:

$$f(x) \approx g(x)$$
$$= \frac{(x - x_1)(x - x_2)}{(x_0 - x_1)(x_0 - x_2)} f_0 + \frac{(x - x_0)(x - x_2)}{(x_1 - x_0)(x_1 - x_2)} f_1$$
$$+ \frac{(x - x_0)(x - x_1)}{(x_2 - x_0)(x_2 - x_1)} f_2$$

Differentiating and setting $x = 0$, we get

$$f_0' \approx \frac{-f_2 + 4f_1 - 3f_0}{2h} \tag{A}$$

Differentiating twice and setting $x = 0$ yield

$$f_0'' \approx \frac{f_2 - 2f_1 + f_0}{h^2} \tag{B}$$

(b) The Lagrange interpolation passing through points $i = -1$, 0 and 1 is

$$f(x) \approx g(x)$$
$$= \frac{(x - x_0)(x - x_1)}{(x_{-1} - x_0)(x_{-1} - x_1)} f_{-1} + \frac{(x - x_{-1})(x - x_1)}{(x_0 - x_{-1})(x_0 - x_1)} f_0$$
$$+ \frac{(x - x_{-1})(x - x_0)}{(x_1 - x_{-1})(x_1 - x_0)} f_1$$

Differentiating once and twice, respectively, and setting $x = 0$ yield

$$f_0' \approx \frac{f_1 - f_{-1}}{2h} \tag{C}$$

$$f_0'' \approx \frac{f_{+1} - 2f_0 + f_{-1}}{h^2} \tag{D}$$

(c) The Lagrange interpolation passing through points at $i = -2$, -1, and 0 is

$$f(x) \approx g(x)$$
$$= \frac{(x - x_{-1})(x - x_0)}{(x_{-2} - x_{-1})(x_{-2} - x_0)}f_{-2} + \frac{(x - x_{-2})(x - x_0)}{(x_{-1} - x_{-2})(x_{-1} - x_0)}f_{-1}$$
$$+ \frac{(x - x_{-2})(x - x_{-1})}{(x_0 - x_{-2})(x_0 - x_{-1})}f_0$$

Differentiating once and twice, respectively, and setting $x = 0$ yield

$$f_0' \approx \frac{3f_0 - 4f_{-1} + f_{-2}}{2h} \tag{E}$$

$$f_0'' \approx \frac{f_0 - 2f_{-1} + f_{-2}}{h^2} \tag{F}$$

Comments: (1) Equations (A), (C), and (E) are all approximations for $f'(0)$, but use different data points. When accuracy of difference approximation is concerned, the general information of the behavior of the error of the Lagrange interpolation is helpful. As discussed in Section 4.3, accuracy of a Lagrange interpolation is the best about the center point. This indicates that Eq.(C) that is obtained by evaluating the derivative of the interpolation formula for the center point is most accurate. The other two equations, (A) and (E), obtained by the derivative evaluated at the leftmost and rightmost points, respectively, are less accurate. (2) Equation (C) is identical to Eq.(6.2.3) that is derived by differentiating the linear interpolation through the two points, $i = -1$ and 1.

Example 6.3

Calculate the first derivative of $\tan(x)$ at $x = 1$ by the five difference approximations derived in this section, Eqs.(6.2.2), (6.2.1), (6.2.3) and Eq.(E) and Eq.(A) in Example 6.1, using $h = 0.1$, 0.05 and 0.02. Then evaluate percent error of each approximation by comparison with the exact value.

Solution

By introducing $f_i = f(1 + ih) = \tan(1 + ih)$ into the five equations, the results in the table of the following page are obtained. The numbers in parentheses in the table are percent errors. Notice that errors of the first two approximations decrease in proportion to h, while errors of the last three approximations decrease in proportion to h^2. Clearly, the rate of reduction of error becomes faster as the order of accuracy becomes higher.

	$h = 0.1$	$h = 0.05$	$h = 0.02$
$[f(1) - f(1 - h)]/h$	2.9724 (13.2)	3.1805 (7.1)	3.3224 (3.0)
$[f(1 + h) - f(1)]/h$	4.0735 (−18.9)	3.7181 (−8.5)	3.5361 (−3.2)
$[f(1 + h) - f(1 - h)]/2h$	3.5230 (−2.8)	3.4493 (−0.69)	3.4293 (−0.11)
$[3f(1) - 4f(1 - h) + f(1 - 2h)]/2h$	3.3061 (3.5)	3.3885 (1.08)	3.4186 (0.20)
$[-f(1 + 2h) + 4f(1 + h) - 3f(1)]/2h$	3.0733 (10.3)	3.3627 (1.83)	3.4170 (0.25)

6.3 TAYLOR EXPANSION METHOD

The Taylor expansion method is an alternative way of deriving difference approximations. It not only derives the difference formulas systematically, but also derives the error terms.

For a derivative of order p, the minimum number of data points necessary to derive a difference approximation is $p + 1$. For example, a difference approximation for the first derivative of a function needs at least two points.

Let us consider derivation of difference approximation for $f'_i = f'(x_i)$ in terms of $f_i = f(x_i)$ and $f_{i+1} = f(x_{i+1})$. The Taylor expansion of f_{i+1} about x_i is

$$f_{i+1} = f_i + hf'_i + \frac{h^2}{2}f''_i + \frac{h^3}{6}f'''_i + \frac{h^4}{24}f''''_i + \dots \qquad (6.3.1)$$

Solving Eq.(6.3.1) for f'_i yields

$$f'_i = \frac{f_{i+1} - f_i}{h} - \frac{h}{2}f''_i - \frac{h^2}{6}f'''_i - \dots \qquad (6.3.2)$$

If we ignore all the terms except the first term on the right side, the forward difference approximation is obtained; it is already shown as Eq.(6.2.1). The terms ignored constitute the truncation error, which is represented by the leading term, $-(h/2)f''_i$. Other terms vanish more rapidly than the leading term when h is decreased. The forward difference approximation is expressed, including the truncation error, as

$$f'_i = \frac{f_{i+1} - f_i}{h} + E \qquad (6.3.3)$$

where

$$E \approx -\frac{h}{2}f''_i$$

The term E indicates that error is approximately proportional to the grid interval h. The error is also proportional to the second derivative f''.

The backward difference approximation for the first derivative using f_{i-1} and f_i is obtained in a similar manner. The Taylor expansion of f_{i-1} is

$$f_{i-1} = f_i - h f_i' + \frac{h^2}{2} f_i'' - \frac{h^3}{6} f_i''' + \frac{h^4}{24} f_i'''' + \dots \qquad (6.3.4)$$

Solving Eq.(6.3.4) for f_i', the backward difference approximation is obtained as

$$f_i' = \frac{f_i - f_{i-1}}{h} + E \qquad (6.3.5)$$

where

$$E \approx \frac{h}{2} f_i''$$

The central difference approximation using f_{i+1} and f_{i-1} may be derived by Taylor expansions of f_{i+1} and f_{i-1}, already given as Eqs.(6.3.1) and (6.3.4), respectively. Subtracting the latter from the former yields

$$f_{i+1} - f_{i-1} = 2h f_i' + \frac{1}{3} h^3 f_i''' + \dots \qquad (6.3.6)$$

where the f_i'' term has been automatically eliminated. By solving for f_i' we get

$$f_i' = \frac{f_{i+1} - f_{i-1}}{2h} - \frac{1}{6} h^2 f_i''' + \dots \qquad (6.3.7)$$

Including the error term, the central difference approximation is expressed as

$$f_i' = \frac{f_{i+1} - f_{i-1}}{2h} + E \qquad (6.3.8)$$

where

$$E \approx -\frac{h^2}{6} f_i'''$$

It is remarkable that, because of cancellation of the f'' term, the error of the central difference approximation is proportional to h^2 rather than h. When h is decreased, the error decreases more quickly than with the other two approximations.

As explained before, a difference approximation for $f_i^{(p)}$ needs at least $p + 1$ data points. As the number of data points increases, a more accurate difference approximation can be obtained. To illustrate the point, we derive a difference approximation for f_i' using f_i, f_{i+1} and f_{i+2}. Since the minimum number of data points for f' is two, we have one extra point than the minimum required. Expansions of f_{i+1} and f_{i+2} are written as

$$f_{i+1} = f_i + h f_i' + \frac{h^2}{2} f_i'' + \frac{h^3}{6} f_i''' + \frac{h^4}{24} f_i'''' + \dots \qquad (6.3.9)$$

$$f_{i+2} = f_i + 2h f_i' + \frac{4h^2}{2} f_i'' + \frac{8h^3}{6} f_i''' + \frac{16h^4}{24} f_i'''' + \dots \qquad (6.3.10)$$

With these two equations, it is possible to cancel the second derivative terms, so that the leading term of the truncation errors is the third-order derivative term. On the other hand, if the third derivative terms in Eqs.(6.3.9) and (6.3.10) were eliminated instead of the second derivative terms, the difference approximation obtained would become less accurate because the leading error term becomes one order lower.

By subtracting Eq.(6.3.10) from 4 times Eq.(6.3.9), we obtain

$$4 f_{i+1} - f_{i+2} = 3 f_i + 2h f_i' + \frac{2h^3}{3} f_i''' + \dots \qquad (6.3.11)$$

Solving the foregoing equation for f_i' yields

$$f_i' = \frac{-f_{i+2} + 4 f_{i+1} - 3 f_i}{2h} + E \qquad (6.3.12)$$

where the error term is given by

$$E \approx \frac{h^2}{3} f_i'''$$

Equation (6.3.12) is the three-point forward difference approximation, which is the same as Eq.(E) in Example 6.2. Its error is of the same order as the central difference approximation.

Similarly, the three-point backward difference approximation may be derived using f_i, f_{i-1} and f_{i-2}:

$$f_i' = \frac{3 f_i - 4 f_{i-1} + f_{i-2}}{2h} + E \qquad (6.3.13)$$

where

$$E \approx \frac{h^2}{3} f_i'''$$

Difference approximations for the second derivative are derived by the same principle. The basic principle is to eliminate the first derivative plus as many derivatives of order 2 or higher as possible.

For illustration, we derive the difference approximation for f_i'' in terms of f_{i+1}, f_i and f_{i-1}. Taylor expansions of f_{i+1} and f_{i-1} are given by Eq.(6.3.1) and Eq.(6.3.4). By adding the two, we get

$$f_{i+1} + f_{i-1} = 2f_i + h^2 f_i'' + \frac{h^4}{12} f_i'''' + \cdots$$

or equivalently

$$f_{i+1} - 2f_i + f_{i-1} = h^2 f_i'' + \frac{h^4}{12} f_i'''' + \cdots$$

Then, truncating after the f'' term and rewriting yield

$$f_i'' = \frac{f_{i+1} - 2f_i + f_{i-1}}{h^2} + E \qquad (6.3.14)$$

The foregoing equation is the central difference approximation for f'', which is the same as Eq.(D) in Example 6.2. The error is represented by

$$E \approx -\frac{h^2}{12} f_i''''$$

Another difference approximation for f_i'' may be derived in terms of f_i, f_{i-1} and f_{i-2} (the minimum number of data points for $p = 2$ is 3). Subtracting 2 times the Taylor expansion of f_{i-1} from that of f_{i-2} results in

$$f_{i-2} - 2f_{i-1} = -f_i + h^2 f_i'' - h^3 f_i''' + \cdots$$

Solving the foregoing equation for f_i'' yields

$$f_i'' = \frac{f_{i-2} - 2f_{i-1} + f_i}{h^2} + E \qquad (6.3.15)$$

with

$$E \approx h f_i'''$$

Equation (6.3.15) is the backward difference approximation for f_i'', which was already derived in Example 6.1. The order of its truncation error is lower than the central difference approximation given by Eq.(6.3.14). The higher accuracy of the central difference approximation is what we predicted in Section 6.2 from the fact that the accuracy of the Lagrange interpolation is the best at the center.

Difference approximations for even higher derivatives can be obtained in a similar way, but derivation becomes increasingly more cumbersome as both the number of terms and the order of the derivative increase. For this reason, a computer program that automatically finds the difference approximation for a given set of data will be useful. Its algorithm is described in Section 6.3.

The difference approximations that are frequently used are listed in Table 6.1.

Table 6.1 Difference Approximations

First derivative

(a) Forward difference approximations:

$$f_i' = \frac{f_{i+1} - f_i}{h} + E, \quad E \approx -\frac{1}{2} h f_i''$$

$$f_i' = \frac{-f_{i+2} + 4f_{i+1} - 3f_i}{2h} + E, \quad E \approx \frac{1}{3} h^2 f_i'''$$

$$f_i' = \frac{2f_{i+3} - 9f_{i+2} + 18f_{i+1} - 11f_i}{6h} + E, \quad E \approx -\frac{1}{4} h^3 f_i''''$$

(b) Backward difference approximations:

$$f_i' = \frac{f_i - f_{i-1}}{h} + E, \quad E \approx \frac{1}{2} h f_i''$$

$$f_i' = \frac{3f_i - 4f_{i-1} + f_{i-2}}{2h} + E, \quad E \approx \frac{1}{3} h^2 f_i'''$$

$$f_i' = \frac{11f_i - 18f_{i-1} + 9f_{i-2} - 2f_{i-3}}{6h} + E, \quad E \approx \frac{1}{4} h^3 f_i''''$$

(c) Central difference approximations:

$$f_i' = \frac{f_{i+1} - f_{i-1}}{2h} + E, \quad E \approx -\frac{h^2}{6} f_i'''$$

$$f_i' = \frac{-f_{i+2} + 8f_{i+1} - 8f_{i-1} + f_{i-2}}{12h} + E, \quad E \approx \frac{1}{30} h^4 f_i^{(v)}$$

Second derivative

(d) Forward difference approximations:

$$f_i'' = \frac{f_{i+2} - 2f_{i+1} + f_i}{h^2} + E, \quad E \approx -h f_i'''$$

$$f_i'' = \frac{-f_{i+3} + 4f_{i+2} - 5f_{i+1} + 2f_i}{h^2} + E, \quad E \approx \frac{11}{12} h^2 f_i''''$$

(e) Backward difference approximations:

$$f_i'' = \frac{f_i - 2f_{i-1} + f_{i-2}}{h^2} + E, \quad E \approx h f_i'''$$

$$f_i'' = \frac{2f_i - 5f_{i+2} + 4f_{i+1} - f_i}{h^2} + E, \quad E \approx \frac{11}{12}h^2 f_i''''$$

(f) Central difference approximations:

$$f_i'' = \frac{f_{i+1} - 2f_i + f_{i-1}}{h^2} + E, \quad E \approx -\frac{1}{12}h^2 f_i''''$$

$$f_i'' = \frac{-f_{i-2} + 16f_{i+1} - 30f_i + 16f_{i-1} - f_{i-2}}{12h^2} + E, \quad E \approx \frac{1}{90}h^4 f_i^{(vi)}$$

Third derivative

(g) Forward difference approximation:

$$f_i''' = \frac{f_{i+3} - 3f_{i+2} + 3f_{i+1} - f_i}{h^3} + E, \quad E \approx -\frac{3}{2}h^2 f_i''''$$

(h) Backward difference approximation:

$$f_i'' = \frac{f_i - 3f_{i-1} + 3f_{i-2} - f_{i-3}}{h^3} + E, \quad E \approx \frac{3}{2}h^2 f_i''''$$

(i) Central difference approximation:

$$f_i'' = \frac{f_{i+2} - 2f_{i+1} + 2f_{i-1} - 2f_{i-2}}{2h^3} + E, \quad E \approx -\frac{1}{4}h^2 f_i^{(v)}$$

6.4 ALGORITHMS TO AUTOMATE DERIVATIONS

The objective of this section is to describe two algorithms to automatically derive a difference approximation using a given set of data points. The first is based on differentiation of the Lagrange interpolation formula, and the second is based on the Taylor expansion.

Suppose that L data points are used and they are numbered as $i = \alpha, \beta, ..., \lambda$ as shown in Figure 6.2. We assume $L \geq p + 1$ where p is the order of the derivative. The abscissas of the data points are $x_i = \alpha h, \beta h, ..., \lambda h$ with $i = \alpha, \beta, ..., \lambda$, where h is a given constant. If $i = \alpha, \beta, ..., \lambda$ are consecutive integers, h becomes the interval size between two consecutive points. In general, $i = \alpha, \beta, ...$ have to be in increasing order but do not have to be integers.

6.4.1 Algorithm 1

The algorithm works easily on MATLAB using `shape_pw` and `polyder`, described in Section 4.5. The Lagrange interpolation fitted at data points $x_\alpha, x_\beta, .. x_\lambda$ with corresponding functional values $f_\alpha, f_\beta, ..f_\lambda$ is

Non-equispaced points:
Total number of points = L

An example with 6 equispaced points:
(L = 6)

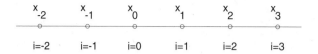

Figure 6.2 Illustration of grid points

$$g(x) = \sum_{i=\alpha,\beta,\dots,\lambda} v_i(x)f_i \qquad (6.4.1)$$

where v_i is a polynomial of x given by

$$v_i(x) = \prod_{\substack{j=\alpha,\beta,\dots,\lambda \\ j \neq i}} \frac{(x-x_j)}{(x_i-x_j)}, \quad \text{for } i = \alpha,\ \beta,\ \dots,\ \lambda \qquad (6.4.2)$$

The p-th derivative of $g(x)$ is written as

$$g^{(p)}(x) = \prod_{i=\alpha,\beta,\dots,\lambda} v_i^{(p)}(x)f_i \qquad (6.4.3)$$

A difference approximation formula may be obtained by setting x to one of $x_i = \alpha h,\ \beta h,\ ..\lambda h$ in Eq.(6.4.3). See Section 4.6 for evaluation of $v_i^{(p)}$.

6.4.2   Algorithm 2

The difference approximation for the p-th derivative of $f(x)$ in terms of f_α, f_β, .. and f_λ may be written in the form:

$$f_0^{(p)} = \frac{a_\alpha f_\alpha + a_\beta f_\beta + \dots + a_\lambda f_\lambda}{h^p} + E \tag{6.4.4}$$

where a_α through a_λ are L undetermined coefficients, $f_\alpha = f(x_\alpha)$ through $f_\lambda = f(x_\lambda)$ are ordinates of the data to be used, and E is the error written by

$$E \approx c_1 h^{L-p} f_0^{(L)} + c_2 h^{L-p+1} f_0^{(L+1)} \tag{6.4.5}$$

In Eq.(6.4.5), the second term is ignored if the first coefficient c_1 is not zero. If it is, the error is represented by the second term.

The essence of the algorithm is to introduce the Taylor expansions of f_i into Eq.(6.4.4) and determine the undetermined coefficients so the error is minimized, or equivalently, the order of E becomes the highest possible.

For simplicity of further explanation, let us assume $p = 1$, $L = 3$, $\alpha = 0$, $\beta = 1$ and $\gamma = 2$. Then, Eq.(6.4.4) becomes

$$f_0' = \frac{a_0 f_0 + a_1 f_1 + a_2 f_2}{h} + E \tag{6.4.6}$$

where a_0, a_1, and a_2 are three undetermined coefficients, and $x_0 = 0$, $x_1 = h$ and $x_2 = 2h$ are abscissas of the data points. Introducing the Taylor expansions of f_1 and f_2 about $x = 0$ into Eq.(6.4.6) yields

$$f_0' = \frac{a_0}{h} f_0$$
$$+ \frac{a_1}{h} [f_0 + h f_0' + \frac{h^2}{2} f_0'' + \frac{h^3}{6} f_0''' + \dots]$$
$$+ \frac{a_2}{h} [f_0 + 2h f_0' + \frac{4h^2}{2} f_0'' + \frac{8h^3}{6} f_0''' + \dots] + E$$

or after reorganizing terms,

$$f_0' = f_0 [a_0 + a_1 + a_2] \frac{1}{h}$$
$$+ f_0' [0 + a_1 + 2a_2]$$
$$+ f_0'' [0 + a_1 + 4a_2] \frac{h}{2}$$
$$+ f_0''' [0 + a_1 + 8a_2] \frac{h^2}{6}$$
$$+ f_0'''' [0 + a_1 + 16a_2] \frac{h^3}{24}$$
$$+ \dots + E \tag{6.4.7}$$

The foregoing equation has three undetermined coefficients, which can be determined by imposing three conditions. To minimize the error, we set the coefficients of f_0, f_0' and f_0'' to 0, 1 and 0, respectively:

$$
\begin{aligned}
a_0 + a_1 + a_2 &= 0 \\
0 + a_1 + 2a_2 &= 1 \\
0 + a_1 + 4a_2 &= 0
\end{aligned}
\tag{6.4.8}
$$

By solving the foregoing equations, the three undetermined coefficients become $a_0 = -3/2$, $a_1 = 2$, and $a_2 = -1/2$.

The higher-order terms in Eq.(6.4.7) that do not vanish constitute the error, namely

$$
E \approx -f_0''' (0 + a_1 + 8a_2)\frac{h^2}{6} - f_0''''(0 + a_1 + 16a_2)\frac{h^3}{24} + \dots
\tag{6.4.9}
$$

By comparing Eq.(6.4.9) to Eq.(6.4.5), c_1 and c_2 in in the latter are found to be

$$
c_1 = -(a_1 + 8a_2)\frac{1}{6}
$$

$$
c_2 = -(a_1 + 16a_2)\frac{1}{24}
$$

which become, by introducing $a_1 = 2$ and $a_2 = -1/2$,

$$
c_1 = -(2 - \frac{8}{2})\frac{1}{6} = \frac{1}{3}
$$

$$
c_2 = -(2 - \frac{16}{2})\frac{1}{24} = \frac{1}{4}
$$

Since the first term of Eq.(6.4.5) is not zero, we ignore the second term and write the error term as

$$
E \approx \frac{1}{3}h^2 f_0'''
\tag{6.4.10}
$$

If the first term of Eq.(6.4.5) becomes zero, the second term would represent the error.

The final result of the present derivation is

$$
f_0' = \frac{-3f_0 + 4f_1 - f_2}{2h} + E
\tag{6.4.11}
$$

where E has been given by Eq.(6.4.10).

   In more general terms, using L data points, we can determine the L undetermined coefficients in Eq.(6.4.4). Thus, the error term becomes proportional to the $(L+1)$th term, or equivalently the L-th derivative, provided that its coefficient is not zero. If it is zero, the error term becomes one order higher.

   The present algorithm works even when the grid indices, α, β, ... are not integers. This means that difference approximation on a nonequispaced grid may be derived by the present algorithm. The algorithm is implemented in `diff_fnd` (see FM 6-1 in Section 6.7).

6.5   DIFFERENCE APPROXIMATION FOR PARTIAL DERIVATIVES

Difference approximation formulas for partial derivatives of multidimensional functions are essentially the same as the numerical differentiation of one-dimensional functions.

   Consider a two-dimensional function $f(x, y)$. The difference approximation for the partial derivative with respect to x, for example, can be derived by fixing y to a constant y_0 and considering $f(x, y_0)$ as a one-dimensional function. Therefore, the forward, central, and backward difference approximations for the preceding partial derivatives may be written, respectively, as

$$\begin{aligned}
f_x &\approx \frac{f(x_0 + \Delta x, y_0) - f(x_0, y_0)}{\Delta x} \\
f_x &\approx \frac{f(x_0 + \Delta x, y_0) - f(x_0 - \Delta x, y_0)}{2\Delta x} \\
f_x &\approx \frac{f(x_0, y_0) - f(x_0 - \Delta x, y_0)}{\Delta x}
\end{aligned} \tag{6.5.1}$$

where f_x means the partial derivative of f with respect to x, or equivalently

$$f_x = \frac{\partial f}{\partial x} \tag{6.5.2}$$

   The central difference approximations for the second derivatives of $f(x, y)$ at (x_0, y_0) are illustrated as

$$\begin{aligned}
f_{xx} &\approx \frac{f(x_0 + \Delta x, y_0) - 2f(x_0, y_0) + f(x_0 - \Delta x, y_0)}{\Delta x^2} \\
f_{yy} &\approx \frac{f(x_0, y_0 + \Delta y) - 2f(x_0, y_0) + f(x_0, y_0 - \Delta y)}{\Delta y^2} \\
f_{xy} &\approx \frac{f(x_0 + \Delta x, y_0 + \Delta y) - f(x_0 - \Delta x, y_0 + \Delta y)}{\Delta x \Delta y} \\
&\quad + \frac{-f(x_0 + \Delta x, y_0 - \Delta y) + f(x_0 - \Delta x, y_0 - \Delta y)}{\Delta x \Delta y}
\end{aligned} \tag{6.5.3}$$

where f_{xx}, f_{yy} and f_{xy} are shorthand notations for

$$\frac{\partial^2 f}{\partial x^2}, \quad \frac{\partial^2 f}{\partial y^2}, \quad \text{and} \quad \frac{\partial^2 f}{\partial x \partial y}$$

respectively.

6.6   NUMERICAL EVALUATION OF HIGH-ORDER DERIVATIVES

The difference approximations discussed in the previous sections are useful to evaluate derivatives of a low order, up to three or four at most. As the order of derivative becomes higher, accuracy of the difference approximations deteriorates quickly because of both truncation and rounding errors.

For a higher-order derivative, the Cauchy integral is recommended, which works for low-order as well as very high-order derivatives accurately. The Cauchy integral is given by

$$f^{(k)}(z_0) = \frac{k!}{2\pi i} \int_C \frac{f(z)}{(z - z_0)^{k+1}} \, dz \tag{6.6.1}$$

where z is a complex variable. The integral is along a closed curve C on the complex plane, in which $f(z)$ is analytic and z_0 is contained. The integration along C is in the counterclockwise direction. Integration on the complex plane is easy with MATLAB. The shape of the curve C is arbitrary, so the most convenient shape is a circle.

The circle centered at z_0 with radius r on the complex plain is

$$z = re^{i\pi\theta} + z_0, \quad 0 \le \theta < 2\pi \tag{6.6.2}$$

where θ is the angle. Substituting Eq.(6.6.2) into Eq.(6.6.1) yields

$$f^{(k)}(z_0) = \frac{k!}{2\pi i} \int_0^{2\pi} \frac{f(re^{i\pi\theta} + z_0)}{e^{i(k+1)\pi\theta}} \, d\theta \tag{6.6.3}$$

Applying the trapezoidal rule, a numerical integration for Eq.(6.6.3) becomes

$$f^{(k)}(z_0) = \frac{k!}{2\pi i} \Delta\theta \sum_{n=1}^{N} \frac{f(re^{i\pi\theta_n} + z_0)}{e^{i(k+1)\pi\theta_n}} \tag{6.6.4}$$

where $\Delta\theta = 2\pi/N$ and N is the number of intervals chosen for the numerical integration along the circle. Equation (6.6.4) may be evaluated by `Cauchy_d`. Its synopsis is

```
y = Cauchy_d('f_name', z0, k)
```

Figure CP-1
Color bars

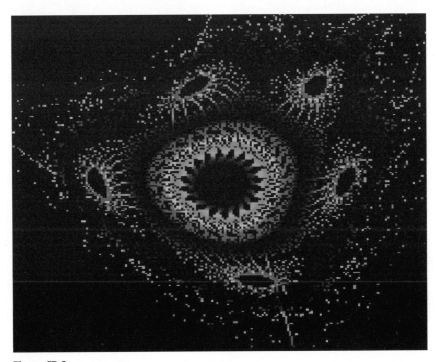

Figure CP-2
Fractal

Figure CP-3
Mobius Trilogy by Ralph Williams

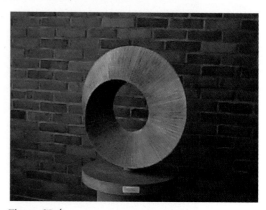

Figure CP-4
Closed Loop Drifter by Ralph Williams

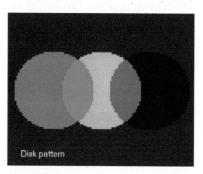

Figure CP-5
Three disks

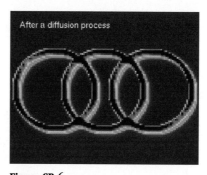

Figure CP-6
Three disks after image processing

Figure CP-7
Footage from *Mystery* (A)

Figure CP-8
Footage from *Mystery* (B)

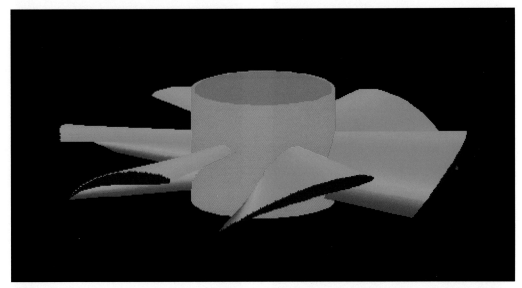

Figure CP-9
Fan rotor

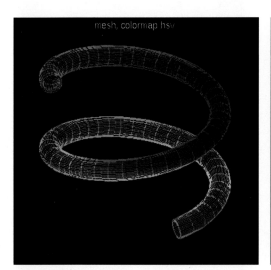

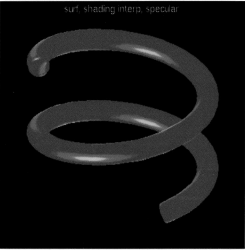

Figure CP-10
Spiral pipes

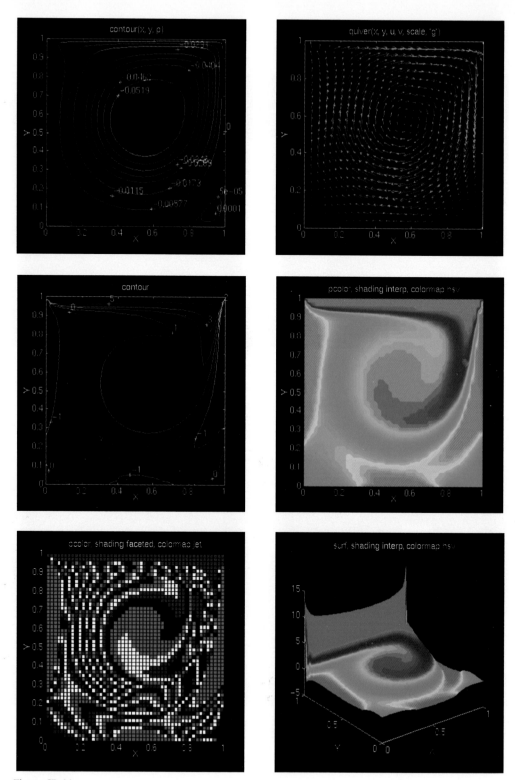

Figure CP-11

Various plots for a driven cavity flow

where 'f_name' is the function name or the m-file name that defines the function to be differentiated, z0 is z_0, and k is the order of the derivative. The values of r and N are selected by default.

We first test Cauchy_d for 1st through 15th derivatives of $\sin(x)$ for $x=0$ by the following script:

```
for k=1:15
    fd = Cauchy_d('sin', 0, k);
    fprintf(' k = %2d, real(fd)=%12.5e, imag(fd)=%12.5e\n', ...
                 k, real(fd), imag(fd))
end
```

The results are:

```
k =  1,   real(fd) =   1.00000e+00, imag(fd) =   2.29794e-18
k =  2,   real(fd) =  -2.20268e-16, imag(fd) =   6.81320e-17
k =  3,   real(fd) =  -1.00000e+00, imag(fd) =   1.32406e-16
k =  4,   real(fd) =  -4.62064e-16, imag(fd) =  -1.07578e-15
k =  5,   real(fd) =   1.00000e+00, imag(fd) =  -3.36210e-15
k =  6,   real(fd) =  -4.88113e-14, imag(fd) =   6.23025e-16
k =  7,   real(fd) =  -1.00000e+00, imag(fd) =   4.09464e-13
k =  8,   real(fd) =  -2.89743e-12, imag(fd) =   5.30509e-13
k =  9,   real(fd) =   1.00000e+00, imag(fd) =  -2.77223e-12
k = 10,   real(fd) =  -1.41163e-10, imag(fd) =   1.83930e-10
k = 11,   real(fd) =  -1.00000e+00, imag(fd) =   3.93545e-09
k = 12,   real(fd) =   3.88622e-09, imag(fd) =  -1.12962e-08
k = 13,   real(fd) =   1.00000e+00, imag(fd) =  -1.52099e-07
k = 14,   real(fd) =  -4.06359e-07, imag(fd) =   1.61043e-06
k = 15,   real(fd) =  -9.99906e-01, imag(fd) =  -3.76529e-03
```

where real(fd) and imag(fd) are real and imaginary parts of the derivative, respectively, the latter of which must be zero if error of the computation is zero. For $k = 1$, the computed derivative is correct. Although the imaginary part computed is not zero, it is a negligibly small rounding error. For order 2, the exact value of the derivative of the sine function is zero. The computed value is within a rounding error. By continuing our evaluation similarly, we find that computed derivative values are good up to order 13. Beyond 13, however, errors seem to increase rapidly as order is increased.

Accuracy of the Cauchy integral is affected by the choice of r and the number of points (in the trapezoidal rule), both of which are fixed in Cauchy_d. Readers are encouraged to investigate its effect, particularly if a very high derivative is computed.

One also is reminded that the Cauchy integral is not valid if a singularity exists within the circle.

Example 6.4

The Taylor expansions of $\tan(x)$ about $x = a$ are written as:

$$\tan(x) = \tan(a) + h\tan'(a) + \frac{h^2}{2}\tan''(a) + \frac{h^3}{6}\tan'''(a) + \ldots \frac{h^n}{n!}\tan^{(n)}(a) + \ldots$$

The truncated Taylor series

$$g_k(x) = \tan(a) + x\tan'(a) + \frac{x^2}{2}\tan''(a) + \frac{x^3}{6}\tan'''(a) + \ldots \frac{x^k}{k!}\tan^{(k)}(a)$$

is called a Taylor polynomial of order k. In order to investigate the convergence of the Taylor polynomials, set $a = 0$ and plot the series for $k = 4$, 6 and 8, for the interval of $-\pi/2 < x < \pi/2$. Plot also $e(x) = \tan(x) - g_k(x)$.

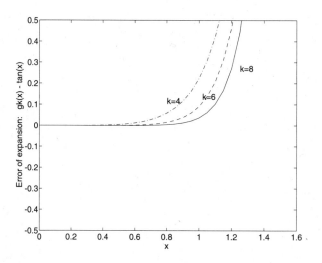

Figure 6.3 Error of truncated Taylor series

Solution

By Cauchy_d we find derivatives of $\tan(x)$ for $x = 0$:

Order of derivative	Derivative for x=0
0	0
1	1
2	0
3	2
4	0
5	16
6	0
7	272
8	0
9	7936
10	0

Figure 6.3 illustrates the error of the truncated Taylor series with $k = 4$, 6 and 8.

6.7   M-FILES

FM 6-1: Difference approximation finder
Purpose: to find a difference approximation formula.
Synopsis: fiff_fnd
　　　　All input data are prompted by the program.

fiff_fnd.m

```
%    Difference Approximation Finder
while 1
clear, clg,clc
    fprintf( '\n=============================================\n' );
    fprintf( ' Difference Approximation Finder  \n' );
    while 1
       km = input( '** Number of points ?  ' );
       if km>1 break; end
       fprintf(' Input is invalid: Repeat.\n')
    end
%
    while 1
       fprintf( 'Input the point indices in row vector form ')
       fprintf( 'like [x x ... x]');   el = input('');
       if length(el) == km;  break; end
       fprintf( ' Number of points do not match with indices')
```

```
      fprintf( ' Repeat your input for indices.')
   end
   kdr = input('** Order of difference scheme to be derived ?' );
   z = 1.0; for  i = 1:kdr;  z = z*i; end
   for k = 1:km+2;    a(k,:) = el.^(k-1); end
   M = a(1:km, 1:km);
   rs = zeros(km,1);   rs(kdr+1) = z;
%  kmp2 = km + 2;
   y = M^(-1)*rs;
           c = a*y;
   u = abs(y);
   for k = 1:km+2
       if k<=km; if u(k)<0.000001, u(k) = 1000;end; end
       if( abs( c(k) ) < 0.00000001 ) c(k) = 0;end
   end
   f_min = min(u);
          cf = y/f_min;
   fprintf( '\nDifference scheme:\n' );
   for  k = 1:km
       finv = 1.0/f_min;
       fprintf( ' +(%8.5f/( %8.5f h^%1.0f))*', cf(k),finv, kdr)
       fprintf( 'f( %3.1fh ) \n',  el(k) );
   end
   fprintf('\nError term\n');
   dd = 1.0;
   for k = 1:km
        dd = dd*k;
   end
   for k = km+1:km+2,
      cm = -c(k);
      %km1 = k - 1;
      nh = k-1-kdr;
      if( k == km+1 & cm ~= 0 )
            fprintf( '    (%7.3f/%7.3f)h^%1.0f f', cm, dd, nh );
            for (i=1:k-1)   fprintf( ''' );
            end
            break
      end
      if( k == km + 2 ),
         fprintf( '\n   +(%7.3f/%7.3f)h^%1.0f f',cm,dd,nh);
           for i=1:k-1
              fprintf( ''' );
           end
       end
       dd = dd*k ;
   end
   fprintf('\n==========================================')
   kont = input( 'Type 1 to continue, or 0 to stop:' );
   if kont ==0, break; end
end
```

FM 6-2: Differentiation by Cauchy integral
Purpose: to compute derivative values of a function.
Synopsis: Cauchy_d('f_name', x, k)
     f_name: name of the function to be differentiated
     x: the abscissa of the function
     k: order of derivative

Cauchy_d.m
```
function f_d = Cauchy_d(f_name, z0, k)
N=2480 + k*10;    r=1;
dth = 2*pi/N;
th=0:dth:2*pi-dth;
z = r*exp(i*th)+ z0;
kf=1; for m=1:k, kf=kf*m; end
f_sum  = dth*sum( feval(f_name, z)./ exp(i*k*th) );
f_d = kf/(2*pi)*f_sum/r^k;
```

FM 6-3: All derivatives of a polynomial interpolation
Purpose: to compute all derivatives of a polynomial interpolation.
Synopsis: poly_drv(xd,yd,a)
     xd: the abscissas of data points fitted by interpolation
     yd: the ordinates of data points fitted by interpolation
     a: x=a at which derivatives are to be evaluated

poly_drv.m
```
function der = poly_drv(xd,yd,a)
m = length(xd)-1;
d = polyfit(xd-a, yd, m);
c = d(m:-1:1);
fact(1)=1; for i=2:m; fact(i)=i*fact(i-1);end
der = c.*fact;
```

PROBLEMS

(6.1) A table of data points for a function $y(x)$ is given:

i	x_i m	y_i m
0	0.0	0.0
1	0.2	7.78
2	0.4	10.68
3	0.6	8.37
4	0.8	3.97
5	1.0	0.0

Evaluate all the derivatives possible at $x = 0$ and $x = 0.5$.

(6.2) The velocity distribution of a fluid near a flat surface is given by

i	y_i m	u_i m
0	0.0	0.0
1	0.002	0.006180
2	0.004	0.011756
3	0.006	0.016180
4	0.008	0.019021

Evaluate all the derivatives of $u(y)$ possible at $y = 0$.

(6.3) Evaluate the first derivative of $y(x) = \sin(x)$ for $x = 1$ by the three different schemes:

(a) $y'(1) \approx [y(1+h) - y(1)]/h$

(b) $y'(1) \approx [y(1) - y(1-h)]/h$

(c) $y'(1) \approx [y(1+h) - y(1-h)]/h$

Evaluate the errors for each of $h = 0.1, 0.05, 0.01, 0.005$, and 0.001 by comparison with the exact values.

(6.4) Calculate $df(x)/dx$, where $f(x) = \sqrt{x}$, for $x = 1$ by the forward, backward, and central difference approximations with $h = 0.1$. 0.05 and 0.025. Evaluate the error of each result by (i) comparison with the exact value, and (ii) using the error term shown in Table 6.1, namely $-(1/2)hf''$, $(1/2)hf''$, and $-(1/6)h^2f'''$, respectively.

(6.5) A difference approximation formula may be derived by differentiating a Lagrange interpolation formula, as described in Section 6.2. Suppose we have, f_{-2}, f_{-1}, f_0 with an equispaced interval, h. Develop a script in MATLAB that finds the coefficients in the difference approximation. Assume that the interval size between two consecutive points equals h. (Each term of the Lagrange interpolation may be transformed to a power form by the `polyfit` command. Then find the coefficients of the derivative of the polynomial.)

(6.6) Derive a difference approximation and the error term for f'_i in terms of (i) f_{i-1} and f_{i+2}, (ii) f_{i-1}, f_i and f_{i+2}, and (iii) f_{i-2} and f_{i+2}. Assume grid points are equispaced.

(6.7) Derive a difference approximation and the error term for f''_i in terms of f_i, f_{i-1} and f_{i-2} (three-point backward difference approximation for f''_i).

(6.8) Repeat Problem 6.2 with the second-order-accurate forward and backward difference approximations:

(a) $f'(1) \approx [-f(1+2h) + 4f(1+h) - 3f(1)]/2h$

(b) $f'(1) \approx [3f(1) - 4f(1-h) + f(1-2h)]/2h$

and evaluate the errors by comparison with the exact value of $f'(1)$.

(6.9) Calculate the first derivative $f'(1)$ for $f(x) = \sin(x)$ by the second-order-accurate forward and backward difference approximations used in Problem 6.6 for $h = 0.1$, $0.05, 0.025$, and 0.001. Then, evaluate the error of each numerical approximation by comparison with the exact value. Plot the result. If an increase of error with reduction of h is observed, explain the reason.

(6.10) A difference approximation for f''' is to be derived in terms of f_{-2}, f_{-1}, f_0, f_1 and f_2 by differentiating the Lagrange interpolation formula. Develop a script in MATLAB that answers the question. (Each term of the Lagrange interpolation may be transformed to a power form by `polyfit`. Then find the coefficients of the derivative of the polynomial.)

(6.11) Evaluate the second derivative of $\tan(x)$ at $x = 1$ by the central difference formula using $h = 0.1, 0.05$ and 0.02. Evaluate the error by comparison with the exact value and show that the error is proportional to h^2.

(6.12) (a) Knowing the error term of

$$f_i' \approx (f_i - f_{i-1})/h$$

estimate the error term for

$$f_i' \approx (f_i - f_{i-2})/2h$$

(b) Accuracy of a difference approximation can be improved by a linear combination of two difference approximations so the lowest order truncation error of each approximation is eliminated. Determine α of the following approximation so the accuracy is optimized:

$$f_i' \approx \alpha(f_i - f_{i-1})/h + (1 - \alpha)(f_i - f_{i-2})/2h$$

(6.13) Determine the optimum value of α for the following equation:

$$f_i'' \approx \alpha(f_{i+1} - 2f_i + f_{i-1})/h^2 + (1 - \alpha)(f_{i+2} - 2f_i + f_{i-2})/(2h)^2$$

Hint: eliminate the leading error of both

$$(f_{i+1} - 2f_i + f_{i-1})/h^2$$

and

$$(f_{i+2} - 2f_i + f_{i-2})/(2h)^2$$

(6.14) Derive the most accurate difference approximations for f_i' and f_i'' in terms of f_{i-2}, f_{i-1}, f_i, f_{i+1} and f_{i+2}. Assume that the data points are equispaced.

(6.15) By applying Taylor expansion, derive the difference approximations for f_i' and f_i'' in terms of f_i, f_{i+1}, f_{i+2} and f_{i+3} with the highest possible accuracy for each. Assume that the grid spacing is constant.

(6.16) A function table is given by

x	f
−0.1	4.157
0	4.020
0.2	4.441

(a) Derive the best difference approximation to calculate $f'(0)$ with the data given above.

(b) What is the error term for the difference approximation?

(c) Calculate $f'(0)$ by the formula you derived.

(6.17) Evaluate the truncation error of the following difference formula:

$$f_i'(x) \approx (-f_{i+3} + 9f_{i+1} - 8f_i)/6h$$

(6.18) Two difference approximations for the 4th derivative are given by

$$f_i'''' = \frac{f_{i+4} - 4f_{i+3} + 6f_{i+2} - 4f_{i+1} + f_i}{h^4} + O(h)$$

$$f_i'''' = \frac{f_{i+2} - 4f_{i+1} + 6f_i - 4f_{i-1} + f_{i-2}}{h^4} + O(h^2)$$

By the Taylor expansion, find the error terms.

(6.19) The velocity distribution of a fluid near a flat surface is given by

i	y_i (m)	u_i (m/s)
0	0.0	0.0
1	0.001	0.4171
2	0.003	0.9080
3	0.006	1.6180

where y is the distance from the surface and u is the velocity. Assuming that the flow is laminar and $\mu = 0.001\ Ns/m^2$, calculate the shear stress at $y = 0$ using data at the following points:

    (i) $i = 0$ and 1

    (ii) $i = 0$, 1, and 2

(6.20) The function table for $f(x, y)$ is given below:

y/x	0.0	0.5	1.0	1.5	2.0
0.0	0.0775	0.1573	0.2412	0.3309	0.4274
0.5	0.1528	0.3104	0.4767	0.6552	0.8478
1.0	0.2235	0.4547	0.7002	0.9653	1.2533
1.5	0.2866	0.5846	0.9040	1.2525	1.6348

(i) Evaluate $\partial f/\partial y$ at $x = 1.0$ and $y = 0$ using the forward difference approximation with an error of order h^2 where $h = 0.5$.

(ii) Evaluate $\partial^2 f/\partial x^2$ at $x = 1.0$ and $y = 1.0$ using the central difference approximation with an error of order h^2 where $h = 0.5$.

(iii) Evaluate $\partial^2 f/\partial x \partial y$ at $x = 0$ and $y = 0$ using the forward difference approximation with an error of order h^2 where $h = 0.5$.

Chapter 7

Roots of Nonlinear Equations

Solutions of a scalar equation, $f(x) = 0$, are called zeros or roots of $f(x)$. In this section, we study the methods, such as the graphic, bisection and Newton iteration, secant, and successive substitution methods, to find real roots of nonlinear equations. If $f(x)$ is a polynomial, we may use `roots` explained in Chapter 4. Even for polynomials, however, the methods written in this chapter often become useful when high accuracy is desired.

We also study application of successive substitution and Newton iteration to simultaneous nonlinear equations.

7.1 GRAPHICAL METHOD

Suppose we wish to find a positive root of

$$f(x) = 0 \qquad\qquad (7.1.1)$$

where

$$f(x) = x \sin(1/x) - 0.2 \exp(-x) \qquad\qquad (7.1.2)$$

If you ask a mathematician to find the solution immediately, he/she will perhaps look at the equation for a minute. After figuring out that, as x approaches 0 from the positive side of x, $\sin(1/x)$ oscillates with an increasing frequency, and becomes singular at $x = 0$, he/she would start sketching $x \sin(1/x)$ and $0.2 \exp(-x)$. After a few trials, a neat graph would be drawn, although it is done by hand drawing on a piece of scratch paper. From the figure, it would be found that there is only one root, approximately 0.4.

After this, a computer program may be used to find a more accurate value; however, the most crucial part of solution has been accomplished by the graphic method. Knowing the behavior of the function, the number of roots, and its approximate value, the rest can be done easily by a computer program, or even with a hand-held calculator.

254

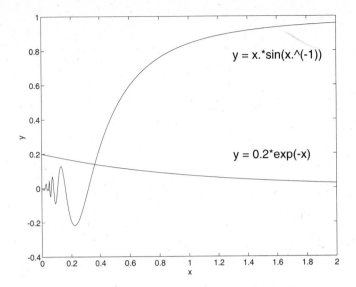

Figure 7.1 Plot of two functions

The approach of the mathematician is exactly what we will do with graphics of MATLAB. Indeed, we can easily plot $x\sin(1/x)$ and $0.2\exp(-x)$, as illustrated in Figure 7.1. Alternatively, $f(x) = x\sin(1/x) - 0.2\exp(-x)$ may be directly plotted as shown in Figure 7.2. The figures show that the root is approximately 0.38. The graphic method can still be used to find a more accurate value by zooming up the plot. It would be more efficient, however, if one of the methods discussed in the following sections is applied.

Example 7.1

The natural frequencies of vibration of a uniform beam clamped at one end is the solution of the following equation:

$$\cos(x)\cosh(x) + 1 = 0 \qquad\qquad\text{(A)}$$

where

$$x = \rho\omega^2 L/EI$$
$$L = \text{length of the beam(m)}$$
$$w = \text{frequency}(\text{s}^{-1})$$
$$EI = \text{flexural rigidity}(\text{Nm}^2)$$
$$\rho = \text{density of the beam material}(\text{kg/m}^3)$$

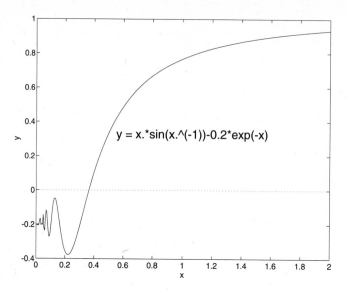

Figure 7.2 Plot of the combined function

Determine approximate values of the lowest three positive roots by the graphic method.

Solution

We first set

$$f(x) = \cos(x)\cosh(x) + 1 \qquad (B)$$

Because we know little of the function, we first plot without limits of y for $0 \le x \le 20$. The plotted graph is shown in Figure 7.3 (see List 7.1 for the script to plot). From this figure, we learn that one root is approximately $x = 17.5$, but also other roots may exist in $0 \le x < 15$.

List 7.1
```
clg;clear
x = 0:0.1:20;
y = cos(x).*cosh(x) + 1;
plot(x,y, x, zeros(x));
xlabel('x'); ylabel('y = cos(x)*cosh(x)+1')
```

While the figure plotted by the foregoing script is still on the screen, the

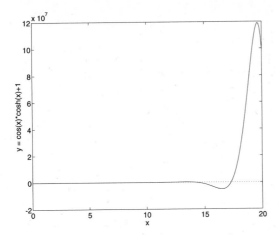

Figure 7.3 Plot of $y = \cos(x)\cosh(x) + 1$

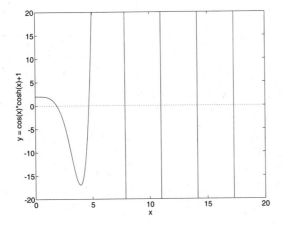

Figure 7.4 Enlarged plot of $y = \cos(x)\cosh(x) + 1$

limits of the graph may be changed by the `axis` command. For example, `axis([0 20 -10 20])` changes the graph to that shown in Figure 7.4.

By reading from Figure 7.4, the three smallest positive roots are found to be $x = 1.8$, 4.6, and 7.8, approximately.

As obvious from the example just described, the graphic method is not without difficulties and pitfalls. One problem is that a graph may be very poorly depicted in some cases. For example, quality of plot becomes poor in the vicinity of a singularity. If a graph is carelessly plotted, special features such as singular points may be hidden, so they sometimes may be confused with roots. If a singularity is suspected, zoom up the graph and then determine if the function is really singular. Another example is that, if a function is plotted with equispaced intervals, fast oscillation may not be captured, so the plotted curve may significantly misrepresent the true function. It is advisable, therefore, to plot the function several times with different zooming and focus until the function is well understood.

7.2   BISECTION METHOD

The bisection method is a simple but robust numerical method for finding one real root in a given interval where the root is known to exist. Its unique advantage is that it works even for nonanalytic functions; however, the method should be used after a graphic analysis.

Suppose that a root of $f(x) = 0$ is located in an interval between $x = a$ and $x = c$ denoted by $[a, c]$, or equivalently $a \leq x \leq c$. The bisection method is based on the fact that, when an interval $[a, c]$ has a root, the sign of $y(x)$ at the two end points are opposite, namely $f(a)f(c) < 0$ (see Figure 7.5). The first step of this method is to bisect the interval $[a, c]$ into two halves, namely, $[a, b]$ and $[b, c]$ where $b = (a + c)/2$ (see mark 1 in Figure 7.5). By checking the signs of $f(a)f(b)$ and $f(b)f(c)$, the half interval that has the root can be found. Indeed, if $f(a)f(b) \leq 0$, then the interval $[a, b]$ including $x = a$ and $x = b$ has the root, otherwise the root is in the other interval $[b, c]$. The new interval containing the root is bisected again. As this procedure is repeated, the size of the interval containing the root becomes smaller and smaller. In each step, the midpoint of the interval is taken as the most updated approximation for the root. The iteration is stopped when the half interval size is less than a given tolerance.

The interval size after n iteration steps becomes

$$\frac{c_0 - a_0}{2^n} \tag{7.2.1}$$

where a_0 and c_0 are initial values of a and c, so the numerator is the initial interval size. Equation (7.2.1) also represents the maximum possible error when the root is approximated by the n-th midpoint. Therefore, if the tolerance for the error is given by τ, the number of iteration steps required is the smallest integer n satisfying

$$\tau \geq \frac{c_0 - a_0}{2^n} \tag{7.2.2}$$

or equivalently

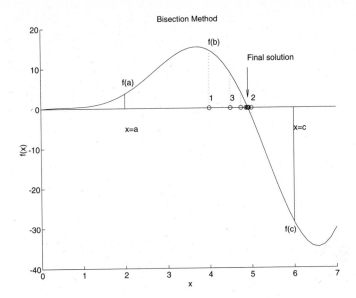

Figure 7.5 Bisection method (Plotted by `bisec_g`)

$$n \geq \frac{\log\left(\frac{c_0 - a_0}{\tau}\right)}{\log(2)} \tag{7.2.3}$$

where τ is the tolerance. For example, if $c_0 - a_0 = 1$ and $\tau = 0.0001$, then $n = 14$.

Two functions, `bisec_g`, and `bisec_n` may be used for bisection computations. The former graphically displays the progress of bisection iteration, the final plot of which is illustrated in Figure 7.5. The latter does not plot a graph but is faster.

The synopsis for `bisec_g` is as follows:

```
bisec_g('f_name', a, c, xmin, xmax, n_points)
```

where `f_name` is the name of the function that defines the equation to be solved, and a and c are end points of the initial interval, `xmin` and `xmax` are minimum and maximum x values of the graph, and `n_points` is the number of points to plot the function. The tolerance is set to $\tau = 10^{-6}$ by default.

The synopsis of `bisec_n` is

```
bisec_n('f_name', a, c)
```

Example 7.2

Find the intersection of the following two functions:

$$y = \sqrt{x^2 + 1}$$
$$y = \tan(x), \quad 0 < x < \pi/2$$

Solution

The problem is equivalent to finding a zero of

$$f = \sqrt{x^2 + 1} - \tan(x), \quad 0 < x < \pi/2 \qquad \text{(A)}$$

By plotting the function, we find the root is approximately $x = 0.9$. To use bisec_n (or bisec_g), we write a function M-file to define Eq.(A):

```
function f = fun_ex2(x)
f = sqrt(1+x.^2) - tan(x);
```

Then, bisec_n is used as

```
bisec_n('fun_ex2', 0.8, 1.0)
```

The output is:

```
Bisection Scheme:
It. a         b         c         f(a)       f(b)       f(c)
 1 0.800000 0.900000 1.000000  0.250986   0.085204  -0.143194
 2 0.900000 0.950000 1.000000  0.085204  -0.019071  -0.143194
 3 0.900000 0.925000 0.950000  0.085204   0.035236  -0.019071
 4 0.925000 0.937500 0.950000  0.035236   0.008660  -0.019071
 5 0.937500 0.943750 0.950000  0.008660  -0.005056  -0.019071
 6 0.937500 0.940625 0.943750  0.008660   0.001838  -0.005056
 7 0.940625 0.942187 0.943750  0.001838  -0.001600  -0.005056
 8 0.940625 0.941406 0.942187  0.001838   0.000122  -0.001600
 9 0.941406 0.941797 0.942187  0.000122  -0.000738  -0.001600
10 0.941406 0.941602 0.941797  0.000122  -0.000308  -0.000738
11 0.941406 0.941504 0.941602  0.000122  -0.000093  -0.000308
12 0.941406 0.941455 0.941504  0.000122   0.000014  -0.000093
13 0.941455 0.941479 0.941504  0.000014  -0.000040  -0.000093
14 0.941455 0.941467 0.941479  0.000014  -0.000013  -0.000040
15 0.941455 0.941461 0.941467  0.000014   0.000001  -0.000013
16 0.941461 0.941464 0.941467  0.000001  -0.000006  -0.000013
17 0.941461 0.941463 0.941464  0.000001  -0.000003  -0.000006
18 0.941461 0.941462 0.941463  0.000001  -0.000001  -0.000003
19 0.941461 0.941462 0.941462  0.000001   0.000000  -0.000001
Tolerance is satisfied.
Final result: Root = 0.941462
```

7.3 NEWTON ITERATION

Newton iteration is an iterative scheme to find a root of a nonlinear equation. It is applicable on the complex domain to find a complex root, as well as extendable to simultaneous nonlinear equations, as described in more detail in Section 7.6.

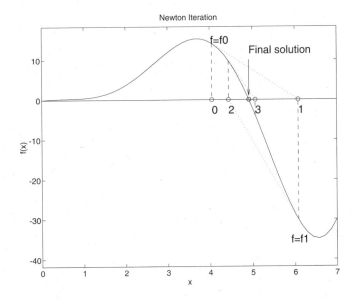

Figure 7.6 Newton iteration

Newton iteration is derived by Taylor expansion. Suppose the problem is to find a root of $f(x) = 0$. The first order truncated Taylor expansion of $f(x)$ about an initial estimate, x_0, is written by

$$f(x) \approx f(x_0) + f'(x_0)(x - x_0) \tag{7.3.1}$$

which is regarded as an approximation for $f(x)$. By setting Eq.(7.3.1) to zero, the next approximation is obtained as

$$x_1 = x_0 - \frac{f(x_0)}{f'(x_0)}$$

The same process is repeated by

$$x_n = x_{n-1} - \frac{f(x_{n-1})}{f'(x_{n-1})} \tag{7.3.2}$$

The algorithm is also graphically illustrated in Figure 7.6. For the initial value x_0, the line passing through (x_0, f_0) tangentially is drawn. The intersection of the tangential line with the x-axis is x_1. Then, the line passing through (x_1, f_1) tangentially is drawn. The same procedure is repeated, using the most updated value as a guess for the next iteration cycle.

Deriving the first derivative of a given function could be cumbersome if not impossible. In such a case $f'(x)$ in Eq.(7.3.2) may be evaluated by a difference approximation rather than analytically. For example, $f'(x_{n-1})$ may be approximated by

$$f'_{n-1} = \frac{f(x_{n-1} + h) - f(x_{n-1})}{h} \tag{7.3.3}$$

or

$$f'_{n-1} = \frac{f(x_{n-1}) - f(x_{n-1} - h)}{h} \tag{7.3.4}$$

where h is a small value (such as $h = 0.001$ for most exercise problems). Equation (7.3.3) and (7.3.4) are the forward and backward difference approximations, respectively. Small errors in the difference approximation have no noticeable effect on the convergence rate of Newton iteration. Accuracy of the final result is not affected by the error of a difference approximation; however, when a singularity is near the root, difference approximation needs to be used with much caution.

Example 7.3

Derive an iterative scheme to find the cubic root of a number based on Newton iteration. Find the cubic root of $a = 155$ by the scheme derived.

Solution

The problem is to find the zero of

$$f(x) = x^3 - a$$

Newton iteration is written as

$$x_{n+1} = x_n - \frac{f(x_n)}{f'(x_n)}$$

$$= x_n - \frac{x_n^3 - a}{3x_n^2}$$

$$= 0.666x_n + \frac{a}{3x_n^2}$$

We set $a = 155$ and an initial guess to $x_0 = 5$. The iteration proceeds as

List 7.1a

```
n       x
0       5
1       5.4
2       5.371834
3       5.371686 (exact)
```

The exact solution is obtained after only three iteration steps. We try again with a much poorer initial guess of $x_0 = 10$:

List 7.1b

```
n       x
0       10
1       7.183334
2       5.790176
3       5.401203
4       5.371847
5       5.371686 (exact)
```

The exact value of the cubic root is obtained with five iteration steps.

Two functions, Newt_g, and Newt_n (listed in Section 7.7), solve nonlinear equations by Newton iteration. The former displays the procedure of Newton iteration graphically, while the latter performs only computations. The synopses are

```
Newt_g('f_name', x0, xmin, xmax, n_points)
Newt_n('f_name', x0)
```

where f_name is the name of the function M-file that defines the equation to be solved, and x0 is an initial guess for the root. The meanings of xmin, xmax, and n_points are the same as for bisec_g.

For illustration purpose, we define the equation to be solved by

$$y = (0.01x + 1)\sin(x) - (x - 0.01)/(x^2 + 1) - 0.0096$$

The foregoing equation is written in an M-file named eqn_1.m listed in FM7-3. Then, we execute Newt_n('eqn_1', 4). The output becomes

```
Newton Iteration
 Type name of the function (enclosed with single quote):
       'eqn_1'
 f_name =
       eqn_1
 Type initial guess of the root: 4
 n=  1, x= 2.36795e+00, y = -1.031e+00,   yd = -6.319e-01
 n=  2, x= 2.92631e+00, y =  3.488e-01,   yd = -6.247e-01
 n=  3, x= 2.82370e+00, y = -9.467e-02,   yd = -9.226e-01
 n=  4, x= 2.82171e+00, y = -1.774e-03,   yd = -8.895e-01
 n=  5, x= 2.82170e+00, y = -4.498e-06,   yd = -8.888e-01
 n=  6, x= 2.82170e+00, y = -9.553e-09,   yd = -8.888e-01
       Final answer = 2.82170e+00
```

The output of Newt_g is identical to that of Newt_n except the former plots a graph of progress. Indeed, Figure 7.6 was plotted by Newt_g('eqn_1', 4, 0 , 7, 50) for this example.

Example 7.4

Imagine a brick wall of thickness 0.05 m. The inner wall temperature of the wall, T_0, is 625 K, but the outer surface temperature, T_1, is unknown. The heat loss from the outer surface is due to convection as well as radiation. The temperature T_1 is determined by the equation

$$f(T_1) \equiv \frac{k}{\Delta x}(T_1 - T_0) + \varepsilon\sigma(T_1^4 - T_\infty^4) + h(T_1 - T_f) = 0 \qquad \text{(A)}$$

where

k: thermal conductivity of the wall, 1.2 W/mK

ε: emissivity, 0.8

T_0:   inner wall temperature, 625 K

T_1:   outer wall temperature (unknown), K

T_∞:   temperature of the surrounding environment, 298 K

T_f: temperature of the air, 298 K

h: heat transfer coefficient, 20 W/m^{2}K

σ: Stefan-Boltzmann constant, 5.67×10^{-8} W/m^{2}K^4

Δx: thickness of the wall, 0.05 m

Determine T_1 by Newton iteration.

Solution

We solve the problem by Newt_g. The equation to be solved is written in a function M-file as shown:

```
List 7.2
function  f = wall_ht(T1)
k =1.2; e = 0.8; Tinf = 298;
Tf=298; h = 20; T0=625;
sig = 5.67E-8 ; wall_thick = 0.05;
f = k/wall_thick*(T1-T0) +e*sig*(T1.^4-Tinf^4)   ...
                        + h*(T1 - Tf);
```

After saving the foregoing function M-file, we execute the following command:

```
Newt_g('wall_ht', 550,400,600, 50)
```

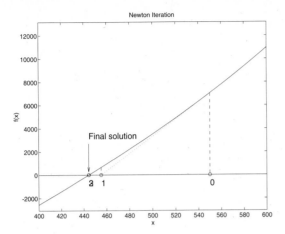

Figure 7.7 $f(T_1)$ vs T_1

The result is:

```
Newton Iteration
  n=   0,   x= 5.50000e+02,   y= 7.03301e+03
  n=   1,   x= 4.55199e+02,   y= 6.58551e+02
  n=   2,   x= 4.44423e+02,   y= 6.44623e+00
  n=   3,   x= 4.44316e+02,   y= 6.27680e-04
  n=   4,   x= 4.44316e+02,   y= 5.70253e-10
  ans =
    444.3157
```

The final answer is $T_1 = 444.3$ K. The graphic output is shown in Figure 7.7, where x and y denote T_1 and $f(T_1)$ respectively.

7.4 SECANT METHOD

The secant method is a variant of Newton iteration. We have used a difference approximation to evaluate f' in Newton iteration; however, f' can also be evaluated approximately using the past two consecutive values of f. The iterative scheme based on this concept is written as

$$x_n = x_{n-1} - f_{n-1} \frac{x_{n-1} - x_{n-2}}{f_{n-1} - f_{n-2}}, \quad n = 2, 3, \dots$$

To start the iteration, x_0 has to be specified. The value of x_1 may be set arbitrarily to $x_1 = x_1 + \Delta x$, where Δx is an arbitrarily small number such as 0.01, for example. Then, the iteration can be continued until a tolerance is satisfied.

Example 7.5

A bullet of $M = 0.002$ kg has been shot vertically into the air and is descending at its terminal speed.[1] The terminal speed is determined by $gM = F_{\text{drag}}$, where g is gravity and M is the mass, and the whole equation is written, after evaluating the constants, as

$$(0.002)(9.81) = 1.4 \times 10^{-5}v^{1.5} + 1.15 \times 10^{-5}v^2 \qquad \text{(A)}$$

where v is the terminal velocity, m/s. The first term on the right side represents the friction drag and the second term represents the pressure drag. Determine the terminal velocity by the secant method. A crude guess is given by $v \approx 30$ m/s.

Solution

The task is to find the root of

$$f(v) = (0.002)(9.81) - 1.4 \times 10^{-5}v^{1.5} - 1.15 \times 10^{-5}v^2 \qquad \text{(B)}$$

We set $v_0 = 30$ and $v_1 = 30.1$, based on the crude guess given, and compute f_0 and f_1 by Eq.(B). The iterative solution is shown below:

```
n         v            f(v)
0      30.00000      1.9620001E-02
1      30.10000      6.8889391E-03
2      30.15411      6.8452079E-03
3      38.62414     -8.9657493E-04
4      37.64323      9.0962276E-05
5      37.73358      9.9465251E-07
6      37.73458     -1.8626451E-09
```

Thus, the terminal velocity is $v = 37.7$ m/s.

7.5   SUCCESSIVE SUBSTITUTION METHOD

The term *successive substitution* method refers to a large class of iterative solution schemes for nonlinear equations. Newton iteration and the secant method may be viewed as an application of successive substitution. Since successive substitution is employed in many numerical algorithms to solve nonlinear equations including differential equations and simultaneous nonlinear equations, we introduce some fundamental aspects of it in this section.

---

[1]Please don't shoot bullets into the air: many people are wounded every year by randomly shot bullets.

If the equation to be solved, $f(x) = 0$, is rearranged to the form

$$x = g(x) \tag{7.5.1}$$

then an iterative scheme may be written as

$$x_n = g(x_{n-1}) \tag{7.5.2}$$

where n is the number of iteration steps and x_0 is an initial guess. This method is called the successive substitution method, or *fixed-point iteration*.

The advantage of this method is its simplicity and flexibility in choosing the form of $g(x)$. The disadvantage, however, is that the iteration does not always converge for an arbitrarily chosen form of $g(x)$. To insure convergence of the iteration, the following condition must be satisfied:

$$|g'(x)| < 1 \tag{7.5.3}$$

Figure 7.8 illustrates how $g'(x)$ affects the convergence of the iterative method. It can be observed that the convergence is asymptotic if $0 < g' < 1$, and oscillatory if $-1 < g' < 0$. Otherwise, the iteration diverges. Furthermore it can be shown easily that the convergence rate becomes fastest as g' approaches 0.

Example 7.6

The function

$$y = x^2 - 3x + e^x - 2 \tag{A}$$

is known to have two roots, one negative and one positive. Find the smaller root by successive substitution.

Solution

By checking the sign of y at $x = -1$ and $x = 0$ (namely $y(-1) = 2.367$ and $y(0) = -1$), we locate the smaller root in $-1 < x < 0$. We rewrite the given equation to

$$x = g(x) = \frac{x^2 + e^x - 2}{3} \tag{B}$$

Then, an iterative scheme is written as

$$x_n = g(x_{n-1}) \tag{C}$$

The first derivative of $g(x)$ satisfies Eq. (7.5.3) in the range of $-1 < x < 0$, so the scheme is convergent. The results of iteration are shown next:

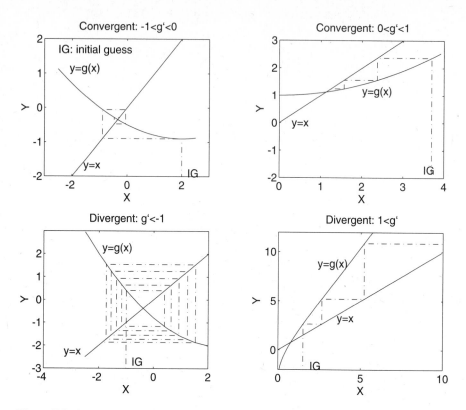

Figure 7.8 Convergence of successive substitution method. (IG denotes an initial guess.)

Iteration Count	Successive Approx.
n	x(n)
0	0 (initial guess)
1	-0.333333
2	-0.390786
3	-0.390254
4	-0.390272
5	-0.390272

Alternative equations are

$$x = -\sqrt{3x - e^x + 2} \qquad\qquad \text{(D)}$$

and

$$x = \sqrt{3x - e^x + 2} \qquad \text{(E)}$$

Equations (D) and (E), however, have discontinuities in the vicinity of the smaller root. Furthermore, the first derivatives of both equations violate the condition of Eq. (7.5.3). Therefore, neither equation works.

One systematic way of finding a form of $g(x)$ is to set

$$g(x) = x - \alpha f(x) \qquad \text{(7.5.4)}$$

so the iterative scheme becomes

$$x_n = x_{n-1} - \alpha f(x_{n-1}) \qquad \text{(7.5.5)}$$

where α is a constant. The constant α may be determined as follows: By substituting Eq.(7.5.5) into Eq.(7.5.3), it is seen that iteration converges when

$$-1 < 1 - \alpha f'(x) < 1 \qquad \text{(7.5.6)}$$

or equivalently

$$0 < \alpha f'(x) < 2 \qquad \text{(7.5.7)}$$

The foregoing equation indicates that first, α must have the same sign as f', and second, the convergence rate is optimal when $\alpha \approx 1/f'$.

The present scheme reduces to Newton iteration if α is set to $1/f'(x_n)$ for each iteration.

Example 7.7

The critical size of a nuclear reactor is determined by a criticality equation. Suppose a simple version of the criticality equation is given by

$$\tan(0.1x) = 9.2e^{-x} \qquad \text{(A)}$$

The solution that is physically meaningful is the smallest positive root satisfying $3 < x < 4$. Determine the smallest positive root.

Solution

We apply the iterative scheme of Eq.(7.5.5) to

$$f(x) = \tan(0.1x) - 9.2e^{-x} \qquad \text{(B)}$$

An approximate value of f' in $3 < x < 4$ is estimated by

$$f' \approx \frac{f(4) - f(3)}{4 - 3} = 0.40299 \qquad (C)$$

Then, the parameter α is set to

$$\alpha = \frac{1}{0.40299} \qquad (D)$$

The iteration of Eq.(7.5.5) converges as follows:

Iteration number n	Iterative solution x
0	4.00000
1	3.36899
2	3.28574
3	3.29384
4	3.28280
5	3.29293
6	3.29292
7	3.29292

7.6   SIMULTANEOUS NONLINEAR EQUATIONS

The necessity to solve simultaneous nonlinear equations occurs rather frequently. We introduce two methods of solving simultaneous nonlinear equations.

Successive substitution iteration: If the given system of nonlinear equations represents a natural phenomenon or engineering system, they often become linear when the magnitude of the solution is small. Such a nonlinear system may be written in the same form as the linear system except that the coefficients are dependent on the solution.

Iterative solution for a nonlinear system based on successive substitution may be written as

$$\mathbf{A}_{n-1}\mathbf{x}_n = \mathbf{y} \qquad (7.6.1)$$

where $\mathbf{A}_{n-1}$ is a matrix representing the coefficients that is computed by the previous solution; $\mathbf{x}_n$ is the n-th iterative solution; and $\mathbf{y}$ is an inhomogeneous term that may be also a function of the solution.

Initially, the coefficient matrix is computed using an initial guess for the solution. Once the coefficient matrix is determined, the equation is solved as a linear system. After the solution is obtained, the coefficient matrix is revised and the equation is solved again. If instability occurs during iteration, use under-relaxation:

$$\mathbf{x}_n = \omega \mathbf{A}_{n-1}^{-1}\mathbf{y} + (1 - \omega)\mathbf{x}_{n-1} \qquad (7.6.2)$$

where ω is an under-relaxation parameter satisfying $0 < \omega < 1$.

Example 7.8

Electric heating elements are connected as shown in Figure 7.9. The resistance of the j-th heating element is a function of temperature and is given by

$$R_j = a_j + b_j T_j + c_j T_j^2 \qquad (A)$$

where a_j, b_j and c_j are constants, and T_j is the temperature of the j-th element, in Kelvin. The temperature of each heating element is determined by

$$I_j^2 R_j = A_j \sigma \left(T_j^4 - T_\infty^4\right) + A_j h(T_j - T_\infty) \qquad (B)$$

where T_∞ is the temperature of the surrounding environment. See Example 7.4 for other notations. Equation (B) is an energy equation that includes the effects of the heat generated, and convection and radiation heat transfer. Discuss how the present problem may be solved.

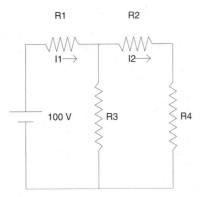

Figure 7.9 Circuit of heating elements

Solution

The electric currents I_1 and I_2 satisfy

$$(R_1 + R_3)I_1 - R_3 I_2 = 100$$
$$-R_3 I_1 + (R_2 + R_4 + R_3)I_2 = 0 \qquad \text{(C)}$$

The foregoing equations are nonlinear because each resistance is a function of temperature, while temperature is, in turn, a function of current and resistance. If the temperature is low, the nonlinear effects vanish and the equations become linear. Therefore, the algorithm may be developed as follows: Solve the electric current equation first with cold values of resistances. Solve Eq.(B) for the temperature. Calculate the resistance of each resistor as a function of temperature by Eq.(A). Repeat solution of Eq.(C) using the updated values of the resistances. The whole procedure is repeated until the solution for every quantity converges.

Newton Iteration: Nonlinear equations may be linearized by Taylor expansion. Suppose the system of equations is in the form

$$f_i(x_1, \ x_2, \dots, x_n) = 0, \ i = 1, 2, \dots n \qquad (7.6.3)$$

where f_i is a nonlinear function of x_j. If we know an initial guess for the solution, the solution may be written as

$$x_j = \hat{x}_j + \Delta x_j \qquad (7.6.4)$$

where $\hat{x}_j$ is the initial guess and Δx_j is an unknown correction. If we expand Eq.(7.6.3) into a first-order truncated Taylor polynomial about $\hat{x}_j$, we get

$$\sum_j \frac{\partial f_i}{\partial x_j} \Delta x_j = -f_i(\hat{x}_1, \ \hat{x}_2, \ \dots \hat{x}_n) \qquad (7.6.5)$$

where the partial derivatives are evaluated with the initial guesses. Equation (7.6.5) may be written in a matrix form as

$$J \Delta x = -f \qquad (7.6.6)$$

where **J** is the Jacobian matrix given by

$$\mathbf{J} = \left[\frac{\partial f_i}{\partial x_j} \right] \qquad (7.6.7)$$

and

$$\Delta \mathbf{x} = \begin{bmatrix} \Delta x_1 \\ \Delta x_2 \\ \cdots \\ \Delta x_n \end{bmatrix} \qquad \mathbf{f} = \begin{bmatrix} f_1(\hat{x}_1, \ \hat{x}_2, \ \ldots \hat{x}_n) \\ f_2(\hat{x}_1, \ \hat{x}_2, \ \ldots \hat{x}_n) \\ \cdots \\ f_n(\hat{x}_1, \ \hat{x}_2, \ \ldots \hat{x}_n) \end{bmatrix} \qquad (7.6.8)$$

The partial derivatives may be evaluated by a difference approximation, for example,

$$\frac{\partial f_i}{\partial x_j} \approx \frac{f_i(\hat{x}_1, \ \ldots, \ \hat{x}_j + \delta x_j, \ldots \hat{x}_n) \ - \ f_i(\hat{x}_1, \ \ldots, \ \hat{x}_j, \ldots \ \hat{x}_n)}{\delta x_j} \qquad (7.6.9)$$

where δx_j is an arbitrarily chosen small value.

Example 7.9

Using the method described in this section, find the solutions of

$$f_1(x, y) = f_2(x, y) = 0$$

where

$$f_1(x, y) = x \exp(xy + 0.8) + \exp(y^2) - 3$$
$$f_2(x, y) = x^2 - y^2 - 0.5 \exp(xy)$$

satisfying $x > 0$.

Solution

We first plot $f_1(x, y) = 0$ and $f_2(x, y) = 0$ in Figure 7.10 by the following script based on the plotting technique mentioned in Section 2.3.

List 7.3
```
clear, clg, hold off
x1 = 0:0.1:2;
y1 = -2:0.1:2;
[x,y] = meshgrid(x1,y1);
f1 = f_f1(x,y) ;
f2 = f_f2(x,y) ;
contour(f1, [0.00, 0.00], x1,y1)
hold on
contour(f2, [0.00, 0.00], x1,y1)
xlabel(x); ylabel(y)
```

f_f1.m
```
function f = f_f1(x,y)
f = x.*exp(x.*y+0.8)   + exp(y.^2)  - 3;
```

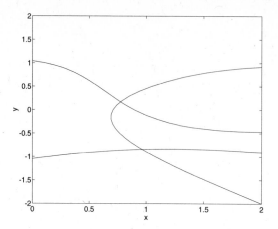

Figure 7.10 Graphic solution for Example 7.9

f_f2.m
```
function f = f_f2(x,y)
f = x.^2 - y.^2 - 0.5*exp(x.*y);
```

The curves in Figure 7.10 indicate that there are two roots in the positive domain of x; one is approximately ($x = 0.8, y = 0.2$) and the other is ($x = 1, y = -0.8$). We find more accurate solutions by Newton iteration. A script is in List 7.4.

List 7.4
```
% Newton Iteration 2D
clear,clg, fprintf('\n')
dx = 0.01; dy = 0.01;
x = input('Initial guess for x? ');
y = input('Initial guess for y? ');
for n=1:50
  s = [x,y];
  xp = x + dx;
  yp = y + dy;
  J(1,1) = (f_f1(xp, y) - f_f1(x,y))/dx;
  J(1,2) = (f_f1(x, yp) - f_f1(x,y))/dy;
  J(2,1) = (f_f2(xp, y) - f_f2(x,y))/dx;
  J(2,2) = (f_f2(x, yp) - f_f2(x,y))/dy;
  f(1) = f_f1(x,y);
  f(2) = f_f2(x,y);
  ds = - J\f';
  x = x + ds(1);
  y = y + ds(2);
fprintf('n=%2.0f,   x=%12.5e,   y=%12.5e', n,x,y)
fprintf('f(1)=%10.2e,  f(2)=%10.2e\n', f(1), f(2))
```

```
        if (abs(f(1))<1.0e-9 & abs(f(2))<1.0e-9), break; end
    end
```

The output of Newton iteration is:

```
Initial guess for x? 1
Initial guess for y? 1
n=1, x= 9.237e-01, y= 5.828e-01 f(1)= 5.77e+00, f(2)=-1.36e+00
n=2, x= 8.086e-01, y= 3.295e-01 f(1)= 1.93e+00, f(2)=-3.43e-01
n=3, x= 7.754e-01, y= 2.009e-01 f(1)= 4.64e-01, f(2)=-1.07e-01
n=4, x= 7.748e-01, y= 1.729e-01 f(1)= 5.81e-02, f(2)=-2.33e-02
n=5, x= 7.749e-01, y= 1.716e-01 f(1)= 1.92e-03, f(2)=-1.26e-03
n=6, x= 7.749e-01, y= 1.716e-01 f(1)= 2.24e-05, f(2)=-1.82e-05
n=7, x= 7.749e-01, y= 1.716e-01 f(1)= 2.69e-07, f(2)=-2.30e-07
n=8, x= 7.749e-01, y= 1.716e-01 f(1)= 3.31e-09, f(2)=-2.87e-09
n=9, x= 7.749e-01, y= 1.716e-01 f(1)= 4.10e-11, f(2)=-3.58e-11


Initial guess for x? 1
Initial guess for y? -1
n=1, x= 9.863e-01, y=-8.815e-01 f(1)= 5.37e-01, f(2)=-1.84e-01
n=2, x= 9.695e-01, y=-8.489e-01 f(1)= 9.53e-02, f(2)=-1.38e-02
n=3, x= 9.687e-01, y=-8.476e-01 f(1)= 3.43e-03, f(2)=-3.75e-04
n=4, x= 9.687e-01, y=-8.477e-01 f(1)=-6.65e-05, f(2)= 1.98e-05
n=5, x= 9.687e-01, y=-8.477e-01 f(1)= 1.45e-06, f(2)=-3.67e-07
n=6, x= 9.687e-01, y=-8.477e-01 f(1)=-3.14e-08, f(2)= 8.20e-09
n=7, x= 9.687e-01, y=-8.477e-01 f(1)= 6.82e-10, f(2)=-1.77e-10
```

A summary of the solutions is:

```
    x = 0.7749, y = 0.1716
    x = 0.9687, y =-0.8477
```

7.7   M-FILES

FM 7-1: Bisection
Purpose: To find a root of a function
Synopsis: `bisec_n('f_name', a, b)`
       `f_name`: the name of the function in single quote signs.
       `a` and `b`: end points of the initial interval
Example: `bisec_n('eqn_w3', 0, 1.3)`

bisec_n.m

```
function bisec_n(f_name, a,c)
f_name
%       a, c : end points of initial interval
%       tolerance : tolerance
%       it_limit : limit of iteration number
%       Y_a, Y_c : y values of the current end points
%       fun_f(x) : functional value at x
fprintf( 'Bisection Scheme\n\n' );
```

```
tolerance = 0.000001;   it_limit = 30;
fprintf( ' It.  a              b              c         fa=f(a)    ');
fprintf( '  fc=f(c)      abs(fc-fa) \n' );
it = 0;
Y_a = feval(f_name, a ); Y_c = feval(f_name, c );
if ( Y_a*Y_c > 0 )
    fprintf( '\n \n Stopped because   f(a)f(c) > 0 \n' );
else
   while 1
      it = it + 1;
      b = (a + c)/2;  Y_b = feval(f_name, b );
      fprintf('%3.0f %10.6f, %10.6f', it, a, b );
      fprintf('%10.6f,  %10.6f, %10.6f', c, Y_a, Y_c );
      fprintf( ' %12.3e\n', abs((Y_c - Y_a)));
      if ( abs(c-a)/2<=tolerance )
         fprintf( '  Tolerance is satisfied. \n' );break
            fprintf( '\n Change a or b and run again.\n' );
      end
      if ( it>it_limit )
         fprintf( 'Iteration limit exceeded.\n' ); break
      end
      if( Y_a*Y_b <= 0 )     c = b;    Y_c = Y_b;
      else                   a = b;    Y_a = Y_b;
      end
   end
   fprintf('Final result: Root = %12.6f \n', b );
end
```

eqn_w3.m

```
function y = eqn_w3(x)
   y = sqrt(x^2 + 1) - tan(x);
```

FM 7-2: Bisection method with graphics

Purpose: To find a root of a function and display the iterative process.

Synopsis: `bisec_g('f_name', a, b, xmin, xmax,n_points )`

    f_name: the name of the function.

    a and b: end points of the initial interval

    xmin, xmax: minimum and maximum x coordinates of the graph

    b_points: number of points used to plot the curve

Example: `bisec_g('dem_bs', 2, 6, 0, 7, 100)` (see Figure 7.5).

bisec_g.m

```
function bisec_g(f_name, a,c, xmin, xmax, n_points)
f_name
%       a, c : end points of initial interval
%       tolerance : tolerance
%       it_limit : limit of iteration number
%       Y_a, Y_c : y values of the current end points
%       fun_f(x) : functional value at x
clg, hold off
```

```
clear Y_a, clear Y_c
wid_x = xmax - xmin;  dx = (xmax- xmin)/n_points;
xp=xmin:dx:xmax;    yp=feval(f_name, xp);
plot(xp,yp); xlabel('x');ylabel('f(x)');
title('Bisection Method'),hold on
ymin=min(yp); ymax=max(yp);wid_y = ymax-ymin;
yp=0.*xp;  plot(xp,yp)
fprintf( 'Bisection Scheme\n\n' );
tolerance = 0.000001;  it_limit = 30;
fprintf( ' It.  a           b           c          fa=f(a)   ');
fprintf( '  fc=f(c)    abs(fc-fa) \n' );
it = 0;
Y_a = feval(f_name, a ); Y_c = feval(f_name, c );
plot([a,a],[Y_a,0]); text(a,-0.1*wid_y,'x=a')
plot([c,c],[Y_c,0]); text(c,-0.1*wid_y,'x=c')
if ( Y_a*Y_c > 0 )  fprintf( '   f(a)f(c) > 0 \n' );
else
   while 1
      it = it + 1;
      b = (a + c)/2;  Y_b = feval(f_name, b );
      plot([b,b],[Y_b,0],':'); plot(b,0,'o')
      if it<4, text(b, wid_y/20, [num2str(it)]), end
       fprintf('%3.0f %10.6f, %10.6f', it, a, b );
      fprintf('%10.6f,  %10.6f, %10.6f', c, Y_a, Y_c );
      fprintf( ' %12.3e\n', abs((Y_c - Y_a) ));
      if ( abs(c-a)<=tolerance )
         fprintf( '  Tolerance is satisfied. \n' );break
      end
      if ( it>it_limit )
        fprintf( 'Iteration limit exceeded.\n' ); break
      end
      if( Y_a*Y_b <= 0 )     c = b;    Y_c = Y_b;
      else                   a = b;    Y_a = Y_b;
      end
   end
   fprintf('Final result: Root = %12.6f \n', b );
end
x=b;
plot([x x],[0.05*wid_y 0.2*wid_y])
text( x, 0.25*wid_y, 'Final solution')
plot([x (x-wid_x*0.004)],[0.05*wid_y  0.09*wid_y])
plot([x (x+wid_x*0.004)],[0.05*wid_y  0.09*wid_y])
```

dem_bs.m
```
function y = dem_bs(x)
y = (1 - x.*cos(x)).*x;
```

FM7-3: Newton iteration with no graphics

Purpose: Solves a nonlinear equation by Newton iteration.

Synopsis: Newt_n('f_name', x0)

  f_name: name of the function that defines the nonlinear equation

  x0: initial guess

Example: `Newt_n('eqn_1', 2)`

Newt_n.m

```
function x = Newt_n(f_name, x0)
% Newton iteration with no graphics
x = x0; xb=x-999;
n=0;   del_x = 0.01;
while abs(x-xb)>0.000001
    n=n+1;    xb=x;
    if n>300 break; end
    y=feval(f_name, x);
    y_driv=(feval(f_name, x+del_x) - y)/del_x;
    x = xb - y/y_driv;
    fprintf(' n=%3.0f, x=%12.5e, y = %12.5e, ', n,x,y)
    fprintf(' yd = %12.5e \n', y_driv)
end
fprintf('\n     Final answer = %12.6e\n', x);
```

eqn_1.m

```
function y = eqn_1(x)
y = (0.01*x + 1).*sin(x) ...
      - (x - 0.01).*(x.^2 +1).^(-1) - 0.0096;
```

FM7-4: Newton iteration with graphics

Purpose: To solve a nonlinear equation by Newton iteration.

Synopsis: `Newt_g(f_name, x0, xmin, xmax, n_points)`

    f_name: name of the function that defines the nonlinear equation

    x0: initial guess

    xmin, xmax: minimum and maximum x coordinates of the graph

    b_points: number of points used to plot the curve

Example: `Newt_g('eqn_1', 2, 0, 5, 50)`

Newt_g.m

```
function x = Newt_g(f_name, x0, xmin, xmax, n_points)
clg, hold off
% Newton_Method with graphic illustration
del_x=0.001;
wid_x = xmax - xmin;   dx = (xmax- xmin)/n_points;
xp=xmin:dx:xmax;     yp=feval(f_name, xp);
plot(xp,yp); xlabel('x');ylabel('f(x)');
title('Newton Iteration'),hold on
ymin=min(yp); ymax=max(yp);wid_y = ymax-ymin;
yp=0.*xp;   plot(xp,yp)
x = x0;    xb=x+999; n=0;
while abs(x-xb)>0.000001
   if n>300 break; end
   y=feval(f_name, x);     plot([x,x],[y,0]); plot(x,0,'o')
   fprintf(' n=%3.0f,   x=%12.5e,   y=%12.5e\n', n,x,y);
   xsc=(x-xmin)/wid_x;
   if n<4, text(x, wid_y/20, [ num2str(n)]), end
   y_driv=(feval(f_name, x+del_x) - y)/del_x;
```

```
    xb=x;
    x = xb - y/y_driv; n=n+1;
    plot([xb,x],[y,0])
end
plot([x x],[0.05*wid_y 0.2*wid_y])
text( x, 0.2*wid_y, 'Final solution')
plot([x (x-wid_x*0.004)],[0.01*wid_y  0.09*wid_y])
plot([x (x+wid_x*0.004)],[0.01*wid_y  0.09*wid_y])
```

PROBLEMS

(**7.1**) Determine approximate values of the solutions of the following equations by the graphic method:

$$\text{(a)} \ \ 0.5 \exp(x/3) - \sin(x) = 0, \ x > 0$$
$$\text{(b)} \ \ \log(1+x) - x^2 = 0$$

(**7.2**) Find all the positive solutions of the following equations approximately by the graphic method:

$$\text{(a)} \ \ \tan(x) - x + 1 = 0, \quad 0 < x < 3\pi$$
$$\text{(b)} \ \ \sin(x) - 0.3e^x = 0, \quad x > 0$$
$$\text{(c)} \ \ 0.1x^3 - 5x^3 - x + 4 + e^{-x} = 0$$
$$\text{(d)} \ \ \log(x) - 0.2x^2 + 1 = 0$$
$$\text{(e)} \ \ x + (x^2 + 3x^{-1}) = 0$$

(**7.3**) Calculate $\tan^{-1}(3.5)$ in the interval $[0,\pi]$ by the bisection method. (*Hint*: solve $\tan(x) = 3.5, 0 \geq x \geq \pi$)

(**7.4**) Repeat Problem 7.1 by the bisection method.

(**7.5**) The surface configuration of the NACA 0012 airfoil of chord length 1 m and maximum thickness of 0.2 m is given by

$$y(x) = \pm[0.2969\sqrt{x} - 0.126x - 0.3516x^2 + 0.2843x^3 - 0.1015x^4]$$

where + and − signs refer to upper and lower surfaces, respectively. The design engineer has to find the following information:

(a) The x coordinate where the airfoil thickness become the maximum.
(b) The x and y coordinates of the airfoil where thickness becomes half of the maximum.

Find the answers by the bisection method.

(7.6) A design engineer has to find the coordinates of the intersections of the NACA 0012 airfoil surface (given in the previous problem) and the curve given by

$$y(x) = 0.2x(x - 0.6)$$

Compute the value by a method of your choice.

(7.7) One kilogram mole of CO is contained in a vessel at $T = 215$ K and $p = 70$ bars. Calculate the volume of the gas using the van der Waals equation of state for a non-ideal gas given by

$$\left(P + \frac{a}{v^2}\right)(v - b) = RT$$

where $R = 0.08314$ bar m^3/(kg mol K), $a = 1.463$ bar m^6/(kg mol)^2 and $b = 0.0394$ m^3/kg. Determine the specific volume v (m^3/kg) and compare the result to the volume calculated by the ideal gas equation, $Pv = RT$. You can choose any solution method.

(7.8) Find the positive roots of the following functions by Newton iteration:

(a) $f(x) = 0.5 \exp(x/3) - \sin(x)$, $x > 0$
(b) $f(x) = \log(1 + x) - x^2$
(c) $f(x) = \exp(x) - 5x^2$
(d) $f(x) = x^3 + 2x - 1$
(e) $f(x) = \sqrt{x + 2} - x$

(7.9) The following equation has two positive roots, one of which is very close to a singular point:

$$y = \exp(x) - 1/\sin(x)$$

(a) Find both positive roots by Newton iteration using analytically differentiated derivative.
(b) Repeat (a) using difference approximation given by Eq.(7.3.3) or Eq.(7.3.4)
(c) State what efforts are necessary for both approaches in order to find the two roots successfully.

(7.10) Two ellipses have zero to four intersections[2] as illustrated in Figure 7.11. The following equations represent two ellipses. Find coordinates of intersections by a graphic method first and then by Newton iteration. *Hint*: Eliminate x or y and work with a single unknown.

$$(x - 2)^2 + (y - 3 + 2x)^2 = 5$$
$$2(x - 3)^2 + (y/3)^2 = 4$$

---

[2]This problem was provided by Professor S.V. Sreenivasan of University of Texas, Austin, TX.

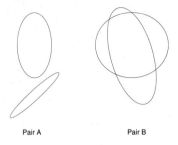

Pair A   Pair B

Figure 7.11 Two ellipses

(7.11) The natural frequencies of vibration of a uniform beam clamped at one end and free at the other end are solutions of

$$\tan(\beta L)\tanh(\beta L) + 1 = 0 \qquad\qquad\text{(A)}$$

where

$\beta = \rho\omega^2/EI$
$L = 1$ (length of the beam), m
ω = frequency, s^{-1}
EI = flexural rigidity, Nm^2
ρ = density of the beam material, kg/m^3

Investigate the β values that satisfy Eq.(A) first by the graphic method and then determine the lowest three values of β satisfying Eq.(A) by Newton iteration.

(7.12) An equimolar mixture of carbon monoxide and oxygen is to attain equilibrium at 300 K and 5 bar pressure. The theoretical reaction is

$$CO + (1/2)O_2 \leftrightarrow CO_2$$

The actual chemical reaction is written as

$$CO + N_2 \rightarrow xCO + (1/2)(1 + x)O_2 + (1 - x)CO_2$$

The chemical equilibrium equation to determine the fraction of remaining CO, namely x, is given by

$$K_p = \frac{(1 - x)\sqrt{10.52 + x}}{x\sqrt{1 + x}\sqrt{P}},\ 0 < x < 1$$

where $K_p = 3.06$ is the equilibrium constant for $CO + (1/2)O_2 = CO_2$ at 3000 K, and $P = 5$ bar. Determine the value of x by Newton iteration.

(7.13) Consider the same chemical reaction as in the previous problem, except that it occurs with the existence of N_2 at atmospheric pressure. The reaction is

$$CO + O_2 + 3.76N_2 \rightarrow xCO + \frac{1}{2}(1+x)O_2 + (1-x)CO_2 + 3.76N_2$$

The equation of equilibrium is

$$3.06 = \frac{(1-x)\sqrt{10.52+x}}{x\sqrt{1+x}}$$

Determine the value of x using Newton iteration.

(7.14) The equation $x^2 - 2x - 3 = 0$ may be reformulated for the successive substitution method as follows:

(a) $x = (x^2 - 3)/2$
(b) $x = \sqrt{2x + 3}$
(c) $x = (2x + 3)/\sqrt{x}$
(d) $x = x - 0.2(x^2 - 2x - 3)$

The solutions of the equation are $x = 3$ and $x = -1$. Determine graphically which formulas above converge when used for successive substitution to find the root, $x = -1$. Verify the results of the graphic approach by the criterion of Eq.(7.5.3). Repeat the same analysis for $x = 3$.

(7.15) Find all the solutions of the equations in Problem 7.2 using successive substitution in the form

$$x = x - \alpha f(x)$$

Hint: Determine α using the gradient of the linear interpolation fitted to the two end points of the interval found in problem 7.4.

(7.16) The friction factor f for the turbulent flows in a pipe is given by

$$\frac{1}{\sqrt{f}} = 1.14 - 2\log_{10}\left(\frac{e}{D} + \frac{9.35}{Re\sqrt{f}}\right)$$

named Colebrook correlation, where Re is the Reynolds number, e is the roughness of the pipe surface, and D is the pipe diameter.[3] (a) Write a computer program to solve the equation for f using the successive substitution method. (b) Evaluate f by running the program for the following cases:

1. $D = 0.1\ m$, $e = 0.0025$, $Re = 3 \times 10^4$
2. $D = 0.1\ m$, $e = 0.0001$, $Re = 5 \times 10^6$

---

[3] See Fox and McDonald, *Introduction to Fluid Mechanics*, 4th ed., John Wiley, 1992

Hint: Rewrite the equation to the following form first:

$$f = \left[1.14 - 2\log_{10}\left(\frac{e}{D} + \frac{9.35}{Re\sqrt{f}} \right) \right]^{-2}$$

Introduce an initial guess to f on the right side. Reintroduce f calculated to the right side again, and repeat this iteration until f converges. The initial guess may be set to zero. The results of the calculations can be checked with a Moody's chart in a fluid mechanics text.

Chapter 8

Curve Fitting to Measured Data

Curve fitting means to fit a function $g(x)$ to a set of given data, (x_i, y_i), $i = 1, 2, ..., L$. The function $g(x)$ can be a polynomial, nonlinear function, or a linear combination of known functions. The function $g(x)$ selected for curve fitting must have a certain number of undetermined coefficients. In general, the number of data points to be fitted, L, is much greater than the number of undetermined coefficients, k. Therefore, the principle of determining the coefficients is based on minimization of the discrepancies between the determined function and the data points and named the *least square method*. In the special case of $L = k$, the curve fitting reduces to an interpolation problem because the fitted curve passes through the data points.

8.1 LINE FITTING

Suppose we desire to fit a linear function to the data set, as illustrated in Table 8.1. The line fitted to a data set is called a *regression line*.

Table 8.1 Sample data set

i	x	y
1	0.1	0.61
2	0.4	0.92
3	0.5	0.99
4	0.7	1.52
5	0.7	1.47
6	0.9	2.03

The linear function is expressed by

$$g(x) = c_1 x + c_2 \tag{8.1.1}$$

where c_1 and c_2 are undetermined constants. Since the number of data points is greater than two, the line cannot be fitted to every point, but is determined by minimizing the discrepancies between the line and data. Deviation of the line from data points is defined by

$$r_i = y_i - g(x_i) = y_i - (c_1 x_i + c_2), \quad i = 1, 2, \dots L \qquad (8.1.2)$$

where L is the total number of data points (6 in this example), and c_1 and c_2 are the constants to be determined.

The sum of the squared deviations is

$$R = \sum_{i=1}^{L} r_i^2 = \sum_{i=1}^{L} (y_i - c_1 x_i - c_2)^2 \qquad (8.1.3)$$

The minimum of R occurs if partial derivatives of R with respect to c_1 and c_2 become zero:

$$\frac{\partial R}{\partial c_1} = -2 \sum_{i=1}^{L} x_i (y_i - c_1 x_i - c_2) = 0$$

$$(8.1.4)$$

$$\frac{\partial R}{\partial c_2} = -2 \sum_{n=1}^{L} (y_i - c_1 x_i - c_2) = 0$$

Equation (8.1.4) may be rewritten as

$$\begin{bmatrix} a_{1,1} & a_{1,2} \\ a_{2,1} & a_{2,2} \end{bmatrix} \begin{bmatrix} c_1 \\ c_2 \end{bmatrix} = \begin{bmatrix} z_1 \\ z_2 \end{bmatrix}, \qquad (8.1.5)$$

where

$$a_{1,1} = \sum_{i=1}^{L} x_i^2$$

$$a_{1,2} = a_{2,1} = \sum_{i=1}^{L} x_i$$

$$a_{2,2} = \sum_{i=1}^{L} 1 = L$$

$$z_1 = \sum_{i=1}^{L} x_i y_i$$

$$z_2 = \sum_{i=1}^{L} y_i$$

The solution of Eq.(8.1.5) is

$$c_1 = (a_{2,2}z_1 - a_{1,2}z_2)/(a_{1,1}a_{2,2} - a_{1,2}a_{2,1})$$

$$c_2 = (a_{1,1}z_2 - a_{2,1}z_1)/(a_{1,1}a_{2,2} - a_{1,2}a_{2,1})$$

An equivalent way of determining the coefficients is to consider the problem as an *over-determined* linear equation, as explained in Section 3.4. If every data point in Table 8.1, for example, satisfies Eq.(8.1.1), we write

$$c_1 x_i + c_2 = y_i, \quad i = 1, 2, ... L$$

or

$$Ac = y \tag{8.1.6}$$

where

$$A = \begin{bmatrix} 0.1 & 1 \\ 0.4 & 1 \\ 0.5 & 1 \\ 0.7 & 1 \\ 0.7 & 1 \\ 0.9 & 1 \end{bmatrix}, \quad c = \begin{bmatrix} c_1 \\ c_2 \end{bmatrix}, \quad y = \begin{bmatrix} 0.61 \\ 0.92 \\ 0.99 \\ 1.52 \\ 1.47 \\ 2.03 \end{bmatrix}$$

Equation (8.1.6) is called an over-determined linear equation because the number of equations, L, is greater than the number of unknowns. To find the solution, Eq. (8.1.6) is premultiplied by the transpose of A:

$$A^t A c = A^t y \tag{8.1.7}$$

Since $A^t A$ becomes a 2-by-2 square matrix, and $A^t y$ becomes a vector of length 2, Eq.(8.1.7) is a regular 2-by-2 problem (indeed, it is identical to Eq.(8.1.5). The solution is obtained by

```
c = (A'*A)\(A'*y)
```

The foregoing solution agrees with Eq.(8.1.6).

An over-determined equation can also be solved in MATLAB simply by

```
c = A\y
```

The same can be achieved by `polyfit`, too. Suppose x and y are the data sets to be fitted, then

```
c = polyfit(x,y,1)
```

will return the coefficients, c_1 and c_2 in the vector c, where "1" in the third place of the argument is the order of polynomial fitted, which is unity for line fitting.

Example 8.1

Determine the regression line for the data in Table 8.1 by (i) solving Eq.(8.1.5), and (ii) using the polyfit command. After the regression line is obtained, examine the deviation of the line from the data.

Solution

We calculate the coefficients of Eq.(8.1.5) as follows:

	a_{21}	z_2	a_{11}	z_1
i	x_i	y_i	x_i^2	$x_i y_i$
1	0.1	0.61	0.01	0.061
2	0.4	0.92	0.16	0.368
3	0.5	0.99	0.25	0.495
4	0.7	1.52	0.49	1.064
5	0.7	1.47	0.49	1.029
6	0.9	2.03	0.81	1.827
Total	3.3	7.54	2.21	4.844

From the foregoing table, we get

$$a_{1,1} = 2.21, a_{1,2} = 3.3, z_1 = 4.844$$
$$a_{2,1} = 3.3, a_{2,2} = 6, z_2 = 7.54$$

Thus, Eq.(8.1.5) becomes

$$\begin{bmatrix} 2.21 & 3.3 \\ 3.3 & 6 \end{bmatrix} \begin{bmatrix} c_1 \\ c_2 \end{bmatrix} = \begin{bmatrix} 4.844 \\ 7.54 \end{bmatrix} \qquad (A)$$

The solution is

$$c_1 = 1.7645, \ c_2 = 0.2862$$

The regression line therefore becomes

$$g(x) = 1.7645x + 0.2862 \qquad (B)$$

Figure 8.1 plots Eq.(B) with the data points.
We now solve the same problem again using the polyfit command. The script has only three lines, as follows:

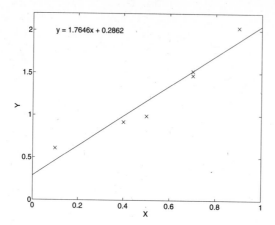

Figure 8.1 The line fitted to the data

```
x = [0.1,   0.4,   0.5,   0.7    0.7    0.9]
y = [0.61, 0.92, 0.99, 1.52, 1.47, 2.03]
c = polyfit(x,y,1)
```

The result is:

```
c =
        1.7646      0.2862
```

which is identical to the coefficients of Eq.(B).

Deviation of the fitted line is analyzed as follows:

i	$x(i)$	$y(i)$	$g = c_1 x + c_2$	Deviation
1	.1	.61	0.4626	0.14738
2	.4	.92	0.9919	-0.07198
3	.5	.99	1.1684	-0.17844
4	.7	1.52	1.5213	-0.00135
5	.7	1.47	1.5213	-0.05135
6	.9	2.03	1.8742	0.15574

8.2 NONLINEAR CURVE FITTING WITH A POWER FUNCTION

For some data types, fitting the power function given by

$$g(x) = \beta x^{\alpha} \qquad\qquad (8.2.1)$$

may be suitable where α and β are undetermined coefficients. To determine the coefficients, we first take the logarithm of Eq.(8.2.1):

$$\log(g) = \alpha \log(x) + \log(\beta) \qquad (8.2.2)$$

With definitions

$$G = \log(g) \qquad (8.2.3)$$
$$c_1 = \alpha \qquad (8.2.4)$$
$$c_2 = \log(\beta) \qquad (8.2.5)$$
$$X = \log(x) \qquad (8.2.6)$$

Eq.(8.2.2) becomes

$$G = c_1 X + c_2 \qquad (8.2.7)$$

Then, the problem is reduced to line regression, as described in Section 8.1. Equation (8.2.7) is fitted to the data set, $(\log(y_i), \log(x_i))$.

Example 8.2[1]

A data set plotted in Figure 8.2 is given by

```
x = [0.15,   0.4,    0.6,    1.01,   1.5,    2.2,    2.4,    2.7,
     2.9,    3.5,    3.8,    4.4,    4.6,    5.1,    6.6,    7.6]
y = [4.4964,5.1284,5.6931,6.2884,7.0989,7.5507,7.5106,8.0756,
     7.8708,8.2403,8.5303,8.7394,8.9981,9.1450,9.5070,9.9115]
```

Fit the data by the power function.

Solution

The MATLAB script may be developed as follows:

List 8.1
```
x = [0.15,   0.4,    0.6,    1.01,   1.5,    2.2,    2.4,    ...
     2.7,    2.9,    3.5,    3.8,    4.4,    4.6,    5.1,    ...
     6.6,    7.6]
y = [4.4964,5.1284,5.6931,6.2884,7.0989,7.5507,7.5106,  ...
     8.0756,7.8708,8.2403,8.5303,8.7394,8.9981,9.1450,  ...
     9.5070,9.9115]
c = polyfit(log(x),  log(y),1)
```

The script yields
```
c =
        0.2093     1.8588
```

[1]This example was provided by Professor Y. Guezennec of The Ohio State University.

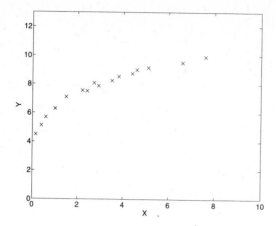

Figure 8.2 Plot of data points

The constants of the power function become

$$\alpha = c_1 = 0.2093$$

$$\beta = \exp(c_2) = \exp(1.8588) = 6.4160$$

Finally, the power form becomes

$$g(x) = \beta x^\alpha = 6.4160 x^{0.2093}$$

The data set and the fitted curve are plotted in three different ways in Figure 8.3.

8.3   CURVE FITTING WITH A HIGHER-ORDER POLYNOMIAL

The principle of least square can be extended to fitting a higher-order polynomial to measured data. An n-th order polynomial is written as

$$g(x) = c_1 x^n + c_2 x^{n-1} + \ldots + c_{n+1} \tag{8.3.1}$$

Deviation of the curve from each data point is

$$r_i = y_i - g(x_i), \quad i = 1, 2, \ldots L \tag{8.3.2}$$

where L is the number of data points. The sum of the squared deviations is

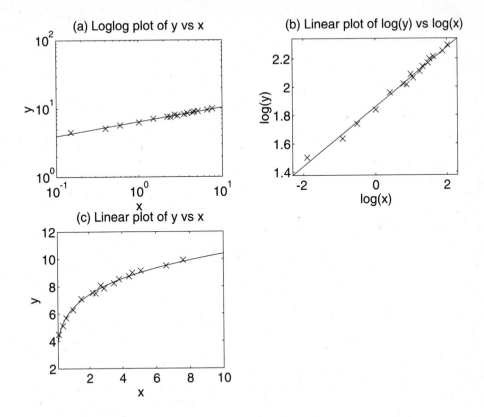

Figure 8.3 Fitted function and data points (plotted in three different ways)

$$R = \sum_{i=1}^{L} r_i^2 \tag{8.3.3}$$

In order to minimize R, we set the partial derivatives of R with respect to c_j to zero:

$$\frac{\partial R}{\partial c_j} = 0, \quad j = 1, 2, ..., n+1 \tag{8.3.4}$$

or equivalently

$$\sum_{j=1}^{n+1} \left(\sum_{i=1}^{L} x_i^{2n+2-j-k} \right) c_j = \sum_{i=1}^{L} x_i^{n+1-k} y_i, \quad k = 1, 2, ... n+1 \tag{8.3.5}$$

or equivalently in matrix form as

$$
\begin{bmatrix}
\sum\limits_{i=1}^{L} x_i^{2n} & \sum\limits_{i=1}^{L} x_i^{2n-1} & \cdot & \sum\limits_{i=1}^{L} x_i^{n} \\
\sum\limits_{i=1}^{L} x_i^{2n-1} & \cdot & \cdot & \sum\limits_{i=1}^{L} x_i^{n-1} \\
\cdot & \cdot & \cdot & \cdot \\
\sum\limits_{i=1}^{L} x_i^{n} & \cdot & \cdot & \sum\limits_{i=1}^{L} x_i^{0}
\end{bmatrix}
\begin{bmatrix}
c_1 \\ c_2 \\ \cdot \\ c_{n+1}
\end{bmatrix}
=
\begin{bmatrix}
\sum\limits_{i=1}^{L} x_i^{n} y_i \\
\sum\limits_{i=1}^{L} x_i^{n-1} y_i \\
\cdot \\
\sum\limits_{i=1}^{L} y_i
\end{bmatrix}
\qquad (8.3.6)
$$

An equivalent way of deriving Eq.(8.3.6) is to start with an over-determined equation. The matrix form of the equation is

$$Ac = y \qquad (8.3.7)$$

where

$$
A = \begin{bmatrix}
x_1^n & x_1^{n-1} & \cdot & 1 \\
x_2^n & \cdot & \cdot & 1 \\
\cdot & \cdot & \cdot & \cdot \\
x_L^n & \cdot & \cdot & 1
\end{bmatrix},
\qquad
c = \begin{bmatrix} c_1 \\ c_2 \\ \cdot \\ c_{n+1} \end{bmatrix},
\qquad
y = \begin{bmatrix} y_1 \\ y_2 \\ \cdot \\ y_L \end{bmatrix}
$$

When $L > n+1$, the equation is over-determined because the number of equations is greater than the number of undetermined coefficients. Premultiplying both sides by A^t yields

$$A^t A c = A^t y \qquad (8.3.8)$$

which equals Eq.(8.3.6) and can be solved as a regular problem by

```
c = (A'*A)\(A'*y)
```

In MATLAB, the solution of Eq.(8.3.7) can be obtained simply by

```
c = A\y
```

As already mentioned in Section 8.1, another equivalent but simpler way of finding coefficents of a polynomial fitted to a data set is by means of `polyfit`:

```
c = polyfit(x,y,n)
```

Example 8.3

Fit the following data set by a quadratic polynomial:

```
x = [0.1, 0.4, 0.5, 0.7, 0.7, 0.9];
y = [0.61, 0.92, 0.99, 1.52, 1.47, 2.03];
```

and plot both data set and the fitted curve.

Solution

We find the coefficients of the quadratic polynomial by the polyfit command, and then plot the curve. A script to complete the answer is as follows:

List 8.2
```
clear, clg
x = [0.1, 0.4, 0.5, 0.7, 0.7, 0.9];
y = [0.61, 0.92, 0.99, 1.52, 1.47, 2.03];
cc = polyfit(x,y,2)
xx = x(1):0.1:x(length(x))
yy = polyval(cc,xx)
plot(xx,yy); hold on
plot(x,y,'x')
axis([0, 1, 0, 3])
xlabel('X')
ylabel('Y')
```

The plot of the result is shown in Figure 8.4.

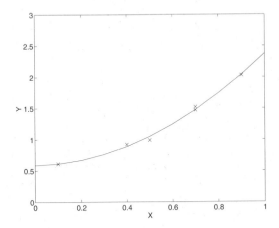

Figure 8.4   Plot of the quadratic polynomial fitted

The linear equations in curve fitting can become ill-conditioned. This occurs if (1) the abscissas of the data points include both very small and very large numbers, or (2) when the order of the polynomial is high. A high-order polynomial is not desirable because the polynomial may oscillate just as a high-order polynomial is not desirable for interpolation.

8.4   CURVE FITTING BY A LINEAR COMBINATION OF KNOWN FUNCTIONS

In fitting a function to data points, a linear combination of any known functions, including polynomials, may be used:

$$g(x) = c_1 f_1(x) + c_2 f_2(x) + c_3 f_3(x) + ... + c_k f_k(x) \qquad (8.4.1)$$

where f_1, f_2, .. are prescribed functions, c_1, c_2, .. are undetermined coefficients, and k is the total number of prescribed functions. By fitting Eq.(8.4.1) to each data point, an over-determined equation is written as

$$Ac = y \qquad (8.4.2)$$

with

$$A = \begin{bmatrix} f_1(x_1) & f_2(x_1) & . & f_k(x_1) \\ f_1(x_2) & f_2(x_2) & . & f_k(x_2) \\ . & . & . & . \\ f_1(x_L) & f_2(x_L) & . & f_k(x_L) \end{bmatrix}$$

$$c = \begin{bmatrix} c_1 \\ c_2 \\ . \\ c_k \end{bmatrix}$$

$$y = \begin{bmatrix} y_1 \\ y_2 \\ . \\ y_L \end{bmatrix}$$

where $L > k$. The coefficients are determined by

```
c = A\y
```

Any function may be used for f in Eq.(8.4.1). Knowledge, experience and trials help select appropriate functions for linear combination.

Example 8.4

Determine the coefficients of the function

$$g(x) = c_1 + c_2 x + c_3 \sin(\pi) + c_4 \sin(2\pi x)$$

fitted to the data in the following table:

x	y
0.1	0.61
0.4	0.92
0.5	0.99
0.7	1.52
0.7	1.47
0.9	2.03

Solution

The solution algorithm is implemented in List 8.3. The curve determined is plotted in Figure 8.5.

List 8.3

```
clc; clear; clg
data=[   0.1   0.61;
         0.4   0.92;
         0.5   0.99;
         0.7   1.52;
         0.7   1.47;
         0.9   2.03]
x = data(:,1);    y = data(:,2);
A(:,1)=ones(x);    A(:,2)=x;    A(:,3)=sin(x);    A(:,4)=exp(x);
c = A\y
xx = 0:0.01:1;
g= c(1)*ones(xx) + c(2)*xx + c(3)*sin(xx) + c(4)*exp(xx);
axis('square');
plot(x, y,'*', xx, g);   xlabel('x'); ylabel('y')
```

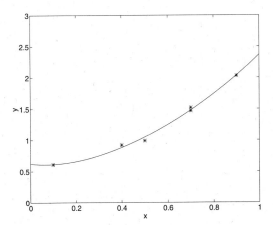

Figure 8.5 Plot of the linearly combined functions

PROBLEMS

(8.1) Determine a line fitted to the following data set by the least square method. (Work by hand calculation first and then verify the answer with `polyfit`.)

i	x_i	y_i
1	1.0	2.0
2	1.5	3.2
3	2.0	4.1
4	2.5	4.9
5	3.0	5.9

(8.2) Using MATLAB, determine a linear function fitted to the following data set by solving an over-determined linear equation. Verify the result by `polyfit`.

i	x_i	y_i
1	0.1	9.9
2	0.2	9.2
3	0.3	8.4
4	0.4	6.6
5	0.5	5.9
6	0.6	5.0
7	0.7	4.1
8	0.8	3.1
9	0.9	1.9
10	1.0	1.1

(8.3) The data set below is to be fitted by

$$y = \alpha \exp(\beta x)$$

Determine the constants. Plot the curve with the data on a linear scale as well as on a log scale.

x	y
0.0129	9.5600
0.0247	8.1845
0.0530	5.2616
0.1550	2.7917
0.3010	2.2611
0.4710	1.7340
0.8020	1.2370
1.2700	1.0674
1.4300	1.1171
2.4600	0.7620

(8.4) Prove that Eq.(8.1.7) is equivalent to Eq.(8.1.5).

(8.5) (a) Fit a quadratic polynomial to the following data set using `polyfit` command.
(b) Plot the determined polynomial with the data.

i	x_i	y_i
1	0	0
2	1	2.3
3	2	4.2
4	3	5.7
5	4	6.5
6	5	6.9
7	6	6.8

(8.6) Repeat the previous problem with 1st order and 3rd order polynomials.

(8.7) Fit polynomials of order 1, 2, and 3 to the following data set and compare deviations of the three polynomials. Plot the polynomial with the data.

x_i	y_i
0	0
.002	0.618
.004	1.1756
.006	1.6180
.008	1.9021

(8.8) Fit a cubic polynomial to the following data. Plot the polynomial with the data.

i	x_i	y_i
1	0	0
2	0.2	7.78
3	0.4	10.68
4	0.6	8.37
5	0.8	3.97
6	1	0

(8.9) Fit

$$g(x) = c_1 + c_2 x + c_3 \sin(\pi x) + c_4 \sin(2\pi x)$$

to the following data. Plot $g(x)$ with the data.

i	$x(i)$	$y(i)$
1	.1	0.0000
2	.2	2.1220
3	.3	3.0244
4	.4	3.2568
5	.5	3.1399
6	.6	2.8579
7	.7	2.5140
8	.8	2.1639
9	.9	1.8358

Chapter 9

Spline Functions and Nonlinear Interpolation

This chapter presents three subjects; namely, b-spline, c-spline, and nonlinear interpolation. The c-spline function consists of piecewise cubic polynomials that fit to given data points. It is suitable to fit a smooth curve to a set of a large number of data points. The cubic b-spline function consists of piecewise cubic polynomials that do not fit to the data poins exactly, but its purpose is to generate smooth curves that are eye-pleasing. The nonlinear interpolation methods are useful when an exponential behavior of the fitted function is desired.

9.1 C-SPLINE INTERPOLATION

An incentive for the *c-spline* (cubic spline) interpolation is illustrated by the question: How can a large number of points on the x-y plane, such as shown in Figure 9.1, be fitted by a smooth curve?

Attempts to fit a single polynomial to a large data set will fail. The reason is that, as the number of points increases, error of the Lagrange interpolation increases rapidly.

The essence of the c-spline interpolation is to apply a cubic polynomial to each interval between two consecutive data points. The first and second derivatives of the cubic polynomials, however, also are required to be continuous across each data point. Therefore, all of the functional value, first derivative and second derivative become continuous in the entire domain. To determine the coefficients of the cubic polynomial for each interval, however, the coefficients for all the intervals must be determined simultaneously.

In order to fit a c-spline function $f(s)$ to data points (s_i, f_i), the following quantities are involved:

$$s_i, \ i = 1, 2, ..., n : \ \text{known}$$
$$f_i, \ i = 1, 2, ..., n : \ \text{known}$$
$$f_i', \ i = 1, 2, ..., n : \ \text{to be determined}$$

$$f_i'', \quad i = 1, 2, ..., n : \quad \text{to be determined}$$

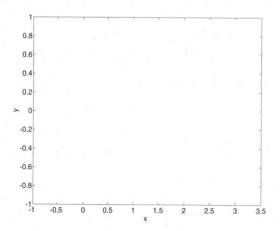

Figure 9.1 Points to be connected by a smooth curve

Consider one interval, $s_i < s < s_{i+1}$ with $h_i = s_{i+1} - s_i$, as shown in Figure 9.2. Using the local coordinate $t = s - s_i$, a cubic polynomial for one interval may be written as

$$f(t) = a + bt + ct^2 + et^3 \tag{9.1.1}$$

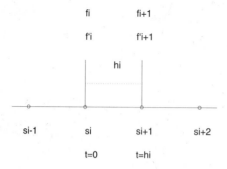

Figure 9.2 An interval between two data points for c-spline

where $0 \leq t \leq h_i$.

We first require $f(t)$ to equal the known value of the function $f(t)$ at $t = 0$ and $t = h_i$:

$$f_i = a \tag{9.1.2}$$

$$f_{i+1} = a + bh_i + ch_i^2 + eh_i^3 \tag{9.1.3}$$

The foregoing two equations are insufficient to determine the four constants, a, b, c, and e. If two more conditions are specified, however, the equations to determine the constants will be closed. These conditions are provided by the requirements that f'' and f' become continuous across each point. If this is achieved, the entire curve will become continuous in the function fitted, first and second derivatives.

The second derivative of Eq.(9.1.1) is

$$f''(t) = 2c + 6et \tag{9.1.4}$$

which becomes, at points i and $i + 1$, respectively,

$$f_i'' = 2c \tag{9.1.5}$$

$$f_{i+1}'' = 2c + 6eh_i \tag{9.1.6}$$

where f_i'' and f_{i+1}'' are values of f'' at i and $i + 1$, respectively, which are yet to be determined. The foregoing two equations can be written as

$$c = f_i'' / 2 \tag{9.1.7}$$

$$e = \frac{f_{i+1}'' - f_i''}{6h_i} \tag{9.1.8}$$

The coefficient a is already given by Eq.(9.1.2). The coefficient b is determined by eliminating a, c, e in Eq.(9.1.3) by Eqs.(9.1.2), (9.1.7), and (9.1.8),

$$b = \frac{f_{i+1} - f_i}{h_i} - \frac{f_{i+1}'' + 2f_i''}{6} h_i \tag{9.1.9}$$

Thus, the cubic polynomial Eq.(9.1.1) is expressed by

$$f(t) = f_i + \left(\frac{f_{i+1} - f_i}{h_i} - \frac{f_{i+1}'' + 2f_i''}{6} h_i \right) t + \frac{f_i''}{2} t^2 + \frac{f_{i+1}'' - f_i''}{6h_i} t^3 \tag{9.1.10}$$

We differentiate Eq.(9.1.10), and set the first derivative of f at $t = 0$ and $t = h_i$ to f_i' and f_{i+1}', respectively,

$$f_i' = -\frac{h_i}{6}\left(f_{i+1}'' + 2f_i''\right) + \frac{1}{h_i}\left(f_{i+1} - f_i\right) \tag{9.1.11}$$

$$f_{i+1}' = \frac{h_i}{6}\left(2f_{i+1}'' + f_i''\right) + \frac{1}{h_i}\left(f_{i+1} - f_i\right) \tag{9.1.12}$$

For the adjacent interval of $s_{i-1} < s < s_i$, Eq.(9.1.12) becomes

$$f_i' = \frac{h_{i-1}}{6}\left(2f_i'' + f_{i-1}''\right) + \frac{1}{h_{i-1}}\left(f_i - f_{i-1}\right) \tag{9.1.13}$$

where $h_{i-1} = x_i - x_{i-1}$. The f_i' of Eq.(9.1.13) must equal that of f_i' of Eq.(9.1.11) for continuity. Eliminating f_i' between the two equations yields

$$h_{i-1}f_{i-1}'' + (2h_{i-1} + 2h_i)f_i'' + h_if_{i+1}''$$
$$= 6\left(\frac{1}{h_{i-1}}f_{i-1} - \left(\frac{1}{h_{i-1}} + \frac{1}{h_i}\right)f_i + \frac{1}{h_i}f_{i+1}\right) \tag{9.1.14}$$

where the equation has been multiplied through by 6.

The foregoing equation can be written for all the points except for the two end points. That is, there are $n - 2$ equations, while the number of undetermined f_i'' is n. Therefore, two additional equations are necessary to determine all the undetermined f_i''s, which may be provided by the boundary conditions. Three ways of specifying boundary conditions at the end points are explained in the following:

(a) Specifying f_i'' at the end points: If we prescribe the values of f_i'' at the two end points, $i = 1$ and $i = n$, the set of equations becomes

$$(2h_1 + 2h_2)f_2'' + h_2f_3''$$
$$= 6\left(\frac{1}{h_1}f_1 - \left(\frac{1}{h_1} + \frac{1}{h_2}\right)f_2 + \frac{1}{h_2}f_3\right) - h_1f_1''$$
$$h_{i-1}f_{i-1}'' + (2h_{i-1} + 2h_i)f_i'' + h_if_{i+1}''$$
$$= 6\left(\frac{1}{h_{i-1}}f_{i-1} - \left(\frac{1}{h_{i-1}} + \frac{1}{h_i}\right)f_i + \frac{1}{h_i}f_{i+1}\right) \tag{9.1.15}$$
$$h_{n-2}f_{n-2}'' + (2h_{n-2} + 2h_{n-1})f_{n-1}''$$
$$= 6\left(\frac{1}{h_{n-2}}f_{n-2} - \left(\frac{1}{h_{n-2}} + \frac{1}{h_{n-1}}\right)f_{n-1} + \frac{1}{h_{n-1}}f_n\right) - h_{n-1}f_n''$$

The foregoing equations constitute $n - 2$ equations for $n - 2$ unknowns, f_i''. When the equations are written in matrix form, the coefficient matrix becomes a special form, called the *tridiagonal matrix*, in which all the elements are zero except the three diagonal lines. Although the equation may be solved by the standard solution for the linear equations, the tridiagonal solution scheme explained in Section 11.3 is significantly more efficient. Although f'' at the end points are not known in most situations, one approach is to assume $f'' = 0$ at the end points. Geometrically, this is equivalent to assuming that the curve becomes a straight line toward the end points.

(b) Extrapolating f'' from inside: Extrapolation of f''_1 from f''_2 and f''_3 is written as

$$f''_1 = (1 + \frac{h_1}{h_2})f''_2 - \frac{h_1}{h_2}f''_3 \qquad (9.1.16)$$

By setting $i = 2$ in Eq.(9.1.14) and eliminating f''_1 by Eq.(9.1.16), we get

$$\left(3h_1 + 2h_2 + \frac{(h_1)^2}{h_2}\right)f''_2 + \left(h_2 - \frac{(h_1)^2}{h_2}\right)f''_3$$

$$= 6\left(\frac{1}{h_1}f_1 - (\frac{1}{h_1} + \frac{1}{h_2})f_2 + \frac{1}{h_2}f_3\right) \qquad (9.1.17)$$

The foregoing equation replaces the first equation of Eq.(9.1.15). A similar equation may be written for point $n - 1$, which replaces the last equation in Eq.(9.1.14). The system of the equation has the same form as Eq.(9.1.15) except for a few coefficients. Therefore, the set of equations may be solved by the same scheme as for **(a)**.

(c) Cyclic boundary condition: The cyclic boundary condition is applied if the first and last data are identical, and the derivatives at these data points are identical also. This occurs if the whole data set represents one cycle of a curve that repeats. A closed curve on a plane may be fitted by the cyclic boundary conditions, for example.

The MATLAB command `interp1` performs a c-spline interpolation (see Section 4.1). Its synopsis is

```
interp1(x,y,xi,'spline')
```

where `x` and `y` are data points in the vector form, and `xi` is a vector of abscissa for which the interpolation is performed. Therefore, the command returns the interpolated `y` values for `xi`.

No boundary conditions are necessary in the argument, but the boundary condition of type (b) explained earlier is assumed. Although the MATLAB Reference Manual does not explain this, we can verify by examining the result of `spline` applied with a test data set. We set test data as:

```
x = [0, 0.5, 2, 3.5, 4]
y = [0, 2,  -2, 2,   0]
```

In order to find the spline function for $0 \leq x \leq 4$, we also set

```
xi = 1:0.05:4
```

which are significantly finer than the test data. We denote the c-spline function for xi by yi. The second derivative of the spline function can be computed from yi by the second-order difference approximation. In Figure 9.3, the spline function (solid curve) and its second derivative (dotted curve), computed from the spline function, are plotted. Notice that the second derivative is linear from $x = 0$ to $x = 2$, spanning two data intervals. The same is the case for the last two intervals. This does not occur unless the second derivative at each end point is linearly extrapolated in spline. The script used to plot Figure 9.3 is listed in List 9.1.

List 9.1

```
clear, clf, hold off
x=0:4;
x(2) = 0.5; x(4)=3.5;x
y = [0 2 -2 2 0]
xp=0:0.05:4; % fine points for which spline
              %    function is to be computed
h = xp(2)-xp(1)
yp = spline(x,y,xp);
n=length(xp)
for i=2:n-1
```

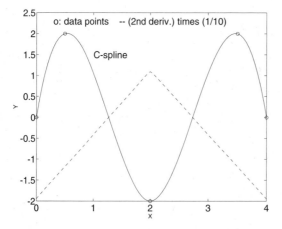

Figure 9.3 Investigation of B.C. (The spline BC in MATLAB is extrapolation)

```
            ypd(i) = (yp(i-1) - 2*yp(i) + yp(i+1))/h^2;
     end
     ypd(1)=ypd(2)*2 - ypd(3);       %for graphics only
     ypd(n)=ypd(n-1)*2 - ypd(n-2);   %for graphics only
     plot(xp,yp,  xp,ypd/10,  '--')
     hold on
     plot(x,y,'o')
     xlabel('X')
     ylabel('Y')
     set(gca, 'FontSize',[18])
     text(1,1.5,'C-spline','FontSize',[18])
     text(0.3,2.3,'o: data points    -- (2nd deriv.) times (1/10)', ...
     'FontSize',[18])
```

Like the Lagrange interpolation, the c-spline interpolation may develop an oscillatory behavior of errors. If abscissas of the data points can be chosen freely, use smaller intervals near the end points as well as where the curvature is high.

Example 9.1

The data points in Figure 9.1 are given by

```
xx =
[-1.0000 -0.8660 -0.5000 -0.0000  0.5000  0.8660   ...
   1.0000  1.0000  1.0402  1.1500  1.3000  1.5400   ...
   1.8280  2.1736  2.5883  3.0860]

yy =
[ 0.0000 -0.2500 -0.4330 -0.5000 -0.4330 -0.2500    ...
  -0.0000  0.0000  0.1500  0.2598  0.3000  0.3000    ...
   0.3000  0.3000  0.3000  0.3000]
```

Determine the spline function that fits the data.

Solution

We use s as a parameter and fit spline functions to x and y separately as functions of s. A script is given in List 9.2. The result is shown in Figure 9.4.

List 9.2
```
clear, clf, hold off
xx = ...
[-1.0000 -0.866 -0.5000 -0.0000  0.5000 0.8660 1.0000 ...
1.0000  1.0402  1.1500  1.3000  1.5400  1.8280  2.1736 ...
2.5883 3.0860]
yy = ...
[0.0000 -0.2500 -0.4330 -0.5000 -0.4330 -0.2500 -0.0000 ...
0.0000 0.1500 0.2598 0.3000 0.3000 0.3000 0.3000 ...
0.3000 0.3000]
s=1:length(xx);sp=1:(length(xx)/100):length(xx);
xp=spline(s,xx,sp);
yp=spline(s,yy,sp);
```

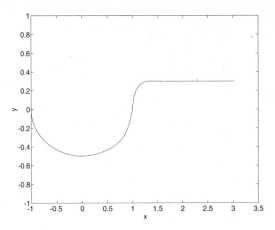

Figure 9.4 C-spline curve on the x-y plane

```
clg
plot(xp,yp); hold on
plot(xx,yy, 'o');xlabel('x'); ylabel('y');
hold off
```

9.2   CUBIC B-SPLINE

The *b-spline* function consists of piecewise polynomials determined by a series of control points, (s_i, p_i), $i = 1, 2, ..., n$. The b-spline function based on cubic polynomials is named cubic b-spline, a sibling of the c-spline studied in the preceding section but with different characters. We call (s_i, p_i) control points, because b-spline does not pass through the points except under special conditions. The b-spline function is useful to generate a smooth curve in design and graphics when artistic impression or a visually comfortable curve is more important than strict fitting. In the remainder of this section, we will discuss mathematical expression and behaviors of the cubic b-spline.

A segment of the cubic b-spline is determined with four consecutive control points, (s_{i-1}, p_{i-1}), (s_i, p_i), (s_{i+1}, p_{i+1}), and (s_{i+2}, p_{i+2}), by

$$f(s) = \frac{1}{6}[(1-t)^3 p_{i-1} + (3t^3 - 6t^2 + 4)p_i$$
$$+(-3t^3 + 3t^2 + 3t + 1)p_{i+1} + t^3 p_{i+2}], \quad 0 \le t \le 1 \quad (9.2.1)$$

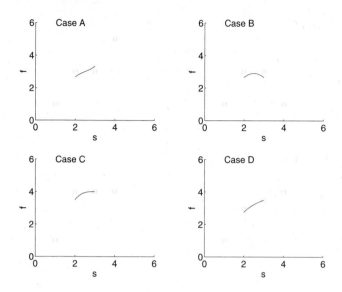

Figure 9.5 Pieces of b-spline determined by four control points

where $t = s - s_i$ is a local coordinate, and $s_i = i$. For $s = s_i$ and $s = s_{i+1}$ (or equivalently $t = 0$ and $t = 1$, respectively), f, f' and f'' have the following values:

$$f(s_i) = \frac{p_{i-1} + 4p_i + p_{i+1}}{6}, \quad f'(s_i) = \frac{p_{i+1} - p_{i-1}}{2}, \quad f''(s_i) = \frac{p_{i+1} - 2p_i + p_{i-1}}{2}$$

$$(9.2.2)$$

$$f(s_{i+1}) = \frac{p_i + 4p_{i+1} + p_{i+2}}{6}, \quad f'(s_{i+1}) = \frac{p_{i+2} - p_i}{2}, \quad f''(s_{i+1}) = \frac{p_{i+2} - 2p_{i+1} + p_i}{2}$$

The cubic b-spline curves determined by four control points are illustrated in Figure 9.5, where s values are set to 1, 2, 3, and 4 while p values are varied from case to case. It is seen that $f(s)$ does not pass through control points in Cases A and B. If three consecutive ordinates are identical, however, as in Case C, or if the three consecutive ordinates change linearly, as in Case D, the curve passes through the middle of the three.

If the number of control points is greater than 4, a series of cubic b-spline curves becomes a single curve, as illustrated in Figure 9.6. The b-spline function, its first and second derivatives all become continuous.

The curve in Figure 9.6 does not pass through any boundary points. By repeating $f = 1$ three times in the beginning of the control points, and repeating

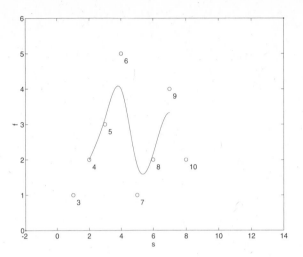

Figure 9.6 A b-spline function determined by 10 control points

$f = 2$ three times at the end of the control points, however, the curve satisfies these boundary conditions, as illustrated in Figure 9.7. The script used to plot Figure 9.7

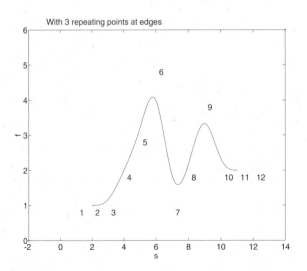

Figure 9.7 The b-spline function satisfying the boundary conditions

is given in List 9.3.

List 9.3

```
clear; clg; hold off
f = [ 1 1 1 2 3 5 1 2 4 2 2 2 ];  m = length(f)
s=1:m;
plot([-2 14], [0 6], '.'); hold on
xlabel('s'); ylabel('f');  plot(s,f,'o')
for k=1:m
  z=int2str(k); sk = s(k); fk=f(k); text(sk+0.2,fk-0.2,z)
end
t = 0:0.1:1; t2=t.^2; t3=t.^3;
for i=2:m-2
  fb = 1/6*((1-t).^3*f(i-1)+(3*t3-6*t2+ 4)*f(i) + ...
       (-3*t3+3*t2 + 3*t + 1)*f(i+1) + t3*f(i+2) );
  plot(s(i)+t,fb)
end
title (' With 3 repeating points at edges')
```

The rule of repeating the same ordinates three times also applies to a control point in the middle. That is, if the curve is required to pass through a point in the middle, repeat that point three times in the control point vector.

We now apply the cubic b-spline on the x-y plane. The control points are given by

$$(x,y): (0,0), (0.2,1), (1,1), (2,0), (2.8,0), (3,1)$$

Assume that the curve is required to pass through the first point $(0,0)$ and the last point $(3,1)$. Each of x and y must be determined as a function of parameter s. Therefore the control points of the s-x space as well as s-y space are set to

```
s =  (1, 2, 3, 4,  5, 6, 7,  8, 9, 10)
x =  (0, 0, 0, 0.2,1, 2, 2.8,3, 3, 3)

s =  (1, 2, 3, 4,  5, 6, 7,  8, 9, 10)
y =  (0, 0, 0, 1,  1, 0, 0,  1, 1, 1)
```

The value x=0, and y=0 are repeated three times in the beginning of the control point vectors, while x=3 and y=1 are repeated three times at the end of the control point vectors. The plot of the curve on the x-y plane is shown in Figure 9.8. Notice that the curve passes through x=y=0 at the left end, while the curve passes through x=3 and y=1 at the right end. The script to plot Figure 9.8 is listed in List 9.4.

List 9.4

```
clear; clg; hold off
y = [0 0 0 1    1 0 0    1 1 1];
x = [0 0 0 0.2  1 2 2.8 3 3 3];
m = length(y); plot([-1 4], [-1 2], '.'); hold on
xlabel('x'); ylabel('y');  plot(x,y,'o')
for k=1:m
```

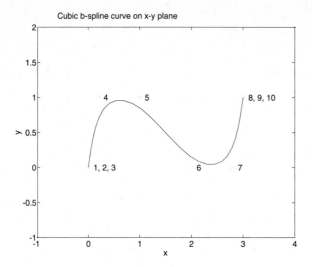

Figure 9.8 The b-spline curve passing through two end points

```
    z=int2str(k); xk = x(k); yk=y(k); text(xk+0.1,yk,z)
 end
 t = 0:0.2:1; t2=t.^2; t3=t.^3;
 for i=2:m-2
    yb = 1/6*((1-t).^3*y(i-1) + (3*t3-6*t2+4)*y(i) + ...
         (-3*t3 + 3*t2 + 3*t + 1)*y(i+1) + t3*y(i+2) );
    xb = 1/6*((1-t).^3*x(i-1) + (3*t3-6*t2+4)*x(i) +  ...
         (-3*t3 + 3*t2 + 3*t + 1)*x(i+1) + t3*x(i+2) );
    plot(xb,yb)
 end
 title(' Cubic b-spline curve on x-y plane ')
```

Example 9.2

The data file `car.dat` specify a side-view profile of an automobile. Plot the data without any modification. Then, smooth out the profile by b-spline.

Solution

Two profiles plotted by List 9.5 are shown in Figure 9.9.

List 9.5
```
clear, clf, hold off
load car.dat
```

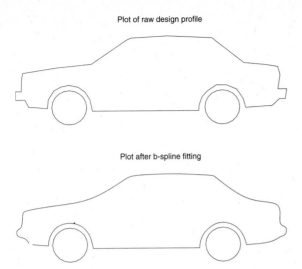

Plot of raw design profile

Plot after b-spline fitting

Figure 9.9 Car profiles before and after b-spline fitting

```
x=car(:,1)'; y=car(:,2)';
subplot(2,1,1)
hold on
plot(x,y) % plot of car profile
dth=pi/10;
th=0:dth:2*pi; xt=1.2*cos(th); yt=1.2*sin(th);
plot(xt+3.7, yt+0.45)    %front tire
plot(xt+14.3, yt+0.45)   %front tire
title('Plot of raw design profile')
axis([-0,20,-0.9,6.0]); axis('off')
disp 'Hit return to plot the profile after smoothing'
pause
subplot(2,1,2)
hold on
m = length(y); plot([-1 4], [-1 2], '.');
x=[x(1),x,x(m)]; y=[y(1),y,y(m)];
m=length(x);
t = 0:0.25:1; t2=t.^2; t3=t.^3;
for i=2:m-2
   yb = 1/6*((1-t).^3*y(i-1) + (3*t3-6*t2+4)*y(i) + ...
        (-3*t3 + 3*t2 + 3*t + 1)*y(i+1) + t3*y(i+2) );
   xb = 1/6*((1-t).^3*x(i-1) + (3*t3-6*t2+4)*x(i) +  ...
        (-3*t3 + 3*t2 + 3*t + 1)*x(i+1) + t3*x(i+2) );
   plot(xb,yb)
end
plot(xt+3.7, yt+0.45), plot(xt+14.3, yt+0.45) % tires
title('Plot after b-spline fitting'); hold off
```

Example 9.3

A ceramic pot image may be created on the screen by k_wheel. The script collects data points clicked on the screen by mouse. The points are used

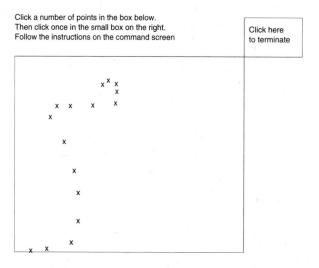

Figure 9.10 Input for pot making

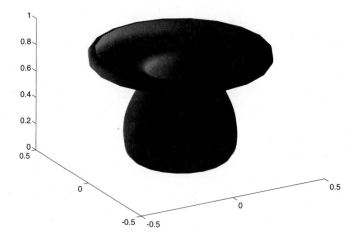

Figure 9.11 The pot image created

as control points for b-spline, and a pot is created by rotating the shape determined by b-spline. Run `k_wheel` and create a pot. (Script of `k_wheel` is listed in Section 9.4)

Solution

To run the script, we type `k_wheel`. Then input the coordinate values by clicking points on the graphic window from the bottom to the top of the pot. When input is completed, click inside the box to terminate input. Figure 9.10 illustrates the points clicked for input.
Figure 9.11 shows the pot image created.

9.3   INTERPOLATION WITH A NONLINEAR FUNCTION

Interpolation by a nonpolynomial function can produce effects different from interpolation by a polynomial. In this section, we present a few applications of exponential functions fitted to a given data set.

In the first approach we use

$$f(x) = a\exp(bx) + c \tag{9.3.1}$$

where a, b and c are undetermined coefficients. With the three free parameters, a, b, and c, Eq.(9.3.1) may be fitted to three data points, (x_i, f_i), $i = 1$, 2, and 3. Setting Eq.(9.3.1) to each data point, we get

$$
\begin{aligned}
f(x_1) &= a\exp(bx_1) + c = f_1 \\
f(x_2) &= a\exp(bx_2) + c = f_2 \\
f(x_3) &= a\exp(bx_3) + c = f_3
\end{aligned}
\tag{9.3.2}
$$

By eliminating c between the first and second equations, we get

$$a = \frac{f_1 - f_2}{\exp(bx_1) - \exp(bx_2)} \tag{9.3.3}$$

Also by eliminating c between first and third equations, we get

$$a = \frac{f_1 - f_3}{\exp(bx_1) - \exp(bx_3)} \tag{9.3.4}$$

Equating the two foregoing equations yields

$$\frac{\exp(bx_2) - \exp(bx_1)}{f_2 - f_1} = \frac{\exp(bx_3) - \exp(bx_1)}{f_3 - f_1} \tag{9.3.5}$$

or by dividing through by $\exp(bx_1)$,

$$\frac{\exp\{b(x_2 - x_1)\} - 1}{f_2 - f_1} = \frac{\exp\{b(x_3 - x_1)\} - 1}{f_3 - f_1} \tag{9.3.6}$$

The constant b is determined by solving the foregoing nonlinear equation by one of the schemes described in Chapter 7. Once b is known, a is evaluated by Eq.(9.3.3), and c by one of the equations in Eq.(9.3.2); for example

$$c = f_1 - a\exp(bx_1) \tag{9.3.7}$$

Example 9.4

A bar of length L is to be cut into 7 sections such that the lengths change monotonically and smoothly from one section to the next. The first section should be 1/12 of the total length L. Determine the length of each section.

Solution

The problem can be restated as follows: Determine a smooth and monotonic function

$$f(s)/L = a\exp(bs) + c \tag{A}$$

where s is a parameter satisfying $0 \le s \le 7$; f is the length of the bar measured from the left end while at $s = 7$, f is equal L; a, b and c are undetermined constants. We summarize the conditions for f as

$$s = 0 : f(0) = 0$$
$$s = 1 : f(1) = L/12 \tag{B}$$
$$s = 7 : f(7) = L$$

Introducing the three foregoing conditions to Eq.(9.3.1) yields

$$a + c = 0$$
$$a\exp(b) + c = 1/12 \tag{C}$$
$$a\exp(7b) + c = 1$$

Eliminating a and c yields

$$\frac{\exp(b) - 1}{1/12} = \exp(7b) - 1 \tag{D}$$

Applying Newton iteration, b is found to be 0.16229 so

$$a = 0.472931, \quad b = 0.16229, \quad c = -0.472931 \qquad \text{(E)}$$

The exponential function determined is plotted in Figure 9.12. Length of each segment becomes as follows:

Section #	Relative length
1	0.083333
2	0.098017
3	0.115288
4	0.135602
5	0.159496
6	0.187601
7	0.220657

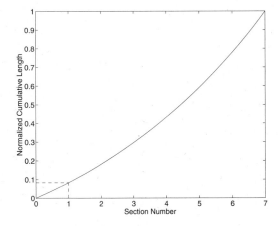

Figure 9.12 Plot of f

List 9.6

```
% A script to plot Figure 9.12
clear, hold off, clg
b = 0.162294
c = 1/12/(1- exp(b))
a = -c
x = 0:0.1:7;
y =  a*exp(b*x) + c;
plot(x,y)
xlabel('s')
ylabel('f(s)/L')
y1 =  a*exp(b) + c
hold on
plot([1,1], [0,y1], '--')
plot([0,1], [y1,y1], '--')
```

Example 9.5

Fit the function

$$y = ae^{-\gamma x} + be^{\gamma x} + c$$

to the following data:

```
x1 = 0,   x2 = 0.01,   x3 = 0.95,   x4 = 1
y1 = 0,   y2 = 0.01,   y3 = 0.8,    y4 = 1
```

where a, b, c and γ are undetermined constants.

Solution

We first define

$$f(x) = ae^{-\gamma x} + be^{\gamma x} + c - y \tag{A}$$

By setting Eq. (A) to each data point, we get four equations:

$$
\begin{aligned}
f_1 &\equiv f(x_1) = a &&+ b &&+ c = 0 \\
f_2 &\equiv f(x_2) = ae^{-0.01\gamma} &&+ be^{0.01\gamma} &&+ c - 0.01 = 0 \\
f_3 &\equiv f(x_3) = ae^{-0.95\gamma} &&+ be^{0.95\gamma} &&+ c - 0.8 = 0 \\
f_4 &\equiv f(x_4) = ae^{-\gamma} &&+ be^{\gamma} &&+ c - 1 = 0
\end{aligned}
$$

The foregoing equations, each of which may be regarded as a function of a, b, c and γ, can be written as

$$f_k(\hat{a} + \delta a, \hat{b} + \delta b, \hat{c} + \delta c, \hat{\gamma} + \delta\gamma) = 0, \quad k = 1 \sim 4 \tag{B}$$

where $\hat{a}$, $\hat{b}$, $\hat{c}$ and $\hat{\gamma}$ are guesses, while δa, δb, δc, and $\delta\gamma$ are unknown corrections, and $a = \hat{a} + \delta a$, $b = \hat{b} + \delta b$, $c = \hat{c} + \delta c$ and $\gamma = \hat{\gamma} + \delta\gamma$. Assuming that the corrections are small, the first-order approximation (using the Taylor expansion) may be written as

$$\frac{\partial f_k}{\partial a}\delta a + \frac{\partial f_k}{\partial b}\delta b + \frac{\partial f_k}{\partial c}\delta c + \frac{\partial f_k}{\partial \gamma}\delta\gamma = -f_k(\hat{a}, \hat{b}, \hat{c}, \hat{a}(\gamma)), \quad k = 1 \sim 4 \tag{C}$$

Equation (C) may be solved as a linear system. The solution is then updated by $a = \hat{a} + \delta a$, $b = \hat{b} + \delta b$, $c = \hat{c} + \delta c$ and $\gamma = \hat{\gamma} + \delta\gamma$. The procedure is iterated using a, b, c and γ as new guesses until δa, δb, δc and $\delta\gamma$ become all zero. The problem is solved by the following script. The function determined is plotted in Figure 9.13.

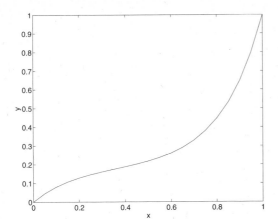

Figure 9.13 Nonlinear function fitted to four data points

List 9.7
```
clear, clf, hold off
a=1;
b=1;
c=1; g = 1;
x1 = 0.01; y1 = 0.01; x2 = 0.95; y2 = 0.8;
for it = 1:20
  A=zeros(4);
  A(1,1)=1; A(1,2)=1; A(1,3)=1; A(1,4) = 0;
  y(1) = -(a + b + c);
  A(2,1) = exp(-g*x1); A(2,2) = exp(g*x1); A(2,3)=1;
  A(2,4) = a*(-x1)*A(2,1) + b*(x1)*A(2,2);
  y(2) = -(a*A(2,1) + b*A(2,2) + c - y1);
  A(3,1) = exp(-g*x2); A(3,2) = exp(g*x2); A(3,3)=1;
  A(3,4) = a*(-x2)*A(3,1) + b*(x2)*A(3,2);
  y(3) = -(a*A(3,1) + b*A(3,2) + c - y2);
  A(4,1) = exp(-g); A(4,2) = exp(g); A(4,3)=1;
  A(4,4) = a*(-1)*A(4,1) + b*(1)*A(4,2);
  y(4) = -(a*A(4,1) + b*A(4,2) + c - 1);
  da=A\y'
  a = a+da(1); b = b+da(2); c=c+da(3); g=g+da(4);
  if sum(abs(da)) < 0.00001, break;end
end
x =0:0.05:1;
yy = a*exp(-g*x) + b*exp(g*x) + c;
clg
plot(x,yy)
ylabel('y'), xlabel('x')
```

The need of dividing a length to a specified number of segments such that the length of the first and last segments are both prescribed and yet the segment lengths change from one end to the other as gradually as possible. This need can be fulfilled by the Vinokur's stretching function.[1] Its algorithm is as follows:

Consider an arc of length L. A point on the arc is measured by the arc length s from one end. Assume also a total of n points is to be distributed along the arc, one at $s = 0$, and another at $s = L$. We assume that the points are numbered by index i and the s value at the points are denoted by s_i, with $i = 1, 2, ...n$. If the desired increment of s between $i = 1$ and $i = 2$ equals Δs_a, while the desired length between $i = n - 1$ and $i = n$ equals Δs_b, then s_i values are determined by

$$s_i = \frac{Lu_i}{A + (1 - A)u_i}$$

where

$$u_i = 0.5 \left[1 + \frac{\tanh\left(\delta(\frac{i-1}{n-1} - 0.5)\right)}{\tanh(\delta/2)}\right]$$

$$A = \sqrt{\Delta s_b/\Delta s_a}$$

In the foregoing equations, δ satisfies

$$\sinh(\delta) = B\delta$$

with

$$B = \frac{L}{(n - 1)\sqrt{\Delta s_a \Delta s_b}}$$

The foregoing equations are computed by `stret_`, listed as FM 9-2. Suppose a line of unit length is desired to be divided into 19 intervals, with the first interval to be approximately 0.01, and the last interval to be approximately 0.02. Then,

```
x = stret_(20, 1, 0.01, 0.02)
```

yields

```
x =
          0   0.0117   0.0277   0.0491   0.0776   0.1147   0.1620
     0.2206   0.2907   0.3711   0.4587   0.5495   0.6385   0.7212
     0.7942   0.8560   0.9064   0.9462   0.9768   1.0000
```

The lengths of the segments are plotted in Figure 9.14.

---

[1] M. Vinokur, "On the stretching Functions for Finite-Difference Calculations," *J. Comput. Phys.*, **50**, 215 (1983)

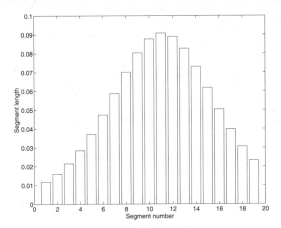

Figure 9.14 Lengths of segments determined by stretching function

Example 9.6

Data points along the upper surface of a prototype airfoil are given by

```
x_af=[1.0000   0.6638   0.4397   0.2900   0.1896   0.1221   ...
        0.0765   0.0455   0.0243   0.0099        0 ]
y_af=[0.0021   0.0668   0.0939   0.1000   0.0946   0.0836   ...
        0.0705   0.0569   0.0431   0.0282        0 ]
```

where the data points start at the the trailing edge and are in counterclockwise order. The chord length of the airfoil is set to unity (nondimensional). The manufacturer desires to partition the upper airfoil surface into 15 intervals so the arc length of the interval at the leading edge is 0.05, and the length of the interval at the trailing edge is approximately 0.1, while the arc length of the segments should change as gradually as possible. Determine the points where the airfoil is cut to pieces, and show the location of the cuts in a plot of the airfoil profile. Assume the airfoil is symmetric about the chord.

Solution

Although data points of only upper half of the surface are given, we can plot the whole profile because the airfoil is symmetric. Figure 9.15 illustrates the airfoil with data points along the upper surface. The arc lengths at the points measured from the trailing edge are then calculated. The coordinates x and y will be expressed as functions of arc length s. The

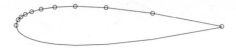

o: given data points

x: points to cut the surface

Figure 9.15 Airfoil profile

total arc length from the trailing edge to the leading edge will be denoted by L. The lengths of arcs to satisfy the manufacturer's need are determined by `stret_` that partitions the length L into 15 segments. The coordinates, x and y, at the points are determined by c-spline. A script to perform the computations is shown in List 9.9.

List 9.9

```
clear,clf
x_af=[1.0000   0.6638   0.4397   0.2900   0.1896   0.1221   ...
         0.0765   0.0455   0.0243   0.0099        0 ];
y_af=[0.0021   0.0668   0.0939   0.1000   0.0946   0.0836   ...
         0.0705   0.0569   0.0431   0.0282        0 ];
m=length(x_af);
x = [x_af, x_af(m-1:-1:1)];   % Whole airfoil profile
y = [y_af, -y_af(m-1:-1:1)];
plot(x,y+0.3)
hold on
plot(x_af,y_af+0.3,'or')
axis([-0.1, 1.1 ,-0.6, 0.6])
n=length(x);
arc(1)=0;   % Arc length measured from trailing edge
for i=2:n
    arc(i)=arc(i-1)+sqrt((x(i)-x(i-1))^2+(y(i)-y(i-1))^2);
end
L = arc(m);
s = stret_(15+1, L,  0.02, 0.02);
xcut=interp1(arc, x, s, 'spline');   % c-spline
ycut=interp1(arc, y, s, 'spline');   % c-spline
plot(x,y-0.3)
plot(xcut,ycut-0.3,'x')
axis([-0.2, 1.1 ,-0.6, 0.6])
text(0, 0.1, 'o: given data points','Fontsize',[18])
```

```
text(0,-0.5, 'x: points to cut the surface','Fontsize',[18])
axis('off')
```

The airfoil arc with the determined points is shown as the second graph in Figure 9.15.

9.4 M-FILES

FM 9-1 Kickwheel ceramic game

Purpose: to collect data of points, and fit them by b-spline and draw a ceramic image

Synopsis: k_wheel. Follow instructions on the screen.

k_wheel.m

```
% Simulation of kickwheel
clear; clg; hold off
axis([0, 1.25, 0,1.2 ])
text(1.02,1.14,'Click here','Color', 'r')
text(1.02,1.09,'to terminate','Color', 'r')
hold on
axis('off')
plot([1,1.25,1.25,1,1],[1,1,1.2,1.2,1])
plot([0,1,1,0,0],[0,0,1,1,0])
text(0,1.2,'Click a number of points in the box below.', ...
                                     'Color', 'g')
text(0,1.15,'Then click once in the small box on the right.', ...
                                     'Color', 'g')
text(0,1.10,'Follow the instructions on the command screen', ...
                                     'Color', 'g')
for n=1:100
[xg,yg]=ginput(1);
if xg>0.99 & yg>0.99, break; end
x(n)=xg; y(n)=yg;
text(x(n),y(n),'x')
end
m = length(y);
xlabel('x'); ylabel('y');  plot(x,y,'o')
for k=1:m
  z=int2str(k); xk = x(k); yk=y(k); text(xk+0.1,yk,z)
end
t = 0:0.25:1; t2=t.^2; t3=t.^3;
lt = length(t); ltm=lt-1;
rs=[]; zs=[];
for i=2:m-2
   yb = 1/6*((1-t).^3*y(i-1) + (3*t3-6*t2+4)*y(i) + ...
       (-3*t3 + 3*t2 + 3*t + 1)*y(i+1) + t3*y(i+2) );
   xb = 1/6*((1-t).^3*x(i-1) + (3*t3-6*t2+4)*x(i) +  ...
```

```
        (-3*t3 + 3*t2 + 3*t + 1)*x(i+1) + t3*x(i+2) );
    plot(xb,yb)
    rs=[rs,xb(1:ltm)];
    zs=[zs,yb(1:ltm)];
end
    rs=[rs,xb(lt)];
    zs=[zs,yb(lt)];
title(' Cubic b-spline curve on x-y plane ')
fprintf('Hit RETURN to proceed')
pause
clg
dth=pi/10;
th=0:dth:2*pi;
for i=1:length(th)
zz(i,:)=zs;
xx(i,:)=rs.*(cos(th(i)) + 0*0.2*cos(5*th(i)));
yy(i,:)=rs.*(sin(th(i))+ 0*0.2*sin(5*th(i)));
end
mesh(xx,yy,zz,zz)
colormap default
caxis([-0.5, 1.5])
shading interp
fprintf('Hit RETURN to proceed')
pause
surfl(xx,yy,zz,[30,30])
fprintf('Hit RETURN to proceed')
pause
caxis([-1,3])
fprintf('Hit RETURN to proceed')
pause
clg
colormap default
[nx,ny,nz]=surfnorm(xx,yy,zz);
r=specular(nx,ny,nz,[30,30], [50,10]);
r=diffuse(nx,ny,nz, [-50,10]);
surface(xx,yy,zz,r*0.3+ 0.1*zz)
view([-30,30])
shading interp
colormap jet
caxis([-0,1])
pause
clg
```

FM 9-2 Stretching and clustering

Purpose: to distribute points with stretching and clustering

Synopsis: `stret_(n,L,ds0,ds1)`

      `n`: total number of points including end points

      `L`: total length

      `ds0`: desired size of first interval

      `ds1`: desired size of last interval

Example: `stret_(20,1,0.01, 0.1)`

stret_.m
```
% Distribution of points with stretching function
function s=stret_(n,L,ds0,ds1)
A=sqrt(ds1/ds0);
B=L/(n-1)/sqrt(ds0*ds1);
if (B<1.0), fprintf('B is less than 1'),pause; end
DL= delta_(B) ;
if DL==0, retern, end
for I=1:n
        X=DL*(I-1)/(n-1) - .5*DL;
        U=.5*(1+tanh(X)/tanh(DL/2.));
        s(I)=U*L/( A + (1.-A)*U);
end
```

delta_.m
```
% Solves sinh(delta)=B*delta by Newton iteration
function DELTA = delta_(B)
if (B<1.0 ),
   fprintf('B IS LESS THAN 1. CODE IS STOPPED IN SUB. DELTA' )
   B=0.0;
return
end
DELTA=0;
K=0;
X=sqrt(6*B-6.);
XB = 0;
x=6.0;
     if (B< 3) x=B;   end
     if (B>=3 & B< 80) x=7. ;end
     if (B>=80 & B<100) x=7.3;end
     if (B>=100 & B<200) x=8.   ;end
     if (B>=200 & B<300) x=8.65;end
     if (B>=300 ) x=8.86;end
X = x;
flag = 0;
while abs(X-XB)>0.000001*abs(X)  ,
     XB=X;
     XP = exp(X);
     XM=1./XP;
     F=XP-XM -B*2.0*X;
     FD=XP+XM -B*2.0 ;
     X= XB-F/FD ;
     K=K+1
       if  (K>40)
          fprintf(' ITERATION LIMIT EXCEEDED.  STOPPED IN SUB.
DELTA')
          flag = 1;return
        end
     if flag==1; return ,end
end
DELTA=X;
```

PROBLEMS

(9.1) Determine the c-spline curve that passes through the following points using the extrapolation boundary conditions. Plot the curve with the data points:

```
x: 0    -0.5   0    1    2    3    3.5   3
y: 0     1     2    2    2    2    1     0
```

(9.2) Determine a closed c-spline curve that passes through the following points. The curve is required to be smooth across the end points. Plot the curve with the data points:

```
x: 0   1    2     3     3.5   3.7   3.5    3      2     1     0
y: 0   1    1.5   1.5   1     0     -1    -1.5   -1.5   -1     0
```

(9.3) Determine a b-spline curve using the following control points. Plot the curve with the data points:

```
x: 0    0    1    1    2     2    4    4
y: 0    1    1    0.5  0.5   2    2    0
```

The curve is required to pass through the end points of the data above.

(9.4) Determine the function

$$f(x) = a\exp(bx) + c$$

that passes through

```
x: 0    1    5
y: 0    2    4
```

(9.5) The pot shown in Figure 9.11 has a hole like a planting pot, which can be seen using a different view angle. Explain how the hole can be closed.

(9.6) Determine the function

$$y = ae^{-\gamma x} + be^{\gamma x} + c$$

that passes through

```
x: 0    1     4     5
y: 0    0.5   3.5   4
```

(9.7) Divide a bar of one unit length into 11 segments such that the first segment length will be 1/20 and the last segment length will be 1/15. The lengths of the segments must change as gradually as possible. Determine the length of all the 11 segments by stret_.

Chapter 10

Initial-Value Problems of Ordinary Differential Equations

Dynamic behaviors of systems are important subjects. A mechanical system involves displacements, velocities, and accelerations. An electric or electronic system involves voltages, currents, and time derivatives of these quantities. In general, the equations used to describe dynamics include unknowns such as displacement or electric current and its derivatives.

An equation that involves one or more ordinary derivatives of the unknown function is called an ordinary differential equation, abbreviated as *ODE*. The order of the equation is determined by the order of the highest derivative. For example, if the first derivative is the only derivative, the equation is called a first-order ODE. Likewise if the highest derivative is second order, the equation is called a second-order ODE.

Problems of solving an ODE are classified into initial-value problems and boundary-value problems, depending on how the conditions at the end points of the domain are specified. All the conditions of an initial-value problem are specified at the initial point. On the other hand, the problem becomes a boundary-value problem if conditions are spread between both initial and final points. The ODEs in the time domain are initial-value problems, so all the conditions are specified at the initial time, such as $t = 0$. The subject of this chapter is the solution of initial-value problems, while the boundary-value problems are discussed in the next chapter.

10.1 FIRST-ORDER ODEs

The initial-value problem of a first-order ODE may be written in the form

$$y'(t) = f(y, t), \quad y(0) = y_0 \qquad (10.1.1)$$

where $f(y, t)$ is a function of y and t, and the second equation is an initial condition without which the solution cannot be evaluated. In the foregoing equation, the first derivative of y is given as a function of y and t, and we desire to compute the unknown function y by numerically integrating $f(y, t)$. If f were independent of y, the computation would be one of the straightforward integrations discussed in Chapter 5. The fact that f is a function of y, however, makes the integration different. If f is a linear function of y, for example

$$f = ay + b$$

with a and b being constant or functions of t, Eq.(10.1.1) is a *linear ODE*. If f is a nonlinear function of y, the equation is called a *nonlinear ODE*. Analytical solution of some ODEs can be found, but the majority of nonlinear ODEs have no analytical solution. This is one of the reasons why numerical methods become important. We solve even linear ODEs by numerical methods, particularly when the ODEs are coupled.

It is hoped that the reader has been exposed to differential equations; however, to those who learn them for the first time, derivations of ODEs are illustrated next.

Example 10.1

Carbon-11 is a radioisotope that disintegrates at the rate of 3.46 %/min, which is equivalent to a half life of 20 minutes. The rate of decay is expressed by $\lambda = 0.0346$ min^{-1} or $\lambda = 2.076$ s^{-1} called decay constant. The initial atomic number density at $t = 0$ is given by N_0 atoms/cm^3. Derive a differential equation for the atomic number density.

Solution

Denoting the number density at t s by $N(t)$, $N(t + dt)$ becomes

$$N(t + dt) = N(t) - \lambda N(t) dt \qquad \text{(A)}$$

where dt is an infinitesimally small time interval. The foregoing equation can be written as

$$\frac{dN}{dt} = -\lambda N(t) \qquad \text{(B)}$$

with the initial condition,

$$N(0) = N_0$$

where N_0 is the number density at $t = 0$.

Comment: Equation (B) is one of the simplest ODEs. Its analytical solution is given by $N(t) = exp(-\lambda t)N_0$. From a practical point of view, there is no need to solve Eq.(B) numerically. We will often use an equation of this type, however, to investigate accuracy of the numerical methods.

Example 10.2

A skydiver of mass M kg jumps into the air from an airplane at $t = 0$. We assume the initial vertical velocity of the sky diver is zero at $t = 0$ and that the skydiver falls vertically. If the aerodynamic drag is given by $F_{air} = Cv^2$ where C is a constant and v is the vertical velocity which is positive downward, derive an ODE to determine the vertical velocity of the diver.

Solution

Applying the Newton's first law, the balance of forces satisfies

$$M\frac{dv(t)}{dt} = -F_{air} + gM \qquad\qquad (A)$$

where v is the diver's velocity (m/s) positive downward and g is the gravity acceleration, 9.8 m/s^2. Equation (A) can be written as

$$\frac{dv(t)}{dt} = -\frac{C}{M}v^2 + g, \qquad v(0) = 0 \qquad\qquad (B)$$

or equivalently

$$v' = f(v, t), \qquad v(0) = 0 \qquad\qquad (C)$$

with

$$f(v, t) = -\frac{C}{M}v^2 + g$$

Comment: The equation may be rewritten in terms of $y(t)$, which is the distance the skydiver fell. The relation between the velocity and height is $v = y'$. Introducing this into Eq.(B) yields

$$\frac{d^2y(t)}{dt^2} = -\frac{C}{M}y'^2 + g$$

which is a second-order ODE with initial conditions, $y(0) = 0$ and $y'(0) = 0$.

Example 10.3

Consider the electrical circuit shown in Figure 10.1. The switch is closed at $t = 0$. Write an equation for current $i(t)$.

Solution

Kirchhoff's first law states that the total of the voltages through a loop is zero; that is

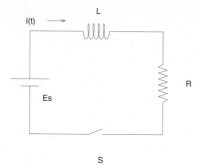

Figure 10.1 Electrical circuit

$$E_L + E_R + E_S = 0 \qquad \qquad \text{(A)}$$

where E_S is the voltage of the source that may be time-dependent, E_L is the voltage across the inductor, and E_R is the voltage across the resistor. Voltages E_L and E_R are given, respectively, by

$$E_L = -L\frac{dI(t)}{dt}$$
$$E_R = -RI(t)$$

where L is self-inductance, and R is resistance. Therefore, Eq.(A) becomes

$$\frac{dI(t)}{dt} = -\frac{R}{L}I(t) + \frac{E_s}{L} \qquad \qquad \text{(B)}$$

The foregoing equation is a first-order ODE and its initial condition is $I(0) = 0$.

10.2   EULER METHODS

The Euler methods are simple methods of solving first order ODEs, suitable particularly for a quick programming because of their great simplicity, although their accuracy is not high. Euler methods include three versions, namely, (a) forward Euler, (b) modified Euler, and (c) backward Euler methods. We study these methods primarily for the sake of understanding the basic concepts of numerical solution for initial-value problems.

10.2.1 Forward Euler Method

The forward Euler method for $y' = f(y, t)$ is derived by rewriting the forward difference approximation,

$$(y_{n+1} - y_n)/h \approx y'_n \tag{10.2.1}$$

to

$$y_{n+1} = y_n + hf(y_n, t_n) \tag{10.2.2}$$

where $y'_n = f(y_n, t_n)$ is used. In order to advance time steps, Eq.(10.2.2) is recursively applied as

$$
\begin{aligned}
y_1 &= y_0 + hy'_0 = y_0 + hf(y_0, t_0) \\
y_2 &= y_1 + hf(y_1, t_1) \\
y_3 &= y_2 + hf(y_2, t_2) \\
&\cdots \\
y_n &= y_{n-1} + hf(y_{n-1}, t_{n-1})
\end{aligned}
\tag{10.2.3}
$$

Example 10.4

Find the velocity of the skydiver in Example 10.2, and plot the solution for $t \leq 20$ s after the skydiver jumps from the airplane. Assume $M = 70$ kg and $C = 0.27$ kg/m. Use $h = 0.1$ s.

Solution

The following script solves Eq.(C) of Example 10.2 by the forward Euler method:

List 10.1
```
clear,clf, hold off
t = 0; n=0; v=0;
C = 0.27; M = 70; g = 9.8; h = 0.1;
t_rec(1)=t; v_rec(1) = v;
while t<=20
    n=n+1;
    v = v + h*( -C/M*v*v + g);
    t = t+h;
    v_rec(n+1) = v;
    t_rec(n+1) = t;
end
plot(t_rec,v_rec)
```

```
xlabel('time (s)')
ylabel('velocity (m/s)')
```

The results are shown in Figure 10.2.

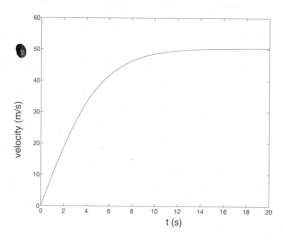

Figure 10.2 Skydiver's velocity

Example 10.5

(a) Solve

$$y' = f(y, t), \quad y(0) = 5 \tag{A}$$

where

$$f(y, t) = -20y + 7 exp(-0.5t) \tag{B}$$

using the forward Euler method with $h = 0.01$ for $0 < t \leq 0.02$. Do this part by hand calculation.

(b) Repeat the same for $0 < t \leq 0.1$ with $h = 0.01, 0.001$ and 0.0001 for $0 \leq t \leq 0.1$ by MATLAB. Evaluate errors of the three calculations by comparison to the analytical solution given by

$$y = 5e^{-20t} + (7 - 19.5)(e^{-0.5t} - e^{-20t}) \tag{C}$$

Solution

(a) The first two time steps of calculations with $h = 0.01$ are

$$t_0 = 0, \qquad y_0 = y(0) = 0$$
$$t_1 = 0.01, \quad y_1 = y_0 + hy'_0 = 5 + (0.01)(-20(5) + 7\exp(0)) = 4.07$$
$$t_2 = 0.02, \quad y_2 = y_1 + hy'_1 = 4.07 + (0.01)(-20(4.07) + \exp(-0.01))$$
$$= 3.326$$

(b) The computational results for selected values of t with three different values of h are shown in the following table:

t	$y(t)$ and percent errors in parentheses		
	$h=0.01$	$h=0.001$	$h=0.0001$
0.01	4.07000 (8.710)	4.14939 (0.771)	4.15634 (0.076)
0.02	3.32600 (14.099)	3.45438 (1.261)	3.46574 (0.125)
0.03	2.73080 (17.117)	2.88650 (1.547)	2.90044 (0.153)
0.04	2.25464 (18.474)	2.42251 (1.687)	2.43771 (0.167)
0.05	1.87371 (18.693)	2.04339 (1.725)	2.05893 (0.171)
0.06	1.56897 (18.158)	1.73362 (1.693)	1.74887 (0.168)
0.07	1.32518 (17.150)	1.48052 (1.616)	1.49507 (0.161)
0.08	1.13014 (15.868)	1.27372 (1.510)	1.28732 (0.150)
0.09	0.97411 (14.453)	1.10474 (1.390)	1.11726 (0.138)
0.10	0.84929 (13.002)	0.96668 (1.263)	0.97805 (0.126)

Comment: Accuracy of the forward Euler method increases with decrease in step size h. It is observed that magnitudes of errors are approximately proportional to h. The errors (in percentage) are due to truncation associated with the forward Euler method. Further reduction of h is not advantageous, however, because computational time becomes longer and rounding error may increase [1]

Although the forward Euler method is simple, it has to be used carefully for two kinds of errors. The first is the truncation error which is mentioned in Example 10.5, and the second is *instability*. The latter occurs when the time constant of the equation is negative (solution approaches zero if source is removed) but time step h is not sufficiently small. A typical equation with a negative time constant is $y' = \alpha y$, with $y(0) = y_0 > 0$ and $\alpha < 0$ (see Example 10.1). The exact solution is $y = y_0 e^{\alpha t}$. The forward Euler scheme for this problem becomes

$$y_{n+1} = (1 + \alpha h)y_n$$

If $0 > \alpha h > -1$, the numerical solution is positive and approaching zero, but if $\alpha h < -1$ the sign of the solution alternates as n is advanced. Furthermore, if $\alpha h > 2$, the magnitude of the solution increases after each step while the sign alternates, and eventually the solution diverges. This erratic behavior of the solution is referred to as instability of the scheme.

---

[1]See Chapters 1 and 9 of Nakamura, *Applied Numerical Methods in C*, Prentice-Hall, 1992

10.2.2   Modified Euler Method

The motivation for the modified Euler method is two fold. First, the modified Euler method is more accurate than the forward Euler method. Second, it is more stable than the forward Euler method.

The modified Euler method is derived by applying the trapezoidal rule to solution of $y' = f(y, x)$:

$$y_{n+1} = y_n + \frac{h}{2}[f(y_{n+1}, t_{n+1}) + f(y_n, t_n)] \tag{10.2.4}$$

If f is a linear function of y, Eq.(10.2.4) may be easily solved for y_{n+1} in a closed form. As an example, let

$$f(y, t) = ay + \cos(t)$$

then, Eq.(10.2.4) becomes

$$y_{n+1} = y_n + \frac{h}{2}[ay_{n+1} + \cos(t_{n+1}) + ay_n + \cos(t_n)]$$

Therefore, solving for y_{n+1} yields

$$y_{n+1} = \frac{1 + ah/2}{1 - ah/2}y_n + \frac{h}{1 - ah/2}\frac{\cos(t_{n+1}) + \cos(t_n)}{2} \tag{10.2.5}$$

If f is a nonlinear function of y, Eq.(10.2.4) becomes a nonlinear function of y_{n+1}, so an algorithm to solve the nonlinear equation should be applied. A widely used method is the *successive substitution method*, which is written as

$$y_{n+1}^{(k)} = y_n + \frac{h}{2}[f(y_{n+1}^{(k-1)}, t_{n+1}) + f(y_n, t_n)] \tag{10.2.6}$$

where $y_{n+1}^{(k)}$ is the k-th iterative approximation for y_{n+1}, and $y_{n+1}^{(0)}$ is an initial guess for y_{n+1}. The iteration is terminated when $|y_{n+1}^{(k)} - y_{n+1}^{(k-1)}|$ becomes less than a prescribed tolerance. If the initial guess is set to y_n, the first iteration step becomes identical with the forward Euler method. If only two iteration steps are used, the scheme becomes the second-order Runge-Kutta method.

The next example shows an application of the modified Euler method to a nonlinear first-order ODE.

Example 10.6

(a) Determine $y(0.1)$ for the following initial-value problem

$$y' = -y^{1.5} + 1, \quad y(0) = 10 \tag{A}$$

by the modified Euler method with $h = 0.1$. Set the tolerance of convergence to 0.00001.

(b) Continue computation by advancing time steps until $t = 0.5$ is reached.

(c) Develop a MATLAB script to compute the solution for $0 < t \le 1$ by both forward Euler and modified Euler methods and plot the results.

Solution

(a) The modified Euler scheme is written

$$y_{n+1} = y_n + (h/2)[-(y_{n+1})^{1.5} - (y_n)^{1.5} + 2] \qquad (B)$$

Its iterative solution based on successive substitution is

$$y_{n+1}^{(k)} = y_n + (h/2)[-(y_{n+1}^{(k-1)})^{1.5} - (y_n)^{1.5} + 2] \qquad (C)$$

where k is the iteration number. The iteration for y_1 starts with the initial guess $y_1^{(0)} = y(0) = 10$, and is continued as follows:

$$y_1^{(1)} = 10 + (0.1/2)[-(10)^{1.5} - (10)^{1.5} + 2] = 6.93772$$
$$y_1^{(2)} = 10 + (0.1/2)[-(6.93772)^{1.5} - (10)^{1.5} + 2] = 7.60517$$
$$y_1^{(3)} = 10 + (0.1/2)[-(7.60517)^{1.5} - (10)^{1.5} + 2] = 7.47020$$
$$y_1^{(4)} = 10 + (0.1/2)[-(7.47020)^{1.5} - (10)^{1.5} + 2] = 7.49799$$
$$y_1^{(5)} = 10 + (0.1/2)[-(7.49799)^{1.5} - (10)^{1.5} + 2] = 7.49229$$
$$\cdots$$
$$y_1 = 10 + (0.1/2)[-(7.49326)^{1.5} - (10)^{1.5} + 2] = 7.49326$$

(b) The computed results for five time steps are:

```
t         y
0.0     10.0000
0.1      7.4932
0.2      5.8586
0.3      4.7345
0.4      3.9298
0.5      3.3357
```

(c) A MATLAB script to obtain the solutions is in List 10.2. In the script, the solution of the forward Euler scheme is denoted by `yf`, while that of the modified Euler scheme is `ym`. The modified Euler equation is solved iteratively by successive substitution method. The number of iteration is limited to 10 times at most. If iteration exceeds 9, a message is printed out.

List 10.2

```
clear, clf, hold off
%===== Forward Euler
yf(1) = 10;  t(1) = 0;   h = 0.1; n=1;
while t(n)<1
   n = n+1; t(n) = t(n-1) + h;
   yf(n) = yf(n-1) +  h*( -yf(n-1)^1.5 + 1);
end
%==== Modified Euler
ym(1) = 10;  t(1) = 0;  h = 0.1; n=1;
while t(n)<1
   n = n+1;  t(n) = t(n-1) + h;
   ym(n) = ym(n-1) +  h*( - ym(n-1)^1.5 + 1);
   for k=1:10      % Successive substitution iteration
      ymb = ym(n);
      ym(n) = ym(n-1) ...
         + 0.5*h*( -ym(n)^1.5 - ym(n-1)^1.5 + 2);
      if abs(ym(n) - ymb) < 0.00001, break
      end
      if k>9,
         disp 'Iteration does not converge after k=9'
      end
   end
end
plot(t,yf,'--', t,ym, '-')
xlabel('t'); ylabel('y');
text(0.1, 1.2, ' ... forward Euler    - modified Euler')
```

The results are shown in Figure 10.3.

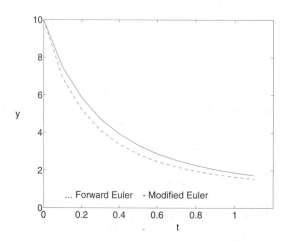

Figure 10.3 Comparison of Euler and modified Euler results

10.2.3   Backward Euler Method

The backward Euler method is based on the backward difference approximation and written as

$$y_{n+1} = y_n + hf(y_{n+1}, t_{n+1}) \tag{10.2.7}$$

The order of accuracy of this method is the same as that of the forward Euler method. Besides, if f is a nonlinear function of y, an iterative scheme (successive substitution) has to be used in each step just as in the modified Euler method. The advantages, however, are (a) the method is unconditionally stable, and (b) positivity of solution is guaranteed when the solution is supposed to be positive.

10.2.4   Accuracy of Euler Methods

Why is accuracy of the modified Euler method higher than that of the forward or backward Euler methods? To find out the reason analytically, let us consider the test equation $y' = \alpha y$. Equation (10.2.4) may then be written for this problem as

$$y_{n+1} = y_n + \frac{1}{2}\alpha h(y_{n+1} + y_n) \tag{10.2.8}$$

or equivalently,

$$y_{n+1} = \frac{1 + \frac{1}{2}\alpha h}{1 - \frac{1}{2}\alpha h} y_n$$

Expanding the foregoing equation yields

$$y_{n+1} = \left(1 + \alpha h + \frac{1}{2}(\alpha h)^2 + \frac{1}{4}(\alpha h)^3 + \cdots\right)y_n \tag{10.2.9}$$

Here we assume that y_n is given. On the other hand, Taylor expansion of the exact solution $(y_{n+1})_{\text{exact}} = \exp(\alpha h)y_n$ is

$$(y_{n+1})_{\text{exact}} = \left(1 + \alpha h + \frac{1}{2}(\alpha h)^2 + \frac{1}{6}(\alpha h)^3 + \cdots\right)y_n \tag{10.2.10}$$

The discrepancy between Eq.(10.2.9) and Eq.(10.2.10) is due to the error generated in $t_n < t < t_{n+1}$, named *local error*. The two equations agree to the second-order term, and the discrepancy is in the order h^3. Thus the modified Euler method is a second-order (accurate) method. Errors are accumulated as time steps proceed. Assuming that a fixed interval of time, h, is used repeatedly, the order of the total error accumulated during a given period of time, say t, equals the number of time intervals times h^3, that is, $(t/h)h^3 = h^2t$. The total of the accumulated errors is named *global error*. Therefore, the order of global error is one order lower than that of the local error.

A similar analysis may be applied to the forward Euler method as well as to the backward Euler method. The following table summarizes the local and global errors of the three Euler methods.

	Forward Euler	Modified Euler	Backward Euler
Order of local error	h^2	h^3	h^2
Order of global error	h	h^2	h

10.2.5   Second-order ODEs

When the highest derivative in an ODE is the second derivative, the equation is called a *second-order ODE*. The second-order ODEs may be written as

$$u''(t) + au'(t) + bu(t) = s(t), \quad u(0) = u_0, \quad u'(0) = u_0' \qquad (10.2.11)$$

where a, b and s are constants or functions of t, u and u', and the second and third equations are initial conditions. Notice that a second-order ODE needs two initial conditions, which are given for $u(0)$ and $u'(0)$. If a, b, and s are independent of u, the foregoing equation is a linear ODE. On the other hand, if any of a, b, and s is a function of u or u', or both, the equation is a nonlinear equation. In this subsection, we study how to solve second-order ODEs by the forward Euler method. We will also learn how to write MATLAB scripts, which can be easily extended to a more accurate method such as the fourth-order Runge-Kutta method.

An important step before applying an Euler scheme is to break up the second-order ODE to a pair of first-order ODEs. Define

$$v = u'$$

then Eq.(10.2.11) may be written as

$$v'(t) + av(t) + bu(t) = s(t), \quad v(0) = u_0'$$

Here, the initial condition in terms of the new variable v comes from the second initial condition in Eq.(10.2.11). Equation (10.2.11) is now equivalently expressed by a set of first-order ODEs as follows:

$$
\begin{aligned}
u' &= f_1(u, v, t), \quad u(0) = u_0 \\
v' &= f_2(u, v, t), \quad v(0) = u_0'
\end{aligned}
\qquad (10.2.12)
$$

where

$$f_1(u, v, t) = v$$

$$f_2(u, v, t) = -av - bu + s$$

A step-by-step computation for the first few time steps are as follows:

$t = h,$
    $u_1 = u_0 + h f_1(u_0, v_0, 0) = h v_0$
    $v_1 = v_0 + h f_2(u_0, v_0, 0) = h(-a v_0 - b u_0 + s(0))$

$t = 2h,$
    $u_2 = u_1 + h f_1(u_1, v_1, h) = h v_1$
    $v_2 = v_1 + h f_2(u_1, v_1, h) = h(-a v_1 - b u_1 + s(h))$

For MATLAB, the computation for each time step may be written in matrix form. We first define $\mathbf{y}$ and $\mathbf{f}$, respectively, by

$$\mathbf{y} = \begin{bmatrix} u \\ v \end{bmatrix} \tag{10.2.13}$$

$$\mathbf{f} = \begin{bmatrix} f_1 \\ f_2 \end{bmatrix} = \begin{bmatrix} v \\ -av - bu + s \end{bmatrix} \tag{10.2.14}$$

Then, the set of equations in Eq.(10.2.12) is written in a single equation as

$$\mathbf{y}' = \mathbf{f}(\mathbf{y}, t)$$

The forward Euler scheme for the foregoing equation is written as

$$\mathbf{y}_{n+1} = \mathbf{y}_n + h\mathbf{f}(\mathbf{y}_n, t_n) \tag{10.2.15}$$

which is the same as Eq.(10.2.2) except that $\mathbf{y}$ and $\mathbf{f}$ are vectors.

Example 10.7

A cubic object of mass M = 10 kg is fixed to the lower end of a spring-damper system (see Figure 10.4). The upper end of the spring is fixed to a structure at rest. The force of damper is $R = -B|u'|u'$, where B is a constant and u is the displacement distance from the initial position in meter. The equation of motion is

$$M u'' + B|u'|u' + ku = 0, \quad u(0) = 0, \quad u'(0) = 1 \tag{A}$$

where k is the spring constant of 200 N/m, and B = 50 Ns^2/m^2.

(a) Calculate $u(t)$ for $0 < t \leq 0.1$ using the forward Euler method with $h = 0.05$ by hand calculations.

(b) Calculate $u(t)$ for $0 < t \leq 5$ s by MATLAB using the forward Euler method with $h = 0.05$. Plot the results.

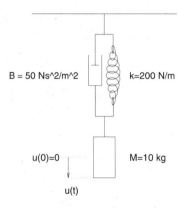

B = 50 Ns^2/m^2   k=200 N/m

u(0)=0   M=10 kg

u(t)

Figure 10.4 A spring-mass system

Solution

Equation (A) may be written as

$$u' = v, \quad u(0) = 0$$
$$v' = -a|v|v - cu, \quad v(0) = 1 \tag{B}$$

where $a = B/M = 5$ and $c = k/M = 20$.

(a):

$t = 0$,
$$u_0 = u(0) = 0$$
$$v_0 = u'(0) = 1$$

$t = 0.05$,

$$u_1 = u_0 + hv_0$$
$$= 0 + (0.05)(1) = 0.05$$
$$v_1 = v_0 + h(-a|v_0|v_0 - cu_0)$$
$$= 1 + (0.05)[-5|1|(1) - (20)(0)] = 0.75$$

$t = 0.1$,

$$u_2 = u_1 + hv_1$$
$$= 0.05 + (0.05)(0.75) = 0.0875$$

$$z_2 = v_1 + h(-a|v_1|v_1 - cu_1)$$
$$= 0.75 + (0.05)\left[-5|0.75|(0.75) - (20)(0.05)\right] = 0.5594$$

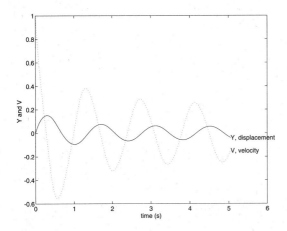

Figure 10.5 Forward Euler solution of mass-spring problem

(b): A script for MATLAB is most easily developed by writing the equations in vector form:

$$\mathbf{y}' = \mathbf{f}(\mathbf{y}, t) \tag{C}$$

where

$$\mathbf{y} = \begin{bmatrix} u \\ v \end{bmatrix}$$

$$\mathbf{f} = \begin{bmatrix} v \\ -a|v|v - cu \end{bmatrix}$$

The forward Euler scheme for the foregoing equation is written as

$$\mathbf{y}_{n+1} = \mathbf{y}_n + h\mathbf{f}(\mathbf{y}_n, t_n) \tag{D}$$

A script to complete the solution is given in List 10.3. The results are shown in Figure 10.5.

List 10.3
```
clear,clf,hold off
h = 0.05; t_max=5; n=1;
y(:,1) = [0; 1];
t(1) = 0;
```

```
while t(n)< t_max
   y(:,n+1) = y(:,n) + h*f_def(y(:,n),t); yb=y;
   t(n+1) = t(n)+h ;
   n=n+1;
end
axis([0 5 -1 1])
plot(t, y(1,:), t, y(2,:),':')
xlabel('time (s)'); ylabel('Y and V  ')
L=length(t);
text(t(L), y(1,L), 'Y, displacement')
text(t(L), y(2,L), 'V, velocity')
```

f_def.m
```
function f = f_def(y, t)
a = 5; c=20;
f = [y(2);  (-a*abs(y(2))*y(2) - c*y(1))];
```

Comment: Since the computation is very easy, we may be tempted to apply the foregoing script for the case with $B = 0$. If you do this, somewhat puzzling results will occur. For $B = 0$, the solution must be purely harmonic; in other words, the oscillation should be a sustaining sinusoidal motion. The computational result of the forward Euler method with $h = 0.05$, however, will show a slowly diverging oscillation because of numerical errors. In order to decrease the error, a substantially smaller h is necessary. This not only increases computing time significantly, but also risks the danger of introducing a significant amount of rounding errors. This is one of the reasons why we should use more accurate methods such as the fourth-order Runge-Kutta method described in Section 10.3.

10.2.6   Higher-order ODEs

The methods described in the preceding subsections may be extended further to higher-order ODEs. For example, consider

$$y''''(t) + ay'''(t) + by''(t) + cy'(t) + ey(t) = g(t) \qquad (10.2.16)$$

where a, b, c, e, and g are constants or known functions of t if the equation is a linear ODE. If the equation is nonlinear, at least one of a, b, c, e, and g is a function of one or more of y, y', y'' and y'''. The initial conditions are given as

$$y(0) = y_0, \quad y'(0) = y_0',$$
$$y''(0) = y_0'', \quad y'''(0) = y_0'''$$

where y_0, y_0', y_0'' and y_0''' are prescribed values.

If we consider each of y, y', y'' and y''' as an unknown variable, Eq.(10.2.16) can be equivalently written as a set of four first-order ordinary differential equations:

$$y' = u, \qquad y(0) = y_0$$
$$u' = v, \qquad u(0) = y_0'$$
$$v' = w, \qquad v(0) = y_0'' \qquad\qquad (10.2.17)$$
$$w' = g - aw - bv - cu - ey, \qquad w(0) = y_0'''$$

Equation (10.2.16) may be equivalently written in a vector form as

$$\mathbf{y}' = \mathbf{f}(\mathbf{y}, t) \qquad\qquad (10.2.18)$$

with

$$\mathbf{y} = \begin{bmatrix} y \\ u \\ v \\ w \end{bmatrix}$$

$$\mathbf{f} = \begin{bmatrix} u \\ v \\ w \\ g - aw - bv - cu - ey \end{bmatrix}$$

The expression of the forward Euler scheme for Eq.(10.2.18) is the same as Eq.(10.2.15).

The numerical methods also may be applied to integro-differential equations. For example, consider

$$y'' + ay + \int_0^t y(s)ds = c, \quad y(0) = y_0, \quad y'(0) = y_0' \qquad (10.2.19)$$

We define u and v as

$$u = y'$$
$$v = \int_0^t y(s)ds \qquad\qquad (10.2.20)$$

the latter of which may be equivalently written, after differentiation, as

$$v' = y, \quad v(0) = 0$$

Then, Eq.(10.2.19) becomes

$$y' = u, \quad y(0) = y_0$$
$$u' = -ay - v + c, \quad u(0) = y_0' \qquad (10.2.21)$$
$$v' = y, \quad v(0) = 0$$

The foregoing equation can be written in the vector form as

$$\mathbf{y}' = \mathbf{f}(\mathbf{y}, t) \qquad (10.2.22)$$

with

$$\mathbf{y} = \begin{bmatrix} y \\ u \\ v \end{bmatrix}$$

$$\mathbf{f} = \begin{bmatrix} u \\ -ay - v + c \\ y \end{bmatrix}$$

For Eq.(10.2.22), the forward Euler scheme is again the same as Eq.(10.2.15).

Example 10.8

The electric current of the circuit shown in Figure 10.6 satisfies the integro-differential equation

$$L\frac{di(t)}{dt} + Ri(t) + \frac{q(t)}{C} = E(t), \quad t > 0 \qquad (A)$$

$$q(t) = \int_0^t i(t')dt' + q(0) \qquad (B)$$

where $q(t)$ is the capacitor charge (coulombs), the switch is closed at $t = 0$, $i = i(t)$ is the current (amperes), and the constants are given by

$$R = 100 \quad \Omega$$
$$L = 200 \quad mH$$
$$C = 10 \quad \mu F$$
$$E = 1 \quad V$$

Initial conditions are $q(0) = 0$ (capacitor's initial charge) and $i(0) = 0$. Calculate the current for $0 < t \leq 0.025$ s with $h = 0.00025$ s.

Solution

Differentiating Eq.(B) yields

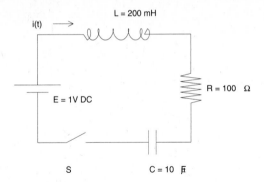

L = 200 mH

i(t)

E = 1V DC

R = 100 Ω

S

C = 10 F

Figure 10.6 Electrical circuit

$$\frac{dq(t)}{dt} = i(t), \quad q(0) = 0 \tag{C}$$

We rewrite Eq.(A) to

$$\frac{di(t)}{dt} = -\frac{R}{L}i(t) - \frac{1}{LC}q(t) + \frac{E(t)}{L}, \quad i(0) = 0 \tag{D}$$

Then, the vector form of the equations is

$$\mathbf{y}' = \mathbf{f}(\mathbf{y}, t) = \mathbf{M}\mathbf{y} + \mathbf{S} \tag{E}$$

with

$$\mathbf{y} = \begin{bmatrix} q \\ i \end{bmatrix}, \quad \mathbf{M} = \begin{bmatrix} 0, & 1 \\ -1/LC, & -R/L \end{bmatrix}, \quad \mathbf{S} = \begin{bmatrix} 0 \\ E(t)/L \end{bmatrix}$$

Computation is performed by the following script, and the results are plotted in Figure 10.7.

List 10.4
```
clear, clf, hold off
R = 100;        %ohm
L = 200e-3;     %H
C = 10e-6;      %F
E = 1;
h = 0.25e-3;
n=1;
t(1)=0; y(:,1)=[0;0];
M=[0,1;-1/(L*C), -R/L]; S = [0;E/L];
while n<101
    y(:,n+1) = y(:,n)  + h*(M*y(:,n)+S);
    t(n+1)   = n*h;
    n=n+1;
```

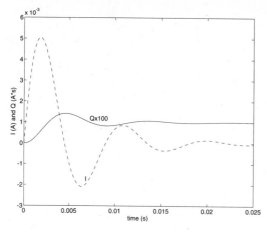

Figure 10.7 Graph of computed results

```
end
plot(t,100*y(1,:),t,y(2,:),'--' )
text(t(30), 119*(y(1,30)), 'Qx100')
text(t(28), y(2,30), 'I')
xlabel('time (s)')
ylabel('I (A) and Q (A*s)')
```

10.3 RUNGE-KUTTA METHODS

A major drawback of the Euler methods is that order of accuracy is low. To maintain a high accuracy requires a very small h, which not only increases computational time but also causes rounding errors.

In Runge-Kutta methods, the order of accuracy is increased using a higher order numerical integration method. A higher accuracy implies that the computed result is more accurate as well as that errors decrease more quickly when h is decreased.

Consider an ordinary differential equation

$$y' = f(y, t), \quad y(0) = y_0 \tag{10.3.1}$$

In order to calculate y_{n+1} with a known value of y_n, we integrate Eq.(10.3.1) in the interval $t_n \geq t \geq t_{n+1}$ to yield

$$y_{n+1} = y_n + \int_{t_n}^{t_{n+1}} f(y, t)dt \tag{10.3.2}$$

Then, Runge-Kutta methods are derived by applying a numerical integration method to the right side of the foregoing equation. In the remainder of this section, the second-, third-, and fourth-order Runge-Kutta methods are explained.

10.3.1 Second-order Runge-Kutta Method

Here we examine application of the trapezoidal rule to the right side of Eq.(10.3.2):

$$\int_{t_n}^{t_{n+1}} f(y,t)dt \approx \frac{h}{2}\left[f(y_n, t_n) + f(y_{n+1}, t_{n+1})\right] \qquad (10.3.3)$$

where $h = t_{n+1} - t_n$. In the foregoing equation, y_{n+1} is not known, so that the second term is approximated by $f(\overline{y}_{n+1}, t_{n+1})$, where $\overline{y}_{n+1}$ is an estimate calculated by the forward Euler method. The scheme derived in this way is called the second-order Runge-Kutta method, and is written as

$$\overline{y}_{n+1} = y_n + hf(y_n, t_n)$$

$$y_{n+1} = y_n + \frac{h}{2}[f(y_n, t_n) + f(\overline{y}_{n+1}, t_{n+1})]$$

or, in a more standard form,

$$k_1 = hf(y_n, t_n)$$
$$k_2 = hf(y_n + k_1, t_{n+1}) \qquad (10.3.4)$$
$$y_{n+1} = y_n + \frac{1}{2}(k_1 + k_2)$$

The second-order Runge-Kutta method is equivalent to the modified Euler method with only two iteration steps.

Example 10.9

The circuit shown in Figure 10.8 has a self-inductance of $L = 50$ mH, a resistance of $R = 20\ \Omega$, and a voltage source of $E = 10$ V. If the switch is closed at $t = 0$, the current $I(t)$ satisfies

$$L\frac{dI(t)}{dt} + RI(t) = E, \quad I(0) = 0 \qquad (A)$$

Find the value of the current for $0 < t < 0.02$ s by the second-order Runge-Kutta method with $h = 0.0001$.

Solution

We first rewrite Eq.(A) as

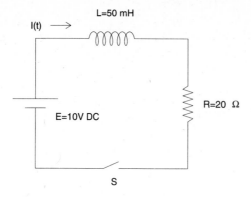

L=50 mH

I(t)

R=20 Ω

E=10V DC

S

Figure 10.8 An electrical circuit

$$\frac{dI}{dt} = f(I, t) \tag{B}$$

where

$$f(I, t) = -\frac{R}{L}I + \frac{E}{L}$$

Then, the second-order Runge-Kutta method becomes

$$k_1 = h\left(\frac{-R}{L}I_n + \frac{E}{L}\right)$$

$$k_2 = h\left(\frac{-R}{L}(I_n + k_1) + \frac{E}{L}\right)$$

$$I_{n+1} = I_n + \frac{1}{2}(k_1 + k_2)$$

Calculations for the first two steps are shown:

$t = 0,$
   $I_0 = 0$

$t = 0.0001,$
   $k_1 = 0.0001[(-400)(0) + 200] = 0.02$
   $k_2 = 0.0001[(-400)(0 + 0.02) + 200] = 0.0192$
   $I_1 = I_0 + (1/2)(k_1 + k_2) = 0 + (1/2)(0.02 + 0.0192) = 0.0196$

$t = 0.0002,$
   $k_1 = 0.0001[(-400)(0.0196) + 200] = 0.019216$
   $k_2 = 0.0001[(-400)(0.0196 + 0.019216) + 200] = 0.018447$

$$I_2 = I_1 + (1/2)(k_1 + k_2) = 0.0196 + (1/2)(0.019216 + 0.018447)$$
$$= 0.038431$$

The remainder of computation is performed by MATLAB (see List 10.5) and the final result of computation is plotted in Figure 10.9.

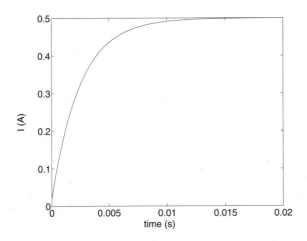

Figure 10.9 Electric current

List 10.5

```
clear, clf, hold off
R = 20;        %ohm
L = 50e-3;     %H
E = 10;        %V
y(1)=0; t(1)=0;
h = 0.1e-3;
n=1;
y_rec(1)=y; t_rec(1)=0;t=0;
RL = R/L;   EL=E/L;
while t(n)<0.02
    k1 = h*fn10_9(y(n), RL, EL);
    k2 = h*fn10_9(y(n)+k1, RL, EL);
    y(n+1) = y(n) + 0.5*(k1+k2);
    t(n+1) = n*h;
    n=n+1;
end
plot(t,y )
xlabel('time (s)')
ylabel('I (A) ')
```

fn10_9

```
function f=fn10_9(I, RL, EL)
f=-RL*I + EL
```

Example 10.10

A thin plate at 200°C (or 473 K) is suddenly placed in a room of 25 K, where the plate is cooled by both natural convection and radiation heat transfer. The following physical constants are given:

$\rho = 300 \text{ kg/m}^3$ (density)
$V = 0.001 \text{ m}^3$ (volume)
$A = 0.25 \text{ m}^2$ (surface area)
$C = 900 \text{ J/kgK}$ (specific heat)
$h_c = 30 \text{ J/m}^2\text{K}$ (heat transfer coefficient)
$\epsilon = 0.8$ (emissivity)
$\sigma = 5.67 \times 10^{-8} \text{ W/m}^2\text{K}^4$ (Stefan-Boltzmann constant)

Assuming the temperature distribution in the metal is uniform, the equation for the temperature is

$$\frac{dT}{dt} = \frac{A}{\rho CV}\left[\epsilon\sigma(297^4 - T^4) + h_c(297 - T)\right], \quad T(0) = 473 \qquad \text{(A)}$$

where T is the temperature in Kelvin. Find the temperature for $0 < t < 180$ s, using the second-order Runge-Kutta scheme with $h = 1$ s.

Solution

The second-order Runge-Kutta scheme is implemented in List 10.6. When the right side of the ODE is a nonliner function like the present problem, it is convenient to write a function M-file to compute the right side of ODE.

List 10.6

```
clear, clf, hold off
ro=300; V=0.001; A = 0.25; C = 900;
hc=30;
epsi=0.8; sig=5.67e-8; n=1;
h = 1; T(1)=473; t(1)=0;
Arcv = A/(ro*C*V);   Epsg = epsi*sig;
while t(n)<180
   k1 = h*fn10_10(T(n),Arcv,Epsg,hc);
   k2 = h*fn10_10(T(n)+k1,Arcv,Epsg,hc);
    T(n+1)  = T(n) + 0.5*(k1 + k2);
    t(n+1)=t(n)  + h;
    n=n+1;
end
plot(t,T);   xlabel('time, sec'), ylabel(' T   (Kelvin)')
```

fn10_10

```
function f = fn10_10(TB,Arcv,Epsg,hc)
y=Arcv*( Epsg*(297^4  - TB^4) + hc*(297-TB));
```

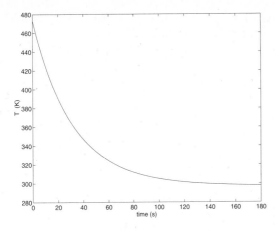

Figure 10.10 Temperature of the metal piece

The results are plotted in Figure 10.10.

10.3.2 Accuracy of Second-order Runge-Kutta Method

Accuracy of the second-order Runge-Kutta method may be analyzed by the test equation

$$y' = f(y, t) = \alpha y \tag{10.3.5}$$

Provided that y_n is given, the exact solution for y_{n+1} is obviously

$$(y_{n+1})_{\text{exact}} = e^{\alpha h} y_n \tag{10.3.6}$$

Its Taylor expansion is

$$(y_{n+1})_{\text{exact}} = [1 + \alpha h + \frac{1}{2}(\alpha h)^2 + \frac{1}{6}(\alpha h)^3 ...]y_n \tag{10.3.7}$$

On the other hand, applying Eq.(10.3.4) to Eq.(10.3.5) yields

$$y_{n+1} = [1 + \alpha h + \frac{1}{2}(\alpha h)^2]y_n \tag{10.3.8}$$

By comparing Eq.(10.3.8) with Eq.(10.3.7), the former is found to be accurate to order h^2 and the discrepancy (error generated in one step) is proportional to h^3. Notice that the second-order Runge-Kutta method is identical to the modified Euler method given by Eq.(10.2.6) with two iteration steps. Order of accuracy of the second-order Runge-Kutta scheme, however, is found to be identical to that of the modified Euler method which requires iterative convergence. This indicates that the iteration beyond the second step in the modified Euler method does not increase order of accuracy. (Indeed, using the second-order Runge-Kutta method with a smaller h is far more effective in improving accuracy than strict iterative convergence.) The accuracy may be analyzed more formally without using a test equation. [2]

10.3.3   Higher-order ODEs

Application of the second-order Runge-Kutta method to a higher-order ordinary differential equation is similar to that of the forward Euler method. For illustration, we consider the second-order differential equation:

$$u'' + au' + bu = q(t), \ u(0) = 1, \ u'(0) = 0 \tag{10.3.9}$$

where a, b, q are constants or functions of t, u, and u'. By defining

$$v(t) = u'(t) \tag{10.3.10}$$

Eq.(10.3.9) can be reduced to a set of coupled first-order differential equations:

$$
\begin{aligned}
u' &= f(u, v, t) = v, & u(0) &= 1 \\
v' &= g(u, v, t) = -av - bu + q, & v(0) &= 0
\end{aligned}
\tag{10.3.11}
$$

The second-order Runge-Kutta method for the foregoing equations is written as

---

[2]Given the value of y_n, the solution of $y' = f(y, t)$ may be expressed by the Taylor expansion of y_{n+1} about t_n as

$$
\begin{aligned}
(y_{n+1})_{\text{exact}} &= y_n + hf + (h^2/2)[f_t + f_y f] \\
&\quad + (h^3/6)[f_{tt} + 2f_{ty}f + f_{yy}f^2 + f_t f_y + f_y^2 f] + O(h^4)
\end{aligned}
\tag{F1}
$$

where all the derivatives of y are expressed in terms of f and the partial derivatives of f at t_n.
  Next, we expand the third equation in Eq.(10.3.4) in a Taylor series:

$$
\begin{aligned}
y_{n+1} &= y_n + hf + (h^2/2)[f_t + f_y f] \\
&\quad + (h^3/4)[f_{tt} + 2f_{ty}f + f_{yy}f^2] + O(h^4)
\end{aligned}
\tag{F2}
$$

Comparison of Eq.(F2) with Eq.(F1) reveals that Eq.(10.3.4) is accurate up to order h^2; in other words, the order of its local error is h^3.

$$k_1 = hf(u_n, v_n, t_n) = hv_n$$

$$m_1 = hg(u_n, v_n, t_n) = h(-av_n - bu_n + q_n)$$

$$k_2 = hf(u_n + k_1, v_n + m_1, t_{n+1}) = h(v_n + m_1)$$

$$m_2 = hg(u_n + k_1, v_n + m_1, t_{n+1})$$

$$= h(-a(v_n + m_1) - b(u_n + k_1) + q_{n+1}) \qquad (10.3.12)$$

$$u_{n+1} = u_n + \frac{1}{2}(k_1 + k_2)$$

$$v_{n+1} = v_n + \frac{1}{2}(m_1 + m_2)$$

For MATLAB implementation, we write the ODEs in the vector form as

$$\mathbf{y}' = \mathbf{f} \qquad (10.3.13)$$

with

$$\mathbf{y} = \begin{bmatrix} u \\ v \end{bmatrix}$$

$$\mathbf{f} = \begin{bmatrix} f \\ g \end{bmatrix} = \begin{bmatrix} v \\ -av - bu + q \end{bmatrix}$$

Then, the second-order Runge-Kutta scheme becomes

$$\mathbf{k}_1 = h\mathbf{f}(\mathbf{u}_n, t_n)$$

$$\mathbf{k}_2 = h\mathbf{f}(\mathbf{u}_n + \mathbf{k}_1, t_{n+1}) \qquad (10.3.14)$$

$$\mathbf{y}_{n+1} = \mathbf{y}_n + \frac{1}{2}(\mathbf{k}_1 + \mathbf{k}_2)$$

In case a, b, and q are constants or functions of only t, Eq.(10.3.13) may be written as

$$\mathbf{y}' = \mathbf{M}\mathbf{f} + \mathbf{S}$$

where

$$\mathbf{M} = \begin{bmatrix} 0 & 1 \\ -b & -a \end{bmatrix}, \qquad \mathbf{S} = \begin{bmatrix} 0 \\ q \end{bmatrix}$$

Then, Eq.(10.3.14) is written equivalently

$$\mathbf{k}_1 = h\left[\mathbf{M}\mathbf{y_1} + \mathbf{S}\right]$$

$$\mathbf{k}_2 = h\left[\mathbf{M}(\mathbf{y_1} + \mathbf{k}_1) + \mathbf{S}\right] \qquad (10.3.15)$$

$$\mathbf{y}_{n+1} = \mathbf{y}_n + \frac{1}{2}(\mathbf{k}_1 + \mathbf{k}_2)$$

Example 10.11

A rectangular box of mass $M = 0.5$ kg is fixed to the lower end of a massless spring-damper system, as illustrated in Figure 10.11. The upper end of the spring is fixed to a structure at rest. The box receives a force of $R = -B du/dt$ from the damper, where B is a damping constant. The equation of motion is

$$Mu'' + Bu' + ku = 0, \quad u(0) = 1, \quad u'(0) = 0 \tag{A}$$

where u is the displacement from the static position, k is the spring constant equal to 100 N/m, and $B = 10$ Ns/m.

(a) Calculate $u(t)$ for $0 < t \leq 0.05$ s, using the second-order Runge-Kutta method with $h = 0.025$ s, by hand calculations.

(b) Calculate $u(t)$ for $0 < t \leq 1$ s, using the second-order Runge-Kutta method with $h = 0.025$ s.

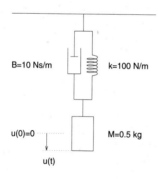

Figure 10.11 A spring-mass system

Solution

Equation (A) may be written as

$$u' = f \equiv v, \quad u(0) = 1$$
$$v' = g \equiv -(B/M)v - (k/M)u, \quad v(0) = 0$$

By setting $a = B/M = 20$ and $b = k/M = 200$, the second-order Runge-Kutta method for Eq.(A) becomes in the form of Eq.(10.3.14);

(a):

$t = 0$,

$\quad u_0 = u(0) = 1$

$\quad v_0 = u'(0) = 0$

$t = 0.025$,

$\quad k_1 = hf(u_0, v_0, t_0) = hv_0 = 0.025(0) = 0$

$\quad m_1 = hg(u_0, v_0, t_0) = h(-20v_0 - 200u_0)$

$\quad\quad = 0.025(-20(0) - 200(1)) = -5$

$\quad k_2 = hf(u_0 + k_1, v_0 + m_1, t_1) = h(v_0 + m_1)$

$\quad\quad = 0.025(0 - 5) = -0.125$

$\quad m_2 = hg(u_0 + k_1, v_0 + m_1, t_1)$

$\quad\quad = h[-20(v_0 + m_1) - 200(u_0 + k_1)]$

$\quad\quad = 0.025[-20(0 - 5) - 200(1 + 0)] = -2.5$

$\quad u_1 = u_0 + (1/2)(0 - 0.125) = 0.9375$

$\quad v_1 = v_0 + (1/2)(-5 - 2.5) = -3.75$

$t = 0.05$,

$\quad k_1 = hf(u_1, v_1, t_1) = hv_1 = 0.025(-3.75) = -0.09375$

$\quad m_1 = hg(u_1, v_1, t_1) = h(-20v_1 - 200u_1)$

$\quad\quad = 0.025[-20(-3.75) - 200(0.9375)] = -2.8125$

$\quad k_2 = hf(u_1 + k_1, v_1 + m_1, t_2) = h(v_1 + m_1)$

$\quad\quad = 0.025(-3.75 - 2.8125) = -0.16406$

$\quad m_2 = hg(u_1 + k_1, v_1 + m_1, t_2)$

$\quad\quad = h[-20(v_1 + m_1) - 200(u_1 + k_1)]$

$\quad\quad = 0.025[-20(-3.75 - 2.8125) - 200(0.9375 - 0.09375)]$

$\quad\quad = -0.9375$

$\quad u_2 = u_1 + (1/2)(-0.09375 - 0.16406) = 0.80859$

$\quad v_2 = v_1 + (1/2)(-2.8125 - 0.9375) = -5.625$

(b): For MATLAB computations, we rewrite the equations as

$$y' = Mf$$

where

$$y = \begin{bmatrix} u \\ v \end{bmatrix}, \qquad Mf = \begin{bmatrix} 0 & 1 \\ -b & -a \end{bmatrix},$$

The script in List 10.7 is developed based on Eq.(10.3.14) applied to the foregoing equation. The results are plotted in Figure 10.12.

List 10.7
```
clear, clf, hold off
M=0.5; k = 100; B=10; a = B/M;
b = k/M; n=1;  h = 0.025;
y(:,1) = [1;0]; t(1)=0; % initial condition
```

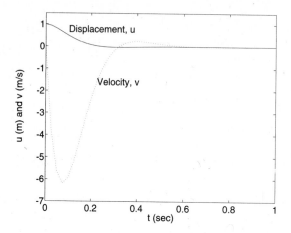

Figure 10.12 Dynamic responses of spring-mass system

```
M=[0,1; -b,-a];
while t(n) <=1
  k1 = h*M*y(:,n);
  k2 = h*M*(y(:,n)+k1);
  y(:,n+1) = y(:,n) + 0.5*(k1 + k2);
  t(n+1) = n*h;
  n=n+1;
end
plot(t,y(1,:),  '-',  t,y(2,:),':');
xlabel('t (s)'),  ylabel(' y and v')
text(0.5, -6.5, '- y, ... v')
```

Comment: The present problem is repeated in Example 10.14 by the fourth-order Runge-Kutta method with application to the case of $B = 0$.

Example 10.12

Motion of an electron in an uniform electromagnetic field is given by[3]

$$m\frac{d\mathbf{V}}{dt} = e\mathbf{V} \times \mathbf{B} + e\mathbf{E} \tag{A}$$

where $\mathbf{V}$ is the velocity vector, $\mathbf{B}$ the magnetic field vector, $\mathbf{E}$ the electric

---
[3]This example was provided by Professor Y. Funato of Suzuka College of Technology, Japan.

field vector, m the mass of electron, e the charge of electron:

Initial condition: $\mathbf{V} = (-10, 2, 0.1) \times 10^5$ m/s
Initial position of electron: $\mathbf{R} = (0, 0, 0)$ m
Magnetic field vector: $\mathbf{B} = (0, 0, 0.1)$ T
Electric field vector: $\mathbf{E} = (0, 2, 0) \times 10^4$ V/m
Mass of electron: $m = 9.1 \times 10^{-31}$ kg
Charge of electron, $e = 1.6 \times 10^{-19}$ c

Solve Eq.(A) by the second-order Runge-Kutta method with $h = 0.5 \times 10^{-11}$ s, for $0 < t \leq 2 \times 10^{-9}$ s, and determine the locus of the electron. Plot trajectory of the electron in a three-dimensional view, and the velocity components as functions of time as well as in the three-dimensional phase space.

Solution

A script may be developed in a straightforward manner using vxv_, which is a function to compute vector product. The solutions computed by the following script are shown in Figure 10.13.

List 10.8

```
clear,clf,hold off
e=1.6e-19;              % Charge of electron, coulomb
m=9.1e-31;              % Electron mass, kg
B=[0;0;0.1]*e/m;        % Magnetic field strength, tesla
E=[0;2e4;0]*e/m;        % Electric field strength, volt/meter
h=0.5e-11;              % Time step, second
v(:,1)=1e5*[-10;2;0.1];
                        % Initial velocity of electron, meter/sec
t(1)=0;                 % Time initialization, sec
xyz(:,1)=[0;0;0];
epm=e/m;
for i=2:400
  t(i)=h*i;
  k1=h*(vxv_(v(:,i-1),B) + E) ;
  k2=h*(vxv_(v(:,i-1)+k1,B) + E) ;
  v(:,i)=v(:,i-1) + 0.5*(k1+k2);
  xyz(:,i)=xyz(:,i-1)+0.5*(v(:,i-1)+v(:,i))*h;
end
figure(1)
plot3(xyz(1,:), xyz(2,:),xyz(3,:))
axis([-5,5,-1,2,0,0.3]*1e-4)
xlabel('X'); ylabel('Y'); zlabel('Z');
figure(2)
plot3(xyz(1,:), xyz(2,:),xyz(3,:))
xlabel('X'); ylabel('Y'); zlabel('Z');
view([0,0,1])
figure(3)
```

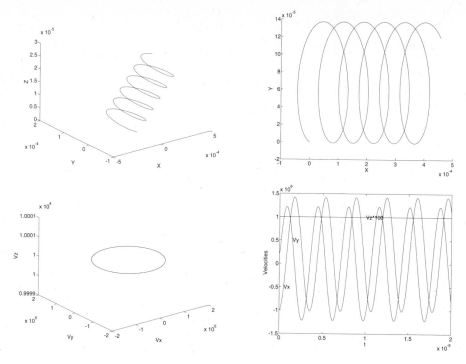

Figure 10.13 Trajectory and velocity of electron

```
plot3(v(1,:), v(2,:),v(3,:))
xlabel('Vx'); ylabel('Vy'); zlabel('Vz');
figure(4)
plot(t,v(1,:),t, v(2,:),t,v(3,:)*100)
xlabel('t'); ylabel('Velocities');
text(t(10),v(1,10), 'Vx')
text(t(30),v(2,30), 'Vy')
text(t(200),v(3,200)*100, 'Vz*100')
```

vxv_.m

```
function c=vtv_(a,b)
% [c] = [a]   x [b]
% a, b, c:  vectors
c=[a(2)*b(3)-a(3)*b(2);
  -a(1)*b(3)+a(3)*b(1);
   a(1)*b(2)-a(2)*b(1)];
```

10.3.4 Third-order Runge-Kutta Method

The third-order Runge-Kutta method is derived by a higher-order numerical integration scheme for the second term of Eq.(10.3.2). Using the Simpson's 1/3 rule, Eq.(10.3.2) may be written as

$$y_{n+1} = y_n + \frac{h}{6}[f(y_n, t_n) + 4f(\overline{y}_{n+1/2}, t_{n+1/2}) + f(\overline{y}_{n+1}, t_{n+1})] \quad (10.3.16)$$

where $\overline{y}_{n+1/2}$ and $\overline{y}_{n+1}$ are estimates because $y_{n+1/2}$ and y_{n+1} are not known. The estimate $\overline{y}_{n+1/2}$ is obtained by the forward Euler method as

$$\overline{y}_{n+1/2} = y_n + \frac{h}{2}f(y_n, t_n) \quad (10.3.17)$$

The estimate $\overline{y}_{n+1}$ may be obtained by

$$\overline{y}_{n+1} = y_n + hf(y_n, t_n)$$

or

$$\overline{y}_{n+1} = y_n + hf(\overline{y}_{n+1/2}, t_{n+1/2})$$

or a linear combination of both

$$\overline{y}_{n+1} = y_n + h[\theta f(y_n, t_n) + (1 - \theta)f(\overline{y}_{n+1/2}, t_{n+1/2})] \quad (10.3.18)$$

Here θ is an undetermined parameter, which will be determined to maximize accuracy of the numerical method. With Eq.(10.3.18), the whole scheme is written in the following form:

$$k_1 = hf(y_n, t_n)$$
$$k_2 = hf(y_n + \frac{1}{2}k_1, t_{n+1/2})$$
$$k_3 = hf(y_n + \theta k_1 + (1 - \theta)k_2, t_{n+1})$$
$$y_{n+1} = y_n + \frac{1}{6}(k_1 + 4k_2 + k_3) \quad (10.3.19)$$

To analyze the accuracy and optimize θ, we apply the foregoing equations to our test equation, Eq.(10.3.5). For Eq.(10.3.5), Eq.(10.3.19) becomes

$$k_1 = h\alpha y_n$$

$$k_2 = h\alpha(1 + \frac{1}{2}h\alpha)y_n$$

$$k_3 = h\alpha\left[1 + \theta h\alpha + (1-\theta)h\alpha(1+\frac{1}{2}h\alpha)\right]y_n \qquad (10.3.20)$$

$$y_{n+1} = \left[1 + h\alpha + \frac{1}{2}(h\alpha)^2 + \frac{1-\theta}{12}(h\alpha)^3\right]y_n$$

Comparing with the expansion of $(y_{n+1})_{\text{exact}}$ given by Eq.(10.3.7), we find that the optimum is $\theta = -1$.

Therefore, the third-order Runge-Kutta method is written as

$$k_1 = hf(y_n, t_n)$$
$$k_2 = hf(y_n + k_1/2, t_{n+1/2})$$
$$k_3 = hf(y_n - k_1 + 2k_2, t_{n+1})$$
$$y_{n+1} = y_n + \frac{1}{6}(k_1 + 4k_2 + k_3) \qquad (10.3.21)$$

The foregoing equations also may be derived without assuming any particular model equation. [4]

10.3.5 Fourth-order Runge-Kutta Method

Derivation of the fourth-order Runge-Kutta method is similar to that of the third-order method, except that one more intermediate step of evaluating the derivative is used. There are several alternative choices for the numerical integration scheme to be used in Eq.(10.3.2). The fourth-order Runge-Kutta method is accurate to the fourth-order term of the Taylor expansion, so the local error is proportional to h^5.

---

[4]Taylor expansions of k_1, k_2 and k_3 in Eq.(10.3.18) are

$$k_1 = hf \qquad (F3a)$$

$$k_2 = hf + (1/2)h^2(f_t + f_y f)$$
$$+ \frac{1}{8}h^3(f_{tt} + 2f_{ty}f + f_y f^2) \qquad (F3b)$$

$$k_3 = hf + h^2(f_t + f_y f)$$
$$+ \frac{1}{2}h^3[f_{tt} + 2f_{ty}f + f_{yy}f^2 + (1-\theta)(f_t + f_y f)f_y] \qquad (F3c)$$

where f and its derivatives are evaluated at t_n. We introduce Eq.(F3) into Eq.(10.3.20) and compare it with the exact value of y_{n+1} in the Taylor series written in Footnote 2. We then find that Eq.(10.3.20) agrees with the Taylor expansion of the exact solution to the third-order term if $\theta = -1$.

The following two versions of the fourth-order Runge-Kutta method are most popularly used. The first version is based on the Simpson's 1/3 rule and is written as

$$k_1 = hf(y_n, t_n)$$
$$k_2 = hf(y_n + k_1/2, t_{n+1/2})$$
$$k_3 = hf(y_n + k_2/2, t_{n+1/2})$$
$$k_4 = hf(y_n + k_3, t_{n+1})$$
$$y_{n+1} = y_n + \frac{1}{6}(k_1 + 2k_2 + 2k_3 + k_4) \qquad (10.3.22)$$

The second version is based on the Simpson's 3/8 rule and is written as

$$k_1 = hf(y_n, t_n)$$
$$k_2 = hf(y_n + k_1/3, t_{n+1/3})$$
$$k_3 = hf(y_n + k_1/3 + k_2/3, t_{n+2/3})$$
$$k_4 = hf(y_n + k_1 - k_2 + k_3, t_{n+1})$$
$$y_{n+1} = y_n + \frac{1}{8}(k_1 + 3k_2 + 3k_3 + k_4) \qquad (10.3.23)$$

Example 10.13

Calculate $y(1)$ for

$$y' = -1/(1 + y^2), \qquad y(0) = 1$$

using the fourth-order Runge-Kutta method with $h = 1$.

Solution
We set

$$f(y, t) = -1/(1 + y^2)$$

with $y_0 = 1$ and $t_0 = 0$. Since we have only one interval, the answer is obtained by

$$k_1 = hf(y_0, t_0) = -1/(1 + 1) = -0.5$$
$$k_2 = hf(y_0 + k_1/2, t_{1/2}) = -1/(1 + (0.75)^2) = -0.64$$
$$k_3 = hf(y_0 + k_2/2, t_{1/2}) = -1/(1 + (0.68)^2) = -0.6838$$

$$k_4 \quad = hf(y_0 + k_3, t_1) = -1/(1 + (0.3161)^2) = -0.9091$$

$$y_1 = y_0 + \frac{1}{6}[k_1 + 2k_2 + 2k_3 + k_4]$$

$$= 1 + \frac{1}{6}[-0.5 - 2(0.64) - 2(0.6838) - 0.9091] = 0.3238$$

Application of the fourth-order Runge-Kutta method to a set of ordinary differential equations is very similar to that of the second-order Runge-Kutta method. For simplicity of explanation, we consider a set of two equations:

$$u' = f(u, v, t)$$
$$v' = g(u, v, t) \tag{10.3.24}$$

The fourth-order Runge-Kutta method for the set of two equations becomes

$$k_1 = hf(u_n, v_n, t_n)$$
$$m_1 = hg(u_n, v_n, t_n)$$
$$k_2 = hf(u_n + k_1/2, v_n + m_1/2, t_{n+1/2})$$
$$m_2 = hg(u_n + k_1/2, v_n + m_1/2, t_{n+1/2})$$
$$k_3 = hf(u_n + k_2/2, v_n + m_2/2, t_{n+1/2})$$
$$m_3 = hg(u_n + k_2/2, v_n + m_2/2, t_{n+1/2})$$
$$k_4 = hf(u_n + k_3, v_n + m_3, t_{n+1})$$
$$m_4 = hg(u_n + k_3, v_n + m_3, t_{n+1})$$
$$u_{n+1} = u_n + \frac{1}{6}(k_1 + 2k_2 + 2k_3 + k_4) \tag{10.3.25}$$
$$v_{n+1} = v_n + \frac{1}{6}(m_1 + 2m_2 + 2m_3 + m_4)$$

If Eq.(10.3.24) is written in the vector form,

$$y' = f(y, t) \tag{10.3.26}$$

where

$$y = \begin{bmatrix} u \\ v \end{bmatrix}$$
$$f = \begin{bmatrix} f \\ g \end{bmatrix} \tag{10.3.27}$$

then, the fourth-order Runge-Kutta scheme is written as

$$k_1 = hf(\mathbf{y}_n, t_n)$$
$$k_2 = hf(\mathbf{y}_n + k_1/2, t_{n+1/2})$$
$$k_3 = hf(\mathbf{y}_n + k_2/2, t_{n+1/2})$$
$$k_4 = hf(\mathbf{y}_n + k_3, t_{n+1})$$
$$\mathbf{y}_{n+1} = \mathbf{y}_n + \frac{1}{6}(k_1 + 2k_2 + 2k_3 + k_4) \qquad (10.3.28)$$

MATLAB scripts implementing the fourth-order Runge-Kutta method can be developed using the form of Eq.(10.3.28); however, if Eq.(10.3.26) can be written in a linear form as

$$\mathbf{y}' = \mathbf{My} + \mathbf{S}$$

then Eq.(10.3.28) is written as

$$k_1 = h[\mathbf{My} + \mathbf{S}]$$
$$k_2 = h[\mathbf{M}(\mathbf{y} + k_1/2) + \mathbf{S}]$$
$$k_3 = h[\mathbf{M}(\mathbf{y} + k_2/2) + \mathbf{S}]$$
$$k_4 = h[\mathbf{M}(\mathbf{y} + k_3) + \mathbf{S}]$$
$$\mathbf{y}_{n+1} = \mathbf{y}_n + \frac{1}{6}[k_1 + 2k_2 + 2k_3 + k_3] \qquad (10.3.29)$$

Example 10.14

(a) Repeat (a) of the problem in Example 10.11 by the fourth-order Runge-Kutta method. (b) Repeat (b) of Example 10.11 for $B = 0$, using MATLAB.

Solution

(a): Referring to Example 10.11, the equations to be solved are

$$u' = f \equiv v, \quad u(0) = 1$$
$$v' = g \equiv -(B/M)v - (k/M)u, \quad v(0) = 0$$

By setting $a = B/M = 20$ and $b = k/M = 200$, the fourth-order Runge-Kutta method for Eq.(A) in Example 10.11 becomes the form of Eq.(10.3.25).

$t = 0,$

$\quad u_0 = u(0) = 1$

$\quad v_0 = u'(0) = 0$

$t = 0.025,$

$\quad k_1 = hf(u_0, v_0, t_0) = hv_0 = 0.025(0) = 0$

$\quad m_1 = hg(u_0, v_0, t_0) = h(-20v_0 - 200u_0)$

$\qquad = 0.025(-20(0) - 200(1)) = -5$

$\quad k_2 = hf(u_0 + k_1/2, v_0 + m_1/2, t_0 + h/2) = h(v_0 + m_1/2)$

$\qquad = 0.025(0 - 5/2) = -0.0625$

$\quad m_2 = hg(u_0 + k_1/2, v_0 + m_1/2, t_0 + h/2)$

$\qquad = h[-20(v_0 + m_1/2) - 200(u_0 + k_1/2)]$

$\qquad = 0.025[-20(0 - 5/2) - 200(1 + 0/2)] = -3.75$

$\quad k_3 = hf(u_0 + k_2/2, v_0 + m_2/2, t_0 + h/2) = h(v_0 + m_1/2)$

$\qquad = 0.025(0 - 3.75/2) = -0.046875$

$\quad m_3 = hg(u_0 + k_2/2, v_0 + m_2/2, t_0 + h/2)$

$\qquad = h[-20(v_0 + m_2/2) - 200(u_0 + k_2/2)]$

$\qquad = 0.025[-20(0 - 3.75/2) - 200(1 - 0.0625/2)] = -3.9062$

$\quad k_4 = hf(u_0 + k_3, v_0 + m_3, t_0 + h) = h(v_0 + m_3)$

$\qquad = 0.025(0 - 5/2) = -0.09765$

$\quad m_4 = hg(u_0 + k_3, v_0 + m_3, t_0 + h)$

$\qquad = h[-20(v_0 + m_3/2) - 200(u_0 + k_3/2)]$

$\qquad = 0.025[-20(0 - 3.90625) - 200(1 - 0.046875)] = -2.8125$

$\quad u_1 = u_0 + (1/6)(0 + 2(-0.0625) + 2(-0.046875) - 0.097656)$

$\qquad = 0.947266$

$\quad v_1 = v_0 + (1/6)(-5 + 2(-3.75) + 2(-3.9062) - 2.8125)$

$\qquad = -3.8541$

$t = 0.05,$

$\quad k_1 = hf(u_1, v_1, t_1) = hv_1 = 0.025(-3.85416) = -0.096354$

$\quad m_1 = hg(u_1, v_1, t_1) = h(-20v_1 - 200u_1)$

$\qquad = 0.025(-20(-3.8541) - 200(0.947265)) = -2.8092$

$\quad k_2 = hf(u_1 + k_1/2, v_1 + m_1/2, t_1 + h/2) = h(v_1 + m_1/2)$

$\qquad = 0.025(-3.8541666 - 2.809244/2) = -0.1314697$

$\quad m_2 = hg(u_1 + k_1/2, v_1 + m_1/2, t_1 + h/2)$

$\qquad = h[-20(v_1 + m_1/2) - 200(u_1 + k_1/2)]$

$\qquad = 0.025[-20(-3.85416 - 2.809244/2) - 200(0.947266 - 0.096354/2)]$

$\qquad = -1.866054$

$\quad k_3 = hf(u_1 + k_2/2, v_1 + m_2/2, t_1 + h/2) = h(v_1 + m_2/2)$

$\qquad = 0.025(-3.85416 - 1.866054/2) = -0.1196797$

$\quad m_3 = hg(u_1 + k_2/2, v_0 + m_2/2, t_1 + h/2)$

$\qquad = h[-20(v_1 + m_2/2) - 200(u_1 + k_2/2)]$

$\qquad = 0.025[-20(-3.85416 - 1.866054/2) - 200(0.947266 - 0.1314697/2)]$

$\qquad = -2.014058$

$\quad k_4 = hf(u_1 + k_3, v_1 + m_3, t_1 + h) = h(v_1 + m_3)$

$$= 0.025(-3.85416 - 2.014058) = -0.146706$$

$$m_4 = hg(u_1 + k_3, v_1 + m_3, t_1 + h)$$
$$= h[-20(v_1 + m_3) - 200(u_1 + k_3)]$$
$$= 0.025[-20(-3.85416 - 2.014058) - 200(0.947266 - 0.1196797)]$$
$$= -1.203821$$

$$u_2 = u_1 + (1/6)(-0.0963541 + 2(-0.131469) + 2(-0.119679)$$
$$-0.146705) = 0.823039$$

$$v_2 = v_1 + (1/6)(-2.809244 + 2(-1.866048) + 2(-2.014058)$$
$$-1.203816) = -5.816375$$

(b): For MATLAB computations, we rewrite the equations to the following form:

$$\mathbf{y}' = \mathbf{M}\mathbf{y}$$

where

$$\mathbf{y} = \begin{bmatrix} u \\ v \end{bmatrix}$$

$$\mathbf{M} = \begin{bmatrix} 0, & 1 \\ -b, & -a \end{bmatrix}$$

List 10.9 is developed based on Eq.(10.3.29) applied to the foregoing equations. The result is shown in Figure 10.14.

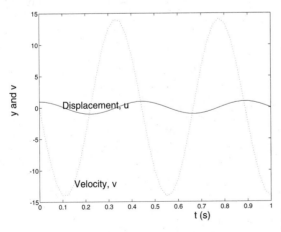

Figure 10.14 Dynamic responses of spring-mass system

List 10.9
```
clear,clg
M=0.5;  k = 100;  B=0;  a = B/M;
b = k/M;  n=0;  t=0;  h = 0.025;
```

```
y(:,1)  = [1;0]; t(1)=0; % initial condition
M=[0,1; -b,-a];
while t<=1
  n=n+1;
   k1 = h*M*y(:,n);
   k2 = h*M*(y(:,n)+k1/2);
   k3 = h*M*(y(:,n)+k2/2);
   k4 = h*M*(y(:,n)+k3);
   y(:,n+1) = y(:,n) + (k1 + 2*k2 + 2*k3 + k4)/6;
   t(n+1) = n*h;
end
plot(t,y(1,:), '-', t,y(2,:),':');
xlabel('t (s)'), ylabel(' y and v')
text(t(5),y(1,5)+0.3,'Displacement, u','FontSize',[18])
text(t(7),y(2,7),'Velocity, v','FontSize',[18])
axis([0,1,-15,15])
```

Comment: Part B is a simple problem but not necessarily trivial (see comments in Example 10.7). Since the solution is analytically known, however, it is a good benchmark problem to examine a solution method.

Example 10.15

The three-mass system is shown in Figure 10.15.[5] The displacements of the three masses satisfy the equations given by

$$M_1 y_1'' + B_1 y_1' + K_1 y_1 - B_1 y_2' - K_1 y_2 = F_1(t)$$
$$-B_1 y_1' - K_1 y_1 + M_2 y_2'' + B_1 y_2' + (K_1 + K_2) y_2 - K_2 y_3 = 0 \qquad (A)$$
$$-K_2 y_2 + M_3 y_3'' + B_3 y_3' + (K_2 + K_3) y_3 = F_3(t)$$

where y_1, y_2 and y_3 are displacements. Constants and initial conditions are

$K_1 = K_2 = K_3 = 1$ (spring constants, N/m)
$M_1 = M_2 = M_3 = 1$ (mass, kg)
$F_1(t) = 0.01,\ F_3(t) = 0$ (force, N)
$B_1 = B_3 = 0.1$ (damping coefficients, Ns/m)
$y_1(0) = y_1'(0) = y_2(0) = 0$ (initial displacement, m)
$y_2'(0) = y_3(0) = y_3'(0) = 0$ (initial velocity, m/s)

Solve the foregoing equations by the fourth-order Runge-Kutta method for $0 \le t \le 30$ s with $h = 0.1$ s.

---

[5]This example was provided by Professor Doebelin of The Ohio State University.

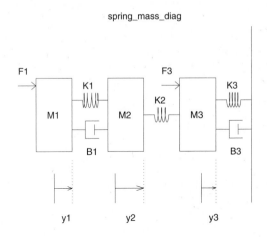

Figure 10.15 Mass-spring system

Solution

We define

$$y_4 = y_1',\quad y_5 = y_2',\quad \text{and}\quad y_6 = y_3' \tag{B}$$

Then, Eq.(A) is written as a set of six first-order ODEs as

$$y_1' = y_4$$

$$y_2' = y_5$$

$$y_3' = y_6$$

$$y_4' = [-B_1 y_4 - K_1 y_1 + B_1 y_5 + K_2 y_2 + F_1]/M_1$$

$$y_5' = [B_1 y_4 + K_1 y_1 - B_1 y_5 - (K_1 + K_2)y_2 + K_2 y_3]/M_2$$

$$y_6' = [K_2 y_2 - B_3 y_6 - (K_2 + K_3)y_3 + F_3]/M_3$$

Equation (C) can be written in matrix form as

$$\mathbf{y}' = \mathbf{f}(\mathbf{y}, t) \tag{D}$$

with

$$\mathbf{y} = \begin{bmatrix} y_1 \\ y_2 \\ y_3 \\ y_4 \\ y_5 \\ y_6 \end{bmatrix}$$

$$\mathbf{f} = \begin{bmatrix} 0 & 0 & 0 & 1 & 0 & 0 \\ 0 & 0 & 0 & 0 & 1 & 0 \\ 0 & 0 & 0 & 0 & 0 & 1 \\ \frac{-K_1}{M_1} & \frac{K_2}{M_1} & 0 & \frac{-B_1}{M_1} & +\frac{B_1}{M_1} & 0 \\ \frac{K_1}{M_2} & -\frac{K_1+K_2}{M_2} & \frac{K_3}{M_2} & \frac{B_1}{M_2} & \frac{-B_1}{M_2} & 0 \\ 0 & \frac{K_2}{M_3} & -\frac{K_2+K_3}{M_3} & 0 & 0 & \frac{-B_3}{M_3} \end{bmatrix} \mathbf{y} + \begin{bmatrix} 0 \\ 0 \\ 0 \\ F_1/M_1 \\ 0 \\ F_3/M_3 \end{bmatrix}.$$

The computational results are shown in Figure 10.16.

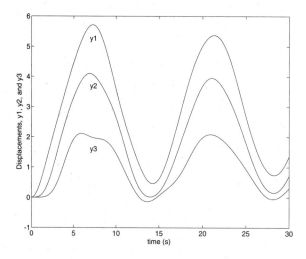

Figure 10.16 Results of computations

List 10.10

```
clear, clg
M1 = 1; M2 = 1; M3 = 1;
K1 = 1; K2 = 1; K3 = 1;
F1 = 0.01; F3 = 0; F = [0, 0, 0, F1/M1, 0, F3/M3]';
B1 = 0.1; B3 = 0.1;
y(:,1)=[0; 0; 0; 0; 0; 0]; t(1) = 0; n=1;
```

```
h = 0.1;
C = [0,       0,         0,        1,      0,      0; ...
     0,       0,         0,        0,      1,      0; ...
     0,       0,         0,        0,      0,      1; ...
    -K1/M1,   K2/M1,     0,      -B1/M1, B1/M1,    0; ...
     K1/M2,-(K1+K2)/M2, K2/M2,   B1/M2, -B1/M2,    0; ...
     0,       K2/M3,  -(K2+K3)/M3,  0,     0,    -B3/M3]
while t<=30
    k1 = h*F3m(y(:,n),       C, F);
    k2 = h*F3m(y(:,n)+k1/2,  C, F);
    k3 = h*F3m(y(:,n)+k2/2,  C, F);
    k4 = h*F3m(y(:,n)+k3,    C, F);
  y(:,n+1) = y(:,n) + (1/6)*(k1 + 2*k2 + 2*k3 + k4);
  t(n+1) = n*h;
  n=n+1;
end
plot(t,y(1:3,:))
text( t(70), y(1,70), 'y1')
text( t(70), y(2,70), 'y2')
text( t(70), y(3,70), 'y3')
xlabel('time (s)')
ylabel('Displacements, y1, y2, and y3')
```

F3m.m
```
function f = F3m(y,C,F)
f = C*y + F;
```

Example 10.16

The behavior of an electric circuit changes significantly depending upon the values of the parts used. Consider the circuit shown in Figure 10.17, for which differential equations are written as

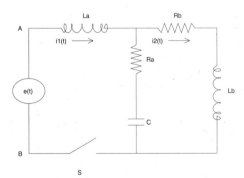

Figure 10.17 Electrical circuit

$$L_a \frac{di_1}{dt} + R_a(i_1 - i_2) + \frac{q(t)}{C} = e(t)$$

$$-\frac{q(t)}{C} - R_a(i_1 - i_2) + R_b i_2 + L_b \frac{di_2}{dt} = 0$$

with

$$q(t) = \int_0^t (i_1(t') - i_2(t'))dt' + q(0)$$

where $e(t) = 0$ except $e(t)=1$ when $0 < t < 0.01$ s, $q(t)$ is the capacitor charge, $i_1(t)$ and $i_2(t)$ are currents; meanings of other notations and units are shown in Figure 10.17. Initial conditions are $i_1(0) = i_2(0) = q(0) = 0$ for all cases. In order to investigate the effects of the parts, solve the equations for the following four sets of constants:

(a) $L_a = 0.01$; $L_b = 0.5$; $R_a = 200$; $R_b = 20$; $C = 0.002$
(b) Same as (a) except $L_a = 0.1$
(c) Same as (a) except $L_b = 0.25$
(d) Same as (a) except $R_a = 20$

Solution

The solutions are obtained by List 10.11. The results are shown in Figure 10.18.

List 10.11

```
clear;clg
subplot(221)
for k=1:4
  e=1;
  if k==1; subplot(221);
      La=0.01; Lb=0.5;    Ra=200; Rb=20;C=0.002; end
  if k==2, subplot(222);
      La=0.1;  Lb= 0.5;  Ra=200 ; Rb=20; C=0.002; end
  if k==3; subplot(223);
      La=0.01; Lb= 0.25; Ra=200 ; Rb=20  ;C=0.002; end
  if k==4; subplot(224)
      La=  0.01; Lb= 0.5; Ra=20 ; Rb=20   ;C=0.002; end
      M=[ -Ra/La,    Ra/La,        -1/(La*C) ; ...
          Ra/Lb, -(Ra+Rb)/Lb,    1/(Lb*C) ;   ...
                1/C,      -1/C,         0        ]
  S=[0;0;0]; x=[0; 0; 0];
  h=0.00005;
  for n=1:101
    t=(n-1)*h;
    %S=[ sin(t*600)*exp(-t*600)/La; 0; 0];
    %S=[ cos(t*600)/La; 0; 0];
    S=[ 1/La; 0; 0];
    if t>0.001, S=[0;0;0];end
    k1=h*(M*x+S);
    k2=h*(M*(x+k1/2)+S);
    k3=h*(M*(x+k2/2)+S);
```

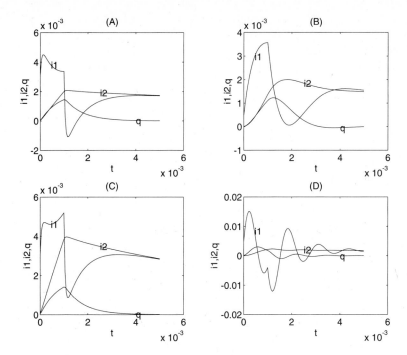

Figure 10.18 Behavior of circuit

```
       k4=h*(M*(x+k3)+S);
       x=x+(k1+k2*2+k3*2+k4)/6;
       x_r(:,n)=x;
       t_r(n)=t;
   end
   plot(t_r, x_r(1:2,:), t_r, x_r(3,:))
   xlabel('t'),ylabel('i1,i2,q')
   L= length(t_r)
   text(t_r(L/10),x_r(1,L/10),'i1')
   text(t_r(L/2),x_r(2,L/2),'i2')
   text(t_r(L*0.8),x_r(3,L*0.8),'q')
   if k==1;title('(A)');end
   if k==2;title('(B)');end
   if k==3;title('(C)');end
   if k==4;title('(D)');end
end
```

10.3.6   Error, Stability, and Time-interval Optimization

The Runge-Kutta methods are subject to two kinds of errors; namely, truncation error and instability. As discussed earlier, the truncation error can be found as the discrepancy between the Taylor expansion of the numerical method and that of the exact solution. The amount of error decreases faster with decrease in h as the order of the method becomes higher. On the other hand, instability is an accumulated effect of the local errors.

To analyze instability of a Runge-Kutta method, let us consider our model equation

$$y' = \alpha y \tag{10.3.30}$$

where $\alpha < 0$. For a given value of y_n, the exact value for y_{n+1} is analytically given as

$$(y_{n+1})_{\text{exact}} = e^{\alpha h} y_n = e^{n\alpha h} y_0 \tag{10.3.31}$$

Notice that, since $\alpha < 0$, $|(y_{n+1})_{\text{exact}}|$ decreases as n (or time) increases.

The numerical solution of Eq.(10.3.30) by the fourth-order Runge-Kutta method, Eq.(10.3.22), becomes

$$k_1 = \alpha h y_n$$

$$k_2 = \alpha h(y_n + k_1/2) = \alpha h(1 + \frac{1}{2}\alpha h)y_n$$

$$k_3 = \alpha h(y_n + k_2/2) = \alpha h(1 + \frac{1}{2}\alpha h(1 + \frac{1}{2}\alpha h))y_n$$

$$k_4 = \alpha h(y_n + k_3) = \alpha h(1 + \alpha h(1 + \frac{1}{2}\alpha h(1 + \frac{1}{2}\alpha h)))y_n$$

$$y_{n+1} = \left(1 + \alpha h + \frac{1}{2}(\alpha h)^2 + \frac{1}{6}(\alpha h)^3 + \frac{1}{24}(\alpha h)^4\right) y_n \tag{10.3.32}$$

Equation (10.3.32) equals the first five terms of the Taylor expansion for the right side of Eq.(10.3.31) about t_n. The amplification factor

$$\gamma = 1 + \alpha h + \frac{1}{2}(\alpha h)^2 + \frac{1}{6}(\alpha h)^3 + \frac{1}{24}(\alpha h)^4 \tag{10.3.33}$$

in Eq.(10.3.32) is an approximation for $\exp(\alpha h)$ of Eq.(10.3.31), so the truncation error and instability of Eq.(10.3.23) both originate from this approximation.

Equation (10.3.33) and $\exp(\alpha h)$ are plotted together in Figure 10.19 for comparison. The figure indicates that if $\alpha < 0$ and the modulus (absolute value) of αh increases, the deviation of γ from $\exp(\alpha h)$ increases; that is, the error of the Runge-Kutta method increases. Particularly, if $\alpha h \leq -2.785$, the method becomes unstable because the modulus of the numerical solution grows while the modulus of the true solution decreases by a factor, $\exp(\alpha h)$, in each step.

In practical applications of the Runge-Kutta method, an optimal time interval can be determined in the following way: For illustration purposes, suppose we

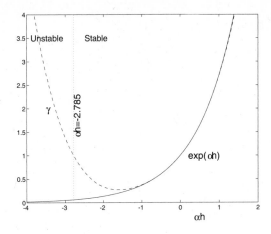

Figure 10.19 Domain of stability

desire to keep the local error of the third-order Runge-Kutta method less than ξ. The local error of the third-order Runge-Kutta method for a test interval h is proportional to h^4, so we express the local error in the form

$$E_h = Bh^4 \qquad (10.3.34)$$

where B is a constant that depends on the given problem. If we apply the same Runge-Kutta method in two steps with time interval $h/2$, the error becomes proportional to $2(h/2)^4$, where the factor 2 is due to accumulation of errors in two steps:

$$2E_{h/2} = 2B(h/2)^4 = (1/8)Bh^4 \qquad (10.3.35)$$

By subtracting Eq.(10.3.35) from Eq.(10.3.34), we get

$$E_h - 2E_{h/2} = Bh^4 - (1/8)Bh^4 = (7/8)Bh^4 \qquad (10.3.36)$$

The left side of the above equation may be evaluated by a numerical experiment; that is, to run the scheme twice starting from the same initial value. In the first run, only one time step is advanced using a trial value for h as the time interval. We denote the result of this calculation as $[y_1]_h$. In the second run, $[y_2]_{h/2}$ is calculated in two time steps using time interval $h/2$. Using the results of those two calculations, the left side of Eq.(10.3.36) is evaluated as

$$E_h - 2E_{h/2} = [y_1]_h - [y_2]_{h/2} \qquad (10.3.37)$$

Eliminating the left side of Eq.(10.3.36) by Eq.(10.3.37) and solving for B yield

$$B = (8/7)([y_1]_h - [y_2]_{h/2})/h^4 \qquad (10.3.38)$$

Once B is determined, the maximum (or optimum) h that satisfies the criterion $|E_h| \leq \xi$ is found by taking the absolute of Eq.(10.3.35) and setting $|E_h| = \xi$:

$$h = (\xi/|B|)^{0.25} \qquad (10.3.39)$$

The present approach has a reminiscence of the Romberg integration explained in Section 5.1.

Example 10.17

Assuming a fourth-order Runge-Kutta method is applied to

$$y' = -y/(1 + t^2), \; y(0) = 1$$

find an optimal step interval satisfying $|E_h| \leq 0.00001$.

Solution

For the fourth-order Runge-Kutta method, the local error is expressed by

$$E_h = Bh^5 \qquad (A)$$

The approach is very similar to Eqs.(10.3.34) through (10.3.39) except that the order of error is five. The error accumulated in two steps using $h/2$ is $2E_{h/2} = 2B(h/2)^5$. The difference between the errors of one-step and two-step calculations, namely $E_h - 2E_{h/2}$, is numerically evaluated by

$$E_h - 2E_{h/2} = [y_1]_h - [y_2]_{h/2} \qquad (B)$$

In the above equation, $[y_1]_h$ is the result of the fourth-order Runge-Kutta method for only one step with h, and $[y_2]_{h/2}$ is the result of the same for two steps with $h/2$. Introducing Eq.(A) into Eq.(B) and solving for B, we have

$$B = (16/15)([y_1]_h - [y_1]_{h/2})/h^5 \qquad (C)$$

Now we actually run the fourth-order Runge-Kutta method for only one step with $h = 1$ starting with the given initial condition, then for two steps with $h/2 = 1/2$. The results are

$$[y_1]_1 = 0.4566667 \quad (\text{one interval only})$$
$$[y_2]_{1/2} = 0.4559973 \quad (\text{two intervals})$$

From Eq.(C) we obtain B as

$$B = (16/15)(0.4566667 - 0.4559973)/(1)^5 = 6.3 \times 10^{-4} \qquad (\text{D})$$

By introducing this into Eq.(A), the local error for any h is expressed by

$$E_h = 6.3 \times 10^{-4} h^5$$

The maximum h that satisfies the given criterion, $|E(h)| < 0.00001$, is

$$h = \left(\frac{0.00001}{6.3 \times 10^{-4}} \right)^{1/5} = 0.44 \qquad (\text{E})$$

10.4 SHOOTING METHOD

The numerical methods for initial-value problems may be used to solve boundary-value problems. This approach is named the *shooting method*.

We consider a second-order ODE

$$\frac{d^2 y(x)}{dx^2} + a \frac{dy(x)}{dx} + by(x) = 0 \qquad (10.4.1)$$

with

$$y(0) = 0, \quad y(1) = 1$$

The foregoing equation has nothing new compared with the second-order ODEs we have seen in this chapter except the second condition is not an initial condition. Since the end conditions are spread between the initial and final points, the equation is called a boundary-value problem.

In order to apply any numerical method for initial-value problems to Eq.(10.4.1), we have to consider Eq.(10.4.1) as if it were an initial-value problem. We will estimate the second initial condition on a trial basis and see if the second boundary condition in Eq.(10.4.1) is satisfied. If not, we will make another guess and try again. This process will be repeated until the end condition is satisfied. Of course, after a few trials, we learn how to estimate the initial condition more skillfully just like in shooting a gun at a target.

Example 10.17

A rod 0.2 m long is placed in a stream of air at 293 K. The temperature at left end at $x = 0$ is fixed at 493 K, but the right end is insulated. The heat is removed from the surface by convection heat transfer. Using the following constants, determine the temperature distribution in the axial direction:

$$k = 60 \text{ W/mK (thermal conductivity)}$$
$$h_c = 20 \text{ W/m}^2\text{K (heat transfer coefficient)}$$
$$A = 0.0001 \text{ m}^2 \text{ (cross sectional area)}$$
$$P = 0.01 \text{ m (perimeter of the rod)}$$

Solution

The heat conduction equation in the axial direction x is written as

$$-Ak\frac{d^2T}{dx^2} + Ph_c(T - 293) = 0, \quad 0 < x < 0.2 \text{ m} \qquad \text{(A)}$$

with the boundary conditions

$$T(0) = 493 \text{ K}, \quad T'(0.2) = 0$$

The present problem is a boundary-value problem (boundary conditions are specified at $x = 0$ and $x = 0.2$ m), but can be solved as an initial-value problem on the trial-and-error basis. By defining

$$y_1(x) = T(x)$$
$$y_2(x) = T'(x)$$

Eq.(A) may be rewritten as a set of two first-order ODE's as

$$y_1' = y_2(x)$$
$$y_2' = (Ph_c/Ak)(y_1(x) - 293) \qquad \text{(B)}$$

Only one initial condition, $y_1(0) = 493$, is known from the boundary conditions (but $y_2(0)$ is not known). So we solve Eq.(A) with trial values for $y_2(0)$ until the boundary condition for the right end, namely $y_2(0.2) = T'(0.2) = 0$, is satisfied. A MATLAB script to perform the computation is developed as List 10.12. When executed, the program asks for the value of $y_2(0)$, then the computed temperature distribution is plotted. By looking at the plot of $y_2(x)$, the next guess may be determined.

We use the fourth-order Runge-Kutta method. After a number of trial-and-errors, we find that $y_2(0) = -2813.57$ satisfies the second boundary condition accurately, as shown in Figure 10.20.

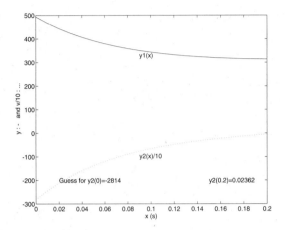

Figure 10.20 Computed results of the shooting method

List 10.12

```
clear, clg
while 1
   y2 = input('Type gradient, y2(0); or -99999 to quit:  ')
   if y2 < -88888, break, end
   A = 0.0001; P=0.01; hc = 120; k = 60; b=293;
   a=P*hc/A/k;
   n=1; x(1)=0; h = 0.01;
   y(:,1) = [493;y2];
    while x<=0.3
      k1 = h*f_shoot(y(:,n),        x(n),      a,b);
      k2 = h*f_shoot(y(:,n)+k1/2, x(n)+h/2,  a,b);
      k3 = h*f_shoot(y(:,n)+k2/2, x(n)+h/2,  a,b);
      k4 = h*f_shoot(y(:,n)+k3,    x(n)+h,    a,b);
      y(:,n+1) = y(:,n) + (1/6)*(k1 + 2*k2 + 2*k3 + k4);
      x(n+1) = n*h;
      if (x(n)-0.2001)*(x(n)-0.1999)<0
         y2_end = y(2,n+1), break,
      end
      n=n+1;
    end
 %  y2_end=(y(1,n+1)-y(1,n))/h;
   plot(x,y(1,:),  '-', x,y(2,:)/10,':');
   xlabel('x (s)'), ylabel(' y:-   and v/10:...')
   text(0.15, -200, ['y2(0.2)=', num2str(y2_end)] )
   text(0.02, -200, ['Guess for y2(0)=', num2str(y2)] )
```

```
text(x(10),    y(1,10)-20, 'y1(x)' )
 text(x(10),    y(2,10)/10-20   , 'y2(x)/10' )
axis([0,0.2,-300,500])
end
```

f_sm
```
function  f = f_shoot(y,x,a,b)
f = [y(2); a*(y(1)-b)];
```

Comment: Although writing a program using the shooting method is easy, much patience is necessary in the trial-and-error effort to determine the initial condition that satisfies the boundary condition at the end point. The boundary-value problem as in this example can be solved much more easily and efficiently by the method described in Chapter 11.

10.5   METHOD OF LINES

Method of lines is another application of numerical methods of initial-value problems to boundary-value problems. The method of lines is suitable particularly for parabolic PDEs.

We consider an unsteady heat conduction equation:

$$\frac{\partial T(x,t)}{\partial t} = \alpha \frac{\partial^2 T(x,t)}{\partial x^2}, \quad 0 < x < H \tag{10.5.1}$$

with the initial condition

$$T(x,0) = T_0$$

and boundary conditions

$$T(0,t) = T_L, \quad T(H,t) = T_R$$

where α is a constant (thermal diffusivity).

In order to derive a solution algorithm, we divide the domain of $0 \le x \le H$ into $K + 1$ equispaced intervals, so the mesh size is $\Delta x = H/(K+1)$. The points are indexed by i and the temperature value at point i is denoted by

$$T_i(t) = T(x_i, t)$$

A semidifference approximation for Eq.(10.5.1) is written as

$$\frac{\partial T_i(t)}{\partial t} = \frac{\alpha}{\Delta x^2} \left(T_{i-1}(t) - 2T_i(t) + T_{i+1}(t) \right), \quad 1 \le i \le K \tag{10.5.2}$$

with boundary conditions

$$T_0(t) = T_L, \quad T_{K+1}(t) = T_R$$

We can now express Eq.(10.5.2) in vector form by

$$\mathbf{T}' = \mathbf{MT} + \mathbf{S} \tag{10.5.3}$$

where

$$\mathbf{T} = \begin{bmatrix} T_1 \\ T_2 \\ T_3 \\ . \\ T_K \end{bmatrix}$$

$$\mathbf{M} = \frac{\alpha}{\Delta x^2} \begin{bmatrix} -2 & 1 & 0 & \cdots & 0 \\ 1 & -2 & 1 & \cdots & 0 \\ 0 & 1 & -2 & \cdots & 0 \\ & & & \cdots & 0 \\ . & . & . & \cdots & 0 \\ 0 & 0 & 0 & \cdots & -2 \end{bmatrix}, \quad \mathbf{S} = \frac{\alpha}{\Delta x^2} \begin{bmatrix} T_L \\ 0 \\ 0 \\ . \\ T_R \end{bmatrix} \tag{10.5.4}$$

The foregoing equation can be solved by one of the Runge-Kutta methods.

Example 10.18

The temperature of a perfectly insulated iron bar 50 cm long is initially at 200°C. The temperature of the left edge is suddenly reduced and fixed to 0°C at $t = 0$ s, but the temperature of the right end is maintained at 200 °C. Plot the temperature distribution at every increment of 200 s until 1000 s is reached. The material properties are

$$k = 80.2 \text{ W/mK (thermal conductivity)}$$
$$\rho = 7870 \text{ kg/m}^3 \text{ (density)}$$
$$c = 447 \text{ kJ/kgK (specific heat)}$$

Solution

We first divide the rod into ten intervals (see Figure 10.21). The thermal diffusivity is calculated by

$$\alpha = \frac{k}{\rho C} = \frac{80.2}{(7870)(447)} = 2.28 \times 10^{-5}$$

The equation to be solved is given by Eq.(10.5.3) with $K = 9$. The values of T_L and T_R in Eq.(10.5.4) are set to $T_L = 0$ and $T_R = 200$, respectively.

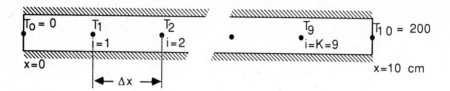

Figure 10.21 An insulated bar

A MATLAB script using the fourth-order Runge-Kutta scheme in the vector given by Eq.(10.3.29) is shown in List 10.13. The results are plotted in Figure 10.22.

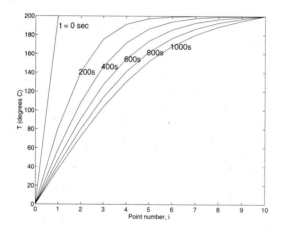

Figure 10.22 Results of method of lines

List 10.13
```
clear, clg, hold off
k=80.2;  ro=7870;c=447;TL=0;TR=200;
alpha = k/ro/c;  Dx=.05;
A=[-2  1  0  0  0  0  0  0  0; ...
    1 -2  1  0  0  0  0  0  0; ...
    0  1 -2  1  0  0  0  0  0; ...
    0  0  1 -2  1  0  0  0  0; ...
    0  0  0  1 -2  1  0  0  0; ...
    0  0  0  0  1 -2  1  0  0; ...
    0  0  0  0  0  1 -2  1  0; ...
    0  0  0  0  0  0  1 -2  1; ...
    0  0  0  0  0  0  0  1 -2]*alpha/Dx^2;
```

```
S=[TL; 0; 0; 0; 0; 0; 0; 0;TR]*alpha/Dx^2;
T=[40;40;40;40;40;40;40;40;40] ;
T=200*ones(T);
n=0; t=0; h=20; m=0;
%
   axis([0,10,0,220])
   j=[0,1:length(T),length(T)+1];
   T_plot=[TL, T',TR];
   plot(j,T_plot)
   text( j(2), T_plot(2),['t=',int2str(t),'s'])
   xlabel('Point number, i')
   ylabel('T (degrees C)')
%
for k=1:5
   for m=1:10
     n=n+1;
     k1 = h*(A*T + S);
     k2 = h*(A*(T+k1/2) + S);
     k3 = h*(A*(T+k2/2) + S);
     k4 = h*(A*(T+k3) + S);
     T = T+(k1 + 2*k2 + 2*k3 + k4)/6;
     t=h*n;
   end
   hold on
   j=[0,1:length(T),length(T)+1];
   T_plot=[TL, T',TR];
   plot(j,T_plot)
   text( j(k+1), T_plot(k+1),int2str(t))
end
```

PROBLEMS

(10.1) Solve the following problems in $0 \leq t \leq 5$ using the forward Euler method with $h = 0.5$ by hand calculation. Repeat the same with $h = 0.01$ by MATLAB. Evaluate the errors by comparing to the exact solutions shown below:

(a) $y' + ty = 1, \quad y(0) = 1$

(b) $y' + 3y = e^{-t}, \quad y(0) = 1$

(c) $y' = (t^2 - y), \quad y(0) = 0.5$

(d) $y' + y|y| = 0, \quad y(0) = 1$

(e) $y' + |y|^{1/2} = \sin(t), \quad y(0) = 1$

Exact Solution:

Case	(a)	(b)	(c)	(d)	(e)
t	y	y	y	y	y
0	1.0000	1.0000	0.5000	1.0000	1.0000
1	1.3313	0.2088	0.4482	0.5000	0.6147
2	0.7753	0.06890	1.7969	0.3333	0.7458
3	0.4043	2.4955E-2	4.9253	0.2500	0.4993
4	0.2707	9.1610E-3	9.9725	0.2000	−0.2714
5	0.2092	3.3692E-3	16.980	0.1666	−2.2495

Hint: Solution of (b) may oscillate with $h = 0.5$, but students are encouraged to try anyway.

(10.2) Solve

$$y''(t) - 0.05y'(t) + 0.15y(t) = 0, \quad y'(0) = 0, \quad y(0) = 1$$

and find the values of $y(1)$ and $y(2)$ using the forward Euler method with $h = 0.5$.

(10.3) Solve the following problems in $0 \leq t \leq 5$ using the forward Euler method with $h = 0.1$ and $h = 0.01$ (write your own program in MATLAB). Evaluate the errors with the exact solutions shown below:

(a) $y'' + 8y = 0, \quad y(0) = 1, \quad y'(0) = 0$

(b) $y'' - 0.01(y')^2 + 2y = \sin(t), \quad y(0) = 0, \quad y'(0) = 1$

(c) $y'' + 2ty' + ty = 0, \quad y(0) = 1, \quad y'(0) = 0$

(d) $(e^t + y)y'' = t, \quad y(0) = 1, \quad y'(0) = 0$

Exact Solution

Case	(a)	(b)	(c)	(d)
t	y	y	y	y
0	1.0	0.0000	1.0000	1.0000
1	−0.9514	0.8450	0.8773	1.0629
2	0.8102	0.9135	0.5372	1.3653
3	−0.5902	0.1412	0.3042	1.8926
4	0.3128	−0.7540	0.1763	2.5589
5	−0.0050	−0.9589	0.1035	3.2978

(10.4) Solve the following equations for $0 < t < 5$ by the modified Euler method:

$$4y' = -3y + 7z + 2t, \quad y(0) = 1$$
$$7z' = -2y + 8z, \quad z(0) = 0$$

Use both $h = 0.01$ and 0.001.

(10.5) A conical tank contains water up to 0.5 m high from the bottom. The tank has a hole of 0.02 m radius at the bottom. The radius of the tank at y is given by $r = 0.25y$, where r is the radius and y is the height measured from the bottom. The velocity of the water that drains through the hole is given by $v^2 = 2gy$, where $g = 9.8$ m/s^2. Using the forward Euler method (use $h = 0.001$ s), find out how many minutes it will take until the tank becomes empty.

(10.6) A circuit, shown in Figure 10.23, has a self-inductance of $L = 100$ mH, a resistance of $R = 20$ kΩ and a DC voltage source of 10 V. If the switch is closed at $t = 0$, the current, $I(t)$, changes in accordance with

$$L\frac{dI(t)}{dt} + I(t)R = E, \ I(0) = 0$$

(a) Find the current I at $t = 1, 2, 3, 4$, and 5 ms by the forward Euler method with $h = 0.01$ ms.

(b) Evaluate the error by comparing the numerical solution to the analytical solution given by $I(t) = (E/R)(1 - \exp(-Rt/L))$.

(c) Investigate the effect of h by repeating the above calculations with $h = 0.1$ ms.

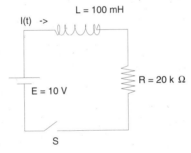

L = 100 mH

I(t) ->

R = 20 k Ω

E = 10 V

S

Figure 10.23 Electrical circuit

(10.7) A U-tube of 0.05 m radius is initially filled with water, but separated by a partition so that the water level of the left vertical part is 0.2 m higher than the water level of the right vertical part. At $t = 0$ the partition is suddenly removed. The water level of the left vertical portion, y_A, measured from the midplane between two surfaces, satisfies

$$L y_A'' = -2gy_A$$

where L is the total length of water in the U-tube, which is assumed to be 1 m, and $g = 9.8$ m/s^2. Ignoring the friction in the tube, calculate the water level by the forward Euler method for $0 < t < 10$ s, and find when y_A reaches minimums and maximums. Use $h = 0.1$ s.

(10.8) Repeat the previous problem assuming that there is friction in the pipe, so that the equation of motion is given by

$$L\ddot{y}_A = -2gy_A - \beta\dot{y}_A$$

where $\beta = 0.8$ m/s. Use $h = 0.001$ s.

(10.9) The number density (number of atoms per cm^3) of iodine-135 (radioisotope) satisfies

$$\frac{dN_i(t)}{dt} = -\lambda_i N_i(t)$$

where $N(t)$ is the number density of iodine-135 and λ_i is its decay constant equal to 0.1044 h^{-1}. If $N_i(0) = 10^5$ atoms/cm^3 at $t = 0$, compute $N_i(t)$ at $t = 1$ h by the modified Euler method. Set $h = 0.05$ h.

(10.10) The decay product of iodine-135 (considered in the previous problem) is xenon-135, and is also radioactive. Its decay constant is $\lambda_x = 0.0753$ h^{-1}. The number density of xenon satisfies

$$\frac{dN_x(t)}{dt} = -\lambda_x N_x(t) + \lambda_i N_i(t)$$

where N_x is the number density of xenon and N_i is the number density of iodine defined in the previous problem. Assuming that $N_x(0) = 0$, develop a program to compute N_i and N_x based on the modified Euler method. (Since the differential equations are linear, use closed form solutions for each time step.) Find the solution for $0 < t \leq 50$ h and plot. Use $h = 0.1$ hr.

(10.11) Find $y(1)$ for the following equation using the second-order Runge-Kutta method with $h = 0.5$:

$$y' = -\frac{y}{t + y^2}, \quad y(0) = 1$$

(10.12) Calculate $y(2)$ for the following equation using the second-order Runge-Kutta method with $h = 1$:

$$y'' + 0.2y' + 0.003y\sin(t) = 0, \quad y(0) = 0, \quad y'(0) = 1$$

(10.13) Find the value of $y(1)$ by solving

$$y'' - 0.05y' + 0.15y = 0, \quad y(0) = 1, \quad y'(0) = 0$$

Use the second-order Runge-Kutta method with $h = 0.5$.

(10.14) Solve the following differential equation

$$2y'' + (y')^2 + y = 0, \quad y(0) = 0, \quad y'(0) = 1$$

by the second-order Runge-Kutta method with $h = 0.5$ and evaluate $y(1)$ and $y'(1)$.

(10.15) An initial-value problem of an ordinary differential equation is given by

$$y''' = -y, \quad y(0) = 1, \quad y'(0) = y''(0) = 0$$

Using the second-order Runge-Kutta method with $h = 0.2$, calculate $y(0.4)$.

(10.16) (a) A 50 gal tank full of water contains salt at a concentration of 10 oz/gal. In order to dilute the salt content, fresh water is supplied at the rate of 2 gal/min. If the tank is well mixed, and the water leaves the tank with the same flow rate, the salt content satisfies

$$y_1'(t) = -(2/50)y_1$$

where $y_1(t)$ is the salt concentration in oz/gal, and t is time in minutes. By the second-order Runge-Kutta method with $h = 1$ min, find out how long it takes until the salt concentration reaches $1/10$ of its initial value.

(b) The water that leaves the tank enters another tank of 20 gal capacity, into which fresh water is also poured at the rate of 3 gal/min and well mixed. The salt concentration in this tank satisfies

$$y_2'(t) = -(5/20)y_2(t) + (2/20)y_1(t), \quad y_2(0) = 0$$

where $y_1(t)$ is the salt concentration of the 50-gal tank of the previous problem. By the second-order Runge-Kutta method, find when the salt concentration of the 20-gal tank reaches its maximum. Assume that the water in the second tank is fresh at $t = 0$.

(10.17) Calculate $y(1)$ by solving the following equation using the fourth-order Runge-Kutta method with $h = 1$:

$$y' = -y/(t + y^2), \quad y(0) = 1$$

(10.18) Find the solution of

$$y'(t) = -1/(1 + y^2), \quad y(0) = 1$$

for $t = 1$ and $t = 2$ using the fourth-order Runge-Kutta method with $h = 0.5$ and $h = 1$.

(10.19) A bullet is shot into the air at a 45 degree angle from the ground at $u = v = 150$ m/s, where u and v are horizontal and vertical velocities, respectively. The equations of motion are given by

$$u' = -cVu, \quad u(0) = 150 \text{ m/s}$$
$$v' = -g - cVv, \quad v(0) = 150 \text{ m/s} \tag{A}$$

where u and v are functions of time, $u = u(t)$, and $v = v(t)$, and

$$V^2 = u^2 + v^2$$
$$c = 0.005 \text{ m}^{-1} \text{ (coefficient of drag)}$$
$$g = 9.8 \text{ m/s}^2 \text{ (gravity)}$$

The equations of motion may be solved by one of the Runge-Kutta methods. The trajectory of the bullet may be calculated by integrating,

$$x' = u, \quad \text{and} \quad y' = v$$

or

$$x = \int_0^t u(t')dt'$$
$$y = \int_0^t v(t')dt' \tag{B}$$

A script based on the forward Euler method to solve Eq.(A) and evaluate Eq.(B) is listed next:

```
clear; clg
u = 150; v=150;  h=.1; c=0.005; t=0;
ub=u; vb=v;
y=0; x=0; n=1;
u_rec(1)=u;   v_rec(1)=v; t_rec(1)=t;
x_rec(1)=x; y_rec(1)=y;
while y>=0
    vel1= sqrt( ub*ub + vb*vb) ;
    k1 = h*(-c*vel1*ub);
    l1 = h*(-9.8-c*vel1*vb);
    u=ub+ k1;    v=vb+l1;
    x=x+h*(ub+u)/2;   y=y+h*(vb+v)/2 ;
    ub=u;    vb=v;
    n=n+1; t=t+1;
    u_rec(n)=u;   v_rec(n)=v; t_rec(n)=t;
    x_rec(n)=x; y_rec(n)=y;
end
plot(x_rec,y_rec)
xlabel('x'); ylabel('y')
```

(a) Run the script and plot the trajectory of the bullet. (b) Rewrite the script using the fourth-order Runge-Kutta method in a vector form. Find the horizontal distance that the bullet reaches with an error less than 0.1 percent error.

(10.20) The solution of $y' = -1/(1 + y^2)$ by the second-order Runge-Kutta method is shown for two different h values.

t	$h = 0.1$ y	$h = 0.2$ y
0.0	1.0000000	1.0000000
0.1	0.9487188	
0.2	0.8946720	0.8947514

(a) Estimate the local error of $y(0.2)$ with $h = 0.1$.

(b) Estimate a more accurate value of $y(0.2)$.

(c) If the local error is required to satisfy $|E_h| < 0.00001$, estimate h.

(10.21) For the equation given by

$$y' = 3y + \exp(1 - t), \; y(0) = 1$$

find an optimal time step for the second-order Runge-Kutta method that satisfies $|E_h| < 0.0001$. (Run the second-order Runge-Kutta method for one interval with a value of h, and rerun for two intervals with $h/2$.)

(10.22) Repeat Problem 10.21 for the fourth-order Runge-Kutta method.

(10.23) By repeating the analysis of Eqs.(10.3.33) through (10.3.39), derive the equation corresponding to Eq.(10.3.38) for the third-order Runge-Kutta method.

(10.24) If the third-order Runge-Kutta method is applied to $y' = -\alpha y$, find in what range of h the method is unstable.

(10.25) The initial temperature of a metal piece is 25°C. The metal piece is internally heated electrically at the rate of $Q = 3000$ W. The equation for the temperature is written as

$$\frac{dT}{dt} = \frac{1}{V\rho c} \left[Q - \epsilon \sigma A \left(T^4 - 298^4 \right) - h_c A(T - 298) \right], \; T(0) = 298 \text{ K}$$

where T is in Kelvin, and

$k = 60$ W/mK (thermal conductivity)

$Q = 50$ W/m (heat generation rate per unit length of the bar)

$\sigma = 5.67 \times 10^{-8}$ W/m^{2}K^4 (Stefan-Boltzmann constant)

$A = 0.25$ m^2 (surface area)

$V = 0.001$ m(volume)

$c = 900$ J/kgK(specific heat)

$\rho = 300$ kg/m^3(density)

$h_c = 30$ J/m^{2}K(heat transfer coefficient)

$\epsilon = 0.8$(emissivity)

Calculate the temperature for $0 < t < 10$ min, by the fourth-order Runge-Kutta method with $h = 0.1$ min.

(10.26) The motion of the mass system illustrated in Figure 10.24 is given by

$$y'' + 2\zeta\omega y' + \omega^2 y = F(t)/M, \quad y(0) = y'(0) = 0$$

where

$$\omega = (k/M)^{1/2} \text{ (undamped natural frequency, s}^{-1})$$
$$\zeta = 0.5 \text{ (damping factor)}$$
$$k = 3.2 \text{ (spring constant, N/m)}$$
$$M = 5 \text{ (mass, kg)}$$
$$F(t) = 0 \text{ (force, N)}$$

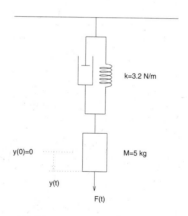

Figure 10.24 Spring-mass system

If $F(t) = 1$ for $0 \le t \le 1$ s, and $F(t) = 0$ for $t > 1$ s, determine the motion of the mass for $0 < t < 10$ s, using the fourth-order Runge-Kutta method.

(10.27) Determine the response of the spring-mass system of the previous problem subject to a triangular force pulse

$$F(t) = 2F_0 t, \ 0 \le t \le 1 \text{ s}$$
$$= 2F_0(1-t), \ 1 \le t \le 2 \text{ s}$$
$$= 0, \ t > 2 \text{ s}$$

where $F_0 = 1$ N. Use the fourth-order Runge-Kutta method and plot the result.

(10.28) Repeat the problem in Example 10.16, except $e(t)$ is changed to

$$e(t) = \sin(1200t)\exp(-1200t)$$

and for $0 < t < 0.01$ s.

(10.29) Solve the following problem by the shooting method based on the fourth-order Runge-Kutta method:

$$Ak\frac{dT^2}{dx^2} + P\sigma(T^4 - 273^4) = AQ, \quad 0 < x < 0.5$$
$$T(0) = 0$$
$$T'(0.5) = 0$$

where A and P are given in Example 10.17, and $\sigma = 5.67 \times 10^{-8}$ w/m²K⁴.
Hint: change $T'(0.5)$ by trial-and-error until $T'(0.5) = 0$ is satisfied.

Chapter 11

Boundary-Value Problems of Ordinary Differential Equations

11.1 INTRODUCTION

For the one-dimensional boundary-value problem of ordinary differential equations, the solution is required to satisfy boundary conditions at both ends of the domain. Definition of boundary conditions is an important part of each boundary-value problem. For example, consider a thin metal rod of length H with each end connected to a different heat source (see Figure 11.1). If heat escapes from the surface of the rod to the air only by convection heat transfer, the equation for the temperature is

$$- A\frac{d}{dx}k(x)\frac{dT(x)}{dx} + h_c PT(x) = h_c PT_\infty + AS(x) \tag{11.1.1}$$

where $T(x)$ is the temperature at distance x from the left end, A the constant cross-sectional area of the rod, k the thermal conductivity, P the perimeter of the rod, h_c the convection heat-transfer coefficient, T_∞ the bulk temperature of the air, and S the heat source. The boundary conditions are

$$T(0) = T_L$$
$$T(H) = T_R \tag{11.1.2}$$

where T_L and T_R are known temperatures at the left and right ends, respectively.
If θ is defined as

$$\theta = T - T_\infty$$

Eq.(11.1.1) may be written as

$$- \frac{d}{dx}k(x)\frac{d\theta(x)}{dx} + \sigma\theta(x) = S(x) \tag{11.1.3}$$

where $\sigma = h_c P / A$ and the equation has been divided by A. The first term represents the conduction of heat, the second term is the removal of heat by convection to the air, and the right side is the heat source.

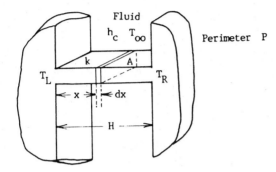

Figure 11.1 A fin connected to two heat sources

Another example of ODE in a similar form is the neutron diffusion equation given by

$$-\frac{d}{dx}D(x)\frac{d\psi(x)}{dx} + \Sigma_a \psi(x) = S(x) \qquad (11.1.4)$$

where ψ is the neutron flux, D is the diffusion coefficient, and S is the neutron source. The meaning of the first term is the diffusion of neutrons, while the second term is the removal by absorption.

In the remainder of this chapter, we consider the equation

$$-\frac{d}{dx}p(x)\frac{d\phi(x)}{dx} + q(x)\phi(x) = S(x) \qquad (11.1.5)$$

or similar equations on cylindrical or spherical coordinates. The first term is the diffusion term, the second is the removal term, and the right side is the source term.

It should be emphasized that Eq.(1.1.5) is a conservation law of diffusion. Indeed, integrating Eq.(1.1.5) in $[a, b]$ yields

$$Z(b) - Z(a) + \int_a^b q(x)\phi(x)dx = \int_a^b S(x)dx \qquad (11.1.6)$$

where

$$Z(x) = -p(x)\frac{d\phi(x)}{dx}$$

is heat flux at x if heat conduction is considered, or neutron current if neutron diffusion is considered. In any case, the first and second terms in the equation above are, respectively, inflow and outflow of the physical quantity associated with ϕ, the third term is the total removal in $[a, b]$, and the right side is the total source in $[a, b]$. Thus, Eq.(11.1.6) represents conservation of the physical quantity in $[a, b]$.

If Eq.(11.1.1) were an initial-value problem, two boundary conditions would be specified at only one boundary, so the numerical solution could proceed from that end to the other by a numerical method such as the fourth-order Runge-Kutta method. Although the solution methods for initial-value problems can be used for boundary-value problems, as illustrated in Chapter 10, they work only on the trial-and-error basis (known as the shooting method; see Example 10.17). An advantage of the shooting method is that an existing program for initial-value problems may be utilized. The shooting method, however, often becomes unsuccessful because it may face numerical instability. Furthermore, its application becomes very difficult if the order of the ODE exceeds two.

A more general way of solving boundary-value problems consists of (a) deriving difference equations and (b) solving all the difference equations simultaneously. In this chapter, we first study the derivation of difference approximations for boundary-value problems and their simultaneous solution.

11.2   BOUNDARY-VALUE PROBLEMS FOR RODS AND SLABS

In this section, we derive finite difference equations for second-order ordinary differential equations with boundary conditions.

In order to explain the principle of the method, we consider the equation

$$-\phi''(x) + q\phi(x) = S(x), \quad 0 < x < H \tag{11.2.1}$$

with the boundary conditions

$$\phi'(0) = 0 \quad \text{(left B.C.)}$$
$$\phi(H) = \phi_R \quad \text{(right B.C.)} \tag{11.2.2}$$

where q is a constant coefficient. By dividing the domain into N equispaced intervals, we obtain a grid, as shown in Figure 11.2, where the grid intervals are $h = H/N$. Applying the central difference approximation (see (f) of Table 6.1) to the first term of Eq.(11.2.1), the difference equation for point i is derived as

$$\frac{-\phi_{i-1} + 2\phi_i - \phi_{i+1}}{h^2} + q\phi_i = S_i \tag{11.2.3}$$

where $\phi_i = \phi(x_i)$ and $S_i = S(x_i)$ and q is assumed to be constant. Multiplying Eq.(11.2.3) by h^2 yields

$$- \phi_{i-1} + (2 + w)\phi_i - \phi_{i+1} = h^2 S_i \qquad (11.2.4)$$

where $w = h^2 q$. The foregoing equation applies to all the grid points except for $i = 1$ and $i = N + 1$.

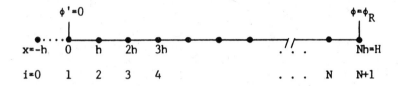

Figure 11.2 One-dimensional grid for a slab

The left boundary condition given by Eq.(11.2.2) is equivalent to a symmetry boundary condition called an *adiabatic* boundary condition in heat transfer. If a hypothetical grid point $i = 0$, located at $x = -h$, is considered, Eq.(11.2.4) for $i = 1$ becomes

$$- \phi_0 + (2 + w)\phi_1 - \phi_2 = h^2 S_1 \qquad (11.2.5)$$

In the foregoing equation, ϕ_0 can be set to $\phi_0 = \phi_2$ because the left boundary condition can be interpreted as

$$\phi_1' \approx \frac{\phi_2 - \phi_0}{2h} = 0$$

Then, dividing the resulting equation by 2 yields

$$(1 + w/2)\phi_1 - \phi_2 = h^2 S_1/2 \qquad (11.2.6)$$

Since $\phi_{N+1} = \phi(H) = \phi_R$ at the right boundary, Eq.(11.2.4) for $i = N$ is written as

$$- \phi_{N-1} + (2 + w)\phi_N = h^2 S_N + \phi_R \qquad (11.2.7)$$

where all the known terms are brought to the right side.

The set of Eqs.(11.2.5), (11.2.4), and (11.2.7) is written together as

$$(1 + w/2)\phi_1 - \phi_2 = h^2 S_1/2$$

$$-\phi_1 + (2 + w)\phi_2 - \phi_3 = h^2 S_2$$

$$-\phi_2 + (2 + w)\phi_3 - \phi_4 = h^2 S_3 \qquad (11.2.8)$$

$$\cdots$$

$$-\phi_{N-1} + (2 + w)\phi_N = h^2 S_N + \phi_R$$

or equivalently in matrix form,

$$\begin{bmatrix} 1 + w/2 & -1 & & & \\ -1 & 2 + w & -1 & & \\ & -1 & 2 + w & -1 & \\ & & \ddots & \ddots & \ddots \\ & & & -1 & 2 + w \end{bmatrix} \begin{bmatrix} \phi_1 \\ \phi_2 \\ \phi_3 \\ \cdots \\ \phi_N \end{bmatrix} = \begin{bmatrix} h^2 S_1/2 \\ h^2 S_2 \\ h^2 S_3 \\ \cdots \\ h^2 S_N + \phi_R \end{bmatrix}$$

$$(11.2.9)$$

The coefficient matrix of Eq.(11.2.9) are all zero except along the three diagonal lines. This special form of the matrix is called a *tridiagonal matrix*, which appears very often in the numerical method for boundary-value problems. Equation (11.2.9) is solved by the tridiagonal solution described in Section 11.3.

Table 11.1 Three Types of Boundary Conditions

Type	Explanation	Examples
Fixed value boundary condition (Dirichlet type)	Functional value of the solution is given.	$\phi(0) = 0$, or $\phi(0) = 1$
Derivative boundary condition (Neumann type)	Derivative of the solution is given.	$\phi'(0) = 0$, or $\phi'(0) = 1$
Mixed boundary condition (Mixed type)	Functional value is related to the derivative.	$\phi'(0) + \alpha\phi(0) = \beta$

Boundary conditions are classified into the three types as shown in Table 11.1. To discuss implementation of a mixed-type boundary condition, suppose both boundary conditions for Eq.(11.2.1) are given by the mixed type, namely

$$-\phi'(0) + f_L\phi(0) = g_L \tag{11.2.10}$$
$$\phi'(H) + f_R\phi(H) = g_R \tag{11.2.11}$$

where f_L, f_R, g_L and g_R are constants. We will consider the grid shown in Figure 11.3 (which is the same as Figure 11.2, except that the last grid point is numbered N rather than $N + 1$).

Figure 11.3 One-dimensional grid

The difference equation, Eq.(11.2.4), is unchanged for $i = 2$ through $N - 1$, but the ones for $i = 1$ and N need to be revised because of the new boundary conditions. We consider the left boundary first. Using the forward difference approximation based on an interval of $h/2$ for Eq.(11.2.1) at $x = 0$ yields

$$-\frac{\phi'(h/2) - \phi'(0)}{h/2} + q\phi_1 = S_1 \tag{11.2.12}$$

Here, $\phi'(h/2)$ is substituted by the central difference approximation,

$$\phi'(h/2) = (\phi_2 - \phi_1)/h$$

and $\phi'(0)$ may be eliminated by using Eq.(11.2.10). Thus we obtain

$$-\frac{(\phi_2 - \phi_1)/h + g_L - f_L\phi_1}{h/2} + q\phi_1 = S_1$$

or equivalently

$$(1 + \frac{w}{2} + hf_L)\phi_1 - \phi_2 = \frac{h^2 S_1}{2} + hg_L \tag{11.2.13}$$

where $w = qh^2$, and all known terms are on the right side.

The difference equation for the right boundary is derived by a similar procedure:

$$- \phi_{N-1} + (1 + \frac{w}{2} + hf_R)\phi_N = \frac{h^2 S_N}{2} + hg_R \tag{11.2.14}$$

The set of Eqs.(11.2.13), (11.2.4), and (11.2.14) forms a tridiagonal equation set.

Example 11.1

Derive difference equations for the following boundary-value problem:

$$-2y''(x) + y(x) = \exp(-0.2x) \tag{A}$$

with the boundary conditions

$$y(0) = 0.1$$
$$y'(10) = -y(10)$$

Assume the grid spacing is unity.

Figure 11.4 Grid for Example 11.1

Solution

We consider the grid shown in Figure 11.4. The difference equations for $i = 2$ through 9 are

$$2(-y_{i-1} + 2y_i - y_{i+1}) + y_i = \exp(-0.2i) \tag{B}$$

where $x_i = i$ is used.

For $i = 1$, the boundary condition $y_0 = y(0) = 1$ is introduced into Eq.(B) to yield

$$5y_1 - 2y_2 = \exp(-0.2) + 0.2 \tag{C}$$

For $i = 10$, we approximate Eq.(A) first by

$$-\frac{2[y'(10) - y'(9.5)]}{1/2} + y(10) = \exp(-2) \qquad \text{(D)}$$

Using the central difference approximation, the term $y'(9.5)$ becomes

$$y'(9.5) = [y(10) - y(9)]/1 \qquad \text{(E)}$$

Introducing Eq.(E) and the right boundary condition $y'(10) = -y(10)$ into Eq.(D) yields

$$-2y_9 + 4.5y_{10} = 0.5\exp(-2) \qquad \text{(F)}$$

Summarizing the difference equations obtained, we write

$$5y_1 - 2y_2 = \exp(-0.2) + 0.2$$
$$-2y_{i-1} + 5y_i - 2y_{i+1} = \exp(-0.2x_i), \text{ for } i = 2 \text{ to } 9 \qquad \text{(G)}$$
$$-2y_9 + 4.5y_{10} = 0.5\exp(-2)$$

where $x_i = i$ is used. The numerical results are shown in Example 11.2.

11.3   SOLUTION OF TRIDIAGONAL EQUATION

We write the tridiagonal equation derived in Section 11.2 in the form

$$\begin{bmatrix} B_1 & C_1 & & & & & \\ A_2 & B_2 & C_2 & & & & \\ & A_3 & B_3 & C_3 & & & \\ & & \ddots & \ddots & & & \\ & & & A_i & B_i & C_i & \\ & & & & \ddots & \ddots & \\ & & & & & A_N & B_N \end{bmatrix} \begin{bmatrix} \phi_1 \\ \phi_2 \\ \phi_3 \\ \cdots \\ \phi_i \\ \cdots \\ \phi_N \end{bmatrix} = \begin{bmatrix} D_1 \\ D_2 \\ D_3 \\ \cdots \\ D_i \\ \cdots \\ D_N \end{bmatrix} \qquad (11.3.1)$$

The solution algorithm, called the tridiagonal solution, is a variant of Gauss elimination and given next.

    (a) Initialize the two new variables:

$$B_1' = B_1, \text{ and } D_1' = D_1$$

(b) Calculate repeatedly the following equations in increasing order of i, until $i = N$ is reached:

$$R = A_i/B'_{i-1}$$

$$B'_i = B_i - RC_{i-1} \qquad (11.3.2)$$

$$D'_i = D_i - RD'_{i-1}$$

for $i = 2, 3, ..., N$.

(c) Calculate the solution for the last unknown by

$$\phi_N = D'_N/B'_N \qquad (11.3)$$

(d) Calculate the following equation in decreasing order of i:

$$\phi_i = (D'_i - C_i\phi_{i+1})/B'_i, \quad i = N - 1, ..., 2, 1 \qquad (11.4)$$

In a computer program, the primed variables B'_i and D'_i need not be distinguished from B_i and D_i, respectively, because B'_i and D'_i are stored in the same memory as for B_i and D_i. Therefore, step (a) is not necessary in real programming.

A function M-file, tri_diag.m, to solve the tridiagonal equation is listed in List 11.2.

List 11.2
tri_diag.m
```
function f = tri_diag(a,b,c,d,n)
for i=2:n
   r=a(i)/b(i-1)
   b(i)=b(i)-r*c(i-1)
   d(i)=d(i)-r*d(i-1)
end
d(n)=d(n)/b(n)
for i=n-1:-1:1
   d(i)=(d(i)-c(i)*d(i+1))/b(i)
end
f=d;
```

When the computation in the function is completed, the solution is returned in array f.

Example 11.2

Solve Eq.(D) in Example 11.1 and plot the results.

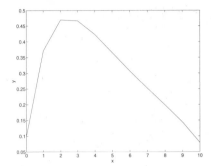

Figure 11.5 Plot of the solution

Solution

The answer is computed by the following script. The solution is plotted in Figure 11.5.

```
clear,clg, y0=0.1;
b(1)=5; c(1)=-2; s(1)=exp(-0.2) + y0;
for i=2:9
a(i)=-2; b(i)=5; c(i)=-2; s(i)=exp(-0.2*i);
end
a(10)=-2; b(10)=4.5; s(10)=0.5*exp(-2);
y=tri_diag(a,b,c,s,10)
plot(0:10, [y0,y])
xlabel('x');ylabel('y')
```

11.4 VARIABLE COEFFICIENTS AND NONUNIFORM GRID

In many problems, the coefficients of the differential equation are space-dependent. Nonequispaced grids are used when the geometry consists of layers of different properties, for example.

The second-order ordinary differential equation for the slab geometry with variable coefficients is written here as

$$- (p(x)\phi'(x))' + q(x)\phi(x) = S(x) \tag{11.4.1}$$

with the boundary conditions given by Eqs.(11.2.9) and (11.2.10). The grid spacing between x_i to x_{i+1} will be denoted by h_i. We assume that p, q, and S in each grid interval are constant and denoted by p_i, q_i, and S_i, respectively, as shown in Figure 11.6.

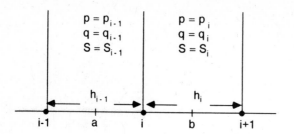

Figure 11.6 Constants in grid intervals

One natural way of deriving difference equations with piecewise-constant coefficients is the method of integration. In this method, Eq.(11.4.1) is integrated from a to b (see Figure 11.6):

$$-\int_a^b (p(x)\phi'(x))'\,dx + \int_a^b q(x)\phi(x)dx = \int_a^b S(x)dx \qquad (11.4.2)$$

where $a = x_i - h_{i-1}/2$, and $b = x_i + h_i/2$ (which are midpoints between i-1 and i, and i and i+1, respectively).

The first term of Eq.(11.4.2) becomes

$$-\int_a^b (p\phi')'\,dx = -(p\phi')_{i+1/2} + (p\phi')_{i-1/2} \qquad (11.4.3)$$

The derivatives on the right side are approximated by the central difference approximation:

$$(p\phi')_{i-1/2} \approx p_{i-1}(\phi_i - \phi_{i-1})/h_{i-1}$$
$$(p\phi')_{i+1/2} \approx p_i(\phi_{i+1} - \phi_i)/h_i \qquad (11.4.4)$$

where $p(x) = p_i$ for $x_i < x < x_{i+1}$. Thus, the first term of Eq.(11.4.2) becomes

$$-\int_a^b (p\phi')'\,dx \approx -\frac{p_{i-1}}{h_{i-1}}\phi_{i-1} + \left(\frac{p_{i-1}}{h_{i-1}} + \frac{p_i}{h_i}\right)\phi_i - \frac{p_i}{h_i}\phi_{i+1}h_i \qquad (11.4.5)$$

The second term of Eq.(11.4.2) becomes

$$\int_a^b q(x)\phi(x)dx \approx (q_{i-1}h_{i-1} + q_ih_i)\phi_i/2 \qquad (11.4.6)$$

where $\phi(x)$ is approximated by ϕ_i. The right side of Eq.(11.4.2) becomes

$$\int_a^b S(x)dx \approx (S_{i-1}h_{i-1} + S_i h_i)/2 \tag{11.4.7}$$

Introducing Eqs.(11.4.5), (11.4.6), and (11.4.7) into Eq.(11.4.2) yields

$$-\frac{p_{i-1}}{h_{i-1}}\phi_{i-1} + (\frac{p_{i-1}}{h_{i-1}} + \frac{p_i}{h_i})\phi_i - \frac{p_i}{h_i}\phi_{i+1} + \frac{(q_{i-1}h_{i-1} + q_i h_i)}{2}\phi_i$$
$$= \frac{S_{i-1}h_{i-1} + S_i h_i}{2} \tag{11.4.8}$$

Equation (11.4.8) can now be written in the form

$$A_i\phi_{i-1} + B_i\phi_i + C_i\phi_{i+1} = D_i \tag{11.4.9}$$

where

$$A_i = -\frac{p_{i-1}}{h_{i-1}}$$

$$B_i = \frac{p_{i-1}}{h_{i-1}} + \frac{p_i}{h_i} + \frac{(q_{i-1}h_{i-1} + q_i h_i)}{2}$$

$$C_i = -\frac{p_i}{h_i} \tag{11.4.10}$$

$$D_i = \frac{S_{i-1}h_{i-1} + S_i h_i}{2}$$

With the boundary conditions given by Eq.(11.2.10) and Eq.(11.2.11), difference equations for the left and right boundary points are also derived by integrating Eq.(11.4.1). Considering the left boundary point, a and b in Eq.(11.4.2) are set to:

$a = x_1$ (the left boundary point)
$b = x_1 + h_1/2$ (the midpoint between x_1 and x_2)

Then, the first term of Eq.(11.4.2) becomes

$$-\int_a^b (p\phi')' dx = -(p\phi')_b + (p\phi')_{ra1} \tag{11.4.11}$$

The first term on the right side is approximated by the central difference approximation,

$$- (p\phi')_b \approx -p_1 \frac{\phi_2 - \phi_1}{h_1} \qquad (11.4.12)$$

The ϕ' in the second term on the right side of Eq.(11.4.11) is eliminated by Eq.(11.2.10). Therefore, Eq.(11.4.11) becomes

$$- \int_a^b (p\phi')' dx \approx -p_1 \frac{\phi_2 - \phi_1}{h_1} + p_1(-g_L + f_L \phi_1) \qquad (11.4.13)$$

The second term and right side of Eq.(11.4.2) become, respectively,

$$\int_a^b q(x)\phi(x)dx \approx \frac{q_1 h_1}{2}\phi_1 \qquad (11.4.14)$$

$$\int_a^b S(x)dx \approx \frac{S_1 h_1}{2} \qquad (11.4.15)$$

Introducing Eqs.(11.4.12) through (11.4.15) in Eq.(11.4.2) yields

$$\left(\frac{p_1}{h_1} + p_1 f_L + \frac{q_1 h_1}{2}\right)\phi_1 - \frac{p_1}{h_1}\phi_2 = \frac{S_1 h_1}{2} + p_1 g_L \qquad (11.4.16)$$

which may be rewritten more compactly as

$$B_1 \phi_1 + C_1 \phi_2 = D_1 \qquad (11.4.17)$$

The difference equation for the right boundary point can be also derived similarly and written as

$$A_N \phi_{N-1} + B_N \phi_N = D_N \qquad (11.4.18)$$

The set of difference equations thus derived, namely Eqs.(11.4.17), (11.4.9) and (11.4.18) becomes exactly the form of Eq.(11.3.1).

Provided that physically correct boundary conditions are imposed and that the coefficient of the removal term is non-negative, the coefficient matrix of the difference equations in the conservation form has the following properties:

(a) the coefficient matrix in Eq.(11.3.1) is symmetric,

(b) the diagonal coefficients are all positive,

(c) A_i and C_i are all negative,

(d) the coefficients in each row satisfy

$$B_i \geq -A_i - C_i$$

with strict inequality for at least one row, and

(e) no part of the equation can be solved independently of other parts.

The inverse of the matrix satisfying all the foregoing conditions is shown to be a positive matrix; that is, all the elements of the inverse matrix are positive. This implies that, if $S_i \geq 0$ with strict inequality for at least one i, the solution is positive everywhere.

11.5   CYLINDERS AND SPHERES

Derivation of difference equations for second-order ordinary differential equations for cylindrical and spherical geometries is very similar to that discussed in Section 11.4. The difference equations for these two geometries will have the form of Eq.(11.3.1).

The second-order ordinary differential equation for cylindrical and spherical geometries may be written as

$$ -\frac{1}{r^m}\frac{d}{dr}p(r)r^m\frac{d}{dr}\phi(r) + q(r)\phi(r) = S(r) \qquad (11.5.1) $$

where

$\quad\quad m = 1$ for cylinder
$\quad\quad m = 2$ for sphere

Notice also that the equation reduces to Eq.(11.4.1) for a slab if $m = 0$.

Considering space-dependent coefficients and a nonequispaced grid, as discussed in the preceding section, we derive difference approximations by the method of integration. That is, to integrate the equation over a cylindrical or spherical control volume, depending on the geometry.

Derivation of difference equations is now shown using the notations for h, p, q, and S defined in Figure 11.6, where p, q, and S are assumed to be constant between two consecutive points. We multiply Eq.(11.5.1) by r^m and integrate from $a = r_{i-1/2}$ to $b = r_{i+1/2}$ which are midpoints of $[r_{i-1}, r_i]$ and $[r_i, r_{i+1}]$, respectively:

$$ -\int_a^b \frac{d}{dr}r^m p(r)\frac{d}{dr}\phi(r)dr + \int_a^b q(r)\phi(r)r^m dr = \int_a^b S(r)r^m dr \qquad (11.5.2) $$

Here, for a cylindrical geometry ($m = 1$), $r^m dr$ represents an infinitesimal volume element divided by $2\pi L$, where L is the height of the circular cylinder. For a spherical geometry, $r^m dr$ represents an infinitesimal volume element divided by 4π. The first term of Eq.(11.5.2) becomes

$$p_{i-1}r_{i-1/2}^m \left[\frac{d}{dr}\phi(r) \right]_a - p_i r_{i+1/2}^m \left[\frac{d}{dr}\phi(r) \right]_b \tag{11.5.3}$$

Using the difference approximation for the derivatives then yields

$$p_{i-1}r_{i-1/2}^m \frac{\phi_i - \phi_{i-1}}{h_{i-1}} - p_i r_{i+1/2}^m \frac{\phi_{i+1} - \phi_i}{h_i} \tag{11.5.4}$$

For the cylindrical geometry, the first term times $2\pi L$ is the total flux of the physical quantity through the cylindrical surface at $a = r_{i-1/2}$, and the second is the same for $b = r_{i+1/2}$. For the spherical geometry, the first term times 4π is the total flux.

The second term of Eq.(11.5.2) may be approximated by

$$\int_a^b q(r)\phi(r)r^m dr \approx (v_L q_{i-1} + v_R q_i)\phi_i \tag{11.5.5}$$

and represents the total removal of the physical property in $[r_{i-1/2}, r_{i+1/2}]$, where for $m = 1$,

$$v_L = \frac{1}{2}[r_i^2 - (r_i - \frac{h_{i-1}}{2})^2] = \frac{h_{i-1}}{2}(r_i - \frac{h_{i-1}}{4}) \tag{11.5.6}$$

$$v_R = \frac{1}{2}[(r_i + \frac{h_i}{2})^2 - r_i^2] = \frac{h_i}{2}(r_i + \frac{h_i}{4}) \tag{11.5.7}$$

and for $m = 2$,

$$v_L = \frac{1}{3}[r_i^3 - (r_i - \frac{h_{i-1}}{2})^3] \tag{11.5.8}$$

$$v_R = \frac{1}{3}[(r_i + \frac{h_i}{2})^3 - r_i^3] \tag{11.5.9}$$

Note here for $m = 1$ that, v_L times $2\pi L$ becomes the volume of a cylindrical cell between $r = r_{i-1/2}$ and $r = r_i$, while v_R becomes the same between r_i and $r_{i+1/2}$. The third term of Eq.(11.5.2) may be approximated similarly by

$$\int S(r)r dr \approx v_L S_{i-1} + v_R S_i \tag{11.5.10}$$

Collecting all the terms, the difference approximation for Eq.(11.5.1) becomes the tridiagonal form.

The difference equations derived in this section are in the conservation form. The coefficient matrix for a cylinder has exactly the same mathematical properties as for the slab geometry (see Section 11.4), so it has a positive inverse matrix.

11.6 NONLINEAR ORDINARY DIFFERENTIAL EQUATIONS

An ordinary differential equation is nonlinear if the unknown appears in a nonlinear form, or if its coefficient(s) depend(s) on the solution. For example, the heat-conduction equation for a cooling fin becomes nonlinear if radiation heat transfer from the surface is involved. The diffusion equation for a chemical species is nonlinear if it has a removal term of which the coefficient is dependent on the density of the species. In a nuclear reactor, properties of the materials are significantly affected by the neutron population when the power level is high, so the governing equation for the neutron flux becomes nonlinear.

Solution of nonlinear boundary-value problems requires iterative applications of a solution method for linear boundary-value problems. Two general methods will be discussed, considering a nonlinear diffusion equation given by

$$ -\phi'' + 0.01\phi^2 = \exp(-x), \quad 0 < x < H \tag{11.6.1} $$

where

$$ \phi(0) = \phi(H) = 0 $$

We note some peculiar aspects of nonlinear boundary-value problems. First, unlike a linear boundary-value problem, existence of the solution is not guaranteed. Second, a nonlinear boundary-value problem can have more than one solution. Indeed, different solutions may be obtained for different initial guesses for an iterative algorithm. Therefore, when a numerical solution is obtained, one must examine whether that solution is physically meaningful.

11.6.1 Successive Substitution

Equation (11.6.1) is now rewritten as

$$ -\phi'' + \alpha(x)\phi(x) = \exp(-x) \tag{11.6.2} $$

where

$$ \alpha(x) = 0.01\phi(x) $$

The method explained here is an extension of the successive substitution method described in Chapter 3, and proceeds as follows:

(a) Set $\alpha(x)$ to an estimate, for example $\alpha(x) = 0.01$.

(b) Solve Eq.(11.6.2) numerically as a linear boundary-value problem (since α is fixed, the equation is linear).

(c) Revise $\alpha(x) = 0.01\phi(x)$ with the updated value of $\phi(x)$ from (b).

(d) Repeat (b) and (c) until $\phi(x)$ in two consecutive solutions agree within a prescribed tolerance.

11.6.2   Newton Iteration

If we denote an estimate for $\phi(x)$ by $\psi(x)$, the exact solution may be expressed as

$$\phi(x) = \psi(x) + \delta\psi(x) \tag{11.6.3}$$

where $\delta\psi(x)$ is a correction for the estimate. Introducing Eq.(11.6.3) into Eq.(11.6.1) gives

$$-\delta\psi'' + (0.01)[2\psi\delta\psi + (\delta\psi)^2] = \psi'' - 0.01\psi^2 + exp(-x) \tag{11.6.4}$$

Ignoring the second-order term $(\delta\psi)^2$ yields

$$-\delta\psi'' + 0.02\psi\delta\psi = \psi'' - 0.01\psi^2 + \exp(-x) \tag{11.6.5}$$

which may be solved as a linear boundary-value problem. An approximate solution for Eq.(11.6.1) is then obtained by $\psi(x) + \delta\psi(x)$. The solution may be further improved by repeating the procedure, using the most updated result as a new estimate. This procedure is an extension of the Newton iteration described in Chapter 3.

Example 11.3

Derive linearized difference equations based on the Newton iteration for Eq.(11.6.1) in the domain $0 < x < 2$ with the boundary conditions $\phi(0) = \phi(10) = 0$ using ten grid intervals. Solve the equations.

Solution

The linearized form of Eq.(11.1.1) is given by Eq.(11.6.5). With the grid spacing $h = 2/10 = 0.2$, the difference equation for Eq.(11.5.5) are written as

$$-\delta\psi_{i-1} + 2\delta\psi_i - \delta\psi_{i+1} + 0.02h^2\psi_i\delta\psi_i$$
$$= \psi_{i-1} - 2\psi_i + \psi_{i+1} - 0.01h^2\psi_i^2 + h^2\exp(-ih) \tag{11.6.6}$$
$$i = 1, 2, ...9$$

where $i = 0$ for $x = 0$, and the equation has been multiplied by h^2. The foregoing equation may be written in the form of Eq.(11.3.1) if we define

$$A_i = -1$$
$$B_i = 2 + 0.02h^2\psi_i$$
$$C_i = -1$$
$$D_i = \psi_{i-1} - 2\psi_i + \psi_{i+1} - 0.01h^2\psi_i^2 + h^2\exp(-ih)$$

We start the Newton iteration by setting an estimate as $\psi_i = 0$ for all the grid points. Then, the difference equations for $i=1, 2, 3, ..9$ are solved by the tridiagonal solution. The iterative solution for the first five grid points is listed next.

```
----------------------------------------------------
Iteration              Grid Points
number     i=1     i=2     i=3     i=4     i=5
----------------------------------------------------
  1       0.0850  0.1406  0.1720  0.1837  0.1792
  2       0.0935  0.1546  0.1891  0.2019  0.1970
  3       0.0943  0.1560  0.1908  0.2038  0.1988
  4       0.0944  0.1561  0.1910  0.2040  0.1990
----------------------------------------------------
```

Example 11.4

The Blasius boundary layer equation is given by

$$y''' + 0.5ff'' = 0 \qquad\qquad \text{(A)}$$

with boundary condtions,

$$f(0) = 0, \quad f'(0) = 0, \quad y'(\infty) = 1$$

The third boundary condition may be replaced by $y'(10) = 1$. Approximate the equation by the finite difference approximation and solve as a boundary value problem.

Solution

Equation (A) may be reduced to a second-order boundary-value problem by defining

$$g(\eta) = f'(\eta) \qquad\qquad \text{(B)}$$

or equivalently

$$f(\eta) = \int_0^\eta g(\tau)d\tau \qquad\qquad \text{(C)}$$

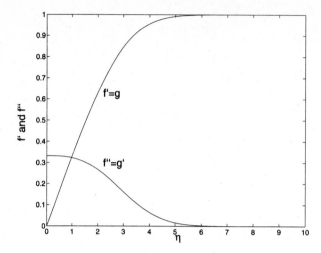

Figure 11.7 Solution of Blasius boundary layer equation

which satisfies the boundary condition, $f(0) = 0$. By introducing Eq.(B) into Eq.(A), we obtain

$$g'' + 0.5fg' = 0 \tag{D}$$

with boundary condtions,

$$g(0) = 0, \quad g(10) = 1$$

Equation (D) is a nonlinear second-order boundary-value problem, and can be solved by successive substitution as follows. The difference approximation for Eq.(D) may be written as

$$\frac{g_{i-1} - 2g_i + g_{i+1}}{(\eta)^2} + 0.5 f_i \frac{g_{i+1} - g_{i-1}}{2\Delta\eta} = 0 \tag{E}$$

where

$$f_i = \sum_{i=1}^{i} \frac{g_{k-1} + g_k}{2} \tag{F}$$

In Eq.(F) the trapezoidal rule is applied with $g_0 = 0$. Equation (E) is solved iteratively as follows:

(a) Assume an initial distribution of g_i, and calculate f_i by Eq.(F).
(b) Solve Eq.(E) by the tridiagonal scheme.
(c) Update f_i by introducing g_i just calculated into Eq.(F).

(d) Repeat (b) and (c) until the solution converges.

The results computed by List 11.2 are shown in Figure 11.7.

List 11.2
blasius.m
```
clear,clf
ni=200;
h=10/ni; h2inv = 1/h/h; hinv=1/h;
eta=h*(1:ni); f=ones(1,ni);
for k=1:9
  for i=1:ni
    a(i) = h2inv - 0.25*f(i)*hinv;
    b(i) = -2*h2inv;
    c(i) = h2inv + 0.25*f(i)*hinv;
    s(i)=0;
  end
  s(ni)=-c(ni);
  g=tri_diag(a,b,c,s,ni);
  f(1)=0.5*g(1)*h;
  for i=2:ni
    f(i)=0.5*(g(i) + g(i-1))*h+f(i-1);
  end
end
if k==1 hold on, end
axis([0,10,0,2])
fdd0 = (-g(2) + 4*g(1))/2/h
fdd(1)= (g(2)-0)/h/2;
for i=2:ni-1
fdd(i)=(g(i+1)-g(i-1))/h/2;
end
fdd(ni) = (3*g(ni) - 4*g(ni-1) + g(ni-2))/h/2;
plot([0,eta],[0,g],[0,eta],[fdd0,fdd])
[[0,eta(20:20:ni)]', [0,g(20:20:ni)]', [fdd0,fdd(20:20:ni)]']
text(2.2, 0.63, 'f'=g', 'Fontsize', [18])
h=text(2.2, 0.3, 'f''=g'', 'Fontsize', [18])
text(5, -0.05, 'h', 'FontName', 'Symbol','Fontsize',[18])
text(-1.0,0.4, 'f' and f''', 'Fontsize',[18],'Rotation',[90])
```

PROBLEMS

(11.1) Derive difference equations for $i=1$ and $i=10$ in Example 11.1 assuming that the boundary conditions are changed to $y'(1) = y(1)$ and $y'(10) = 0$.

(11.2) Derive difference equations for

$$-(p(x)\phi'(x))' + q(x)\phi(x) = S(x), \quad 0 < x < H$$

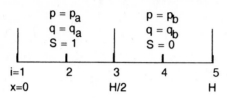

Figure 11.8 Grid and constants (P11.2)

$$\phi'(0) = \phi(H) = 0$$

The geometry, grid, and constants are shown in Figure 11.8. Grid spacings are $h = H/4$ for all the intervals.

(11.3) Repeat the previous problem assuming that the grid spacing for the first two intervals is h_1 and that for the last two intervals is h_2.

(11.4) The differential equation for a flexible cable, 50 m long, fixed at two ends, is given by

$$y''(x) = -w(x)/T, \quad y(0) = y(50) = 0$$

where x is in meters, $y(x)$ is displacement of the wire measured from the level of the end points of the wire (positive downward), T is the horizontal component of tension (5000 kg) and $w(x)$ is the load distribution given by

$$w(x) = 20(1 + \exp(x/25)) \text{ kg/m}$$

Determine the shape of the cable. (Use 10 grid intervals.)

(11.5) Consider a cooling fin with variable cross-sectional area and variable perimeter. Assuming that the temperature across any cross-section perpendicular to the axis is uniform, the temperature in the axial direction is the solution of the equation

$$-(kA(x)T'(x))' + P(x)h_cT(x) = P(x)h_cT_\infty$$

where k is the thermal conductivity, $P(x)$ is the perimeter, $A(x)$ is the cross-sectional area, and T_∞ is the temperature of the surroundings. The boundary conditions are given by

$$T(0) = 100°C$$

$$-kT'(H) = h_c(T(H) - T_\infty)$$

where H is the length of the fin, and h_c is the convection heat-transfer coefficient. Solve the above problem, assuming the following constants:

$$h_c = 30 \text{ w/m}^2\text{K}$$

$$H = 0.1 \text{ m}, \quad k = 100 \text{ w/mK}, \quad T_\infty = 20°\text{C}$$

$$A(x) = (0.005)(0.05 - 0.25x) \text{ m}^2$$
$$P(x) = A(x)/0.005 + 0.01 \text{ m}$$

(Use 10 grid intervals.)

(11.6) The boundary condition in the form of Eq.(11.2.10) becomes numerically equivalent to $\phi(0) = 0$ if g_L is set to 0 and f_L is set to a very large value such as 10^{10}. What values for g_L and f_L make Eq.(11.2.10) equivalent to $\phi(0) = 2$?

(11.7) Consider a cylindrical unit cell in a light water nuclear reactor consisting of a fuel pin and moderator, as shown in Figure 11.9:

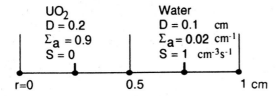

Figure 11.9 Unit cell (P11.7)

The thermal neutron flux in the cell satisfies the neutron diffusion equation given by

$$-\frac{1}{r}\frac{d}{dr}Dr\frac{d}{dr}\phi(r) + \Sigma_a\phi(r) = S(r)$$

where D is the diffusion coefficient, Σ_a is the absorption cross-section and S is the neutron source. The constants for UO_2 and H_2O are shown in the figure. The boundary conditions are

$$\phi'(0) = \phi'(1) = 0$$

(a) Using five grid points for the whole domain with a constant interval of 0.25 cm, derive difference equations for each grid point.

(b) Solve the difference equations derived in (a) by the tridiagonal solution.

(11.8) For a slab material of thickness 0.2 cm, the left side is perfectly insulated, but the right surface temperature is fixed at 0°C. The slab has a distributed heat source. The temperature equation is given by $-T''(x) = q(x)/k$. Develop a program to compute the temperature distribution using 10 grid intervals. Assuming the thermal conductivity is $k = 30$ W/m²K, run the program for the following two heat source distributions:

(a) $q(x) = 200$ kW/m³

(b) $q(x) = 100\exp(-10x)$ kW/m³

Compare the results with analytical solutions shown next:

(a) $T(x) = (10/3)(0.04 - x^2)$

(b) $T(x) = 0.033(e^{-2} + 2 - 10x - e^{-10x})$

(11.9) The diffusion equation for a cylindrical geometry is given by

$$-\frac{1}{r}(p(r)r\phi'(r))' + q(r)\phi(r) = S(r)$$

Considering the three grid points as shown in Figure 11.10, difference equations may be derived by integrating the equation from the midpoint between $i - 1$ and i to the midpoint between i and $i + 1$. Assuming the coefficients are constants as illustrated in the figure below and grid spacings are not uniform, derive the difference equations by integrating in the volume between a and b.

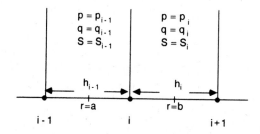

Figure 11.10 Cylindrical geometry (P11.9)

(11.10) The equation for the displacement of a circular membrane loaded with a constant pressure P (see Figure 11.11) is given by

$$y''(r) + \frac{1}{r}y'(r) = -P/T, \quad 0.2\text{ m} \le r \le 0.5\text{ m}$$

where r is the radial coordinate, y is the displacement of the membrane (positive downward), T is tension (400 kg/m), and the pressure is given as $P = 800$ kg/m². The boundary conditions are $y(0.2) = y(0.5) = 0$. Determine the displacement of the membrane, $y(r)$.

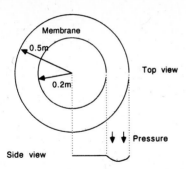

Figure 11.11 A membrane under pressure

(11.11) The spherical body of a material of radius 0.05 m is heated with a heat source distributed by

$$S(r) = 300 \exp[20(r - 0.05)]$$

where r is radius in meter, and the unit of S is W/m^3. The surface of the sphere is exposed to air. Heat escapes to the surrounding air by convection with the heat-transfer coefficient, $h_c = 20 \ W/m^2K$. At steady state, the temperature distribution is the solution of the equation,

$$-\frac{1}{r^2}\frac{d}{dr}r^2 k\frac{d}{dr}T(r) = S(r)$$

The boundary conditions are

$$T'(0) = 0$$
$$k' = h_c(T_\infty - T(R)), \quad T_\infty = 20 \ _0C$$

(a) Write the difference equations for the temperature using four equally spaced grid intervals.

(b) Solve the difference equations by the tridiagonal solution.

(11.12) One end of a rectangular cooling fin of length $H = 0.1$ m is attached to a heat source of 200°C. The fin transfers heat by both radiation and convection to the environment of 20°C. Assuming the fin and environment are both black bodies, the temperature of the fin satisfies the nonlinear diffusion equation

$$-AkT''(x) + Ph_c(T(x) - T_\infty) + P\sigma(T^4(x) - T_\infty^4) = 0$$

where

$k = 120 \ W/mK$ (thermal conductivity)

$A = 1.5x10^{-4} \ m^2$ (cross-sectional area of the fin)

$P = 0.106$ m (perimeter of the fin)

$h_c = 100 \ W/m^2K$ (convection heat-transfer coefficient)

$\sigma = 5.67x10^{-8} \ W/m^2K^4$ (Stefan-Boltzmann constant)

$T_\infty = 293$ K (temperature of the environment)

The boundary conditions are given by

$$T(0) = 500 + 273 \text{ K}$$
$$T'(H) = 0$$

where the right end of the fin is assumed to be perfectly insulated.

(a) Derive difference equation for the above differential equation using 10 equally spaced grid intervals.

(b) Solve the difference equation by means of the successive substitution.

(c) Repeat (b) using Newton iteration.

(11.13) Solve the following equation by the Newton iteration:

$$-\phi''(x) + [2 + \sin(\phi(x)]\phi(x) = 2, \quad \phi(0) = \phi(2) = 0 \qquad (11.6.7)$$

Use 20 mesh intervals.

(11.14) In a chemical reactor, the density of a material is governed by

$$-\phi''(x) + 0.1\phi'(x) = \exp(1 + 0.05\phi^2), \quad 0 < x < 2 \qquad (11.6.8)$$

Boundary conditions are $\phi(0) = 0$ and $\phi'(2) = 0$. With 10 equally spaced grid intervals, solve the equation by (1) successive substitution, and (2) Newton iteration.

Appendix A

Colors

A color may be defined by mixing three basic colors: red, green, and blue, and expressed by a triplet (r, g, b), where r, g, and b represent the relative intensities of the basic colors, red, green, and blue, respectively. The highest value is 1 and the lowest 0 for each basic color. Ten examples of color definitions by triplets are given below:

	r	g	b
white	1	1	1
red	1	0	0
yellow	1	1	0
green	0	1	0
cyan	0	1	1
gray	0.5	0.5	0.5
dark red	0.5	0	0
blue	0	0	1
aquamarine	0.5	1	0.83
black	0	0	0

Color map: Color map is an n-by-3 matrix. Each row is a triplet of the three colors. The default value of n in MATLAB is 64. The first row corresponds to the minimum value of the color axis and the last row the maximum. By defining different intensity distribution of the three basic colors, different color maps are developed. Some predetermined color maps in MATLAB are

```
hsv, cool, hot, jet, gray, flag
```

where hsv stands for the *hue saturation value* color set.

The color map for the hsv color is illustrated in Table A.1. A color map may be displayed in graphic form by rgbplot. The intensities of three colors in hsv color map are plotted in Figure A.1. The actual colors of several color maps are illustrated in color plates similar to Figure A.2. To assign a color map to a figure, use colormap; for example, colormap jet or colormap(jet) sets the current color map to jet.

413

Color axis: Color axis is a one-dimensional coordinate with its minimum and maximum. The minimum and maximum can be prescribed by `caxis([cmin, cmax])`. The minimum value of color axis points to the first row (or the first index) in the color map and the maximum value of color axis points to the last row (or the last index). Unless `cmin` and `cmax` are specified by `caxis`, the lowest color index is automatically set to the minimum value of the color data in `mesh`, `surface` and similar commands.

Table A.1 The rgb color map

Color Index	Red	Intensities Green	Blue
1	1.0000	0	0
2	1.0000	0.0938	0
3	1.0000	0.1875	0
4	1.0000	0.2812	0
5	1.0000	0.3750	0
6	1.0000	0.4688	0
7	1.0000	0.5625	0
8	1.0000	0.6562	0
9	1.0000	0.7500	0
10	1.0000	0.8438	0
11	1.0000	0.9375	0
12	0.9688	1.0000	0
13	0.8750	1.0000	0
14	0.7812	1.0000	0
15	0.6875	1.0000	0
16	0.5938	1.0000	0
17	0.5000	1.0000	0
18	0.4062	1.0000	0
19	0.3125	1.0000	0
20	0.2188	1.0000	0
21	0.1250	1.0000	0
22	0.0312	1.0000	0
23	0	1.0000	0.0625
24	0	1.0000	0.1562
25	0	1.0000	0.2500
26	0	1.0000	0.3438
27	0	1.0000	0.4375
.	.	.	.
.	.	.	.
59	1.0000	0	0.5625
60	1.0000	0	0.4688
61	1.0000	0	0.3750
62	1.0000	0	0.2812

```
63      1.0000          0     0.1875
64      1.0000          0     0.0938
----------------------------------
```

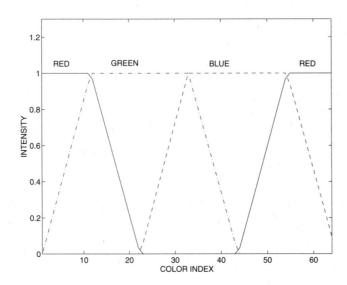

Figure A.1 RGB plot of HSV color map

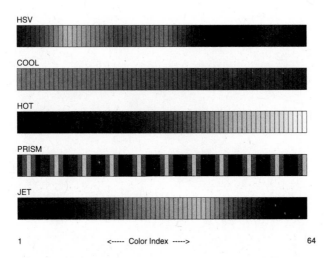

Figure A.2 Color bars (see color plates for a color print)

Multiple color maps: Only one color map can be assigned to a figure. Often, however, it becomes desirable to use multiple color maps to finish a figure. This conflicting situation can be resolved by developing a composite color map. For example, if `cool`, `hot`, and `jet` are all necessary in a single figure, make the composite color map by combining them into a single color map, such as

```
ccm=[ cool(64); hot(64); jet(64)]
```

The color map `ccm` becomes a matrix of 192-by-3, and the top 64 rows correspond to `cool`, the next 64 rows to `hot`, and the last 64 to `jet`.

One word of caution is not to omit 64 in the definition of `ccm`, for the following reason: Once the length of the color map other than 64 is used, the default length of the color map is also changed to that value. In the present case, the default length of color maps becomes $64 \times 3 = 192$ in the next call, so that even the length of `hsv` or `jet` becomes 192, unless their lengths are specified. If `ccm` is computed without 64 for the second time, its length becomes 192×3. In a few times of repeat, the computer memory and disk space are exhausted.

List A.1 that plots the color bars in Figure A.1 is an example of using a composite color map.

List A.1

```
% col_bar.m
clear,clf
C=[hsv(64);cool(64);hot(64);prism(64);jet(64)];
colormap(C);  hold on
for M=1:5
  for i=1:64;
    for j=1:2
      x(i,j)=(i-1)/63;
      y(i,j)=(j+8)*1.1 - (M-1)*2.2;
      z(i,j)=i+64*(M-1);
      if i==1 z(i,j)=z(i,j)+0.0001;end
      if i==64 z(i,j)=z(i,j)-0.0001;end
    end
  end
  surface(x,y,z, z)
end
text(0, 2.4+0.1,'JET')
text(0, 4.6+0.1,'PRISM')
text(0, 6.8+0.1,'HOT')
text(0, 9.0+0.1,'COOL')
text(0,11.2+0.1,'HSV')
axis([0,1,0,12]) ; axis('off')
text(0.3,0,' <-----  Color Index  -----> ')
text(1,0,'64')
text(0,0,'1')
```

Appendix B

Drawing of Three-Dimensional Objects

Developing a complicated three-dimensional object as a single surface or mesh is usually very difficult or inefficient. Instead, the object may be assembled using parts that can be easily developed as a single surface or mesh. The coordinate set of x, y, and z for a part may be developed using a local coordinate system. In order to locate the parts at appropriate positions, rotation, translation, and scaling of the coordinates of each part are necessary. The objectives of this appendix are first, to introduce basic methods for moving objects and second, to illustrate a few objects developed.

MOVING OBJECTS IN 3-D SPACE

Transformation of origin: Suppose a part of the whole object is defined in a local coordinate system (x, y, z). If the origin of the local system is translated by (x_a, y_a, z_a), the new coordinates (x, y, z) become

$$\bar{x} = x + x_a$$
$$\bar{y} = y + y_a \qquad \qquad \text{(B.1)}$$
$$\bar{z} = z + z_a$$

Change of scale: If the scale in the local system is changed by a scale factor α, the new coordinates in the local system are

$$\bar{x} = \alpha x$$
$$\bar{y} = \alpha y \qquad \qquad \text{(B.2)}$$
$$\bar{z} = \alpha z$$

Rotation about the x-axis: If the local system is rotated clockwise θ degrees about the x-axis, the new coordinates become

$$\overline{x} = x$$
$$\overline{y} = \cos(\theta)y - \sin(\theta)z \qquad (B.3)$$
$$\overline{z} = \sin(\theta)y + \cos(\theta)z$$

Rotation about the y-axis: If the local system is rotated clockwise θ degrees about the y-axis, the new coordinates become

$$\overline{x} = \sin(\theta)z + \cos(\theta)x$$
$$\overline{y} = y \qquad (B.4)$$
$$\overline{z} = \cos(\theta)z - \sin(\theta)x$$

Rotation about the z-axis: If the local system is rotated clockwise θ degrees about the z-axis, the new coordinates become

$$\overline{x} = \cos(\theta)x - \sin(\theta)y$$
$$\overline{y} = \sin(\theta)x + \cos(\theta)y \qquad (B.5)$$
$$\overline{z} = z$$

Three functions to rotate a system are

List B.1
rotx_.m

```
function [xd,yd,zd]=rotx_(x,y,z,th)
cosf=cos(th*pi/180);sinf=sin(th*pi/180);
xd =x;
yd =   cosf.*y - sinf.*z;
zd =   sinf.*y + cosf.*z;
```

roty_.m

```
function [xd,yd,zd]=roty_(x,y,z,th)
cosf=cos(th*pi/180);sinf=sin(th*pi/180);
yd =y;
xd =   cosf.*x + sinf.*z;
zd = - sinf.*x + cosf.*z;
```

rotz_.m

```
function [xd,yd,zd]=rotz_(x,y,z,th)
cosf=cos(th*pi/180);sinf=sin(th*pi/180);
xd =   cosf *x - sinf *y;
yd =   sinf *x + cosf *y;
zd =z;
```

Example B.1 Fan Rotor

Figure B.1 illustrates a fan rotor that consists of one cylindrical shaft and six blades. In List B.2, a mesh for a blade is developed by an array of section profiles. The cross-sectional profile of the blades is first developed in b_design.m. The mesh for a blade is expressed by a triple of x, y, and z.

Then, the rotor can be constructed by copying the blade to five other locations after rotations. The shaft is developed as a hollow cylinder.

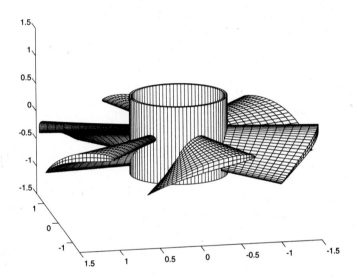

Figure B.1 Fan rotor

List B.2
fan_rot.m

```
%  Plots a fan rotor (Fig.B.1)
clear,clg   %ref: t_blade.m
colormap jet
r=0.601:0.1:2;
imax=length(r);
dth=pi/16;
th=-2*dth:dth:2*dth;
[th,zb]=b_design;
jmax=length(th);
%          minz=-0.5, maxz=0.1
%          minth=-0.4, maxth=0.4
for i=1:imax
for j=1:jmax
x(i,j)=r(i)*cos(th(j));
```

```
y(i,j)=r(i)*sin(th(j));
z(i,j)=zb(j);
end
end
zc=z;
for i=imax-1:imax
for j=1:jmax
x(i,j)=r(imax-2)*cos(th(j));
y(i,j)=r(imax-2)*sin(th(j));
if i== imax, z(i,j)=(zb(j)+zb(jmax+1-j))*0.5;, end
zc(i,j)=1;
end
end
hold on
for k=1:6
angl=60*k
[xb,yb,zb] = rotz_(x,y,z,angl);
mesh(xb,yb,zb, zc)
end
axis([-1.5,1.5,-1.5,1.5,-1.5,1.5])
[xc,yc,zc]=cylinder(0.595,80);
xc(2,:)=xc(1,:);
yc(2,:)=yc(1,:);
zc(1,:)=-ones(size(xc(1,:)))*0.7;
zc(2,:)=ones(size(xc(1,:)))*0.7;
colr=0.7*ones(size(zc));
mesh(xc,yc,zc, colr*0.6)
mesh(xc*0.95,yc*0.95,zc, colr*0.99)
view([-100,20])
```

b_design.m

```
function [thb,zb]=b_design
% Analytical airfoil section design
minz=-0.5;
maxz=0.1;
minth=-0.4;
maxth=0.4;
r=0.4;
dth=pi/32;
th=0:dth:2*pi;
x=r*cos(th);
y=r*sin(th).* (x+0.5).*(5-x)/15  ...
        - (x+0.4).*(x-0.4)+ (0.6/0.8)*(x)-0.2 ;
thb=x;
zb=y;
```

Example B.2   Spiral Pipe

A pipe is constructed by connecting an array of circles (see Figure B.2). Because all circles are identical except for locations and orientations, they can be drawn by translating and rotating one reference circle drawn at the origin on the x-y plain. The reference unit circle on the x-y plane is expressed by points on the circle. The circle is rotated first about the x-axis and then about the z-axis. The pipe is drawn by List B.3.

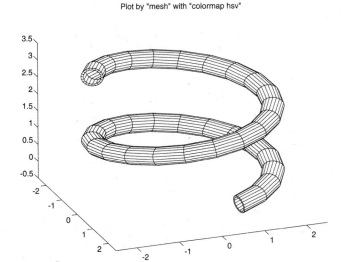

Plot by "mesh" with "colormap hsv"

Figure B.2 Spiral pipe

List B.3
pipe_.m

```
clear,clf,hold off
%-------Construction of basic pipe cross-section (circle)
dth=pi/10;
th=0:dth:2*pi;
x=0.25*cos(th);y=0.25*sin(th);z=0.25*zeros(size(x));
%-------Spiral shape of axis of pipe
ths=0:dth:pi*3.5;
xs=2*cos(ths);ys=2*sin(ths);zs=zeros(size(xs))+ 0.3*ths ;
m=length(xs)  ;
%-------Construction of pipe section to axial direction
for i=2:m
  xn=xs(i)-xs(i-1)  ;
  yn=ys(i)-ys(i-1)  ;
  zn=zs(i)-zs(i-1)  ;
  rn=sqrt(xn^2+yn^2+zn^2);
  el=acos(zn/rn)*180/pi;
  az=0;
  rxy=sqrt(xn^2+yn^2);
  if xn==0,  xn=1e-10;end
  az=atan2(yn,xn)*180/pi;
```

```
     [xd,yd,zd]=rotx_(x ,y ,z ,-el);
     b=-(az+90);
     [xp(i,:),yp(i,:),zp(i,:)]=rotz_(xd,yd,zd,b);
     xp(i,:)=xp(i,:)+xs(i);
     yp(i,:)=yp(i,:)+ys(i);
     zp(i,:)=zp(i,:)+zs(i);
   end
 %------------ Pipe structure is now in xpp,ypp,zpp
 xav=sum(xp(2,:))/length(xp(2,:));
 yav=sum(yp(2,:))/length(yp(2,:));
 zav=sum(zp(2,:))/length(zp(2,:));
 xp(1,:)=xav*0.2+ xp(2,:)*0.8;
 yp(1,:)=yav*0.2+ yp(2,:)*0.8;
 zp(1,:)=zav*0.2+ zp(2,:)*0.8;
 j=m-1;
 xav=sum(xp(j,:))/length(xp(j,:));
 yav=sum(yp(j,:))/length(yp(j,:));
 zav=sum(zp(j,:))/length(zp(j,:));
 xp(m,:)=xav*0.2+ xp(j,:)*0.8;
 yp(m,:)=yav*0.2+ yp(j,:)*0.8;
 zp(m,:)=zav*0.2+ zp(j,:)*0.8;

 xpp=xp;
 ypp=yp;
 zpp=zp;
 %-------------------------------------
 colormap hsv
 mesh(xpp,ypp,zpp)
 view([70,30])
 axis([-2.5 ,2.5 ,-2.5 ,2.5 ,-.5,3.5])
 title('Plot by "mesh" with "colormap hsv" ')
```

Example B.3   Airplane

An airplane frame (see Figure B.3) is developed by putting five parts together.
The fuselage is first developed by an array of circles. One side of the main wing
is developed by function wing_2d, which uses NACA0012 airfoil (see Problem
7.5). The ladder and stabilizer are essentially copies of the main wing after scaling,
rotation, and translation.

List B.4
plane_.m

```
clear, clg     % Next part develops fuselage
dth=pi/16; fuselen=6;  thf=pi:-dth:pi/2;
xa = 0:0.5:fuselen
xt=fuselen+0.25:0.25:fuselen+2;
dxt = 1.4/(length(xt)-0)  ;
yt = -1+dxt:dxt:0.4;
length(yt)
xft=[cos(thf),xa, xt]
yft=[sin(thf)- 0.3*sin(2*thf).^4, ones(size(xa)),...
                                  ones(size(yt))];
```

Commuter Airplane

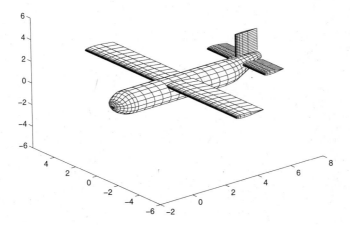

Figure B.3 Airplane

```
xfb=[cos(thf),xa,xt]
yfb=[-sin(thf),-ones(size(xa)),yt ];
k=length([thf, xa])
yfb(k)=( yfb(k-1)+yfb(k+1))/2
xc =(xfb+xft)/2;
yc = (yfb+yft)/2;
L=length(xc);
for i=1:L
   if xc(i)<0   yc(i)=0;  end
end

a=0.5;  b=0.5;
dth=pi/8;   th=0:dth:2*pi; jmax=length(th);
xr=cos(th); yr=sin(th);
L=length(xc);
for i=1:L
  xr=cos(th);
  yr=sin(th);
  a = (yft(i)-yc(i))/(-yfb(i) + yc(i));
  b = (-yfb(i)     +yc(i));
  for j=1:jmax
      y(i,j)=yr(j)*b+yc(i);
      if th(j)<pi    y(i,j)=yr(j)*b*a + yc(i); end
    x(i,j)=xr(j)*b;
    z(i,j)=xc(i);
```

```
      end
   end
   mesh(z, x,y)
   axis([-2 8 -6 6 -6 6])
   hold on
   [xw,yw,zw] = wing_2d          % Airfoil section profile
   F = 1.7;
   xw=F*xw; yw=F*yw; zw=F*zw;
   [x1,y1,z1] = rotz_(xw,yw,zw,90);
   [x2,y2,z2] = rotx_(xw,yw,zw,180);
   [x2,y2,z2] = rotz_(x2,y2,z2,270);
   mesh(x1+2,y1-0.5,z1+ 0.7);
   mesh(x2+2,y2+0.5,z2+ 0.7);
   mesh(0.8*x1+6.6,0.5*z1-0,-0.3*y1+1.2)
   pause
   mesh(0.7*x1+6.6,0.3*y1-0.7,0.9*z1+ 0.7);
   mesh(0.7*x2+6.6,0.3*y2+0.7,0.9*z2+ 0.7);
   caxis([-3,1])
   axis([-2 8 -6 6 -6 6])
   title('Commuter Airplane')
   caxis([-2, 2])
   colormap(hsv)
```

wing_2d.m

```
   function [zw,xw,yw] = naca0012
   x=0:0.1:1;
   n=length(x);
   for k=1:30
      for i=2:n-1
         x(i)=0.5*x(i-1)+0.4*x(i+1);
      end
   end
   for i=2:n
      x(n+i-1)=x(n-i+1);
   end
   y=0.2969*sqrt(x) - 0.126*x - 0.3516*x.^2  + ...
         0.2843 * x.^3 - 0.1015*x.^4;
   for i=n+1:length(y)
      y(i)=-y(i);
   end
   jmax=15
   for j=1:jmax
      for i=1:2*n-1
         xw(i,j)=x(i);
         yw(i,j)=y(i);
         zw(i,j)=0.3*(j-1);
      end
   end
   yw(:,jmax)=zeros(size(yw(:,jmax)));
   zw(:,jmax)=zw(:,jmax-1);
```

Example B.4   A lobe of oscillating liquid jet

A three-dimensional view of an oscillating liquid jet lobe is developed and displayed using the `surfl` command. The script is shown in List B.5 and the view is plotted in Figure B.4.

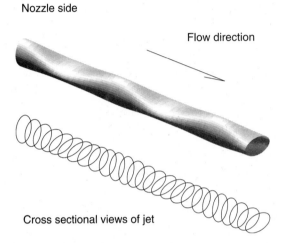

Figure B.4 A lobe of oscillating liquid jet

List B.5
lobe_.m

```
% Plots a lobe of liquid jet.
clear, clf
hold on
dth=2*pi/40;
th=0:dth:2*pi;
r = ones(size(th));
colormap gray
for n=1:51
    b=n-1;
    x(n,:)=cos(th)*(1-0.25*cos(b*0.3));
    y(n,:)=sin(th)*(1+0.25*cos(b*0.3));
    z(n,:)=n*0.3*ones(size(th));
    m=n+9;
    if floor(m/2)*2 == m
        plot3(z(n,:), x(n,:), y(n, :)-5)
    end
end
surfl(z,x,y+2, [-10, 60])
axis([0 13 -5 15 -10 5])
```

```
shading flat
view([10 -10 10])
text(5.2, 8.4,3, ' Flow direction')
text(-5, 8, 'Nozzle side')
xd= [5, 10, 9];
yd=[5,5, 4.5];
zd=[ 3,3,3];
plot3(xd, yd, zd)
axis('off')
text(10,-15, -2,'Cross-sectional views of jet')
hold off
```

Appendix C

Movie

Showing time-dependent phenomena is a natural application of movie. Movie can also be used to show complicated objects from different angles and with different zooming rates. The principle of movie is simple; that is, to show a series of figures or images. This appendix shows how to make and play movies, with an illustration.

Making movie by MATLAB is simple and a great fun. In essence, it consists of only three commands, `getframe`, `moviein`, and `movie`. In order to adjust the axis of the graphic window from which frames are taken and the one in which the movie is played, however, a few more commands are necessary. Since movie is a sequence of figures or images, you must think about how to prepare them.

MATLAB COMMANDS TO MAKE MOVIE

Getframe: `getframe` captures a movie frame from the current axis of a figure. A frame is written in a column vector. It uses one of the following formats:

```
geframe
getframe(h)
```

With the first format, the entire current axis is captured. In the second format, h is the handle to the root, a figure, or axes. Therefore, `getframe(h)` gets a frame from object (or the window of the handle) h.

Moviein: `M = moviein(n)` initializes a matrix M to hold n frames of a movie based on the current figure window. The matrix M has enough rows to store n copies of the output from getframe, one frame in each column. `M = moviein(n, h)` initializes matrix M based on the window of the handle h.

Movie: `movie(M)` plays the movie in matrix M once. It can also take one of the following formats:

```
movie(M,n)
movie(M,n,fps)
movie(h,M,n,fps)
```

```
movie(h,M,n,fps,loc)
```

Command movie(M,n) plays movie n times. If n < 0, the movie is played n times, but the play in the even times is backward. Parameter fps in the third format specifies the number of frames per second. Without fps, the default is 1 frame per second. Parameter h is the handle of figure or axis where the movie is to be played. The parameter loc in the fourth format is a vector of length 4 that specifies the location of the movie relative to the left bottom corner of the current window. Only the first two elements are used, the first is the pixel number counted from the left and the second is the pixel number counted from the bottom.

Example C.1   Rotating Ball

The colored surface of a ball is rotated around its x-axis. List C.1 illustrates the script.

List C.1
movie_1.m
```
clear clf
h=figure(8)
fprintf('AJUST SCREEN SIZE MANUALLY')
fprintf('(A 3 inch square is suggested.)\n')
fprintf('Hit RETURN after ajustment\n')
pause
M=moviein(10,gcf);
dth=pi/10; th=0:dth:pi; fi=0:dth:2*pi;
nk=length(th); nj = length(fi);
for j=1:nj
  for k=1:nk
    x(k,j) = sin(th(k)) *cos(fi(j));
    y(k,j) = sin(th(k))* sin(fi(j));
    z(k,j) =cos(th(k));
  end
end
[xd,yd,zd] = rotx_(x,y,z, 30);
axis([-1.5 1.5 -1.5 1.5 -1 1])
c=zd;
for k=1:11
  kk=36*k;
  [xd,yd,zd] = rotx_(x,y,z, kk);
  surf(xd,yd,zd,c)
  M(:,k) = getframe(gcf);
end
n=10; fps=10; save m_ball M n fps
```

In order to play the movie:
```
gcf;cla;clf
load m_ball
loc=[30,30,0,0];
movie(gcf,M,n,fps,loc)
```

Appendix D

Image Processing

IMAGE IN MATLAB

An image in MATLAB[1] is an m-by-n matrix of color tiles, which is defined by an m-by-n image matrix. The entries of the image matrix are color numbers (color indices) in the color map. For example, consider a 3-by-3 matrix:

```
W=[1 2 3; 2 3 2; 3 2 1]
```

and an associated colormap of length 3:

```
map = [1 0 0; 0 1 0; 0 0 1]
```

where the first raw (first triplet) is red, the second green, and the last blue. Then

```
W=[1 2 3; 2 3 2; 3 2 1]
map = [1 0 0; 0 1 0; 0 0 1]
image(W)
colormap(map)
```

will produce a 3-by-3 color tile pattern like

```
red     green   blue
green   blue    green
blue    green   red
```

Here, the order of tiles is the same as in the matrix (first index of `W` increases downward). Note, however, that if `hold on` is effective, the vertical order of image is reversed (first index increases upward).

The image may be displayed also by `pcolor`. More details of `image` and `pcolor` commands are described next.

Image: `image` displays an image in the figure window. Its formats include

---

[1]Image processing as described in this appendix does not need the MATLAB Image Processing Toolbox. Basic information on the relevant commands can be found, therefore, in *MATLAB Reference Guide* as well as *The student Edtion of MATLAB, Version 4 User's Guide*, Prentice-Hall 1995. If Image Processing Toolbox is available, however, see C. M. Thompson and L. Shure, *MATLAB Image Processing TOOLBOX*, The Math Works, 1995

```
image(W)
image(x,y,W)
h=image(W)
```

The first format `image(W)` displays matrix `W` as an image. Each element of `W` specifies the color of a rectangular tile in the image.

The second format `image(x,y,W)` is useful only if tic marks with coordinate values need to be printed, where `x` and `y` are vectors and specify the labeling of x and y axes. Only the first and last elements of `x` and `y` are used for the axis limits. Commands `image(W)` and `image(x,y,W)` produce exactly the same image except that the tic marks are altered by the latter.

The third format `h=image(W)` returns a handle of objects associated with `image`. In order to see a list of image object properties and their current values, execute `set(h)`. Parameters to specify additional properties of the image can be added after `W` in the arguments of the `image` command. Command `image` uses a special view angle of [0, 90]. That is, the first index of `W(i,j)` increases vertically downward, and the second horizontally. If `hold on` is effective, however, the first index increases upward.

The `shading` and `caxis` commands do not work with `image`.

Pcolor: It stands for seudocolor (checkerboard) plot. The formats are

```
pcolor(W)
pcolor(x,y,W)
h=pcolor(W)
```

Command `pcolor(W)` displays a pseudocolor or "checkerboard" plot of matrix `W`. The first row of `W` becomes the bottom of the figure (reverse of `image(W)` unless `hold on` is used). If `view(0,-90)` is applied, its vertical order becomes identical with that of `image`. The values of the elements of `W` specify the color in each cell of the plot. The `shading` and `caxis` commands are both applicable to `pcolor`. Indeed, `shading faceted` is its default mode, in which each cell has a constant color and the last row and column of `W` are not used. Furthermore, the tiles are separated by black lines. When the size of tiles becomes small, the black lines may dominate the color tiles and tend to darken the image. The black lines may be removed by using `shading flat`. With another option, `shading interp`, colors in a tile are changed continuously by the bilinear interpolation, so the whole image becomes smooth. With the default mode of `caxis`, the smallest and largest elements of `W` are assigned the first and last colors given in the color table; colors for the remainder of the elements in `W` are determined by table-lookup within the remainder of the colormap. By `caxis` command, however, the color range can be changed.

Here is an easy way for the reader to experiment with `image` and `pcolor`; that is, to plot an image of a random matrix by running the following script:

List D.1
rand_im.m

```
% Plots image of random matrix
m=input('m=  ');
n=input('n=  ');
W = ceil(64*rand(m,n));
    % Generates a m-by-n random matrix.
colormap(hot)
image(W);
```

Multiplication of the random matrix by 64 is necessary because the random numbers from `rand` are between 0 and 1. On the other hand, the color indices are between 1 and 64. Therefore, `ceil(64*ran(m,n))` is used to produce a matrix of random numbers from 1 to 64. Try a small number of tiles, such as 5-by-5 (m = n = 5) or 20-by-30 (m = 20, n = 30) first, then a larger one such as 50-by-50. If you have a professional version of MATLAB, try 200-by-300. After the display with the `hot` color map is completed, the colormap can be changed to any other colormap as often as desired. Try `colormap jet`, `colormap cool`, `colormap hsv` and `colormap flag` from the command window. Unlike `pcolor`, the commands `caxis`, `shading flat` and `shading interp` are not applicable to `image`.

Once you understand what works and what doesn't with `image`, replace `image` by `pcolor` in List D.1 and run. Unlike `image`, the `caxis`, `shading` and `view` commands work. For example, with `view(0,-90)`, the top and bottom of the `pcolor` image are flipped. Also, with `caxis([-100, 100])`, the color range in the image is narrowed. Apply `shading interp` as well as `shading flat`. You should notice that with `shading flat`, the black lines that separate tiles are removed, so the image becomes much brighter than with the default option `shading faceted`. With `shading interp`, the image becomes smooth.

SAVING AND LOADING IMAGES IN STANDARD FORMAT

The standard image data in MATLAB consist of an image matrix `W` and an associated colormap `map`. To save an image in the standard format,

```
save filename W map
```

In order to load the file,

```
[W, map] = load filename
```

EXPORT AND IMPORT OF IMAGE FILES

There are many possible reasons why transporting image files between MATLAB and other software becomes inevitable. A few typical examples of reasons are as follows:

(a) Painting, drawing, and photographic images developed on other software need to be reprocessed by MATLAB.

(b) Figures or images developed using MATLAB may be displayed or reprocessed by other software. Geometries of objects may be developed by MATLAB, taking advantage of ample choices of mathematical functions and interpolating tools. On the other hand, editing an existing image or touching it up with colors may be easier in some other software application.

(c) Capturing graphics in postscript form is not possible in many other graphic software programs. Therefore, you may wish to import images into MATLAB in order to create a postscript file.

(d) In some situations, printing of images would be easier with another image processing or painting software than directly from MATLAB.

Unless Image Processing Toolbox is used, the only format to import and export image files from and to other software is in the raw image format.[2]

The raw image can be read into MATLAB by `imread`. Almost any image format can be converted to and from the raw format by Alchemy. An `gif` file, `image04.gif`, for example, can be converted to the raw format by

```
alchemy -r -c 128 -z 4 image04.gif
```

which creates the `image04.raw` file, where
       `-r` : produces a "raw" file;
       `-c 128`: limits the color map length to 128 colors;
       `-z 4` : sorts colormap by luminance.
The image of this file can be displayed in MATLAB by

```
[W,map] = imread('image04.raw');
colormap(map)
image(W)
```

If Alchemy can be accessed directly from MATLAB (by an appropriate path), the foregoing processes can be combined into one script, as follows:

```
alchemy -r -c 128 -z 4 image04.gif
[W,map] = imread('image04.raw');
colormap(map)
image(W)
```

---

[2]The raw image files are produced by the Image Alchemy program developed by Handmade Software, Inc. This program allows one to convert to and from many different formats, including TARGA, ADEX, FOP, EPS, GIF, Gem VDI, ILBM, Vivid IMG, JPEG, HP RTL, PBM, Stork, PALette, AutoLogic, Macintosh PICT, MTV, SGI, QDV, PCX, PCL, HSI Raw, Erdas Image, Sun RASter, Grasp, TIFF, QRT Raw, Utah RLE, Windows BMP, and WPG.

   The price of Image Alchemy varies, depending on the platform. Its price for the PC is the least expensive and is comparable to the price of MATLAB student edition. The address is Handmade Software, Inc., 15951 Los Gatos Blvd., Suite 7, Los Gatos, CA 95032, Phone: (408) 358-1292, Fax: (408) 358-2694, Internet: hsi@netcom.COM.

The reverse of `imread` is `imwrite`. A MATLAB image data may be converted to a `gif` file by

```
[W,map] = load image_data
imwrite(W,map,'filename.raw')
!alchemy -g filename.raw filename.gif
    % converts to GIF
```

Example D.1   A picture from a digital camera

The photographs in Figure D.1 show the sculptures titled *Mobius Trilogy* (left)[3] and *Closed Loop Drifter* (right) by Ralph Williams, which were taken by Quick100[4] and downloaded to a PC. The format of the images from the digital camera was `qtk`, which was first converted to the `tif` format by the Quick100 software, and then to the raw image form by Alchemy. Finally, it was displayed by MATLAB (see also color plates).

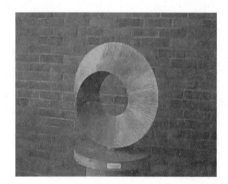

Figure D.1 Mobius Trilogy (left) and Closed Loop Drifter (right) by Ralph Williams

Example D.2   A picture from a VCR

The pictures in Figure D.2 are from the *Mystery* program on PBS.[5] The program was available on a VCR tape recorded by a home video recorder. The images were captured from the video tape and digitized on Macintosh in the `pic` format, and then were converted to `gif` format for PC using PhotoShop on Macintosh, and further to the raw format by Image Alchemy.

---

[3]German mathematician A.G.R. Mobius first described a surface that twists in such a way that its top side is continuous with its underside and so, in effect, it has only one side.

[4]A digital camera manuactured by Apple that takes photographs in an electronic form. Permission to display these photographs has been obtained from Mr. R. Williams.

[5]Permission has been obtained from WGBH, Boston MA.

Figure D.2 Scenes from PBS Mystery Theater program (see also color plates)

ELEMENTS OF IMAGE PROCESSING

Because an image consists of a matrix of color indices and an associated colormap, the image can be altered in many different ways by modifying the matrix and the colormap. Changing color and changing contrast are most elementary image processing. Changing color scheme alone can often provide different information from the same image file. Image Processing Toolbox has numerous tools for image processing. In the remainder of this section, we describe fundamental aspects of a few elementary image-processing techniques.

Example D.4   Edge Extraction and Diffusion

Figure D.3 displays an image of overlapping circular disks plotted by List D.2.

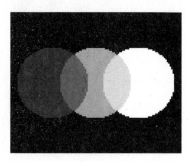

Figure D.3 Three disks

List D.2
disk_ptn.m

```
% disk_ptn.m   Plots three disks by pcolor.
clear;clf
map=jet;
```

```
colormap(map)
disp 'For Student Edition users, ni < 25'
%ni=input('ni = ')
ni=100;
nj= ni*1.20;
ic1=ni/2; ic2=ni/2; ic3=ni/2;
jc1=nj/4; jc2=nj/2; jc3=nj/4*3;
W=ones(ni,nj);
ni20=ni/4;
for i=1:ni
  for j=1:nj
    r1 = sqrt((i-ic1)^2 + (j-jc1)^2);
    r2 = sqrt((i-ic2)^2 + (j-jc2)^2) ;
    r3 =  sqrt((i-ic3)^2 + (j-jc3)^2);
    if r1  <  ni20  W(i,j)=20; end
    if r2  < ni20 , W(i,j)=40; end
    if r3  < ni20 , W(i,j)=60; end
    if r1< ni20 & r2 < ni20,   W(i,j)=30; end
    if r2< ni20 & r3 < ni20,   W(i,j)=50; end
  end
end
pcolor(W);
shading flat;
save disksda W map ; axis('off')
text(ni/10,ni/10,'Disk pattern','FontSize',[18])
```

Edges of disks may be identified by sudden changes of color index in the image matrix w. For example,

$$c(i,j) = [w(j,i) - w(j-1,i)]^2 + [w(j,i) - w(j+1,i)]^2$$
$$+[w(j,i) - w(j,i-1)]^2 + [w(j,i) - w(j,i+1)]^2$$

will become zero unless the tile (i,j) is not ajacent to an edge, but becomes nonzero if it is. The edge pattern image illustrated in Figure D.4 is drawn by List D.3.

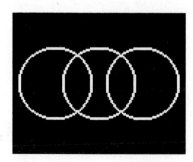

Figure D.4 Edges of three disks

List D.3
disk_edg.m

```
% disk_edg.m    Plots edges extracted from three disks.
clear,clf
load  disksda    %reads W and map
[ni,nj]=size(W);
colormap(map)
c = zeros(size(W));
for i=2:ni-1
for j=2:nj-1
 c(i,j)= (W(i-1,j)-W(i,j))^2 + (W(i+1,j)-W(i,j))^2 ...
    + (W(i,j-1)-W(i,j))^2 + (W(i,j+1)-W(i,j))^2;
  if c(i,j) > 0, c(i,j) = 55; end
end
end
image(c);axis('off')
text(ni/10,ni/10,'Extracted edge pattern','FontSize',[18])
save edgeda c map
```

The edge pattern may be diffused by applying a diffusion operator, or equivalently, by solving the following equation:

$$(4 + \alpha)d_{j,i} = d_{j-1,i} + d_{j+1,i} + d_{j,i-1} + d_{j,i+1} + c(j,i) \qquad \text{(D.1)}$$

where α is a parameter to control how far the diffusion effect reaches. The higher α is, the shorter the distance of diffusion. An iterative solution scheme based on Gauss-Seidel method is written as

$$(4 + \alpha)d_{j,i}^{(t)} = d_{j-1,i}^{(t)} + d_{j+1,i}^{(t-1)} + d_{j,i-1}^{(t)} + d_{j,i+1}^{(t-1)} + c(j,i) \qquad \text{(D.2)}$$

where t is the iteration number. For image processing, a strict convergence is not necessary. In fact, a small number of iteration steps will achieve the diffisuion effect.

A variant of the foregoing processing is the *convective-diffusion* effect produced by

$$(2 + a)d_{j,i}^{(t)} = d_{j+1,i}^{(t-1)} + d_{j,i+1}^{(t-1)} + c(j,i) \qquad \text{(D.3)}$$

The foregoing scheme diffuses the image only in one direction from edges. List D.4 displays the diffused pattern in Figure D.5. Its colored version is in the color plate pages.

List D.4
edge_dif.m

```
% edge_dif.m    Edges of three disks after diffusion.
clear,clf
load  edgeda
[ni,nj]=size(c);
d=c;
```

Figure D.5 Three disks after diffusion

```
colormap(map)
for iter=1:7
for i=2:ni-1
for j=2:nj-1
 d(i,j)= (d(i-1,j)+d(i,j) + d(i,j-1)+d(i,j) + c(i,j))/(4+0.1);
 end
end
end
end
image(d)

text(ni/10,ni/10,'After a diffusion process','FontSize',[18])
axis('off')
```

Example D.5   Fractal

Figure D.6 displays a fractal image plotted by List D.4 based on the Henon's model[6]:

$$x_{n+1} = ax_n - b\left(y_n - x_n^2\right)$$

$$y_{n+1} = bx_n + a\left(y_n - x_n^2\right)$$

where $a = 0.24$ and $b = 0.9708$.

The same fractal image becomes significantly different if the color scheme is altered, as illustrated in the color plates.

List D.5
fractal_.m

```
%fractal_.m   Fractal image plot by Henon's model.
clf,clear, W=ones(201,201)*64; colormap(hot)
hold on
```

---

[6]H. Lauwerier, *Fractals*, Princeton University Press, 1991

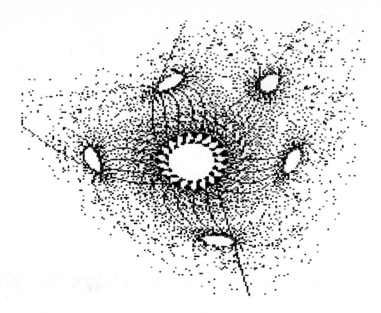

Figure D.6 A fractal by Henon's model

```
L=1;
for y=0.1:0.01:1
  L=L+10;
  for x=.1;0.01; 1.2 ;
    L=L+1; if L>64 L=1; end
    a=0.24; b=0.9708; alph=76.1135;
    for n=1:100
      xb=x;yb=y;
      x=a*xb-b*(yb-xb^2);
      y=b*xb + a*(yb-xb^2);
      if abs(x)>10 | abs(y)>10 break;end
      nx = fix((real(x)+1)* 100);
      ny = fix((real(y)+1)* 100);
      if nx<1 nx=1;end; if nx>200 nx = 200;end
      if ny<1 ny=1;end; if ny>200 ny=200; end
      W(nx,ny) = L;
    end
  end
end
image(W); axis([1,200,1,200]); axis('off'); hold off
```

Appendix E

Graphical User Interface

The reader probably has used menu-driven software more than once. Almost all commercially developed programs are operated by menus. Microsoft Windows is an example. Macintosh programs are all menu-driven. MATLAB itself is menu-driven. Graphical user interface (abbreviated GUI)[1] makes a program friendly. The objective of this appendix is to describe an easy introduction to graphical user interfaces that can be programmed with MATLAB. MATLAB GUI also can help Fortran and C programmers because Fortran and C programs can be operated from MATLAB GUI.[2]

This appendix describes how to develop GUIs. Demonstration scripts in this appendix not only will help you understand the explanations, but also could be used as templates when readers develop their own GUI-based programs .

The GUI panel is developed in a figure window, and consists of the following components:

(a) User interface menu.

(b) User interface control devices.

(c) Axes to display plots or images.

FLOW OF OPERATIONS WITH GUI

With a GUI, the flow of computing is controlled by the actions on the interface. While the flow of commands in a script is predetermined, the flow of operations with a GUI is undetermined. The commands to create a user interface is written in a script. Once the script is executed, however, the user interface remains on the screen even after execution of the script is completed. The user's interaction with the interface starts there and continues until the interface is closed.

Figure E.1 shows the basic concept of software operation with a GUI. When a selection is made on a menu, the program records the value of that selection, and

---

[1] See *MATLAB: Building a Graphical User Interface* by MathWorks.
[2] See more details of linking Fortran and C with MATLAB in *MATLAB External Interface Guide* by MathWorks

executes the commands prescribed in the call-back string. User interface menu, pushbutton, popup menu, slider, and editable text are all devices to control software operations.

Upon completion of instructions in the call-back string, control is returned to the interface, so the next selection from the menu can be made. This cycle is repeated until the GUI is closed.

The call-back string consists of a single or a sequence of MATLAB commands, or a function call. Using a function call is preferred, particularly when more than a few commands are necessary in the call-back string.

In order to understand how to write a GUI, the reader needs to understand only five commands, `uimenu`, `uicontrol`, `get`, `set`, and `axes`. Nonetheless, what makes these commands rather complicated is that there are so many different ways of using the commands. Writing all kinds of situations is impossible, because

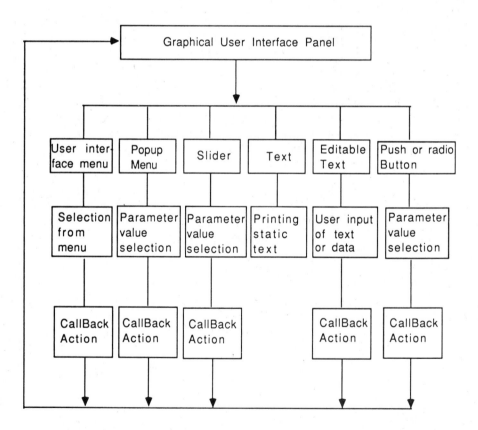

Figure E.1 Flow of operations with GUI

it would take too much space and be very cumbersome to read. Therefore, this appendix tries to explain only basic elements of GUI through examples. The readers should refer to *MATLAB: Building a Graphical User Interface* for more detailed information of the commands.

Here is one suggestion to make understanding GUI easy. Run one or two sample GUI scripts in this appendix first. This is easy if the M-files in the diskette for this book have been installed to your computer. Then try to understand the commands in the script. Trying to alter the scripts is an excellent method for fast learning. There are eighteen demonstration programs in this appendix. To run a program in this appendix, type the name in the command window (assuming all the M-files in the diskette have been installed to your computer, or run the program directly from the diskette):

```
GuiDm_n
```

where $n = 1, 2 .. 18$.

USER INTERFACE MENU

The user interface menu is a menu or a group of menus in the top of a figure window. A menu rolls down when clicked by a mouse and shows a list of options. When a selection is made from the list, another level of menus may also roll down (if the menu is so designed).

A user interface menu is specified by `uimenu`. Its synopsis is as follows:

```
m1 = uimenu(gcf, ...
    'Label','label string 1',...
    'Position', [priority number (integer)],...
    'BackgroundColor',[r,g,b],...
    'CallBack','call-back string')
m2 = uimenu(gcf, ...
    'Label','label string 2',...
    'Position', [priority number (integer)],...
    'BackgroundColor',[r,g,b],...
    'CallBack','call-back string')
m3 = uimenu(gcf, ...
    'Label','label string 3',...
    'Position', [priority number (integer)],...
    'BackgroundColor',[r,g,b],...
    'CallBack','call-back string')
```

Here, three menus in one figure window are assumed. In the commands, `m1`, `m2`, ... are handles of the menus which often become necessary in `CallBack` as well as in other commands. The arguments after `gcf` are called *properties* of menu and have the following meaning:

(a) `'Label'`,`'label string'` specifies the label of the menu that appears in the menu.

(b) `'Position'`, `k`, determines the sequential position of the label in the menu, where `k` is an integer of the priority order.

(c) `'BackgroundColor'`,`[r,g,b]` specifies the color of the menu background.

(d) `'CallBack'`,`'call-back string'` specifies the commands to be executed upon selection of the label.

In the foregoing synopsis, the lines of `Position` and `BackgroundColor` may be omitted if the default settings are acceptable. Furthermore, `CallBack` is not necessary if the menu is followed by a list of selections that opens when the menu is clicked.

Other properties also may be specified; however, the best way to learn such properties is to execute the `get(handle)` command after the `uimenu` command is executed, where `handle` must be like `m1` or `m2` in the earlier synopsis explanation. The `get(handle)` returns the current properties of the menu, most of which are set by default, but can be changed in the arguments of `uimenu` command statement.

The items for selections in the menu are also entered by `uimenu`. Considering the selection list for the first menu with handle `m1`, the synopsis involving three choices is as follows:

```
m1sA = uimenu(m1, ...
    'Label','Selection A',...
    'CallBack','call-back string')
m1sB = uimenu(m1, ...
    'Label','Selection B',...
    'CallBack','call-back string')
m1sC = uimenu(m1, ...
    'Label','Selection C',...
    'CallBack','call-back string')
```

All the three selections belong to the first menu with handle `m1`. Properties `Position` and `BackgroundColor` are omitted, but can be included if desired.

Property `CallBack` here is important if the `uicontrol` is for the terminal level of the menu. The `call-back string` is a string that consists of a command, a set of commands, or a function call. All the computational jobs to be performed upon selection are specified in the string. The instruction(s) may range from a single command to multiple commands. For simplicity of programming, however, it is desirable to write only a few commands, including one function call, in the call-back string. All details of the computations can be written in an M-file.[3]

---

[3]The M-file can be a function M-file as well as a nonfunction M-file. In either case, `'call-back string'` is replaced by `'M-file name'`. The difference between using a function M-file and a

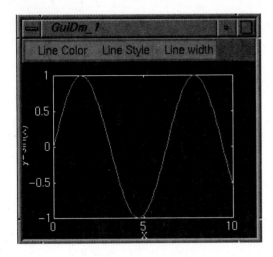

Figure E.2 User interface menu

A simple menu-driven program GuiDm_1 plots $y = \sin(x)$ as illustrated in Figure E.2. The user can change style of the curve, color and line width[4] from the menu.

GuiDm_1.m

```
%GuiDm_1.m  Illustrates user interface menu.
close, clear
figure(1)
set(gcf,'Position',[100,300,300,220],...
    'NumberTitle','off',...
    'Name','GuiDm_1')
x=0:0.1:10;, y=sin(x);
p=plot(x,y);xlabel('x');ylabel('y=sin(x)');
stl = uimenu(gcf,...
      'Label','  Line Style',...
      'BackgroundColor',[0.8, 0.8, 0.8],...
      'Position',2);
clr = uimenu(gcf,...
      'Label','  Line Color',...
      'BackgroundColor',[0.8, 0.8, 0.8],...
      'Position',1);
lw = uimenu(gcf,...
      'Label','  Line width',...
      'BackgroundColor',[0.8, 0.8, 0.8],...
```

nonfunction M-file is as follows. If a function M-file is used, the variables necessary in the function M-file must be given as arguments, because the variables in the calling M-file are not visible from the function M-file otherwise. On the other hand, if a nonfunction M-file is used, all the variables are visible from the called M-file. See more information in the M-file explanation in Chapter 1.

[4]Line width did not change in the MATLAB version that the author used.

```
            'Position',3);
    solid = uimenu(stl, ...
        'Label', 'Solid',...
        'CallBack','set(p,''LineStyle'',''-'')')
    dotted = uimenu(stl, ...
        'Label', 'Dotted',...
        'CallBack','set(p,''LineStyle'','':'')')
    yellow = uimenu(clr,...
        'Label', 'Yellow',...
        'BackgroundColor',[0.9, 0.9, 0.1],...
        'CallBack','set(p,''Color'',''y'')')
    green = uimenu(clr, ...
        'Label','Green',...
        'BackgroundColor',[0.1, 0.9, 0.1],...
        'CallBack','set(p,''Color'',''g'')')
    red = uimenu(clr,...
        'Label', 'Red',...
        'BackgroundColor',[0.9, 0.1 , 0.1],...
        'CallBack','set(p,''Color'',''r'')')
    solid = uimenu(lw, ...
        'Label', '0.5',...
        'CallBack','set(p,''LineWidth'',0.5)')
    dotted = uimenu(lw, ...
        'Label', '1.0',...
        'CallBack','set(p,''LineWidth'',1.0)')
```

Notice that texts in the call-back strings must be enclosed with double quote signs.
   Another example, GuiDm_2, plots one of the following functions at the user's choice from the menu:

(a) $y = \sin(x)$

(b) $y = \exp(-x)$

(c) $y = \cos(x^2)$

(d) $y = \exp(-x^2)$

Figure E.3 was plotted by GuiDm_2 (but the opened menu could not be shown).

GuiDm_2.m

```
%GuiDm_2  Demonstration of selecting equation form menu.
close, clear
fg=figure(1)
set(fg, 'Position',[150 150 350 250],...
    'NumberTitle','off',...
    'Name','GuiDm_2')
x=0:0.1:10;, y=sin(x);
p=plot(x,y);xlabel('x');ylabel('y=sin(x)');
stl = uimenu(gcf,...
```

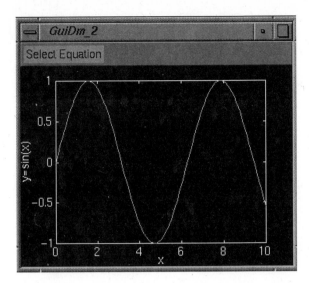

Figure E.3 Selection by menu

```
        'Label','Select Equation',...
        'BackgroundColor',[0.8, 0.8, 0.8])
F1   = uimenu(stl, ...
        'Label', 'y=sin(x)',...
        'CallBack',...
   'plot(x,sin(x));xlabel(''x'');ylabel(''y=sin(x)'')')
F2   = uimenu(stl, ...
        'Label', 'y=exp(-x)',...
        'CallBack',...
   'plot(x,exp(-x));xlabel(''x'');ylabel(''y=exp(-x)'')')
F3   = uimenu(stl, ...
        'Label', 'y=cos(x^2)',...
        'CallBack',...
        [
        'plot(x,cos(x.^2));',...
        'xlabel(''x'');ylabel(''y=cos(x.^2)'')'...
        ])
F4   = uimenu(stl, ...
        'Label', 'y=exp(-x.^2)',...
        'CallBack',...
        [
        'plot(x,exp(-x.^2));',...
        'xlabel(''x'');ylabel(''y=exp(-x.^2)'')'...
        ])
```

The reader might combine the two foregoing scripts into one for exercise.

USER INTERFACE CONTROL

MATLAB user interface control is specified by the `uicontrol` command. User interface control has much similarity with user interface menu, but the former includes many styles. Its synopsis is

```
k=uicontrol('Style','style spec',...
            'String','display string',...
            'Value', [value],...
            'BackgroundColor',[r,g,b],...
            'Max',[value],...
            'Min',[value],...
            'Position',[ left,bottom,width,height],
            'Callback','call-back string')
```

where `'style spec'` is one of the following strings:

```
popup
push
radio
checkbox
slider
edit (editable text)
text (static text)
frame
```

Properties in `uicontrol` are similar to those in `uimenu`. The new properties that appear for the first time are:

(a) `'Value',value`: specifies default value of setting. For on/off switches, the value is 0 or 1. For a slider, it can be any value between the minimum and the maximum.

(b) `'Min', value`: sets the minimum value. Its meaning differs depending on the style.

(c) `'Max',value`: sets the maximum value. Its meaning differs depending on the style.

There are many more properties that can be written in the `uicontrol` commands just like the properties of `uimenu`, although in programming we desire to minimize the number of properties to make the script simple. To find more about the additional properties, investigate using the `get` command.

In the following subsections, the styles will be explained in more detail.

Static Text

A static text can display some symbols, messages, or even numeric values in a GUI, and can be placed at a desired location. There is no call-back string with a static text. An example of a static text is shown here:

```
k1=uicontrol('Style','text',...
             'String','static text displayed',...
             'Position',[ 20, 50, 140, 30])
```

The contents of a static text displayed can be changed as needs occur. This is done by the `set` command. For example, execute the following command from the command window while the foregoing sample of `uicontrol` command is in effect:

```
set(k1, 'String','A revised string is here now.')
```

To display numeric value(s) as a static text, write `num2str(n)`, where `n` is a numeric value, in place of `'static text displayed'` after `'String'`. The output of GuiDm_3 is the top half of Figure E.4.

GuiDm_3.m
```
close; clg
h1=figure(1);
set(h1,'Position',[300,300,400,200],...
'NumberTitle','off',...
'Name','GuiDm_3  Numeric Value')
k1=uicontrol('Style','text',...
             'String',num2str(pi),...
             'Position',[ 20,50,140,30])
```

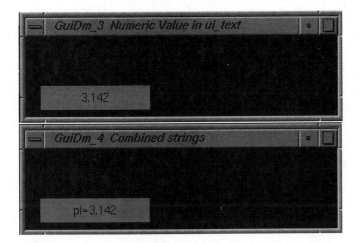

Figure E.4 Results of GuiDm-3.m and 4.m

If multiple strings are to be displayed as a combined string, use brackets. For example, the second half of Figure E.4 is plotted by GuiDm_4.

GuiDm_4.m

```
% GuiDm_4  Combined strings in text.
close; clg
h1=figure(1);
set(h1,'Position',[300,300,400,100],...
'NumberTitle','off',...
'Name','GuiDm_4  Combined strings')
k1=uicontrol('Style','text',...
            'String',['pi=',num2str(3.14159)],...
            'Position',[ 20,10,140,30])
```

Popup menu

A popup menu is different from the user interface menu because the popup menu can be located anywhere in the figure window, while the user interface menu is located only at the top.

Suppose the popup menu is to offer a choice among A, B, C, and D. GuiDm_5.m illustrates how to write `uicontrol` for the popup menu. In order to run the script, a function `task_1` is also necessary.

When GuiDm_5 is executed, a figure window will open with a small white label at the top left corner of the window (see Figure E.5). If the mouse is clicked while the pointer is within the white box, a menu will pop up in the middle of the figure window. Click A, B, C, or D, then a short message such as

```
C is selected.
```

will be printed out on the command screen. For simplicity of illustration, no other operation is performed, but `task_1` can be much longer. Selections can be repeated until `Close` is selected in the menu.

GuiDm_5.m

```
%GuiDm_5 Demonstration of popup menu.
clg
h1=figure(1)
set(h1,'Position',[100,100,300,200],...
        'NumberTitle','off', ...
        'Name','GuiDm_5  Demo of Popup Menu')
k1=uicontrol('Style','Popup',...
            'String','A|B|C|D|Close',...
            'Value',  1,...
            'Position',[ 20,150,140,30], ...
            'Callback','task_1(h1,k1)')
```

task_1.m

```
%task_1.m
function task_1(h,k)
val = get(k,'Value');
```

```
     if val == 1, fprintf('A is selected\n')
  elseif val == 2, fprintf('B is selected\n')
  elseif val == 3, fprintf('C is selected\n')
  elseif val == 4, fprintf('D is selected\n')
  elseif val == 5, close(h)
  end
```

Here, meanings of arguments for `uicontrol` in GuiDm_5.m are as follows:

(a) `'Style'`, `'Popup'`: the style of user control is popup menu.

(b) `'String'`, `'A|B|C|D|Close'`: strings in the menu are A, B, C, D, and `Close`.

(c) `'Value'`, `3`: selects the third selection C as default.

(d) `'Position'`, `[20,150,140,30]`: position of the menu is at (20, 150) in pixel units in the figure window, and size of the menu is (140,30) in pixel units.

(e) `'Callback'`, `'task_1(h1,k1)'`: when the popup menu is selected, command `task_1` is executed, where `task_1` is the function M-file.

Upon a selection on the popup menu (for example, we assume C is selected), function `task_1` is entered and `val` is drawn. In the arguments of `task_1`, h and k are handles of the current figure and `uicontrol`, respectively. Command `val=get(k,'Value')` captures the value selected in the menu window, and `val` becomes 1 for A, 2 for B, etc. In this example, a message `'C is selected'` is printed out on the command window. If `val=5`, the figure window (of handle h) is closed and the GUI disappears. Otherwise, program returns to the user interface, and the same procedure can be repeated.

The figure window in the foregoing example (see Figure E.5) is awkward, however. Indeed, the size of the figure window is too large just for the menu, and more messages for users are desirable. In order to improve the figure window, we create GuiDm_6. The figure window size is reduced, while the background color is changed to green. The `uicontrol` with handle j is to print out a message above the popup menu. Run GuiDm_6 to see the improvements (see Figure E.6).

GuiDm_6.m
```
% GuiDm_6 Shows improvements of GuiDm_5.
h1=figure(2)
set(h1,'Position',[30,50,280,100], ...
    'Color',[0,0.5, 0.5],'Name','GuiDm_6');
j=uicontrol('Position',[ 0,60,250,30], ...
    'String','Select from A, B, C, D or Close');
k=uicontrol('Style','Popup',...
            'String','A|B|C|D|Close',...
            'Position',[ 0,30,100,30], ...
            'Callback','task_1(h1,k)');
```

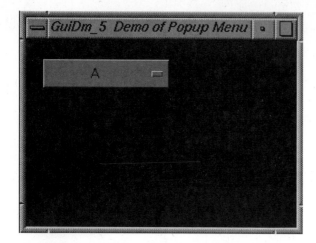

Figure E.5 Popup menu (1)

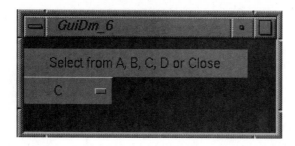

Figure E.6 Popup menu (2)

In the two foregoing examples, the call-back string is task_1; however, the contents of task_1 may be written directly in the call-back string. An example is

GuiDm_7.m

```
%GuiDm_7  Illustrates a long call-back string.
clg
h1=figure(2)
set(h1,'Position',[30,50,280,100], ...
    'Color',[0,0.5, 0.5],'Name','GuiDm_7',...
    'NumberTitle','off')
j=uicontrol('Position',[ 0,60,250,30], ...
    'Style','text',...
    'String','Select from A, B, C, D or Close')
k=uicontrol('Style','Popup',...
            'String','A|B|C|D|Close',...
            'Position',[ 0,30,100,30], ...
  'Callback',...
  [ ...
```

```
'val = get(k,''Value'');',...
'    if val == 1, fprintf(''A is selected\n''),',...
'elseif val == 2, fprintf(''B is selected\n''),',...
'elseif val == 3, fprintf(''C is selected\n''),',...
'elseif val == 4, fprintf(''D is selected\n''),',...
'elseif val == 5, close(h1),',...
'end' ...
])
```

Notice in the foregoing example, the call-back string is written in a row vectors of strings.

Push Button

GuiDm_8 illustrates application of a push button, and its result is in Figure E.7.

GuiDm_8.m

```
%GuiDm_8  Push Button
close;clg
h1=figure(1)
set(h1,'Position',[130,550,280,100], ...
    'Color',[0,0.5, 0.5],...
    'Name','GuiDm_8 Push Button',...
    'NumberTitle','off')
j=uicontrol('Position',[0,60,250,30], ...
    'Style','pushbutton',...
    'String','Push here to plot sin(x)' ,...
    'Callback',...
    [
    'h2=figure(2);x=0:0.1:10;plot(x,sin(x));,',...
    'xlabel(''x''),ylabel(''y''),'...
    'set(h2,''Position'',[130,310,280,200])'
    ])
```

When executed, the window on the top side of Figure E.7 opens first. If pushbutton is pushed then, a new figure window (second window in Figure E.7) will open with a plot of $y = \sin(x)$. If you wish to quit the interface, type `close` in the command window.

Check Box

Check box is designed to provide on/off operations. The following script plots the sine function and creates a small check box at the top of the graph (see Figure E.8). The check box toggles appearance of the axis. The on/off positions are recorded in `Value` which can be found by `get(handle, 'Value')`. The commands `axis on` and `axis off` to toggle axis are written in the call-back string.

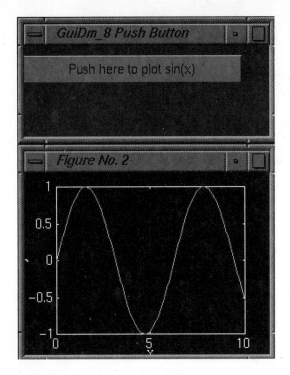

Figure E.7 Push button

GuiDm_9.m

```
%GuiDm_9  Check Box
close;clg
h1=figure(2)
set(h1,'Position',[130,450,300,200], ...
    'Color',[0,0.5, 0.5],'Name','GuiDm_9',...
    'NumberTitle','off')
hold on
x=0:0.1:10;plot(x,sin(x))
j=uicontrol('Position',[ 5,0,250,15], ...
    'Style','checkbox',...
        'Value',1,...
    'String','Push here to toggle axis' ,...
    'Callback',...
    [ ...
      'if get(j,''Value'')==0, axis off; ',...
      'elseif get(j,''Value'')==1, axis on, end' ...
    ])
```

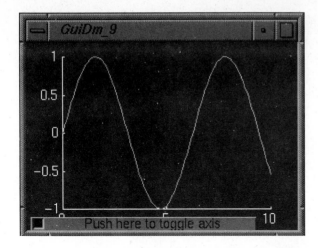

Figure E.8 Check box

Radio Button

When only one radio button is used, there is no functional difference from a check box. On the other hand, radio buttons as a group are intended to be mutually exclusive (that is, if one button is on, all other buttons become off), while check boxes are independent from each other. This exclusive feature of radio buttons can be realized, however, only by the user's own programming in the call-back strings (see *MATLAB: Building a Graphical User Interface*).

Slider

The slider is an analog device to change a parameter. The script of GuiDm_10 illustrates application of sliders (see Figure E.9). The script is to demonstrate how an RGB color is affected by intensities of the three components, R, G, and B. The intensities are changed by sliders.

GuiDm_10.m
```
%GuiDm_10  RGB color demonstration
clf, clear
h6=figure(1);
clf
R=0;G=0.4,B=0;
set(h6,'Position',[60, 300,380,380],...
    'Name','GuiDm_10 RGB Demo',...
    'NumberTitle','off',...
    'Color',[ 0. 0.0 0.])
ah=axes( 'Position', [0.4 0.1, 0.55 0.50],...
    'Box', 'on', ...
    'Color',[R,G,B],...
```

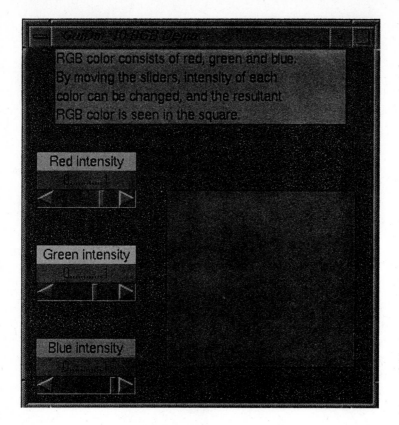

Figure E.9 Slider

```
    'XColor',[0,0,0],'YColor',[0,0,0])
%==============================
t1 = uicontrol(gcf,'Style','text', ...
    'String',...
        'RGB color consists of red, green and blue. ',...
    'HorizontalAlignment','Left',...
    'Position',[30,360,320,20],...
    'BackgroundColor',[0.8 0.8 0.8]);
t2 = uicontrol(gcf,'Style','text', ...
    'String',...
        'By moving the sliders, intensity of each ',...
    'HorizontalAlignment','Left',...
    'Position',[30,340,320,20],...
    'BackgroundColor',[0.8 0.8 0.8]);
t3 = uicontrol(gcf,'Style','text', ...
    'String',...
        'color can be changed, and the resultant  ',...
    'HorizontalAlignment','Left',...
```

```matlab
        'Position',[30,320,320,20],...
        'BackgroundColor',[0.8 0.8 0.8]);
t4 = uicontrol(gcf,'Style','text', ...
    'String',...
        'RGB color is seen in the square.  ',...
    'HorizontalAlignment','Left',...
    'Position',[30,300,320,20],...
    'BackgroundColor',[0.8 0.8 0.8]);
%=============================Slider for Blue
b1 = uicontrol(gcf,'Style','text', ...
    'String','Blue intensity',...
    'Position',[10,50,110,20],...
    'BackgroundColor',[0.6,0.6,0.8]);
b2 = uicontrol(gcf,'Style','text',...
    'String','0............1',...
    'Position',[10,30,110,20]);
b3 = uicontrol(gcf,...
    'Style','slider',...
    'Min' ,0,'Max', 1, ...
    'Position',[10,10,110,20], ...
    'Value', B,...
    'CallBack', ...
    'B=get(b3,''Value'');set(ah,''Color'',[R,G,B])');
%=============================Slider for Green
g1 = uicontrol(gcf,'Style','text', ...
    'String','Green intensity',...
    'Position',[10,150,110,20],...
    'BackgroundColor',[0.6,0.8,0.6]);
g2 = uicontrol(gcf,'Style','text',...
    'String','0............1',...
    'Position',[10,130,110,20]);
g3 = uicontrol(gcf,...
    'Style','slider',...
    'Min' ,0,'Max', 1, ...
    'Position',[10,110,110,20], ...
    'Value', G,...
    'CallBack', ...
        'G=get(g3,''Value'');set(ah,''Color'',[R,G,B])');
%=============================Slider for Red
r1 = uicontrol(gcf,'Style','text', ...
    'String','Red intensity',...
    'Position',[10,250,110,20],...
    'BackgroundColor',[0.8,0.6,0.6]);
r2 = uicontrol(gcf,'Style','text',...
    'String','0............1',...
    'Position',[10,230,110,20]);
r3 = uicontrol(gcf,...
    'Style','slider',...
```

```
'Min' ,0,'Max',1, ...
'Position',[10,210,110,20], ...
'Value', R,...
'CallBack', ...
    'R=get(r3,''Value'');set(ah,''Color'',[R,G,B])');
```

Notice that slider values are captured using get with 'Value'.

Editable text

The editable text device allows the user to write a string input. Numeric values in vector or matrix form may be written as a string through the same device, which is converted to numeric values by str2num command.

An example of uicontrol for the editable text is:

```
ed1 = uicontrol(gcf, 'Style','edit', ...
        'Position', [10,260, 110,20],...
        'CallBack','inp_txt=get(ed1,''String'')')
```

The key words in the foregoing command are 'Style', 'edit', and get (handle,'String') which captures the text input. The following program (GuiDm_11) reads the user input of a matrix from the editable text (see Figure E.10), and computes eigenvalues of the matrix. The eigenvalues are printed on the command window.

GuiDm_11.m

```
% GuiDm_11   Editable Text
close,clg
h1=figure(2)
set(h1,'Position',[130,450,480,150], ...
    'Color',[0,0.5, 0.5],'Name','GuiDm_11 Editable Text')
ed0 = uicontrol(gcf, 'Style','text', ...
        'Position', [110,60, 260,40],...
```

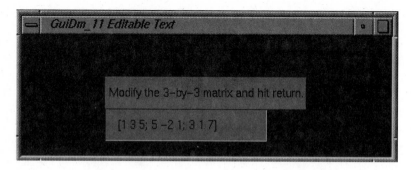

Figure E.10 Input of numbers through editable text

```
            'String',...
            ' Modify the 3-by-3 matrix and hit return.')
  ed2 = uicontrol(gcf, 'Style','edit', ...
            'Position', [110,20, 210,40],...
            'String','    [1 3 5; 5 -2 1; 3 1 7]',...
            'CallBack',['inp_txt=get(ed2,''String''),',...
            'eigenvalues=eig(str2num(inp_txt))'])
```

With the revised script, GuiDm_12, the eigenvalues are printed as static text within the GUI (see Figure E.11).

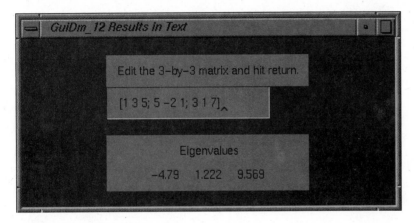

Figure E.11 Displaying results in static text

GuiDm_12.m
```
% GuiDm_12    Results as static text
close,clg
h1=figure(2)
set(h1,'Position',[130,350,480,210], ...
      'Color',[0,0.5, 0.5],'Name','GuiDm_12 Results in Text',...
      'NumberTitle','off')
axis('off'); hold on
ed0 = uicontrol(gcf, 'Style','text', ...
            'Position', [110,150, 260,40],...
            'String',...
            ' Edit the 3-by-3 matrix and hit return.')
ed1 = uicontrol(gcf, 'Style','text', ...
            'Position', [110,50, 260,40],...
            'String',' Eigenvalues')
ed2 = uicontrol(gcf, 'Style','text', ...
            'Position', [110,20, 260,40],...
            'String',' ')
ed3 = uicontrol(gcf, 'Style','edit', ...
```

```
'Position',  [110,110,  210,40],...
'String','    [1 3 5; 5 -2 1; 3 1 7]',...
'CallBack',...
['axis off; inp_txt=get(ed3,''String'');',...
'eigen=eig(str2num(inp_txt));',...
'ans=[num2str(eigen(1)),''      '',',...
'num2str(eigen(2)),''      '',',...
'num2str(eigen(3))];',...
'set(ed2,''String'',ans) '])
```

Frames

The `frame` style may be used to group devices such as radio buttons or check boxes.

MULTIPLE AXES

In developing a graphical user interface, it often becomes necessary to plot one or more graphs within the user interface. The `subplot` command may be used for this purpose, but the `axes` command is more flexible and allows versatile options for programmers.

The `axes` command opens an axis at a specified location within a figure window. Although multiple axes may be opened in a figure window by `axes`, we

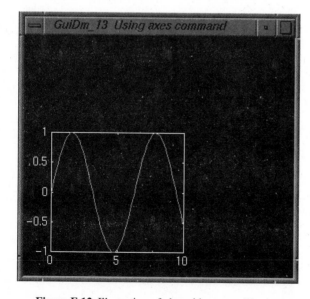

Figure E.12 Illustration of plot with `axes` (1)

first consider only one axis. The following script plots, as shown in Figure E.12, a figure at the lower-left corner of the figure window:

GuiDm_13.m

```
% GuiDm_13: Illustrates axes command.
close,h1=figure(1),clf
set(h1,'Position',[300,300,350,300],...
        'NumberTitle','off',...
        'Name','GuiDm_13  Using axes command')
x=0:0.1:10;
axes('Position',[0.1, 0.1, 0.5, 0.5]);
plot(x,sin(x))
```

The location and size of the axis is specified by a vector following `Position`. The values in the vector have the same meaning as in `uicontrol` except the values are in the normalized scale (maximum is unity). The location and the size can be changed using different values in the position parameters.

The true power of the `axes` command is that it can open multiple axes at chosen locations. Although `subplot` can do the same, the sizes and locations of the subplots cannot be changed freely.

GuiDm_14 plots sin(x) in the middle level of the left side and exp($-x$) at the right bottom (see left side of Figure E.13).

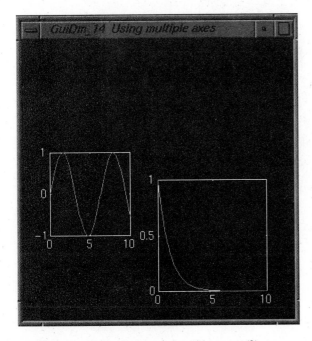

Figure E.13 Illustration of plot with `axes` (2)

GuiDm_14.m

```
%GuiDm_14:  Illustrates multiple axes.
close,h1=figure(1),clf
set(h1,'Position',[300,300,350,350],...
       'NumberTitle','off',...
       'Name','GuiDm_14  Using multiple axes')
x=0:0.1:10;
axes('Position',[0.1, 0.3, 0.3, 0.3]);
plot(x,sin(x));
axes('Position',[0.55, 0.1, 0.4, 0.4]);
plot(x,exp(-x))
```

How can the first axis be reactivated as the current axis so the graph may be revised by adding more curves or by erasing and redrawing? The answer is to use the subplot command to point to the desired axis. To do this, we have to use the handle assigned to each axis. The GuiDm_15 plots two functions in each axis, as illustrated in Figure E.14.

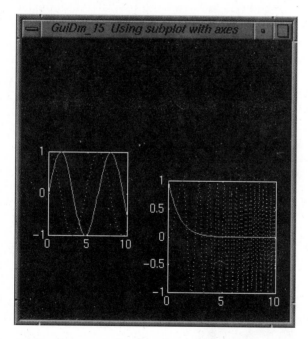

Figure E.14 Illustration of plot with axes (3)

GuiDm_15.m

```
% GuiDm_15  Using subplot with axes.
close,h1=figure(1),clf
```

```
set(h1,'Position',[300,300,350,350],...
        'NumberTitle','off',...
        'Name','GuiDm_15  Using subplot with axes')
x=0:0.1:10;
h1=axes('Position',[0.1, 0.3, 0.3, 0.3]);
plot(x,sin(x));
h2=axes('Position',[0.55, 0.1, 0.4, 0.4]);
plot(x,exp(-x))
%
subplot(h1)
hold on; plot(x,cos(x),':'); hold off
%
subplot(h2)
hold on; plot(x,sin(x.*x),':'); hold off
```

APPLICATIONS

We illustrate three GUI applications that incorporate combinations of different devices.

Application E.1

Here, we develop a script GuiDm_16 that displays a sphere (see Figure E.15) with choices for:

Color map: hsv, flag, jet, and cool
Type of display: mesh, surface, and surfl
Shading: faceted, flat, and interp

GuiDm_16.m

```
%GuiDm_16  GUI to show 3D plots
clf, clear
h6=figure(1);
set(h6,'Position',[60, 300,380,380],...
        'Color',[ 0. 0.0 0.],...
        'NumberTitle','off',...
        'Name','GuiDm_16    3D plots')
[x,y,z]=sphere(10);
axes( 'Position', [0.4 0.2, 0.55 0.55],...
        'Box', 'on', 'Color','k')
surf(x,y,z,-z);
%============================Slider control
txt_sl1 = uicontrol(gcf,...
        'Style','text', ...
```

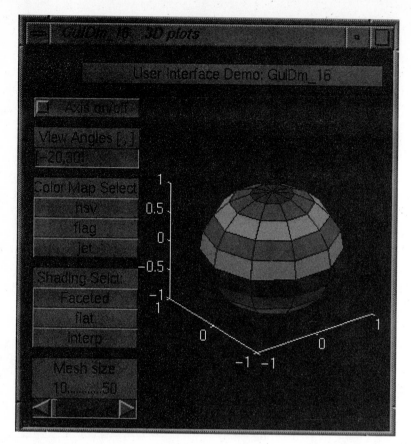

Figure E.15 A 3-D plot in a GUI

```
        'String','Mesh size',...
        'Position',[10,50,110,20]);
txt_sl2 = uicontrol(gcf,...
        'Style','text',...
        'String','10............50',...
        'Position',[10,30,110,20]);
txt_sli = uicontrol(gcf,...
        'Style','slider',...
        'Min' ,10,'Max', 50, ...
        'Position',[10,10,110,20], ...
        'Value', -30,...
        'CallBack',...
   ['clear x y z; ',...
    ' [x,y,z]=sphere(ceil(get(txt_sli,''Value'')));',...
```

```
      ' surf(x,y,z,-z)'...
  ]);
%============================== Shading selection
push0=uicontrol(gcf, ...
        'Style','text',...
        'Position', [10,140, 110,20],...
        'String','Shading Select:   ',...
        'Value',0);
sym(1)=uicontrol(gcf,...
        'Style','push',...
        'Position', [10,80,110,20], ...
        'String','interp', ...
        'CallBack','shading interp ');
sym(2)=uicontrol(gcf, 'Style','push',...
        'Position', [10,100,110,20],...
        'String','flat',...
        'CallBack','shading flat ');
sym(3)=uicontrol(gcf, 'Style','push',...
        'Position', [10,120, 110,20], ...
        'String','Faceted',...
        'CallBack','shading faceted ');
%============================== Color Map Selection
push3=uicontrol(gcf, 'Style','push',...
        'Position', [10,170, 110,20], ...
        'String','jet',...
        'CallBack','colormap(jet)');
push2=uicontrol(gcf, 'Style','push',...
        'Position', [10,190, 110,20],...
        'String','flag',...
        'CallBack','colormap(flag)');
push1=uicontrol(gcf, 'Style','push',...
        'Position', [10,210, 110,20], ...
        'String','hsv',...
        'CallBack','colormap(hsv)');
push0=uicontrol(gcf, 'Style','text',...
        'Position', [10,230, 110,20], ...
        'String','Color Map Select:',...
        'CallBack','dummy=0');
%============================== View Angle Input
edtx0=uicontrol(gcf, 'Style','text',...
        'Position', [10,280, 110,20], ...
        'String', 'View Angles [ , ]');
edtx1=uicontrol(gcf, 'Style','edit', ...
        'Position', [10,260, 110,20],...
        'String','[-20,30]',...
        'CallBack',...
        ['v_ang=str2num(get(edtx1,''String''));',...
         'view(v_ang) ']);
```

```
%=============================== Axis on/off
ckbox=uicontrol(gcf, 'Style','checkbox',...
        'Position', [10,310, 110,20], ...
        'String','Axis on/off', ...
        'CallBack',...
        ['ckv= get(ckbox,''Value'');if ckv==1,',...
         'axis on,elseif ckv==0, axis off, end ']);
%============================== Top title
title=uicontrol(gcf, 'Style','text',...
        'Position', [60,345, 310,20], 'String',...
        'User Interface Demo: GuiDm_16');
```

Application E.2

We revisit the electrical circuit of Example 10.16 and reorganize the script using GUI. The values of La, Lb, and Ra are determined by sliders, while Rb and C are selected from a popup menu. The circuit diagram and the ODE solutions are displayed in the GUI (see Figure E.16).

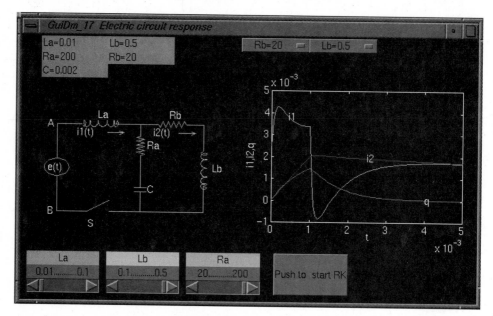

Figure E.16 GUI-guided circuit analysis

GuiDm_17.m
```
% GuiDm_17    Electric Circuit Analysis
```

```
clf, clear
h6=figure(1);
clf
R=0;G=0.4,B=0;
set(h6,'Position',[60, 300,680,380],...
    'Name','RGB_demo',...
    'NumberTitle','off',...
    'Color',[ 0. 0.0 0.])
ah=axes( 'Position', [0.05 0.25, 0.4 0.50],...
    'Box', 'on', ...
    'Color',[R,G,B],...
    'XColor',[0,0,0],'YColor',[0,0,0])
ah2=axes( 'Position', [0.55 0.3, 0.42 0.50],...
    'Box', 'on', ...
    'Color',[R,G,B],...
    'XColor',[0,0,0],'YColor',[0,0,0])
subplot(ah); APE_circ  %calling APE_circ (diagram)
La=0.01; Lb=0.5;Ra=200;Rb=20;C=0.002;
subplot(ah2); APE_rk(La, Lb, Ra, Rb ,C);
                        %calling 2nd RK
%=============================
t1 = uicontrol(gcf,'Style','text', ...
    'String',...
        ['La=',num2str(La)],...
    'HorizontalAlignment','Left',...
    'Position',[30,360,100,20],...
    'BackgroundColor',[0.8 0.8 0.8]);
t1B= uicontrol(gcf,'Style','text', ...
    'String',...
        ['Lb=',num2str(Lb)],...
    'HorizontalAlignment','Left',...
    'Position',[130,360,100,20],...
    'BackgroundColor',[0.8 0.8 0.8]);
t2 = uicontrol(gcf,'Style','text', ...
    'String',...
        ['Ra=',num2str(Ra)],...
    'HorizontalAlignment','Left',...
    'Position',[30,340,100,20],...
    'BackgroundColor',[0.8 0.8 0.8]);
t2B = uicontrol(gcf,'Style','text', ...
    'String',...
        ['Rb=',num2str(Rb)],...
    'HorizontalAlignment','Left',...
    'Position',[130,340,100,20],...
    'BackgroundColor',[0.8 0.8 0.8]);

t3 = uicontrol(gcf,'Style','text', ...
    'String',...
```

```
        ['C=',num2str(C)],...
    'HorizontalAlignment','Left',...
    'Position',[30,320,100,20],...
    'BackgroundColor',[0.8 0.8 0.8]);
%==============================Slider control
b1 = uicontrol(gcf,'Style','text', ...
    'String','La',...
    'Position',[10,50,110,20],...
    'BackgroundColor',[0.8,0.8,1]);
b2 = uicontrol(gcf,'Style','text',...
    'String','0.01............0.1',...
    'Position',[10,30,110,20]);
b3 = uicontrol(gcf,...
    'Style','slider',...
    'Min' ,0.01,'Max', 0.1, ...
    'Position',[10,10,110,20], ...
    'Value', La,...
    'CallBack', ...
    ['cla;La=get(b3,''Value'');',...
     'set(t1,''String'',[''La='',num2str(La)]);',...
    ])
%==============================Slider for Green
g1 = uicontrol(gcf,'Style','text', ...
    'String','Lb',...
    'Position',[130,50,110,20],...
    'BackgroundColor',[0.8,1,0.8]);
g2 = uicontrol(gcf,'Style','text',...
    'String','0.1............0.5',...
    'Position',[130,30,110,20]);
g3 = uicontrol(gcf,...
    'Style','slider',...
    'Min' ,0.1,'Max', 0.5, ...
    'Position',[130,10,110,20], ...
    'Value', Lb,...
    'CallBack', ...
    ['cla;Lb=get(g3,''Value'');',...
     'set(t1B,''String'',[''Lb='',num2str(Lb)]);',...
    ])
%==============================Slider for RED
r1 = uicontrol(gcf,'Style','text', ...
    'String','Ra',...
    'Position',[250,50,110,20],...
    'BackgroundColor',[1,0.8,0.8]);
r2 = uicontrol(gcf,'Style','text',...
    'String','20............200',...
    'Position',[250,30,110,20]);
r3 = uicontrol(gcf,...
    'Style','slider',...
```

```
      'Min' ,20,'Max',200, ...
      'Position',[250,10,110,20], ...
      'Value', Ra,...
      'CallBack', ...
      ['cla;Ra=get(r3,''Value'');',...
      'set(t2,''String'',[''Ra='',num2str(Ra)]);',...
      ])
%================================= Push button
r1 = uicontrol(gcf,'Style','Push', ...
      'String','Push to  start RK',...
      'Position',[380,10,110,60],...
      'CallBack',...
      'disp([La,Lb,Ra,Rb,C]);APE_rk(La,Lb,Ra,Rb,C)');
```

APE_circ.m

```
% APE_circ.m   Draws an electric circuit diagram
cla
hold off
%axis('square')
axis([-0.3,4,-0.5,2.5]);
hold on
%battery_(0.1, 0.2, [0.0, 0], [0.0, 2]);
text(0-0.2 ,0, 'B')

text(0-0.2,2, 'A')
switch_(0.5, 1, [0,0], [2,0]);
capacitor_(0.1, 0.3, [2,0], [2,1])
resist_(6,0.5,   0.2, [2,1], [2,2]);
coil_(6,0.4, 0.07, [0,2],[2.,2]);
%coil_trad(4, 0.3, [0.8,2],[2.2,2]);
line_([2,0],[3.5,0])

resist_(6,0.5,   0.1, [2,2], [3.5,2]);
coil_(6,0.4, 0.07, [3.5,2],[3.5,0]);
text(2+0.19, 0.5,'C')
text(2+0.19, 1.5,'Ra')
text(0.8,-0.3,'S')
text(3.7,1,'Lb')
text(1., 2.2, 'La')
text(2.7, 2.2, 'Rb')
text(-0.2, 1.0,'e(t)')
text( 0.5,2.-0.2, 'i1(t)');
arrow_(0.4, [1.2, 2-0.2], [1.6, 2-0.2] )
text( 2.3,2.-0.2, 'i2(t)');
arrow_(0.4, [2.9, 2-0.2], [3.3, 2-0.2] )
axis('off')

line_([0,0], [0,0.8])
```

```
line_([0,1.2], [0,2])
ellip_( 0, 1, 0.3, 0.2)
```

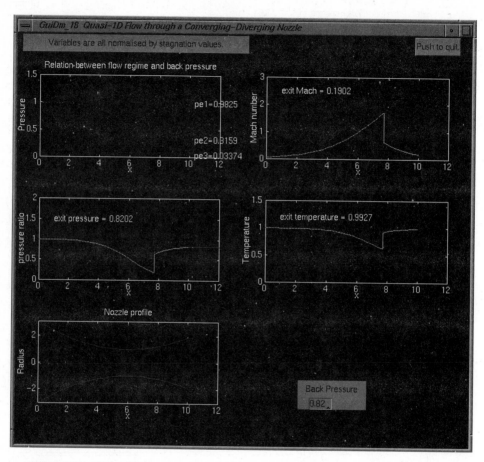

Figure E.17 GUI-guided analysis for nozzle aerodynamics

Application E.3

Nozzles for gas flows are used in many aerodynamic devices; for example, jet engine, rocket, and wind tunnel. Here, we consider converging-diverging nozzles to produce a supersonic flow.

Those who studied fluid dynamics should know how to compute the Mach numbers in the nozzle, using the isentropic air table and the normal shock table. The GuiDm_18 simulates the flow of air in a converging-diverging nozzle using

GUI (see Figure E.17). (The list of GuiDm_18 is not printed here because it is lengthy, but it is available on the diskette.) Although the nozzle configuration is hard coded, it can be changed easily by modifying the M-file. The only user input is the back pressure of the nozzle, which is specified through an editable text window. As soon as the back pressure is written and the return key is hit, graphical results are displayed.

Index

MATLAB® Technical Computing Environment

MATLAB is the companion software to **Numerical Analysis and Graphic Visualization With MATLAB** by S. Nakamura (Prentice Hall, 1996). The *Numerical Analysis and Graphic Visualization Toolbox*, consisting of MATLAB M-files, has been created by the author to illustrate the concepts presented in the text.

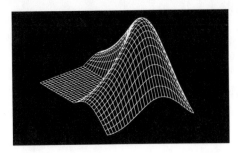

- **MATLAB Application Toolboxes** add functions for symbolic math, signal processing, control design, neural networks, and other areas.

- **The Student Editions** of MATLAB and SIMULINK are available for use on students' own personal computers.

- **Educational discount plans** support classroom instruction and research.

- **Classroom Kits** provide cost-effective support for PC or Mac teaching labs.

- **MATLAB-based books** use MATLAB to illustrate basic and advanced material in a wide range of topics.

NAME _____

TITLE _____

COMP./UNIV. _____

DEPT. OR M/S _____

STREET _____

CITY/STATE/ZIP _____

PHONE _____

FAX _____ EMAIL _____

WHERE DID YOU PURCHASE THIS BOOK? _____

Computer platform – check all that apply:
☐ PC/Macintosh ☐ UNIX Workstation ☐ VAX/Supercomputer

▶ **For the fastest response, fax this card to:**
(508) 653-6284, or call us at (508) 653-1415.

I am interested in The MathWorks product information for:

☐ Simulation ☐ Control System Design ☐ Math & Visualization
☐ Signal Processing ☐ Symbolic Math ☐ Educational Discounts
☐ System Identification ☐ Chemometrics ☐ Classroom Kits
☐ Neural Networks ☐ Optimization ☐ Student Editions
☐ Statistics ☐ Image Processing ☐ MATLAB Books

Send me the free *Numerical Analysis and Graphic Visualization Toolbox* disk for my: (check one) ☐ PC ☐ Macintosh

The MATH WORKS Inc.

BUSINESS REPLY MAIL
FIRST CLASS MAIL PERMIT NO. 82 NATICK, MA

POSTAGE WILL BE PAID BY ADDRESSEE

The MathWorks, Inc.
24 Prime Park Way
Natick, MA 01760-9889